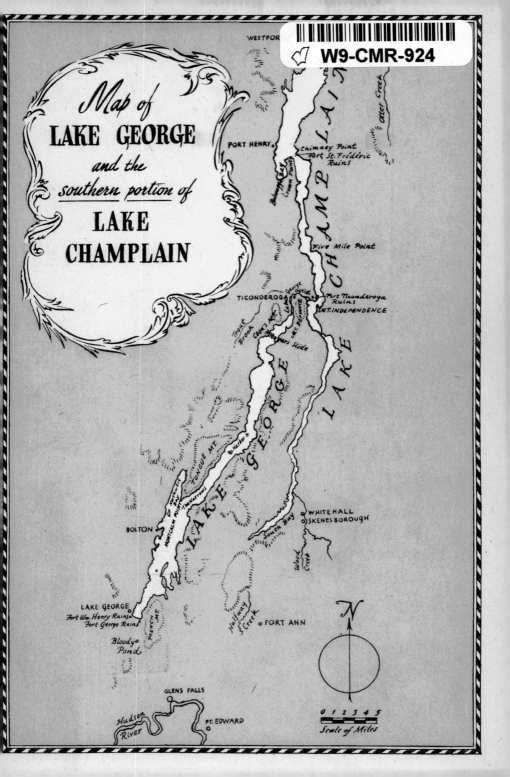

Map of
LAKE GEORGE
and the
southern portion of
LAKE CHAMPLAIN

WESTPORT

PORT HENRY

Otter Creek

Chimney Point
Fort St. Frédéric Ruins

Bulwagga Bay
Crown Point

Five Mile Point

LAKE CHAMPLAIN

TICONDEROGA
Lake George Outlet
Fort Ticonderoga Ruins
MT. INDEPENDENCE

Trout Brook
COOK'S MT.
MT. DEFIANCE
Roger's Slide

LAKE GEORGE

Harbor Is.

TONGUE MT.
THE NARROWS
MONTCALM POINT

BOLTON

WHITE HALL
SKENESBOROUGH

South Bay

Wood Creek

LAKE GEORGE
Fort Wm. Henry Ruins
Fort George Ruins

FRENCH MT.

Halfway Creek

FORT ANN

Bloody Pond

N

GLENS FALLS

Hudson River

FT. EDWARD

0 1 2 3 4 5
Scale of Miles

Frederic F. Van de Water

THE AMERICAN LAKES SERIES

Published:

In Preparation:

LAKE CHAMPLAIN AND LAKE GEORGE

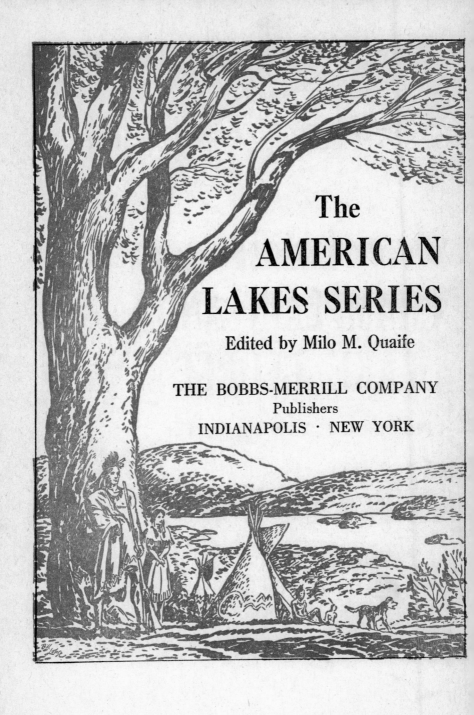

The
AMERICAN
LAKES SERIES

Edited by Milo M. Quaife

THE BOBBS-MERRILL COMPANY
Publishers
INDIANAPOLIS · NEW YORK

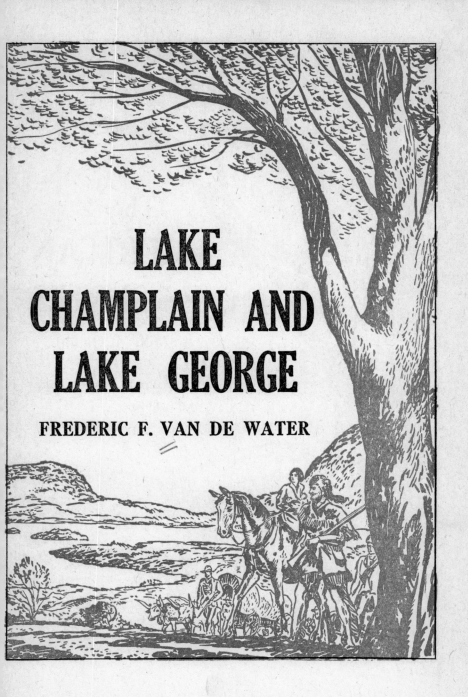

LAKE CHAMPLAIN AND LAKE GEORGE

FREDERIC F. VAN DE WATER

First Edition

To

STERLING AND CAROLYN

with abiding affection

EDITORIAL INTRODUCTION

KING FRANCIS I established a French paper claim to most of North America by sending the Italian navigator, Giovanni Verrazano on a voyage of exploration of the American coast line in 1524. For the St. Lawrence Gulf and Valley the paper claim became a reality three-quarters of a century later when Champlain in 1608 founded the city of Quebec. Eagerness to explore his realm led him in 1609 to accompany an Indian war party upon a raid against their ancient enemies, the Iroquois. The route taken led up the St. Lawrence to the mouth of the Richelieu and then southward up the Richelieu. So the party came in time to the lake of which Champlain became the white discoverer, and which has ever since borne his name. Advancing still southward up the lake, the party came to the vicinity of Ticonderoga where an army of Iroquois warriors was encountered and easily defeated; after which the raiders hastily retired and Champlain returned to Quebec.

So Lake Champlain became a roadway of war to its first European discoverer, as it had doubtless been to the natives of America for uncounted generations of time. To Champlain at this juncture two fascinating geographical opportunities were presented. He might prosecute the westward quest for the Indies by pushing up the St. Lawrence or the Ottawa to the Great Lakes, or he might continue the southward thrust, begun in 1609, toward the Hudson and its outlet in New York Harbor. Force of circumstances dictated the pursuit of the first alternative; within half a dozen years Champlain himself visited Huron and Ontario, and before his death in 1635 Superior and Michigan had been discovered and the westward trend of New France over the interior of the Continent had been determined. Champlain never returned to the lovely lake he had first discovered; and the exploration and settlement of the Hudson Valley were left to the subjects of other nations.

One can never resolve with assurance the might-have-beens of history, but the probable results for the future, had Champlain pushed southward to the Hudson and established French control of New York at a time when the only English settlement in America was the starving Jamestown colony, are sufficient to intrigue the imagination.

As it turned out, the French became seated in the St. Lawrence Valley while a congeries of English colonies occupied the coastal plain stretching southward from Acadia. In 1689 the mother countries entered upon their second One Hundred Years' War—actually continued for a century and a quarter. Save for naval attacks by sea, the rival American colonies could most readily get at each other by conducting raids along the natural highway which the Hudson-Champlain-Richelieu route provided. Each nation appealed for the support of the red warriors, and while Americans commonly regarded such conduct by the French as peculiarly heinous, it is worthy of passing note that the first newspaper established in the English colonies was suppressed by the authorities after its initial issue because the editor had dared to comment unfavorably upon their conduct in enlisting red allies to ravage the settlements and massacre the settlers of French Quebec.

Although Britain conquered Canada in 1760 peace on the old frontier was momentary. When the American colonies revolted and Canada was held loyal to the English Crown, the new adversaries kept up the interminable warfare for another half century. Land-hungry settlers began the occupancy of Champlain's shores soon after the downfall of New France, but not until the War of 1812 ended were their homes safe from destruction or their scalps from inconsiderate barbering.

Since 1815 the beautiful Valley, hemmed between the towering Adirondacks on the west and the gentler Green Mountains to the eastward has been devoted to the arts of peace, save for the modified warfare of smugglers and "Revenuers" which seems likely to continue as long as the varying regulations of Canada and the United States create economic inducements to violate them. Meanwhile the country has been denuded of its primeval forests, farms have been developed and in their turn worn out, and increasing dependence has been lodged in the Valley's one permanent source of wealth, its surpassing scenic and recreational attractions for eastern America's teeming millions.

The martial history of the Champlain-George region has been many times recounted, most effectively for the French-English period by the masterly pen of Parkman. But the story of the region in its entirety, from the glacial age to the present time, richly deserves a comprehensive recital, and to this the present volume in *The American Lakes Series* is devoted.

If devotion to authorship is an inheritable characteristic, Frederic F. Van de Water would seem to afford as good an illustration of this fact as can readily be found. His maternal grandmother, Mary Virginia Terhune, made the pen name "Marion Harland" famous throughout America, and all three of her children who survived to maturity "made their living with ink and paper." One of them was Albert Payson Terhune, prolific journalist, novelist and writer, who is possibly best remembered as the lovable author of stories about dogs. Another, Virginia Terhune Van de Water, wrote numerous novels and serials, served the New York *American* as editorial writer and contributed articles to many magazines. Her son Frederic, our present author, has likewise written many volumes in the several fields of fiction, biography and history. As a journalist he has done "practically everything on a newspaper except set type." As an author he humorously claims as his chief distinction the fact that he has "never even tried to write a play."

A dozen years ago he settled down upon a Vermont farm, and most of his work, literary as well as agricultural, has since had a Vermont background. That the literary work supports the agricultural, rather than vice versa, seems to be clearly indicated by a recent Macedonian appeal for help published as a want ad in a Burlington newspaper. Accomplished journalist and writer, Mr. Van de Water has long since become an earnest student of regional history. Perhaps his most notable published work in this field thus far, at any rate the one he has "sweated over most," is *The Reluctant Republic,* the story of Vermont's birth and existence as an independent nation. To this (and other) serious works is now added *Lake Champlain and Lake George,* whose qualities, we confidently predict, will appreciably increase the reputation both of the author himself and of The American Lakes Series.

M. M. QUAIFE
Detroit Public Library

TABLE OF CONTENTS

TABLE OF CONTENTS—*Continued*

LIST OF ILLUSTRATIONS

LIST OF ILLUSTRATIONS—*Continued*

LAKE CHAMPLAIN AND LAKE GEORGE

SAILBOATING ON LAKE GEORGE AT THE LAKE GEORGE CLUB

THE CHAMPLAIN BRIDGE CONNECTING FORT ST. FRÉDÉRIC RUINS AND CROWN POINT

Chapter 1

Stage Setting

After a Beginning at which men can only guess, land that, ages thence, was to become the western rim of the Champlain Valley and the hills that frame Lake George rose above the surrounding earth.

The world is two billion years old—more or less. A definite age, even if it could be fixed, would mean little since the human mind has limits beyond which it fails. The length of two billion years is past our understanding.

Magnify the smallest human unit of time, of which a minute holds 60 and an hour, 3,600, until a single second's passage represents the lapse of an entire year in this globe's history.

By this ratio, the white discoverer found Champlain five minutes and 37 seconds ago; it is an hour and a half since civilization dawned over Egypt; the earliest ape man existed last week but it still is almost 60 years of seconds, each a year long, since the molten rock of which the Adirondacks are a worn remnant appeared.

The mountains on Champlain's west shore and around Lake George are in general the stumps of incredibly venerable peaks that were minor appendages to the mass that extruded from earth during the birth throes of the North American continent to spread north, east and west. That mass, now an eroded plateau of granitic rock reaching to the Arctic Ocean on either side of Hudson's Bay, is called by geologists the Canadian shield.

Along the edges of the shield, the ocean through ages deposited sediment that solidified into such soft rock as limestone, sandstone, shale.

Unimaginable forces struggled within the young earth. Time, like the human eye, foreshortens distances. In the remoteness of a billion—even a million—years, what seem to have been swift cataclysms may have been achieved only by an imperceptibly minute advance in the millennium. However deliberate these reactions, geology reveals immense risings and fallings and great lateral movements of the earth's crust.

Perhaps four hundred million years ago, toward the end of the Ordovician Period, such a thrust, developing probably from the southeast, jammed the softer, sedimentary rock laid down in the sea against the edge of the obdurate Canadian shield. The granitic mass held. It was the assaulting material that buckled and lifted itself in the east. Out of that consequent highland, the White, Green and Berkshire Mountains were wrought.

It may have been this immense collision which caused upon the shield that crooked fracture geologists call Logan's Fault. This long displacement extends up the present valley of the St. Lawrence from Gaspé and then, turning south, runs along the eastern shore of the present Lake Champlain. Additional and possibly later local faulting in the Lake George area created the ancestors of some of its present eminences—French Mountain, south of the lake, and the flatiron bulk of Tongue Mountain whose tip guards Northwest Bay.

What was to become the Champlain-George Valley remained, for perhaps two hundred million years following the assault upon the Canadian shield, a comparatively stable, probably dry plateau.

During the late Cenozoic Period, only a few million years ago, long after the last dinosaurs had perished and the ancestors of modern mammals had appeared, the land to the east of the present Champlain-George Valley was folded into a rough resemblance to its present terrain. The Adirondack region also was affected and it is probable that, during this disturbance, the valley that Lake George now occupies was formed.

A trough also was created at the feet of the Adirondacks, and through its length, fed by the drainage from these ancient and the newer hills to the east, flowed a river, ancestor of the lake to be. Its course probably was not northward, as Champlain water now moves, but into the ancestor of the present Hudson.

Streams also were born in the depression that modern Lake

George fills. One probably flowed southward from what is now Northwest Bay and, through a now vanished gap between Pilot Knob and French Mountain, escaped into lowlands beyond. The other rose north of the intruding shoulder of Tongue Mountain, which then constituted the divide, and may have run past Rogers Rock and into a no longer existing gap, to join the rivers in the Champlain trough.

The world grew cold a million years ago. In the north, summer's feeble warmth failed to melt the previous winter's snow. This deepened yearly and its weight, increasing storm by storm, turned the buried snow to ice and, pressing ever more heavily, moved that ice ponderously southward along the course of least resistance.

Thus began the Pleistocene Epoch, the Great Ice Age, a recurrent cosmic seizure of chills and fever. Four times the ice mass advanced and receded. We live today in the latest of those withdrawals. No man can tell whether the glacial invasion will come again.

The fourth forward movement overwhelmed New England and extended into the Atlantic beyond Long Island, New York. The advancing ice did not resemble the mountain glaciers of Alaska and the Alps but was a vast, slow-moving plain, perhaps ten thousand feet thick that, as it crept onward, extinguished all life and overrode the tallest mountains.

Rock, pried out by its passage and frozen fast, shod the invading mass that also gathered into its bowels additional earth material. The ice and its acquired tools filed mountaintops, dug deeper the valleys, plowed and gouged new contours into the land. It scored the trough at the foot of the Adirondacks and routed all movable material from the valley of the future Lake George.

It is only one hundred thousand years since the latest withdrawal of the ice began. Whatever its rate of invasion, it has been calculated that in the Connecticut Valley the retirement, as the world grew warm again, was at the rate of a little less than a mile each twenty years.

As the ice sheet melted and shrank, emancipated water flooded land already depressed by the enormous weight of its now diminishing burden while an untold tonnage of rock debris that the glacier had carried forward was left on the earth's surface. Long after mountains had risen above the dwindling ice, the lowlands still were covered. Valleys still harbored lobes of the glacier when the highlands had been freed.

The Lake George depression had been scoured clean by the invading ice. It had planed off and carried away the height of land at Tongue Mountain, hitherto the divide. In its retreat, the glacier completed the creation of what has become the modern lake. At the south end of the French Mountain-Pilot Knob gap, through which one earlier river may have passed, the retiring ice sheet dumped a great mass of sand, gravel and rock, blocking the stream's probable course and creating what is today the height of land between the Lake George and the Hudson Valleys. At what is now the lake's north end, another vast deposit of earth material dammed the second and probably northward-running stream.

Thus, Lake George came into being. While earth was steeped in ice water, the lake level was possibly two hundred feet higher than it is today. Gradually, it assumed its present size as the excess drained away. It was to suffer no such transformations as its larger neighbor endured.

At the nose of the melting glacier lobe that filled the trough we now call the Champlain Valley, the present lake's grandfather, Lake Vermont, was born.

The retreating ice sheet imposed revisions and amendments upon the terrain of the whole Champlain area, creating smaller lakes and ponds in sites it had dug during its advance, altering the surface by dumping haphazardly its massive burden of earth material and turning streams out of old into new courses its advance had graven.

As the Lake Vermont glacial lobe withdrew, the lake itself became greater in length and width than the Champlain of today, filling the lowlands between the Green and Adirondack mountain walls and reaching past the headwaters of the modern lake at Whitehall to immerse the low divide at Fort Ann and pour into the Hudson, first below Schuylerville, later at Fort Edward.

Lake Vermont had begun to decrease in size before the valley was wholly clear of ice, for the overflow now bore off more water than the dwindling lobe could furnish. It is probable that while the lower St. Lawrence still was blocked, the current of the shrinking, ancient lake was reversed and its waters were discharged through approximately its present outlet.

The whole area had been lowered by the unthinkable weight it had borne; ocean had been swollen by a vast inpouring from the glacial melting. When the St. Lawrence barrier finally dissolved, salt water, reversing the river's flow, invaded the Champlain Valley. The estuary thus created, the Champlain Sea, extended no farther south than Whitehall.

Present Champlain yields evidence of its oceanic past. Bones of seals, walruses and the skeleton of a whale have been found on its shores. The silvery smelts that emerge from the depths late each winter to spawn in rivers were once salt-water creatures.

Other fish of the lake must have had a marine origin. The ling or cusk is a fresh-water cod; the Champlain sheepshead is a close relative of the sea-bred drum.

Earth rose as the weight of the ice sheet vanished, but the elevation was not uniform. The land lifted more rapidly in the north and at last bore up above St. Lawrence's water level the barrier through which Champlain's outlet, the Richelieu River, now flows.

The newborn lake thus was cut off from immediate intimacy with the St. Lawrence whose basin, also rising, was ridding itself of the encroaching sea. Streams that fed Champlain washed away the last traces of salt some twenty thousand years ago—which, as geology measures time, is only as day before yesterday to the normal span of human life.

No one can be certain that the land still is not infinitesimally tilting. A further rise of less than six inches to the mile would again reverse the lake's course and turn it to flowing southward through the ancient Whitehall-Fort Ann-Fort Edward channel.

In time unrecorded, Champlain's bed underwent radical change. Some undetermined disturbance caused a break in the land along the west lake shore. It dropped sharply, as a trap door falls, using Logan's Fault as a hinge. The lake bottom shelves off gradually from the east shore today but on the west side it deepens abruptly and bluffs and cliffs mark the line of fracture.

Logan's Fault still may be a formative factor in Champlain's future. Twice in the last ten years, minor adjustments along the dislocation have created perceptible temblors. These may have been faint echoes of the tremendous 1663 quake when, with due allowance for the extravagance of contemporary French reports, forests were overthrown and streams were cast from their ancient beds into new courses. Mont Trembleau, in Chesterfield on the lake's west shore, and Point aux Trembles on the St. Lawrence may be names reminiscent of that catastrophe. Diminishing shocks were felt for many years afterward. There is no certainty that Logan's Fault finally has been stabilized.

Out of cosmic travail—establishment, disruption, recreation—Champlain and George, the linked and lovely lakes, came into being. Their present tranquillity is paradoxical. The ostensibly peace-haunted waters, being where they are and as they are, have served as a reiterant provocation to war.

For the first two hundred years of George's and Champlain's recorded existence, and still farther back through the dimness of Indian tales, the principal traffic of the lakes was martial; the chief enterprise of the area they drained was battle. Their nature and their situation bent history and channeled the course of empire. Lake Champlain is shaped like a battered and dented cornucopia, or a malformed carrot with a long thin taproot. Its over-all length from its headwaters at Whitehall to the northern beach of Missisquoi Bay is 107 miles, of which 5 lie over the border in Canada. Its greatest width is 12 miles in the general latitude of Burlington, Vermont.

The lake has some eighty islands, most of them clustered in the mouth of the northward-opening cornucopia and varying in size from twelve-mile-long Grand Isle and North Hero, with their wind-swept, snake-fenced farmsteads, to crumbs of rock too small to afford a foothold for a single tree.

For a hundred miles of its length, Champlain's channel forms the New York-Vermont boundary line. Its area is 490 square miles of which 322 lie in Vermont, 151 in New York and 17 in Canada. The lake's greatest depth is 399 feet, 2 miles north of Split Rock Point. Its normal surface is 95 feet above sea level. Its greatest recorded height, March 28, 1936, was 100.89 feet; its lowest, November 23, 1908, was 92.04.

Champlain Valley's rivers, born in the guardian mountains of either shore, come down from the highlands over falls that pioneer settlers eagerly exploited for mill power. On the Vermont side of the Canadian border, the Missisquoi and then the Lamoille—a careless early cartographer's misspelling of "la mouette," the sea gull—flow through drowned land to union with the lake. The Winooski, with a lusty mill town of the same name at its falls, runs a winding course south of these, and the final stream of stature on the east shore is Otter Creek, navigable as far inland as the high rock ledge over which it plunges at Vergennes.

The Chazy is northernmost of New York's contributing rivers. Uplake are the Saranac which nourished the infant Plattsburg, the Salmon and the Ausable. The quick brown water of this last was turned from its ancient bed by glacial blocking and has cut deep through sandstone a new fantastically carved gorge for itself. South of the Ausable, the Boquet enters the lake.

These are the only watercourses entitled to the rank of rivers and all of them empty into the lower half of Champlain. Beyond the Otter and the Boquet, only inconsiderable streams come down from the imminent hills.

The Richelieu River sedately carries Champlain's overflow northward through lowlands and past successive wooded islands to go down in foam at the Chambly Rapids and empty into the St. Lawrence at Sorel, downstream from Montreal. A canal now skirts the swift water. Another canal leads inland from Whitehall at the lakehead and follows the ancient bed of Pleistocene Lake Vermont to reach the Hudson and the New York Barge Canal at Fort Edward.

Where Champlain narrows toward its outlet, a causeway and

drawbridge bear motor, and a trestle and drawbridge carry rail traffic between Alburg, Vermont, and Rouses Point, New York. Northward, on the west shore the haggard, gray bulk of Fort Montgomery rises, its dead interior laid bare by the removal of its east wall to supply fill for the motor causeway. Immediately to the south, low islands crowned by foliage tangle the lake in a Venetian intricacy of lagoons, bays and straits.

The channel skirts the rock-rimmed verdure of Isle La Motte, swallow-haunted North Hero and Grand Isle. Beyond them, thrusting out from the New York shore, wooded Cumberland Head guards the bay where Plattsburg's steeples lift through foliage. Over the islands, the far peaks of the Green Mountains rear like lower, darker clouds.

Oblong Valcour Island, standing green on its pedestal of wave-worn rock, lies in the foreground and beyond it stretches the brilliance of Champlain's greatest breadth. In blowing weather, the water is an intense blue; in calm, it cherishes infinite cool, silken hues that are shot with fire as the sun goes west.

The lake reveals here its cornucopia shape. Southward, the shores perceptibly reach toward each other while from either hand, blue ranges advance out of the dim distance toward the water. The Adirondacks circle the Plattsburg plain to stand at Port Kent on Champlain's edge and pile up dusky, blunt pyramids and uneven domes in the south. Beyond the farther strand, where Burlington's mellow houses lie, elm-shaded, along the slope above her bay, the Green Mountains' more fluent ridges slant lakeward from the northeast and mount to the aloof, nose-tilted profile of Mansfield.

Thence, to the south, Champlain dwindles steadily in width. Islands grow infrequent and shores are less deeply indented. The Vermont ranges remain in mid-distance beyond a rolling, dark-soiled lowland where dairy farms and orchards flourish but the Adirondacks still crowd down to the shore. Between the great cloven stone, revered by the Iroquois, at the tip of Split Rock Point and Thompson's Point on the Vermont side, the lake is less than a mile wide.

South of the waterside, iron-mining center of Port Henry, a low, oblong cape juts from the New York shore, and the skeletal remains of old forts protrude through a sparse turf. The current dimples and swirls beneath the tall gray bridge that leaps three-eighths of a mile of water between Crown and Chimney Point, and on the west shore stands a pale granite lighthouse—monument to the lake's discoverer.

Past these narrows, Champlain gradually assumes the aspect of a wide, torpid river, nowhere much more than a mile in breadth and with water that, in wet seasons, grows turgid as the Missouri's.

The narrowing lake extends past the Ticonderoga plain, where the donjon keeps of tall, white silos lend a medieval air to a fair countryside, to another wider and taller cape thrusting out from the west shore. On the promontory's spine rises the Pell family's reconstruction of the stronghold the French built here and called Fort Carillon. The English renamed it Fort Ticonderoga.

The rugged bulk of Mount Defiance looms south of the fort on the New York shore and across the water is the lower height of Mount Independence. Flowing north, east and then southeast from the head of Lake George, the outlet of the lesser lake runs a sickle-shaped course about Mount Defiance and through Ticonderoga village to empty into the larger water at the foot of the declivity the revived fort crowns.

Champlain, south of Ticonderoga, degenerates into an increasingly murky, continually narrower creek moving sluggishly past wooded highlands and through bordering marshes. It skirts the sheer bluff of Bald Mountain below Whitehall and has its source in the muddy anticlimax of South Bay, curving south and west beyond the mill town.

Champlain begins as a swamp, continues as a stream and swells into a torpid river before it becomes a full-statured lake—a lovely lake that lyrically combines light and shade, sky, water and enfolding hills; a short-tempered lake, prone to smash serenity with sudden thunderstorms or pour down its funneled length unheralded gusts that overturn the canoes and boats of the unwary. Its smaller kinsman is less protean, less volatile.

Lake George is 30 miles long and its greatest breadth, east and west from Montcalm Point, is 3.25 miles. Its surface of 44.44 square miles is 317 feet above mean sea level, 212 feet higher than Champlain. George's greatest measured depth, close to the shore of Buck Mountain, is 187 feet. More than 200 small islands are set in the clear, blue-green water. Tall hills encircle the lake. Springs and small mountain brooks nourish it.

The narrow water, stretching from the white beach and dark pines at its head, through the crowding islands of the Narrows, to where its overflow plunges across the first low barrier in its outlet, has the riverlike aspect of upper Champlain but a graver, more constant beauty.

The larger lake has a blithe tranquillity; the lesser, an ecclesiastical calm imposed by protective mountains whose ridges, apple green in sunlight, and dusky blue in shadow, swoop and soar against the sky, while their bases stand deep in lucid water.

Beauty that a state has cherished and preserved is Lake George's chief present importance. The rapids down which its outlet pours have locked the lake to commerce. Canals at either end of Champlain have expedited trade. None has been built for George. It is a waterway running from a place of small consequence to another of no great significance. When wars ended in the Champlain-George Valley, the critical importance of the smaller lake perished also, as though powers committed to paradox had created the fair water for one fell purpose.

The comely lakes that Champlain and Jogues named were to suffer in the two centuries after their christening protracted violences. The gentleman adventurer who first broke the hills' silence with gunfire; the priest who went up the smaller lake to martyrdom, opened the region to widespread war.

The valley already had been plentifully bloodstained when the French discovered it. The geological development of the area had ordained that this water-paved corridor through the ranges should become a highway for conflict.

For generations before Champlain, elm-bark canoes of the Iroquois, the Confederacy of Five Nations who claimed proprietorship of both lakes, had borne war parties to the Huron and Algonquin villages in the north. Birch-bark canoes had carried Algonquin and Huron south on retaliatory raids. Small, savage forays had set the pattern for things to come.

The French gathered power in Canada. The Dutch, and then the English, crept north from the beginnings of Albany. The land seemed so vast and formless that even the greed of men could not encompass it, yet from the beginning, pioneer peoples were flung against each other across leagues of wilderness in wars that were loyal, needless responses to European struggles. If the existence of the lakes had not ordained otherwise, French and English settlers might have lived through reiterated transatlantic strife in approximate peace.

Empty country separated the frontier settlements—multiple ranges clothed in primeval forest, difficult and trackless—but there was one breach in the forbidding rampart. Between the long curves of the Green Mountains and the abrupter angles of the Adirondacks, lay the Champlain-George Valley offering easy passage by water north and south and, at its lower, forked end, a choice of two roads to the English settlements.

The French could advance, the retaliating English could move north, from the head of Lake Champlain or the head of Lake George. From the greater lake's South Bay, the light-draft barges called bateaux could move still farther southward up Wood Creek. When the water shoaled, a distance of from six to ten miles, depending on the season's rainfall, lay between the creek and the Hudson, where Fort Edward stands today. By mileage, this was the easier road, but the ground was low and marshy. Malaria and dysentery waited for expeditions along this route. In time, careful men came to prefer the alternate course.

This second warpath led through Lake George. There was a two-mile carry from Champlain to the lesser lake and at its head fourteen miles of further marching over sandy soil and through pine forest. It was the longer yet the more salutary way.

Land and water had fixed the type for the wars that were to roll up and down the Champlain-George Valley. Here was no opportunity for deception; no chance for spacious maneuverings and flank attacks. The advance must come directly and must be met frontally. Invasion, to move at all, must follow the shining course of the lakes.

Geography molds and directs humanity's courses. The geological present that men misidentify as stability had set the stage in the Champlain-George Valley long before the lurid drama was conceived. The production was to be influenced radically by the background against which Champlain and Jogues, Abercromby and Montcalm, Ethan Allen and Benedict Arnold, St. Clair and Burgoyne, Macdonough and Downie and unnumbered thousands of lesser players were to act their parts. These in no small measure were to be determined in scope and impact by the very form of the valley. Valcour Island and Cumberland Head, Crown Point and Ticonderoga, South Bay and Wood Creek; the outlet and the head of Lake George were to shape and, to a great degree establish, human destiny.

Thus it came about that the valley with its long, narrow waters and the neighboring, difficult ranges, stamped its own distinct imprint on the history of a continent and, less immediately, of a planet.

All this had been ordained before the coming of Samuel de Champlain.

Chapter 2

The Seed Is Sown

FROST covered the ground, October 3, and on November 18 came a great fall of snow. Two Frenchmen died of dysentery that month and many of the Montagnais Indians who camped about the little palisaded fort between the bluff and the river also perished. The captain of the tiny stronghold thought they had killed themselves by gorging on half-cooked eels.

All this and other matters the captain carefully wrote down during the dire ensuing winter. He had a great if overcredulous curiosity concerning this vast new land that was to be won for France. For five years now, aship and ashore, he had explored its wastes and, in the previous summer of 1608, had built this log-walled outpost below the majestic cliffs that the Indians called Quebec.

Seventy-three years earlier, in 1535, the Breton sailor, Jacques Cartier, had ventured this far, and farther, up the St. Lawrence, alert for the demons and griffons with which the tall forests notoriously were populated. Since then, French attempts at colonization had accomplished little more than to establish a semi-permanent fur-trading station at Tadoussac, down-river. This new settlement of Quebec between the bluffs—where the snows lay ever deeper—and the river—now filled with groaning, shouldering floes—would endure, its founder had resolved, if a man of its garrison survived the winter. Before spring arrived, that survival had become doubtful.

The scurvy that had shriveled earlier attempts at settlement did not come until February. It killed ten of the remaining twenty-six men and dysentery slew five more. By the commandant's order, the surgeon performed autopsies on several; then the surgeon also perished. Thereafter, the inquiring mind of Samuel de

29

Champlain was left to grope without scientific aid for cause of the scourge. He recorded his belief that it was due to vapors rising from the recently cleared forest soil.

Champlain in the year of the founding of Quebec was forty-one years old, a seaworn gentleman of a good Saintonge family with a passion for discovery. He had turned from the profession of sailor to measure and map land that seemed as illimitable as ocean, for the glory of France and whatever incidental profit should accrue to him and his partner, Pontgravé, a merchant of St. Malo.

The founder of the infant and ailing outpost was a sunny, energetic person with an active and ambitious mind which had run so far ahead of the winter of 1608-1609 that it seems not to have dwelt at all on what must have been a gruesome ordeal.

"On the 5th of June, a shallop arrived at our settlement with Sieur des Marais, a son-in-law of Pontgravé, bringing us tidings that his father-in-law had arrived at Tadoussac on the 28th of May. This intelligence gave me much satisfaction as we entertained hopes of assistance from him. Only eight out of the twenty-eight at first forming our company were remaining, and half of these were ailing."[1]

Apparently, he thought less of the death and of the agony than of a project urged by a chief of the Huron who had visited the stockaded huts during the previous year and had invited their commandant to join, in the summer now arriving, an expedition against the deadly enemy of Canada's Indians, the People of the Long House, the terrible Iroquois Confederation.

Five tribes composed this union which was at once mystical and intensely practical. The stockaded villages of the allies, which white men later were to call "castles," stretched across upper New York from Lake Erie to the Hudson. The Senecas held the western door of the Long House. Thence, easterly, dwelt the Cayuga, Onondaga, Oneida and the Canienga, whom the Dutch and English misnamed "Mohawk."

In warfare, the Long House people were valiant and wholly merciless. They were semi-cannibalistic savages who yet had evolved an intricate and skillfully contrived system of national gov-

FATHER ISAAC JOGUES

The intrepid and courageous Catholic missionary, Father Jogues, was the first European to see Lake George. He named it Lac du St. Sacrement, but an English soldier, moved by patriotism, later changed the name to Lake George.

Derick Photo, Courtesy of the Department of Conservation and Development

JESUIT CHAPEL, ISLE LA MOTTE

Photo from Division of State Publicity, New York State Department of Commerce

LAKE GEORGE FROM ABOVE LAKEHEAD

ernment whose checks and balances may have indirectly influenced in the years to come the white dream of an American republic. Union augmented Iroquois power and increased, if possible, their rapacity.

These human wolves raided the St. Lawrence Valley from land that no white man yet had seen. The expedition the Huron and their allies, the Algonquin and Montagnais, planned to launch against the Five Nations would follow an already long-employed water route—up a river, through a great lake and a lesser beyond and by portage toward another stream which led to the sea.

Discovery, adventure, statecraft were embodied in this enterprise. Champlain hurried down-river to Tadoussac, conferred with Pontgravé and, in a shallop with twenty men, hastened upstream again and on June 18, with some Montagnais Indians added to his company, set out from Quebec.

They traveled seventy-five miles against the current before Champlain found his Indians, some two or three hundred savages, Huron and Algonquin, armed and painted for war.

It appeared, however, that war was not their immediate purpose and after a conference Champlain and his party were obliged to turn about and accompany their allies down-river again so that the warriors might view the splendors of the white men's new town and, incidentally, be entertained by its occupants.

In the days of feasting and dancing that followed arrival at Quebec, Pontgravé and more men came up from Tadoussac and on June 28, the reinforced expedition set out again. On July 1, Pontgravé and the bulk of the white force "for certain reasons," which may have included a fear of Indian treachery, returned to Quebec and Tadoussac while Champlain in one shallop with eleven men accompanied the war party farther.

At the mouth of the stream then known as the Rivière des Iroquois, later to be called in succession the St. Louis, the Sorel and, finally, the Richelieu, there was further delay and defection. The majority of the warriors decided to go home with the goods they had obtained in trade at Quebec. Only twenty-four canoe crews, sixty men in all, still yearned to face the Iroquois. Champlain's shallop accompanied them and soon met with new difficulties.

The Indians had assured their allies that passage through the river and into the lake beyond was clear and navigable. Forty-five miles up-river, Champlain faced the long, tumbling flow of the Chambly Rapids, about which, it was clear, even canoes must be carried. It would be impossible to transport a heavier craft.

A more short-tempered or less enterprising spirit, seeing how the expedition melted away before him, would have abandoned it and returned to Quebec. Champlain seems to have hesitated but he found it impossible "to go back without seeing a very large lake, filled with handsome islands," of which his unreliable guides had told him. He decided to continue with two volunteers. The shallop and the rest of the crew retired to Quebec. The depleted war party carried the canoes for three miles around the most violent stretch of the rapids.

The actual date when a canoe bore Champlain out upon the lake that bears his name is uncertain. He seems to have been, on this expedition at least, a more enthusiastic than accurate narrator, writing "June" when he obviously meant "July" and vice versa and showing a haphazard disregard for the sequence of the month's days. It is probable that the party got around the Richelieu rapids on July 12 and entered the lake forty-eight hours later. Before then, the character of the advance had changed radically.

It was enemy country beyond the rapids and the bivouac that night was a tribute to the prowess of the Long House warriors. Bark lean-tos were raised as usual, but the expedition worked for two hours thereafter, felling trees and building about the camp a barricade left open only toward the beach where their canoes were drawn up. Three canoeloads of Indians paddled farther upstream to search for signs of the Iroquois.

Upon the scouts' return, the entire party slumbered without posting sentries, much to the scandal of Champlain who protested without avail. Men, the warriors told him, who worked all day could not be expected to sit up all night as well.

The explorer was offended additionally by the conduct of the war party's medicine man who erected a lodge, covered it with a robe and, entering, consulted the tribal deities to the accompaniment of loud gibberish and a violent shaking of the structure while the rest of the company waited for an augury "seated on their buttocks like apes." Champlain's remonstrances again were vain.

He was impressed far more by the fashion in which the Indians planned their battle array. Sticks, each representing a man, were thrust into a level piece of ground and the warriors, after studying the model, arranged themselves in like formation, and continued to do so at each camping place they occupied.

The military adaptability of the Indian is shown by the swift change from the close-order fighting of this time to the ambush and surprise, hit-and-run strategy they employed a generation later when they had learned the power of firearms.

On the following day, the canoes continued upstream, threading a course between wooded islands "with abundance of fowl and such animals of the chase as stags, fallow deer, fawns, roebucks, bears and others." The next morning, probably July 14, the flotilla entered the lake that still bears its discoverer's name.

It may have been the wonder spread before Champlain, as the canoes went past Grand Isle and wide water shone beyond, that unsettled still further his never too extreme accuracy. Sheer beauty may have impelled him to see everything magnified, for he declared the lake was from two hundred and forty to three hundred miles long and that the "four fine islands" near its outlet were thirty, thirty-six and forty-five miles in length—two, three or fourfold exaggerations.

The discoverer also professed to see snow on the long Green Mountain ranges rolling up to the climax of Mount Mansfield, but none on the higher angles of the Adirondacks. The Indians with openhanded inaccuracy akin to Champlain's assured him that in the land which was to become Vermont the Iroquois dwelt "and that there were beautiful valleys in these places with plains productive of grain, such as I have eaten in this country, together with many kinds of fruit without limit," though since the explorer's time small evidence of Indian occupation or cultivation has been found in interior Vermont, where "productive plains" were at that time nonexistent.

Champlain set a capstone of fantasy upon misinformation by dwelling at length upon the habits of the "chaousarou," a native fish said to reach a length of ten feet, two and a half feet of which was a toothed beak. When hungry, he assures us, the creature held his bill above water until some obliging bird perched on it to be devoured.

They were deep in hostile country now and henceforth journeyed only at night, hiding their canoes before dawn and resting quietly in the depths of the woods during the day. The dread that the Iroquois cast over all their foes began to afflict this expedition. It mounted until Champlain fortunately dreamed that he saw the enemy drowning in the lake.

"This, upon being related, gave them so much confidence that they did not doubt any longer that good was to happen to them."

That night, which Champlain says was July 29, they met the enemy. A dark promontory which the Iroquois knew by the resounding name "Ticonderoga" thrust out into the starlit water from the western shore and off its tip the flotilla suddenly made contact with a war party of Iroquois, probably Mohawk, moving north in elm-bark canoes.

After the first outburst of yelling, the affair was conducted with an elaborate observance of protocol which later association with the whites abolished. Champlain's allies lingered offshore, holding their canoes together by poles stretched from gunwale to neighbor's gunwale. The enemy landed and immediately began construction of a breastwork.

Presently, when the invaders had armed themselves, they sent two canoes shoreward. Their occupants, acting as heralds, challenged the breastwork builders to combat.

"The latter replied that they wanted nothing else; but they said that, at present, there was not much light, and that it would be necessary to wait for daylight, so as to be able to recognize each other; and that, as soon as the sun rose, they would offer us battle. This was agreed to by our side."

The two parties, afloat and ashore, enlivened their dark vigil by screeching insults and challenges at each other. When the owl-like hooting paused, Champlain may have heard the sound of Lake George water, foaming down through the outlet, for his narrative says that he visited the rapids on the morrow.

The Frenchmen each lay hidden in a separate canoe. They had put on the light armor they carried and had loaded their arquebuses. At sunrise, the invaders moved in and landed. Champlain's white companions stole to the left through the woods. He himself was hidden in the mass of men who advanced toward the barricade.

The Iroquois, apparently encouraged by the small size of the attacking force, issued from their breastworks, formed ranks and moved forward; tall, stalwart men with shields of cedar and breastplates of twigs that were bound together by plant fibers. Three chiefs, distinguished by tall feathers in their scalp locks, led the red phalanx. Its disciplined deliberation greatly delighted Champlain, whose allies now opened their ranks and thrust him to the fore.

The Iroquois halted abruptly and stared at the strange figure in the gleaming raiment. Some of them raised their bows. Champlain leveled his arquebus and fired. The clap of the shot echoed through the hills that, in years to come, were to roll back the sounds of a myriad heavier explosions. The four balls with which the arquebus had been charged killed two of the chiefs and wounded a warrior.

The Iroquois wavered, rallied and, as Champlain made haste to load, launched a cloud of arrows. At this instant, one of the ambushed Frenchmen fired from the woods. The enemy broke and ran. Champlain, pursuing, killed more by his second shot. His triumphantly screeching allies overtook and captured a dozen of the fugitives.

For three hours, thereafter, the enraptured victors reveled, stuffing themselves with the Iroquois' abandoned supplies, singing and dancing. It must have been during this interval that Champlain inspected the lower rapids of the Lake George outlet.

The triumph ended abruptly and the haste of the victors' departure was like flight. They still feared the Iroquois too greatly to tarry longer in enemy territory. Not until their paddles had thrust twenty-four miles of water behind them, did they go ashore.

Here in the firelight, Champlain witnessed with horror the common aftermath of Indian battle that many Frenchmen were to suffer in the years ahead—the slow destruction of a prisoner with every ingenuity that could intensify and prolong anguish.

The triumphant Huron, Algonquin and Montagnais chose a victim, recited to him the savageries the Iroquois had committed upon prisoners of their own, promised him no better fate and dared him, if he had the courage, to sing. The victim lifted his voice.

"But," Champlain writes, "it was a very sad song."

The torturers went to work with firebrands, knives and teeth. Champlain sickened and turned away. His allies, belatedly recognizing his displeasure, granted him the privilege for which he already had begged and permitted him to shoot the mutilated wretch through the head. The dead man's heart was cut out and slices of it were thrust into the mouth of another captive, his brother. What remained of the body was dismembered, disemboweled and cast into the lake.

After such shambles, the party re-embarked and continued the retreat. Their prisoners kept up a valiant singing "with no more hopes for the future than he had had who was so wretchedly treated."

The expedition broke up after it had passed the falls of the Richelieu. The Huron and Algonquin started with their share of the prisoners for their own country. The Montagnais went on toward Quebec with Champlain. The dread of Iroquois reprisal hung so heavily over these creatures that when, on a stormy midnight, one of them woke from a dream in which he had been pursued by Long House warriors, he and his companions broke camp immediately and hid till daylight in the tall reeds which bordered the dilation of the St. Lawrence the French called Lake St. Peter.

Champlain, for diplomatic reasons, accompanied the Montagnais to Tadoussac and witnessed their homecoming and its subsequent ghastliness. The Indians gave him as a farewell gift, the head and the arms of one of their prisoners to send to his king.

The expedition had won for Samuel de Champlain other prizes, material and immaterial, welcome and unwelcome. He had discovered not only the long, lovely lake to which he had given his name but he also had been the first white man to set foot on the territory later to be called New York and to see the land that was to become Vermont.

Had Champlain gone as an explorer, not a raider, he might have followed the route of which the Indians had told him, discovering Lake George, passing over the Great Carrying Place from the head of the lesser lake to the southward flowing river and voyaging down this to the sea. If all these possibilities had been accomplished, the white-lilied flag might have waved from Manhattan Island when, on September 3 in this same year, 1609, a shoe-shaped little craft named *Half Moon* came up the bay.

Instead, Champlain went as an ally of red warriors and opened for his nation only that watery warpath along which the power of France crept sluggishly forward for almost a century and a half before its final recoil and collapse. He won, by this foray, the friendship of Canadian Indians at the cost of Iroquois enmity. It was a heavy price that New France paid for generations in installments of fire and blood. Historians have deplored Champlain's action, yet it is difficult to see how he could have done otherwise.

The enmity between the Long House Confederation and the red men of Canada was innate and deadly. If the French were to keep and strengthen their slight hold on the vast land, statecraft and common sense demanded that they gain the friendship of the inhabitants of New France. An enemy, however rapacious, south of the St. Lawrence was preferable to more immediate and numerous foes about the little stockades.

There is no evidence that other Frenchmen visited Champlain's namesake for almost a generation. The mind of its discoverer reached westward and, when the exigencies of the colony permitted, he made brief explorations toward lakes that the Indians knew and legendary waterways beyond that might be, at last, the sea route to India. Champlain looked on much that no other white man had seen and solidified French alliance with the Canadian tribes by further skirmishes with the Iroquois.

The Dutch crept up the Hudson and established, where Albany was to rise, a log-walled trading post, Fort Nassau. Hither came Mohawk and, later, Oneida to barter furs for beads and kettles and axes and, most important of all, guns that would give them equality with their new enemies, the French.

On December 20, 1620, Captain Christopher Jones set ashore from his *Mayflower* a hardheaded, stiff-necked company at a place they named Plymouth. Half of the colonists died before winter was spent but the remnant and their brethren who followed increased mightily and, with the English collective and individual hunger for land, spread and possessed the soil.

Quebec, now twelve years old, still had less than fifty French inhabitants and most of these were factors for merchants more intent on profits from the fur trade than on winning a continent for France. They were a dissolute and brawling crew, Catholic and Huguenot alike, and they compelled Champlain to spend much time regulating the colony's affairs while his spirit fretted for more spacious adventures and discoveries.

The slow growth of the stunted settlement was halted brutally in 1629. England, then engaged on an early installment of its serial war with France, sent a fleet under Admiral David Kirke up the St. Lawrence. Quebec fell, and with it all New France, but the British, initiating a custom they were to follow in wars to be, gave back the territory in 1632 and, in the following year, Champlain returned to his own again.

He no longer was executive for profit-seeking merchants, but for Richelieu, the great cardinal himself, who had taken over administration of the affairs of New France. There was power and wisdom behind Champlain now, but he was worn by privation and journeyings, and his mind turned increasingly toward another undiscovered country. The Jesuits who had been sent to stamp out heresy in the colony and redeem heathen souls found the erstwhile explorer gratifyingly devout. Samuel de Champlain died on Christmas Day, 1635.

He was a brave and eager explorer, not a statesman; a seeker, not a settler. Much of which he dreamed he was compelled to leave undone. He never saw again the fair, hill-enfolded water to which he gave his name, and the French, reaching westward, were laggard in exploiting it. They left the lake to lie for years ignored, deserted, untraveled save by the elm-bark canoes of the Mohawk, graving brief broad arrows as the war parties paddled north to pursue an ancient feud intensified by Samuel de Champlain.

[1] The quotations in the present chapter are from Champlain's *Voyages,* edited by W. L. Grant (New York, 1907).

Chapter 3

Martyr's Progress

CHARLES HUALT DE MONTMAGNY, a devout soldier whose piety surpassed his military skill, ruled at Quebec in Champlain's stead. He encouraged the westward extension of Jesuit missions and tried less successfully to stem the hostile Iroquois.

With the handful of troops allowed him by a niggardly king, Montmagny accomplished little of secular importance beyond involuntarily bestowing a Mohawk translation of his surname upon all subsequent governors of New France. The Iroquois called him and his successors "Onontio"—Great Mountain. Montmagny labored desperately against his red enemies and brought forth a mouse.

The Long House warriors had begun a purposeful campaign to bring about, not the defeat and subjugation, but the wholesale extermination of Algonquin, Huron and, eventually, their French allies.

Champlain's participation in earlier Indian fights may have been a minor contribution to this new Iroquois fury but other factors were also responsible and were to heighten the outbursts. Something new had been added to an age-old feud. The Dutch at their trading posts along the Hudson were offering guns and lesser luxuries in exchange for furs.

Hitherto, the simple and rapacious Indian had looked on the beasts of the wilderness only as sources of raiment and food. Now, pelts could be exchanged for immensely valuable things, especially guns, and suddenly beavers, bears and their kindred had turned into animate legal tender.

The bigoted and prudential French permitted only thoroughly converted Indians to acquire firearms. The tolerant Dutch never weighed the religious beliefs of their customers, wherefore the Five

Nations equipped themselves with trade muskets far more rapidly than their enemies.

Iroquois ambition, always most satisfactorily expressed by blood-letting, mounted as the warriors grew sure of their new power. They yearned for still greater riches and, since the fur supply dwindled in their own territory, turned with increased ferocity against Canada. Here dwelt not only the hereditary enemies of the Long House but also a limitless number of fur-bearing animals. By destroying the human residents in that region, the Iroquois would pay off old blood debts and at the same time fall heir to an inexhaustible bank account.

Each summer more war parties ranged north via the lakes. Month by month the butchering, the burning, the broiling, dead or alive, for cannibalistic feasts increased. Villages of Huron and Algonquin were wiped out. Ambushes continually were set for the unwary. One such lurked in the tall reeds bordering that widening of the St. Lawrence called Lake St. Peter on August 2, 1642, and watched a little fleet of heavily laden canoes move into the trap.

The Huron who paddled the craft swung them shoreward to avoid the thrust of the current and the faces of the three white men in the company grew plain to slit eyes watching through the reeds. Two of the French wore civilian attire; the third, a black robe. Father Isaac Jogues of the Society of Jesus was returning with supplies for the lately established mission to the Huron on Georgian Bay. With him were two lay attachés of the order, René Goupil and Guillaume Couture. In all of them burned zeal to bring the heathen to Christ. That fervor never blazed with a purer flame than in the breast of Father Isaac Jogues.

He was a native of Orleans and now thirty-five years old with six years of missionary service behind him; a slender, bearded figure; shy, with a sensitive face and a gentle manner. Frail though he appeared, he had amazing stamina and was so fleet of foot that, at the mission, he had outrun all Indians. His swiftness might have saved him as the painted Mohawks raised the war yell and thrust their canoes from the reeds.

Trade muskets spouted smoke. The rearmost in the trapped flotilla beached their craft and ran. The Frenchmen and the Christian Huron held off the attack for a moment, but another wave of Mohawk canoes issued from the reeds on the river's far side and took them in the rear. There was wrestling and screeching in the shallows as Huron and French tried to fight their way to shore. Goupil and several Indians were taken; Father Jogues shook off his pursuers and was free.

He sank down among the reeds but his liberty was brief and self-ended. Through the haphazard lattice of his hiding place he saw that his friends and his own converts had been made prisoner.

" 'Could I indeed,' I said to myself, 'abandon our French and leave these good Neophytes and these poor Catechumens without giving them the help which the Church of my God had entrusted to me?' "[1]

Isaac Jogues, who was not unacquainted with what Iroquois captivity meant, walked out of the reeds and joined the prisoners.

There was harrying and hunting up and down the riverbank as the Mohawk flushed their cowering victims. Couture, who also had escaped, turned back to find Father Jogues. An Indian shot at him and missed. The Frenchman returned the fire and killed his assailant as four other Mohawk leaped upon him.

They bore him down and in their rage strove to destroy him piecemeal where he lay, ripping his clothes away, tearing out handfuls of his hair, mangling his hands with their teeth. Jogues broke from his captors, plunged into the worrying pack and covered his friend's body with his own. A war club stunned him. When he revived his fingers too were gnawed and Goupil's were served likewise.

While the hunt went on, while more wretched fugitives were dragged from their hiding places, the priest administered baptism with bleeding hands to those of his pagan fellow prisoners who would accept it. One, an old man, had his brains dashed out, just after he had received the rite. The rest of the captives, twenty-two in all, were bound, thrust into canoes and the Mohawk war party turned homeward.

So began the first stage in Isaac Jogues' long and dolorous way to martyrdom and sainthood. They journeyed a hot and weary time and camped that night at the Richelieu's mouth where the town of Sorel was to stand. They paddled upstream to the foot of the rapids. Here the captives were laden and driven over the portage. The priest, recognized by the Mohawk as the chief of their prisoners, suffered a double share of the burden and abuse.

"Therefore I take pleasure in infirmities, in reproaches, in necessities, in persecutions, in distresses for Christ's sake; for when I am weak, then I am strong."

Strength remained with him during the brutalities of that journey through the river and up Lake Champlain. Seven days they traveled and on the eighth the homeward-bound Mohawk met a larger war party of their brethren, traveling north. Wild screeching rose, muskets were fired in salute and the combined groups beached their canoes to amuse themselves with the captives.

Grinning warriors formed a long double line. The war clubs beat upon the prisoners who ran the gantlet. The war clubs fell most furiously upon Father Jogues and he, the fleetest of them all, was struck down and could not rise. They revived him by chewing his fingers again and thrusting firebrands against the most sensitive parts of his body. The Huron chief, whom the French called Eustache, was used still more hideously.

There was no respite for the priest that night. The younger warriors found entertainment in enlarging his wounds, plucking strands from his beard.

"I would be too tedious if I should set down in writing all the rigors of my sufferings."[2]

On the morrow the Mohawk bands separated. The outward-bound party paddled north to attack and be beaten back from the half-completed stockade the distracted Montmagny was building at the mouth of the Richelieu to protect the war-scourged colony. Father Jogues' captors went on up the lake to create on their homeward way an insoluble problem.

The priest's own account of his journey throws no clear light on the route his party took to the Indian villages on the Mohawk.

They may have followed the streamlike, swamp-bordered arm of Champlain into South Bay; they may have journeyed by way of Ticonderoga, up the outlet and into Lake George itself.

If the latter course were taken, Father Jogues actually discovered Lake George in 1642—if he were not too prostrated by his recent torture to be aware of it. If the party proceeded by way of South Bay and Wood Creek, the priest could not have looked on the lake till four years later. Historians are inclined now, on no direct evidence, to accept the latter date.

On August 15, after thirteen days of travel and torment, Father Jogues and the other maimed and burdened prisoners reached Osseruenon, the first of the Mohawk's three palisaded towns. The villagers swarmed screaming out to meet them and formed two lines. The reeling captives were thrust once more through the ordeal of the gantlet. Again the priest fell, to lie stunned and bleeding beneath the flailing clubs.

He was dragged into the settlement and flung with Goupil, who also had been knocked senseless, and the sturdier Couture upon a platform in the center of the village. Dark, frantic faces screeched derision at them; missiles were hurled and at last an Algonquin woman, a captive and a Christian, was compelled to climb the scaffold and saw off the priest's left thumb with a clamshell. That night, the three men lay pegged out in a hut, while Mohawk children dropped live coals on their bare bodies.

The torture at Osseruenon endured for two more days. It was resumed at Andagaron, two miles up-river, and finally at Teonontogen, last of the Mohawk towns, where the priest was hung by his wrists until he fainted.

At Teonontogen, four Huron, more recently taken, were exposed on the scaffold with the French, and Father Jogues in the midst of torment won them to Christ. He baptized two with dew that clung to corn a Mohawk had thrown at him; the others with water dipped from a brook on their return journey to Osseruenon. Here, Couture, whose vigor and endurance had excited admiration, was adopted into the tribe. Father Jogues and Goupil were kept as slaves.

The village mocked and abused and starved them, imposing on maimed bodies labor that was properly the work of squaws. Amid the scorn and maltreatment, the two went their patient way, furtively baptizing infants, teaching children to make the sign of the cross.

" 'Even unto this present hour, we hunger and thirst and are naked and are buffeted and have no certain dwelling place. And labor, working with our own hands; being reviled, we bless; being persecuted, we suffer it.' "

The two took deep comfort in their companionship, since the encouragement they exchanged bound each more firmly to his Lord. Then Goupil was slain as he walked by Father Jogues' side. A Mohawk saw the man teach an Indian child to cross itself and, believing this was witchcraft, stole up behind the lay brother and split his skull. Goupil fell, crying upon Christ.

His body was cast into a ravine where, before Father Jogues could find it, beasts had stripped it. The priest assembled the bones and, muttering the service for the dead, hid them in a hollow tree.

Winter now added its cold and privation to the dirt and the stench and the endless brutality yet Father Jogues still survived, an unkempt, maimed figure in tattered skins who, when the snow kept his masters indoors, stole away to the forest. There, kneeling in the drifts before the great tree upon which he had hacked a cross, he gave thanks for the souls he had been permitted to save and prayed for strength that he might increase the harvest. Seventy Mohawk were secretly baptized; many Huron prisoners were converted before his captivity ended.

He seems to have regarded slavery less as an ordeal than as service to his Lord. The Dutch were aware of his presence in Osseruenon and made attempts to ransom him. Couture urged him to flee to them. The priest refused. By tarrying here he might bring salvation to many otherwise doomed.

Spring came and the Iroquois raged into Canada again. Raiders returned to Osseruenon with fresh captives and the village was filled with screaming and the thick smoke of the torture fires. Many of the victims before they died received baptism from the broken hands of him who felt his own death could not be far away. Soon, some war party would return defeated and find solace in slowly destroying the French priest.

A warrior begged of him a writing to the commander of the French fort at Three Rivers. Father Jogues sensed treachery behind the request and his letter, set down on paper a Dutch trader had given him, warned the garrison to be on its guard.

The priest was at Fort Orange, later to be renamed Albany, still a slave attending upon his masters, when tidings came thither from Osseruenon of the defeat of the war party that had borne his letter to Canada. The commander at Three Rivers had read the missive and straightaway had opened fire on the Mohawk. These, having returned, now were screeching for the life of their betrayer.

Arendt von Corlaer, commanding at Fort Orange, urged Father Jogues to save himself. A ship lay in the Hudson that would bear him to New Amsterdam. He could sail from there for France. It would be death to return to the Mohawk village. The priest hesitated.

He dedicated that night to prayer, seeking to learn his Master's will. On the morrow, he suffered the Dutch to rescue him.

The way that had been shown Father Jogues was long and sore. In Manhattan, William Kieft, the director general, treated him kindly, outfitted him and supplied him with passage overseas. The voyage was stormy. At Falmouth, while the crew was ashore, pirates boarded the ship and stripped the priest of all his property, including hat and coat. He begged a Breton captain for passage to France. On Christmas Day, he was set ashore near Brest.

"In journeying often, in perils of waters, in perils of robbers, in perils by the heathen, in perils in the wilderness, in perils in the seas."

The torment and the travail were over now. Here were respite and security and peace, but a greater need than his weary body's oppressed Father Jogues. He spent the night in a peasant's cottage and on the morrow sought the nearest church to cleanse a spirit long deprived of confession and communion. Thereafter he traveled to the Jesuit College in Rennes and sought audience with the rector as "a poor man from Canada."

"What of Father Jogues?" the rector asked at once. "Have the Iroquois slain him?"

"He is at liberty," the stranger said, kneeling, "and it is he, my Reverend Father, who speaks to you."[3]

Joyous tumult sped through the college. Excitement possessed the seminarians, then awe, then reverence as they looked upon the frail body, scarred and maimed for Christ's sake. The pious jubilation the tale of Father Jogues' mission awoke swept across France and onward to the Vatican. Anne of Austria, Queen of Louis XIII, knelt to kiss the broken hands.

Praise and adulation could not heal one wound in the soul of Father Jogues. His mutilations barred him by Church law from celebrating Mass. No longer could he completely serve his Lord. Pope Innocent X by special dispensation restored him fully to the priesthood, yet still the spirit of Father Jogues was troubled.

Perhaps he remembered the divine reproach to the Apostle Peter as he fled from martyrdom at Rome. Had not Isaac Jogues, the least of Christ's servants, been equally craven in permitting the Dutch to save him from certain death?

"*Quo vadis, Domine?*"

In the spring of 1646, Father Jogues went back to the Jesuit mission at Quebec.

He found the colony reeling from the continued attacks of the implacable Iroquois. Montmagny had built Fort Richelieu at the mouth of the river which now bears that name. It had proved a minor annoyance to the war parties and nothing more. The Indians landed well above the stockade and carried their canoes through the woods, launched them again below the fort and proceeded with their prospering intention to extirpate wholly the Huron and Algonquin.

New France, unable to wage effective counter war, tried desperately to employ diplomacy. Young Algonquin and Huron warriors in the summer of 1644 captured three Mohawk and, bringing them to the fort at Three Rivers, began at once to torture them.

Champfleur, commandant and a farseeing man, intervened and prevailed on them to suspend their sport until the governor arrived.

Montmagny, by dint of much persuasion and trade goods, induced the Algonquin to surrender their slightly damaged prisoner. The Huron obstinately refused to part with their two and carried them off into their own country. The French healed their Mohawk's wounds and treated him with an almost overanxious consideration.

In the spring of 1645, the renowned Algonquin warrior, Pieskaret, set an ambush at the outlet of Lake Champlain and succeeded in taking two more Mohawk alive. These he delivered, intact, to Montmagny.

The governor held a long, appealing counsel with his trio of captives, and the juniors, assured by their senior that they were not to be burned, professed in gratitude an abiding desire for peace. The juniors were held at Three Rivers while the Mohawk purchased the year before was sent home to contrive an armistice. He reappeared on July 5 with two more Indians and Guillaume Couture, Father Jogues' old associate.

The council at Three Rivers was blown about by the high winds of Indian oratory which was followed by the exchange of belts, the bestowal of gifts. At its conclusion, the emissaries went home. They came back to Three Rivers with sachems of the tribe who, at another, longer council solemnly declared peace with all remaining Canadian Indians.

Montmagny had scant opportunity to relax in satisfaction. He had overlooked the fact that, in pledging the Mohawk to abstain from war, the ambassadors had spoken for only one of the Confederacy's Five Nations. The Mohawk were at peace with New France—or they said they were, though when Montmagny withdrew the garrison from the fort on the Richelieu, unidentified marauders burned it. On the other hand, Oneida, Onondaga, Cayuga and Seneca still rapidly were carrying on the destruction of Algonquin and Huron.

All the following winter, increasingly frantic appeals for rescue came to the lately complacent governor. When spring returned it was rumored that the supposedly placated Mohawk were about to take the war trail again. Montmagny sought a messenger to go and remind the waverers of their pledge. Couture had returned to the Mohawk villages with the ambassadors, but one who knew these Indians with an even more painful intimacy had just come back to the colony. Father Isaac Jogues was elected to carry the governor's message and also to clear the way for the establishment of a Mohawk mission at Osseruenon.

The outraged body of the priest must have quailed at the prospect of fresh exposure to its tormentors but his mind, though darkened by apprehension of death, did not waver.

"Would you believe," he wrote to Father Jerome Lalement, vicar general of the Jesuits in Canada, "that, on opening the letters from your Reverence, my heart was, as it were, seized with dread at the beginning? . . . Poor nature which remembered the past trembled, but our Lord, through His goodness has calmed it and will calm it still further."[4]

In early May the priest left Three Rivers, accompanied by Jean Bourdon, engineer to the governor, two Algonquin, laden with gifts, and four friendly Mohawk as guides and escorts.

The journey revived in a sensitive mind all the horror of that earlier passage up the Richelieu into Champlain. At Ticonderoga, the party canoed up the outlet, carried around the clangorous rapids and, May 30, 1646, launched their craft on clear, blue-green water, hemmed in by grave hills.

The sanctity that beauty grants uplifted the sensitive mind of the priest. The wilderness silence was marred only by the plunge and tinkling recovery of the paddles. The canoe bore him deeper into the grave enchantment wrought by towering peaks, dark reflections and the sun's long light, the lyrical alternation of wooded points and tranquil little bays. He saw the fir-crowned islands stand like shaggy cattle, belly-deep in the water of the Narrows, and the gulls that slanted across the peaceful sky were white and fair as the dove of the Holy Spirit.

It was Corpus Christi Eve and the priest, exercising a discoverer's right, named the lovely lake, not for himself but in honor of a faith which few, since Christ, have served more faithfully. He christened it Lac du St. Sacrement—the Lake of the Holy Communion.

From the water's head, they made the long carry to the Hudson, tarried briefly with Father Jogues' rescuers at Fort Orange and then went up the Mohawk to the reminiscent horror of Osseruenon. No screeching rabble swarmed out to form a gantlet for the priest now. He was received with dignity; peace orations were duly delivered, belts were exchanged.

Yet the Mohawk seemed anxious to be rid of their onetime slave. They urged him to make haste lest he fall foul of war parties of the other, still embattled nations. Father Jogues left a chest containing churchly articles that the mission-to-be would require and suffered his unwilling hosts to speed his departure.

The priest returned to Canada late in June. On August 26, he bade farewell to Father Lalement and set out for Osseruenon to establish the mission there. He may have been ordered thither; it is more likely that he begged, with the memory of his earlier flight still rankling, to return to his place of torment.

Jean Lalande, a lay brother, and a few Huron began with him a journey that soon grew dark with omen. A friendly Mohawk whom they encountered brought ill news. Pestilence had raged through Osseruenon since the embassy's departure and had been attributed to the chest the priest had left there. Mohawk anger against the French, particularly against Father Jogues, was burning again. They were about to pick up the war hatchet once more.

"Go back," the Indian warned. The priest went on. The terrified Huron deserted. Father Jogues and Brother Lalande pressed forward alone toward their martyrdom.

The end came quickly. Mohawk captured them as they crossed the Great Carrying Place and bore the twain to Osseruenon. Young and old ran out to beat the prisoners with clubs and fists. Strips were flayed from the priest's back to determine whether his were indeed a wizard's flesh. That night, he was summoned to a chief's dwelling and, bending to enter, was smitten with an ax and slain.

On the morrow, Lalande was slaughtered. The skulls of the martyrs were placed on the palisade of Osseruenon.

*"For I think that God hath set forth us the apostles last, as it
were appointed to death; for we are made a spectacle unto the
world, and to angels, and to men."*

A shrine has been established to a gentle, valiant spirit at Auries-
ville, New York, near the site of the ancient Indian village. Mir-
acles wrought here brought about, June 21, 1925, the beatification
of Father Isaac Jogues and Brothers René Goupil and Jean Lalande. They were canonized, three of the first eight American
saints, June 29, 1930, by Pope Pius XI.

Long before this, all material trace of its discoverer had been
erased from Lake George. The lovely name he had bestowed on
the lovely water had been abolished by a truckling courtier who
wished to command himself to a physically and mentally fat-
headed British monarch. No point or bay or island perpetuated
the memory of Father Isaac Jogues.

After many years, the region has received him again. The
largest island in the Mother Bunch group, near the lake's north
end, has been rechristened Isle de Lac du St. Sacrement and the
State of New York has established Charles Keck's heroic statue
with its mutilated hands and eager, bearded face, close beside the
place where the martyr landed for his last dark journey.

---

[1] R. G. Thwaites (ed.), *The Jesuit Relations* (Cleveland, 1898), xxxi, 3.
[2] *Ibid*, 33.
[3] *Ibid*, 105.
[4] *Ibid*, 107.

Chapter 4

The Iroquois Strike

THE pause in Mohawk hostilities that Montmagny and other hopeful men had called peace collapsed into new and fiercer war. The Mohawk, having slain Father Jogues and Brother Lalande, threw themselves into a conflict the four other nations of the Confederacy never wholly had abandoned. Attack after attack was launched at Canada, like arrows shot into a dazed and stumbling beast.

Lake George and Lake Champlain carried a heavy northbound traffic of warriors, by canoe while the water remained open, thereafter by snowshoe over the ice. Beyond this easy road to war that the Mohawk traveled, Oneida and Onondaga, Cayuga and Seneca swarmed down upon the westward creeping frontier of New France to slay and burn and torture and, vanishing briefly, to come again.

Men who had known only the slow, heavy battles of Europe were dazed by this deft, insatiable fury. It exploded ambushes about the unwary and out of seeming tranquillity launched obliteration on the villages of the hapless Canadian tribes. This was mass murder rather than conflict; war not aimed at conquest but at the enemy's extinction.

The white population of New France, a bare two thousand now, had neither strength nor skill to stem the red hurricane. The Indian allies of the French fought back with a doomed hopelessness. One by one they went down—the Huron, the Neutral and the Erie nations, as well as sundry Algonquin clans—and existed as entities no more.

No trading company, even when headed by the great Cardinal could prevail against this ferocity. In 1663 Old France moved to rescue New. The Richelieu charter was abolished and Canada became a royal province, direct property of Louis XIV. The customary bureaucracy that administered all French colonies took office at Quebec in 1665.

Daniel de Rémy, Sieur de Courcelles, a soldier of energy and daring, was the governor. The intendant, who was to control internal colony affairs and also was expected to spy assiduously on the governor, was Jean Baptiste Talon. The colony's plight was so critical, the danger from the Iroquois so great, that Alexandre de Prouville, Marquis de Tracy, lieutenant general and viceroy over all the American dominions of the Most Christian King, had accompanied his subordinates to Canada and had brought along a regiment of line infantry, the Carignan-Salières.

This outfit had learned something of ruthlessness during its late service in the Turkish wars. It was to obtain a postgraduate education in the New World.

The immediate necessity was to protect interior New France from further Iroquois attacks. Details of the Carignan-Salières began at once the construction of three forts on the Richelieu. The palisades of Fort St. Louis rose below the stream's rapids, where Chambly now stands. Another stockade, Fort Ste. Thérèse, was established upstream beyond the portage, while the old Fort Richelieu at the river's mouth was rebuilt.

The need was urgent and the new leaders of New France, with a defensive system established, immediately began to stage a campaign to snatch the initiative from the Mohawk. Inexperienced valor moved them to launch it in the dead of winter when the snow-covered ice of Champlain and George stretched its wide, white road deep into Indian territory. In January 1666 Courcelles, 300 regulars and 200 habitants set out upon this reckless journey.

The veteran campaigners against the Turk learned in their first few miles of snowshoe plodding over the frozen Richelieu much of the calm brutality Canadian winters inflict. Soldiers who were crippled by frostbite in the early stages of the march were exchanged for sound men at the Richelieu forts.

The column reached the outlet of Champlain and moved out upon the lake's shining desert. Here the unhampered wind bit deeper and the expedition hugged the lee shore, crawling along with smoking breath and weeping eyes toward the piebald mountains that closed in at the south.

Blue-cloaked forest runners guided the groaning advance over the groaning ice, for the Algonquin guides who had been unwilling members of the expedition had seized the opportunity to get themselves prudentially and helplessly drunk at Fort Ste. Thérèse.

There were days of blinding clarity, there were days of swarming snow, but the cold never relaxed. Regulars who waddled on the unfamiliar webs must have thought often of the superior merits of Transylvania's plains. The snow lay four feet deep by the time they reached Lake George.

They threaded their way through the smothered islands and reached the forest at the lake's head. Here, the advance guard went astray, leading the numb and weary column southward and away from the Mohawk villages that were Courcelles' goal. The governor, in consequence, encountered only a single war party that, retreating fleetly before sixty regulars who had been sent in blundering pursuit, laid a deft ambush. Smoke spouted from the thickets, and when it had cleared and the brief fury was spent, ten men and a lieutenant lay dead and their slayers had vanished.

The groping column found itself on Saturday, February 20, close to the little, four-year-old village that Arendt van Corlaer, a leading citizen of Albany, had established and named for himself. Later, it was to be known as Schenectady.

Courcelles encamped his men in a wood. He was afraid to let them enter the cabins for fear he never would be able to drag them from warmth and shelter again. He obtained food from the gaping Dutch villagers and more from the three envoys who arrived from Albany on the morrow to find out why he was trespassing on the Duke of York's territory. Thus Courcelles learned that New Netherlands had become an English province.

Dutch kindness to the invaders had a tragic aftermath. Van Corlaer received them so warmly that Courcelles begged him to make New France a return visit. The Dutchman was on the way to Canada the following year, when his canoe overturned and he

was drowned in Lake Champlain near what now is called Corlaer's Bay. A quarter of a century after the settlers of the little village had dealt hospitably with spent men, another French column
burned Schenectady and massacred its inhabitants.

February thaw and rain made Courcelles fear that the lake ice
would melt and his retreat would be cut off. He led his weary
column northward and straightway the cold closed in again.
Mohawk, following at a safe distance, cut off a few stragglers but
the bitter weather slew more. Sixty men had died of exposure by
the time the survivors reached the Richelieu forts.

The expedition had wrought scant damage to the enemy but the
penetration of Frenchmen so deep into Indian territory made the
already blood-glutted Mohawk pause and think. If it had happened once, it might happen again and more disastrously. Envoys
appeared in Canada the following spring and professed a desire
for peace. While the negotiations were in progress a war party
ambushed Frenchmen who were hunting near Champlain's outlet,
killed one Chazy, nephew to Tracy, and took the viceroy's cousin,
Leroles, and several others prisoner.

The pardonably indignant Tracy imprisoned the red envoys and
ordered Captain Sorel and 300 men to pursue the murderers. The
punitive expedition had scarcely been launched when it met peni-
tent Indians returning with Leroles and the other captives. The
recent outrage was ignored and negotiations were resumed but at
a feast to the Mohawk one of them so far forgot his table manners
as to boast that he had killed Chazy. Tracy promptly hanged him,
jailed the other emissaries and prepared to get on with the war.

That summer, the French established the first white settlement
on Champlain as a jumping-off place for further expeditions to
the south. On the oblong island, rimmed with gray rock and
crowned by trees, that guards the lake's outlet, Tracy ordered Captain Pierre de St. Paul, Sieur de la Motte, or la Mothe, of the Carignan-Salières Regiment to establish a fort, dedicated to Ste. Anne.

La Motte built log bastions, surrounded by a palisade 96 by 140
feet. It was finished in July and a chapel also was raised to Ste.
Anne. The establishment was neither a legitimate settlement nor

a permanent. It was an outpost, designed for war. Sometime in the 1670's, the French deliberately destroyed it, burning the buildings after removing everything of value, but the name of the builder still adheres to this island of quiet farmhouses and disciplined meadows. In September of 1666, Tracy moved again against the Mohawk.

The viceroy was old, fat and gouty but his wrath had overcome his infirmities and, though Courcelles accompanied him, he himself led the expedition. The Carignan-Salières Regiment, habitants and Indians to the number of 1300 followed him up the Richelieu and launched their 300 bateaux and canoes upon Champlain, first of the many flotillas that would bear white men south toward war in the next century and a half and the most completely successful of them all.

The column endured privations. When it had landed at the head of George, a hundred miles of up and downhill trail still separated it from the Mohawk towns but the guiding Indians were skillful and screened the little army so well that no attack was made upon it, no ambush was laid during the toilsome march. Courcelles was smitten by cramps and had to be borne in a litter. The venerable Tracy's gout returned and he too had to be carried. Rations gave out, but the men subsisted on chestnuts and pushed on through the frost-painted woods until, after a forced march in a night of wind and rain, the column debouched into a clearing where stood the first of the Mohawk villages.

Drums beat the charge, the army swept forward and the already cowed red garrison fled. Tracy pressed his pursuit and his display of armed might completely terrified the Mohawk. He captured three more villages equally bloodlessly and late in the afternoon moved on to Andaraquay, largest and strongest of the Mohawk "castles." This had been deserted. Tracy burned it and on the morrow faced about and moved homeward, destroying on the return march the towns he had captured earlier.

Autumn storms buffeted the flotilla during its passage down the lakes. Some boats were upset and a few men drowned but the army returned, sodden yet triumphant, to Fort Ste. Anne and moved on from there to exulting Quebec. The power of the Mohawk temporarily had been broken. Their homes had been burned, their food supply destroyed. That winter Tracy sent messages to the Five Nations, demanding an end to the conflict and promising otherwise to hang all the Mohawk he still held prisoner.

In the following spring, the scurvy-smitten garrison of Fort Ste. Anne saw elm-bark canoes approach from up the lake and prepared to do battle, but this was not a war party. These were placating emissaries, coming to beg for peace.

The ensuing council was briefer and less diplomatic than its forerunners. Tracy showed a blunt willingness to carry the war further if hostilities did not end at once. The awed envoys offered belts, made solemn pledges and—more important—gave hostages to the French. The peace then established endured without another general conflict for twenty years.

Tracy's demonstration of waxing French power alarmed others than the Iroquois. One clear-sighted man viewed the armed trespass on what the English deemed their own territory with apprehension. Governor Richard Nicolls of New York, while the French punitive column tarried within his province, heatedly begged the governors of the New England colonies to join with him and exterminate the invaders, justifying his plea by the fact that a fresh installment of the Anglo-French war was in progress overseas.

The other governors declined, fearing that their own Indian population, which they still were industriously exterminating, would side with the French. Nicolls had to content himself with writing severe letters to Tracy until the establishment of temporary peace in Europe ended the correspondence.

New York's governor had sensed what the rest of the self-centered English colonials ignored. Tracy's expedition was more than a mere trespass; it was an augury of greater invasions to come.

The time was at hand when the ambitions of the American colonists, English and French, were to run far beyond actual settlement and, in response to renewed war in Europe, armies were to grapple bloodily for vast stretches of territory neither contestant required or was strong enough to occupy. The Champlain-George Valley was the easiest road whereby French and English could get at each other's throats. It was shortly to channel the course and direct the fate of empires.

Nicolls, in a foggy way, had felt this. The first man to recognize explicitly the importance of the lakes to the future of New France came to govern Canada in 1672.

Louis de Buade, Count de Frontenac, was a soldier's son, godson of Louis XII, and had himself served in the army since he was fifteen. He was now fifty-two but scandal whispered that he had been sent to rule this distant province of his king largely because of his prowlings about Madame de Montespan, a more immediate possession of Louis XIV. Gossip also tittered that he found a frontier existence and strife with the Iroquois preferable to life with the difficult wife whom he had left behind.

Indians did not accept the countess' unflattering opinion of her lord. Frontenac had a vehement will, a military skill and a gusty energy that ensured his popularity with savages. He was less fortunate in his dealings with Canadian officialdom, fought with his intendant, even strove against the theocracy of New France and, after a notable clash of wills and purposes, was ignominiously recalled in 1682.

He departed when his presence was most needed, for the Iroquois, having whiled away the period of peace with New France by destroying the Andastes and the Illinois tribes, now found themselves with no neighbors left to conquer but the Canadians, or the English.

The Five Nations were unwilling to appease their permanent bloodthirst by attacking their white neighbors whose trading posts and settlements were creeping from Albany up the Hudson and Mohawk Valleys. These folk were sources of the rum, the powder, balls, guns and other blessings of civilization the Iroquois craved. It would be better to assail the French and their red allies. The English frontier in Maryland and Virginia might also, the Confederacy decided, be attacked with impunity.

This crisis had been developing before the recall of Frontenac, and on the arrival of his successor, Le Febvre de la Barre, was placed, smoking-hot, in his lap.

Seneca had begun to kill French traders in western New France and were threatening war against the Ottawa and Winnebago tribes. Cayuga, Oneida and Onondaga were burning and slaughtering in Virginia and Maryland. The English believed, with no warrant whatever, that these attacks were inspired by French Jesuit missionaries. The French held that the Confederacy's threatening attitude toward New France was furthered by English counsel, English rum and English muskets.

The distracted La Barre launched an expedition against the Seneca, which degenerated into negotiations that settled nothing. The council that Francis Howard, Baron Effingham and governor of Virginia, and Colonel Thomas Dongan, governor of New York, held with the Confederacy at Albany in 1684 was more productive. Gifts, oratory and innate hostility to the French persuaded the Iroquois to declare a formal alliance with King Charles II. Despite French efforts which seduced many individuals from that loyalty, the Confederacy for a long time thereafter was a more or less reliable weapon in English hands.

Dongan laid hold upon it immediately and encouraged his new allies to attack the French. In Canada, the blundering La Barre was succeeded by Jacques René de Brésay, Marquis de Denonville who was filled with piety and a prodigious zest for letter writing.

Denonville immediately undertook to subdue Dongan by a correspondence that must have kept expresses paddling furiously up and down the lakes all summer. He reproached the New York governor for inciting the Iroquois against the French and charged him with sending traders into Canada territory to debauch the Indians. The chief satisfaction Denonville obtained from this bombardment by letter was a statement from New York's governor that he was a firm believer in free trade and that English rum was no more harmful a beverage than French brandy.

As a warrior, Denonville was even less successful. He raided Seneca territory and burned an evacuated village or so with all the unhappy consequences that befall him who overturns a beehive. The Seneca called on the other four nations, Dongan encouraged the attack and on August 5, 1689, 1500 warriors swept down upon Lachine, nine miles above Montreal on the St. Lawrence, abolished it and raged up to the walls of Montreal itself, burning, killing and occasionally dining on a captive under the eyes of the terrified citizens.

It was not until October that the main body withdrew, taking with it ninety prisoners, some of whom they burned on the river's far shore. Raiding parties continued to stab and hack at the region during the following winter.

At this nadir of Canada's power and pride, additionally depressing news came from overseas. James II, the quasi-friend of France had been dethroned. Mary, his daughter, and her Dutch husband, William, had succeeded him and the nations of Europe were regrouping themselves for still another war. The Iroquois, alone, had brought New France to her knees. A strong man was needed to save her from complete prostration in the coming conflict.

In late July 1689, Frontenac, reinstated as governor, had sailed for Canada. He bore with him a plan whereby Lakes Champlain and George might be employed to make France supreme in the New World.

Chapter 5

Design for Conquest

THE thing that had driven thousands in flight from Europe was moving westward to overtake them. The recurrent wars of the Old World were spreading to encompass the New. Conflicts that established by their treaties fresh grievances which begot new campaigns had become the nations' prime industry and the need of the standing armies that had supplanted the old feudal levies drew upon entire populations.

"With this transformation in the character of armies, the actual snatching of men for wars and the fear of being snatched made life a genuine terror for innumerable men of military age, their families, and young marriageable women. Moreover the death and destruction spread by wars on a large scale made 'the art of war' so practiced more terrible to non-combatants. For all such reasons British and European workers in town and country, as well as yeomen and merchants, could regard the perils and hardships of resettlement in America, in a strange land, as offering trials slight in comparison."[1]

The wilderness in which the harried had sought peace was about to become the site of wars more savage than Europe's. In the year 1690, a colonial struggle of French against English began. It endured, with truces that only emphasized history's gift for bloody repetition, seventy years. The paroxysms of King William's War, Queen Anne's War, King George's War, the French and Indian War were followed by two conflicts between the British and their erstwhile colonial subjects.

In each of these, the Lake Champlain-Lake George Valley played a critical role. In each, the advances and repulses, the attacks and counterthrusts were to be stamped with a drearily repetitive quality which the mountain-hemmed, easily navigated, deeply penetrating waterway decreed.

The fundamental plan that later generals were to try for another hundred and twenty-five years and might be called "The Frontenac Pattern" had been, in 1689, approved and stingily implemented by Louis XIV before the leathery, vehement old soldier returned to Quebec, September 12. Actually, it was less the creation of any military mind than a dictation by geography.

It had been decided in Paris that the Carignan-Salières Regiment and whatever Indians and habitants Frontenac might marshal were to attack the English by way of Champlain and George, moving up the larger lake in bateaux and canoes, carrying past the rapids of St. Sacrement's outlet and marching from the lesser lake's head to the Hudson.

Thence, the little army was to sweep downstream upon Albany and its outlying settlements. When these had fallen, the invaders were to descend the river to lately rechristened New York. French men-of-war, hovering offshore, were to enter the harbor and co-operate with Frontenac's command in storming the town, whose capture would split the English colonies in twain.

Such was the Frontenac pattern, though he never fulfilled it. None of the subsequent soldiers who adopted it with minor variations was markedly successful. There was something delusive about this apparently easy highway to conquest. It was one of the projects that look enticingly simple on paper but, in practice, are difficult to the point of impossibility. No host that ever attempted the passage was powerful enough to accomplish it. The original exponent of invasion by way of the lakes found his plan wholly frustrated by the time he reached Canada.

Storms had delayed the warships that brought Frontenac and his retinue back to New France and the season was too far advanced for naval and land forces to co-operate in the projected campaign. Furthermore, until the Iroquois could be induced to change their loyalty or at least to remain neutral, a general attack upon the English was impossible.

Frontenac spent months in wheedling and, when necessary,

FORT TICONDEROGA—THE MAIN GATE

FORT TICONDEROGA—THE BASTION

DEER SWIMMING LAKE GEORGE

fighting the Confederacy but succeeded only in seducing individuals from the enemy's cause. The attack, when at last he mounted it, consisted of raids after the Indian fashion rather than the military invasion King Louis had prescribed.

Groups of forest runners and Christianized Indians assembled in 1690 at Montreal, Three Rivers and Quebec to ravage the English frontier. The Three Rivers group destroyed the Salmon Falls settlement in New Hampshire; the Quebec party joined with the Three Rivers to take Fort Loyal, where Portland, Maine, now stands. The Montreal expedition, which started first, was aimed at Albany.

D'Ailleboust de Mantet and Le Moyne de Sainte-Hélène, already distinguished as bushfighters, led their little snowshoed force of 120 woodsmen and ninety-odd converted Iroquois up the Richelieu. They were tough, hard-bitten men, at home in the wilderness and they drew on every ounce of their resource before the expedition ended.

Midway along Champlain's shining desert, difficulty arose, as usual, with the Indians. They halted suddenly and demanded where they were going. Mantet told them to Albany and roused a storm of dissent that Gallic exhortations to honor and glory could not subdue. It was, the Iroquois insisted with justice, too strong a town for so small a force to attack. The ensuing weather decided the argument in their favor.

Until now, the wilderness-wise column had made good time, but a thaw set in with a warm rain that turned the snow into pudding. Beyond the head of St. Sacrement, the column reached the point where the trail forked, one prong leading to Albany, the other to the little village of Schenectady. The spent and sodden raiders headed for the lesser settlement.

After nine days' more floundering, they were still six miles from Schenectady and might have perished in the slush and mud if it had not grown cold. The trail froze hard. Snow squalls hid the expedition as it reeled on. Darkness had fallen, February 8, when it came in sight of the village. Mantet had planned to attack later that night but his men were too nearly exhausted to tarry.

No one saw them as they advanced upon the place that earlier had extended kindness to another French force. The villagers, deriding the idea of danger, had set as sentinels on the stockade twin effigies of snow and had left the gates open. Mantet and his starvelings stormed on.

No mercy was shown to either sex or any age. The French and their allies "rypt up women with chyld, throwed children into the flame, dashed others agt doorposts till their brains stuck to it."[2]

There was no defense. When the fury had ended, sixty men, women and children had been killed outright and between eighty and ninety were captives. Thirty Mohawk who had been visiting the village were treated most courteously. Mantet explained to them that he was visiting deserved punishment only on the English and Dutch.

Schenectady was burned and the raiders fled with their captives. Fifty men from Albany and 150 Mohawk followed them north. The whites gave out at Crown Point, but the Indians pursued farther, killed 6 of the retreating force and took 12 prisoners.

The triple raid upon the English had been designed by Frontenac to break the spirit of his enemies. It had, like all atrocities, a directly opposite effect. The frontier was thoroughly alarmed, and henceforth for a space patrols scouted the lakes to watch for further French attack.

On March 30, Captain Abraham Schuyler, grandfather of the Revolutionary general, ranged north over Champlain's wet ice to the mouth of Otter Creek, built a lookout there and, venturing farther to Chambly on the Richelieu, killed two villagers and took one prisoner.

Meanwhile the outraged colonists were preparing for war. A fleet was gathering at Nantasket, Massachusetts, which in May was to wrest Port Royal and all Acadia from France. Expresses were summoning the governors of New England to a conference in New York.

The plan adopted at this gathering was the prototype of many subsequent. An army was to be assembled at Albany that would advance down Lake Champlain upon Montreal. It was not a mighty host. New York furnished 400 men and the Massachusetts Bay, Plymouth and Connecticut colonies 350 more. Fitz-John Winthrop, a veteran of Cromwell's army, son of the governor of Connecticut and later governor himself, was placed in command of the expedition which made up in dissension and intercolony jealousy for what it lacked in size.

In Canada, Frontenac was laboring furiously to meet the retaliation he himself had invited, strengthening the walls of Quebec, making peace with his adversaries in the government, even appearing, hatchet in hand, to join the war dances of his Indian allies.

The English colonies had been brusquely refused any aid from England in a war that had been of England's making. Even Massachusetts' wistful request for powder and ball to shoot Frenchmen was ignored. New France at least had a regiment of regulars in service. Her adversaries had no professional troops. For them it was to be a wholly amateur conflict with even more than the normal amateur bungling.

The quarrelsome levies that assembled in Albany seemed as willing to fight one another as the French. By the time Winthrop marched them up the Hudson, smallpox and dysentery were at work. Disease in the wars of this era always slew more men than bullets. The ailing army followed swampy Wood Creek to the south end of Lake Champlain, where the grimed brick buildings of Whitehall now rise, and malaria was added to its accumulating ills. For all its ineptitude, the expedition was establishing a pattern that larger hosts would imitate.

The doughty sea captain, Sir William Phips, whose fleet had taken Acadia, was reconditioning it for an attack upon Quebec by way of the St. Lawrence. Winthrop had engaged to move down the lake, capture Montreal and join the naval expedition in the reduction of the French capital. Similar strategy, applied seventy years later, wrought the final downfall of New France. The plan collapsed at the outset, now.

The Iroquois, who had promised to join in the campaign, were frightened off by smallpox. Some Mohawk and Oneida did appear. The other tribes kept prudently away.

Furthermore, when the army reached the muddy water of Champlain's South Bay and the way into Canada lay unobstructed before them, it was discovered that no boats were available to bear them north. The canoes of the few Indians could not carry even so small a force and, since it was too late in the season for elm bark to peel, no more craft could be built. Winthrop was forced to turn about, probably with a secret sigh of thankfulness, lead what portion of his army still could walk to Albany, and let Phips attack Quebec, alone.

Captain John Schuyler, before Winthrop retreated, received permission to raid down Champlain with 29 still belligerent white men and 120 Indians. The habitants of the little village of La Prairie near the Richelieu's mouth were gathering the harvest when Schuyler's men leaped upon them and paid an installment on the Schenectady debt by killing or capturing some 25 men and women.

In October, Phips failed before Quebec and his battered fleet got back to Boston piecemeal through the autumn's storms. The first of seventy years' war ended in more Iroquois bushwhackings and murders. The remainder of the opening conflict, which his extremely unbenefited subjects named "King William's War," produced no more large troop movements such as French and English had furthered at its outset. Both sides were exhausted and impoverished. Only the Iroquois went on energetically with the business of slaughter.

Major Peter Schuyler, in the summer of 1691, with Indian aid launched another redoubtable attack upon La Prairie. One hundred and twenty English and Dutch and 146 Indians paddled with him down Champlain. A storm forced them to beach their canoes at Ticonderoga and there they built a breastwork of stones for their own protection, first of the several fortifications that occupied the site.

Schuyler went on, moving only by night and lying concealed during the day, to the lake's outlet and dropped down the Riche-

lieu to ten miles above Chambly's fort where he hid his canoes
and worked his way farther through a drizzling rain. For all his
care, his advance had been detected and the French had thrown a
strong force about La Prairie's stockade. Two battalions of the
Carignan-Salières had camped to the right; Canadians and Indians, to the left. Before dawn on the morning of August 11,
Schuyler attacked, 226 men against more than 700.

He charged the Canadian-Indian contingent first, killed many
and drove the rest to the refuge of the fort. He sent a volley into
the advancing regulars and scattered them. As they reformed,
Schuyler withdrew, retreating deliberately along the Chambly
trail. The French were too shaken by the savage, brief assault to
pursue, but Valrenne, commander of the Chambly garrison, had
been told by his scouts that an enemy force had passed and had
moved out with 160 regulars and Canadians, as well as a large
number of converted Indians, to take the invaders in the rear.

Schuyler, retiring, ran head-on into Valrenne's command. The
fight that followed ignored all the usual tactics of forest warfare.
The English were blown back, gathered themselves and came
again. Men fought breast to breast in the wet woodland, firing
their enemies' shirts by their muskets' blasts, clubbing their pieces
when they were empty. At last, by the weight and fury of their
attack, Schuyler's men burst through the French center, wheeled
to right and left, scattered the enemy and went on to their canoes.
They carried their wounded but left forty dead behind. The
French loss was materially greater.

Henceforth, the English were content to let their Iroquois allies
take over the offensive. The stinging Indian attacks continued
despite Frontenac's increasingly frantic efforts to placate or punish
the tormentors. He accomplished neither until, in January 1693,
he tore in desperation a leaf from Tracy's and Courcelles' book and
determined to visit upon the Mohawk villages the fate he already
had imposed upon Schenectady.

Mantet, with 625 followers, marched up Champlain to find and
destroy the winter-bound Indian towns. On February 16 he struck,
capturing in succession 3 stockaded communities, killing 30 and

taking over 300 men, women and children. The villages were burned and the column with its unwieldy number of prisoners immediately began the long journey from the Mohawk River to the St. Lawrence.

After two days' march, ingeniously mendacious Mohawk scouts hailed the expedition from a safe distance, hallooing that the English were following but only to parley, since peace had been declared in Europe. Mantet scoffed at this tale but, to his consternation, his own converted Indians believed it and insisted on waiting for the pursuers to catch up. Mantet was forced to tarry but he dropped trees to form a breastwork, still believing the English purpose was neither candid nor peaceful.

The French commander was right. When Peter Schuyler, with 500 settlers and Iroquois, finally appeared, he immediately constructed a barricade of his own and from behind it opened fire on the French. Thrice, with flurries of whooping, Mantet and his followers breasted the fog of English musketry in charges that, each time, failed. Damp snow fell deliberately and then so thickly that it hid one barricade from the other. Behind this screen, the French stole away and Schuyler, ill-provisioned, was forced to pause for more supplies before he could press the chase.

So he waited, dining with his white followers on stewed moccasins while his red allies fed more heartily on boiled Frenchmen. When other food arrived at last, it was too late to resume pursuit, particularly since Mantet had sent word that he intended to kill his prisoners if attacked again.

Punishment dealt by the weather was almost as severe on the French as Schuyler could have wished. A thaw set in, so long and intense that the column had difficulty in crossing the Hudson's cracking floes and, on reaching St. Sacrement, found the lake ice too rotten for passage. The French were forced to march through sodden snow and dripping forests the length of St. Sacrement's brutally difficult shore line and when, drenched and reeling, they reached the store of food they had left at the outlet, they found that most of it had been spoiled by the unseasonable warmth.

The weak made a wretched camp here. The stronger went on

to Montreal and sent back relief. Frontenac hailed the expedition's accomplishment as a triumph but the aspect of the column that straggled back down the lake was not victorious. Its members had, for the moment at least, blunted the edge of the Mohawk war hatchet. Raids down the lakes and into Canada dwindled. Frontenac was careful not to provoke his most bitter enemies again, but occupied himself for the rest of the war in scorching the New England frontier. Peace came to both hemispheres in 1697, a year before the leonine old soldier died at Quebec.

The English colonies had fought the first of the French wars with no assistance, except for some impractical advice from the mother country. The ending found them exhausted, physically, financially. Furthermore, it now appeared that the monarch in whose name New England had taken Acadia looked on that capture as a presumptuous and regrettable mistake, for the peace treaty promptly returned the entire region to France.

If the settlers had gained by the conflict no new reason to esteem war, the Iroquois, who were war's devotees, had still sounder cause for resentment. Half the Confederacy's fighting men had died in attacks upon New France, which still was strong and whole. Over and beyond scalp bounties, the Five Nations had won nothing by their sacrifice.

A not unreasonable suspicion crept into Indian minds that the Confederacy was being duped. The Iroquois were never again to espouse the cause of their ally, the British Crown, with such complete devotion. Before and during the next war, which began in 1702, the Five Nations were frantically wooed by both English and French. None of the tribes deserted entirely their original loyalty, yet many individuals joined their late adversaries and were converted by the missions at Caughnawaga on the St. Lawrence, and elsewhere.

Throughout the new war, named by her loyal subjects for Queen Anne, the French strove to provoke the Iroquois as little as possible and sent their raiding parties against the already charred New England frontier instead of launching them up the lakes. The English, however, again prepared to drive into Canada by way of

Champlain. This time, the exhausted colonies were encouraged by definite promise of aid from overseas.

The plan established in London called for the assembly of 1200 militia from Massachusetts, Rhode Island and New Hampshire at Boston where, in May 1709, a fleet was to appear to carry them to Quebec. The naval attack was to be geared to an advance down Champlain. Colonel Francis Nicholson, a professional soldier and late governor of Virginia, was to lead this expedition which was to consist of levies from Connecticut, New York, New Jersey and Pennsylvania. They were to move north on news of the fleet's arrival at Quebec.

The colonies involved showed an unfilial disregard for this project of the mother country. New Jersey sent a small cash payment but no troops. Pennsylvania was entirely deaf to the summons.

The forces that New York and Connecticut consented to supply were mutually recriminatory and thoroughly undisciplined. Furthermore, though Queen Anne trustfully expected every Iroquois to do his duty, only a suspicious few of the Confederacy appeared.

The unenthusiastic army that Nicholson led north from Albany numbered no more than 1500 but its commander advanced by the proper military method. He established forts to protect his supply line, one at Saratoga, another—Fort Nicholson—within the present town of Fort Edward, and a third which later was named Fort Ann on Wood Creek. Nicholson cut a road from this stockade to the Hudson and, leading his men on to South Bay, built bateaux and canoes while he waited word from the fleet.

Meanwhile his men contracted a virulent dysentery, due, according to some, to the fouled waters of Wood Creek which they drank; according to others, to the rawhides and other offal that the Indians cast into the stream, purposely to poison their comrades in arms.

Tidings of the concentration at the head of Lake Champlain came to the new governor of Canada, Philippe de Vaudreuil, who straightway sent 1500 men under one Ramesay up the lake to attack. The French landed above Crown Point and worked their way south through the lakeside forest, skirmishing with English patrols. In the course of the movement, Ramesay, who seems to have been spectacularly barren of leadership or woodcraft, managed to lose his army and wandered alone and desolately through the wilderness until he stumbled on his command again and, in great relief, conducted it back to Canada where there would be less danger of mislaying it.

Nicholson after long and empty waiting was forced to fall back to Albany while he still had enough sound men to bear the ill. The New England troops, summoned by Britain to Boston, camped there till October 11, when word came from overseas that the ships expected in May would not arrive that year. They had been sent to Portugal instead of America.

A small fleet did appear belatedly in 1710. Five frigates convoyed the provincial transports that carried 1500 New England militia north to attack Port Royal again. It was captured for the second time. In 1711, Britain revived the established pattern and summoned the colonies to still another move against Quebec.

A fleet, calamitously commanded by Admiral Sir Hovendon Walker, arrived at Boston, added 1500 provincial troops to the 5 regular regiments it had aboard and set sail for the St. Lawrence. Meanwhile, the long-suffering Colonel Nicholson assembled 2300 settlers and Indians at Albany and once more toiled up the Hudson and over the road he had built 2 years before to Wood Creek. Again, at the creek's swampy mouth, he and his men waited among the mosquitoes for the word that the fleet had appeared before Quebec.

Tidings more disastrous than those that, in 1709, had sent Nicholson's first command homeward, arrived at last. Walker, by inane seamanship, had managed to pile ten of his vessels on rocks in the Gulf of St. Lawrence and, terrified lest the rest of his craft should be trapped by ice in the river—it was then mid-August—had sailed back to Boston.

Legend recites plausibly that the ill-starred Colonel Nicholson on receiving the news cast his wig on the ground and jumped up and down on it, crying, "Treachery! Roguery!"

He then led his troops by the now familiar way back to Albany. By the Treaty of Utrecht in 1713, Britain obtained the Hudson Bay region, Newfoundland and twice-captured Acadia which was renamed Nova Scotia.

King George's War began in 1744. In the following year, a force of New England provincials, to the astonishment of all concerned, captured the great new fortress of Louisbourg that the French had built on Cape Breton Island. Otherwise, colonial enthusiasm for the conflict was limited and the Iroquois displayed even less.

A pushing young Irishman, William Johnson, whose vigor and fair dealing had endeared him to the Mohawk, induced some warriors of that nation to raid down the Champlain Valley as far as the St. Lawrence. Their attacks were feeble echoes of earlier Iroquois onslaughts. So many members of the Five Nations had gone over to the French by now that the Confederacy shrank from a conflict that would be, in essence, civil war.

New France earnestly encouraged this neutrality and aimed most of its war parties against New England, where lately rebuilt cabins were burned and frontier families were massacred. The punishment its neighbors endured could not distract the New York Assembly from the squabble it was carrying on with Sir George Clinton, the governor. The legislature was more eager to humiliate him than to oppose the French and, to this end, refused to send any troops beyond Albany or to strengthen the frontier forts.

Thus, when on the night of November 28, 1745, 500 raiders under the partisan, Marin, swept down on the Saratoga stockade and the huddle of settlers' cabins that had grown up around it, the raiders killed 30 persons, captured 100, burned fort and dwellings and retired unscathed. Albany was bared by this destruction and the legislature hastily voted money to restore the Saratoga defenses.

A feeble structure was raised and garrisoned for a time by Colonel Peter Schuyler's regiment. When supplies were withheld, the troops marched back to Albany to avoid starvation, first burning the new fort to the subsequent surprise of another party of raiders who had come up the lakes from Canada for the same purpose and who reached their destination to find nothing but smoking embers.

It was a dull war, drearily repeating the ancient story of bushwhacking and murder. Rigaud de Vaudreuil, town major at Three Rivers, launched one more considerable expedition, secretly designed to destroy Schenectady again. He left Montreal with 500 French and 200 Indians, largely Iroquois converts, August 3, 1746. It was not until his fleet of canoes had advanced far up Champlain that he confided to his command the purpose of the expedition.

The Indians instantly objected. Schenectady was too close to the Mohawk towns and, if it were sacked, some of their own relatives might get hurt. Vaudreuil was forced to revise his plan, paddle the length of Champlain to Wood Creek and after a cross-country march, to lay siege to Fort Massachusetts, near what is now North Adams. The garrison which the absent Captain Ephraim Williams commanded consisted at the time of one sergeant and twenty-one men, half of whom were prostrated by dysentery. The fort quickly surrendered.

The war smoldered on, with minor flarings of massacre, and died out entirely in 1748. Louisbourg, whose capture the British evidently considered irregular since it had been accomplished by mere provincials, was restored to France. Much blood and treasure had been spent, nothing commensurate had been gained by the wretched reiteration of the little vicious conflicts but they had established patterns to be followed with new energy to a decision in the final, greater war, still to come.

---

[1] Charles A. and Mary R. Beard, *Basic History of the United States* (Philadelphia, 1944), pp. 13-14.

[2] Letter of Jacob Leisler to the Governor of the Barbadoes, in *Documentary History of New York*, edited by E. B. O'Callaghan (Albany, 1850), I, 194.

Chapter 6

Tragedy of Errors

THE Champlain-George Valley was still a wilderness, beautiful and empty; a delectable, deadly land. France claimed it by discovery. England advanced a more clouded title: The area, or most of it, was Mohawk territory. The Iroquois were allies of the British King. Therefore, and not quite logically, the lakes and their shores belonged to the Crown.

Here was ground for endless argument that long remained in the realm of diplomatic theory, since the valley was left completely unsettled for almost a century after Father Jogues had found and named Lake St. Sacrement. It was inviting, accessible territory but it was kept sterile by repeated wars.

The vigor and military ambition of New France impelled it to begin occupation of the area. When King George's War ended in 1748, Canadians had established several footholds on Lake Champlain; the British, none.

The French dreamed of empire and reached to obtain it. The English colonies were less avid and more deliberate. They still had war-blackened frontiers within their own indisputable boundaries. They were, furthermore, a consolidating people who assimilated what they had acquired before they grasped for more. They, also, were growing more intent on upholding their rights against His Majesty's authority than they were in acquiring more territory for him.

New France was a feudal system. Its source was the king. His vassals sought more land, not primarily for settlement and tillage but to extend the dominions in America of His Majesty. "Glory" was a word absent from English and Dutch colonials' lexicons—which is the chief reason many British generals formed so low and erroneous opinions of provincial fighting ability.

74

The English had founded, when King George's War had ended, no permanent settlement north of Albany. A few valiant or unwary had raised their cabins in the shadows of the Hudson forts or the stockades that guarded Nicholson's road to Wood Creek but when the militia garrisons retired from these the temporary settlers departed also. The French pushed their frontier southward up the valley and worked to pin it down.

A low headland, some seventy miles south of Champlain's outlet, thrust out toward a bluff on the west shore. The French had named it "Pointe à la Chevelure"—literally "Hair of the Head Point" but by Canadian connotation "Scalp Point." The English, by mistranslation, called it "Crown Point."

North of the present bridge's west abutment, there are outcroppings of dark limestone which are the bones of an earlier fort and a mound surmounted by gray ruins that were once a later one. A stone has been found among the rubble. Its dim inscription indicates that on August 19, 1730, Michel d'Agneau, Sieur de Douville, with 30 men, here began a stockade. A year later, St. Luc de la Corne, the bitter partisan leader, added to the works which were named Fort St. Frédéric, probably for Frédéric de Maurepas, then French naval minister.

The site was well chosen. A musket ball would carry almost from shore to shore. The fort's guns closed the lower lake to anything but the strongest invasion and, implicitly, included this segment of Champlain within New France. New York's governors protested repeatedly to Quebec against what they insisted was trespass upon His British Majesty's domain but correspondence was the limit of their immediate objection. The New York Assembly still showed a far heartier willingness to fight with whomever ruled at Albany than against the French.

Crown Point was strengthened further in 1734 and 1742. When Peter Kalm, the Swedish naturalist, saw Fort St. Frédéric in 1749, it was a grim, dark, rock fortification, cannon-studded, with a high watchtower, a windmill that also served as a second lookout, a chapel and barracks of stone. The stronghold was an outpost of empire and, to apprehensive British statesmen, an augury of further encroachment. Ahead lay more wilderness through which the French might advance unimpeded, since the English colonists showed no inclination to occupy and defend it.

George Clarke, governor of New York, saw the menace of the empty frontier and strove to remedy it by publishing an early real-estate prospectus in which the area south of Lake George was praised as an Eden, with no reference whatever to metaphorical serpents. Captain Laughlin Campbell, an ambitious Scot, was firmly hooked. He visited the land and received from Clarke assurances that if he would provide settlers, a grant of 30,000 acres in the region now occupied by Argyle, Greenwich and Fort Edward would be his, free of all charges except those of survey and quitrents. Campbell believed him, sold his ancestral estate, and in 1738 brought over from Scotland 423 settlers-to-be.

Here was material for the establishment of a buffer community that might oppose further French encroachment but Clarke meanwhile had revolted against the idea of giving Campbell something for practically nothing, no matter how much the gift served British interests. He and his associates, in the traditional manner of New York's colonial officials, demanded that Campbell grant them rights in the domain promised him. Campbell refused. The Assembly sided with him, and during the legislative brawl that followed the offer was withdrawn and the would-be colonists scattered.

France, meanwhile, was attempting settlement of the Champlain region with only a little more success. Lake-shore grants of more than 800 square miles were made, not to individual settlers but to members of the Canadian noblesse who were to provide tenants and develop their properties within a stipulated time. In most cases, the seigneurs were unable to comply and their grants reverted to the Crown. François Foucault, a member of the Quebec council, made more vigorous attempts than his associates, with no more permanent result.

A hammerheaded cape that the French called "Pointe à l'Algonquin" juts out from Champlain's east shore, just south of the lake's outlet. Its neck is swamp, but its tip is higher ground, and here in

1731 Foucault began a village, building a stone windmill, starting to erect a church but failing in his enterprise for lack of settlers. He tried again ten years later, induced eleven persons to join him there briefly and failed once more. The site is still called Windmill Point.

On the seigniory granted Sieur de Beauvais in the present town of Swanton, a huddle of cabins grew up about the sawmill that was established at the falls of the Missisquoi River. This village was the longest lived of any of the French settlements for it endured humbly and obscurely until 1775.

A third and probably larger community took root and flourished for a space across the narrow water from Fort St. Frédéric and in the comforting shelter of its guns. When the fort was evacuated, toward the end of the final French war, this settlement perished also. Indians burned the deserted cottages whose chimneys, standing tall and black on the headland, bestowed on it its current name—Chimney Point.

No village could hope for permanence on Champlain's shore while war's tide washed back and forth through the valley. Until peace was assured, sensible men preferred to live where their scalps were more secure and forces were gathering now for a vaster conflict. It was to observe patterns already established, but it also was to be distinguished from earlier conflicts by other characteristics besides its massiveness.

Heretofore, colonial struggles had been the reflex responses of peoples, who originally had no grievance against each other, to wars of European origin. The new strife was of native growth. It was waged in America for a year before Britain and France declared war overseas.

The French and Indian War was not a conflict that would end with the gain or loss of a few patches of territory. It was fought for ownership of most of a continent. Elsewhere than in the Champlain-George Valley, the wilderness no longer thrust a reassuring isolation between the American subjects of French and British kings. The two nations were beginning to press against each other and the pressure bred heat, and the heat, explosion.

The farsighted French were drawing about the hitherto self-centered British colonies a *cordon sanitaire*. Missionaries and explorers had led the way; troops had followed, moving far to the west, then cutting south across the natural course of British expansion. The French were on the Great Lakes. They held the Mississippi and were at New Orleans and now, in the Ohio country, their bayonets were pressing against the backs of the English colonies, while in the Champlain Valley, Fort St. Frédéric menaced the New York and New England frontier.

The rising alarm of colonial authorities was receiving for the first time concerned hearing in London. Academically, peace still endured, yet there was new activity in French and British navy yards and a hurried marshaling of troops. The squadron that stood out from England in January 1755 bore Major General Edward Braddock and the 44th and 48th Foot toward Virginia. The sails that brightened the sea in May were those of the larger French fleet that carried battalions of La Reine, Bourgogne, Languedoc, Guienne, Artois and Béarn—3,000 men under Johann Erdmann, Baron Dieskau—toward Quebec. Before they sailed, Braddock and the colonial governors had met at Alexandria, Virginia, and had planned a triple attack against the encroaching French.

The British general with his regulars and provincial troops was to sweep triumphantly westward against Fort Duquesne in the Ohio country. A colonial force under Governor William Shirley of Massachusetts was to move upon the enemy's works at Niagara while a third army, composed of New England, New York and New Jersey militiamen, was to assemble at Albany, go up the Hudson, cross to Lake George and sweep down the valley to take Fort St. Frédéric.

In July, 3,000 men from this last expedition were camped about Albany. William Johnson, now His Majesty's Superintendent for Indian Affairs and assiduously seeking further aggrandizement, had arrived to take command of this unmilitary host, a disheveled assemblage of farmers and small tradesfolk, undisciplined and so thoroughly filled with provincial pride and suspicion that the canny Johnson had had himself commissioned major general by each of the six governors whose people were represented, so that none might question his authority.

Phineas Lyman, a lawyer and an erstwhile tutor at Yale, was second in command. Connecticut had refused any troops unless he was granted that rank. Here, too, were Colonel Ephraim Williams of Massachusetts, Captain Philip Schuyler of New York, Lieutenant John Stark of the New Hampshire levies, and a private in the Connecticut militia named Israel Putnam.

Only a person of great tact and greater ambition would have ventured to command such a cross-grained, frowzy assemblage and it required all of Johnson's Irish cajolery to hold the unruly and mutually antagonistic elements together. He had greater difficulty in enlisting Iroquois, since the previous conflicts had indicated to Indian eyes that the French were the better warriors, but a few Mohawk joined him here with the fat old war chief whom the English called Hendrick.

The army sweltered in the July heat and the New Hampshire troops, unprovisioned by their province, might have starved if the Albany men had not been charitable. The levies took unkindly to military strictures and, though church services were frequent, their speech was reprehensible.

"We are a wicked, profane army," Colonel Williams wrote, "especially the New York and Rhode Island troops. Nothing to be heard among a great part of them but the language of Hell."[1]

Though there were heavy doses of psalm singing, daily prayers and sermons twice a week, conditions rapidly grew worse in the gloomy colonel's opinion. He noted:

"As to rum, it won't hold out nine weeks. Things appear most melancholy to me."[2]

This dismal augury may have impelled him to make the will whereby he left an endowment to establish a school that became Williams College.

The drab host moved out at last, creeping upstream to the Great Carrying Place where a stockaded storehouse was begun and named Fort Lyman. It groped down Wood Creek toward South Bay and, when Johnson, a wholly amateur soldier, changed his mind, returned and began hacking a road through the tall, dark forest toward the head of St. Sacrement.

News of what had befallen Braddock's more professional and powerful expedition on the Monongahela dampened the inconsiderable military ardor of the Fort St. Frédéric expedition. These same dire tidings, plus a deficiency in supplies, compelled Shirley to abandon his campaign against Niagara. Johnson's army was the sole source left in the field and its commander now began a long-enduring appeal for reinforcements. Nevertheless, when axmen and stump-grubbers had cleared a way to the lake, the bulk of the command went forward, leaving 500 men under Colonel Joseph Blanchard of New Hampshire to complete and garrison Fort Lyman. Campfires on the night of August 27 cast red reflections out over the water which Johnson, hopefully thinking of his king, immediately had rechristened "Lake George."

The expedition camped on the beach, with its right flank close to a swamp, its left anchored to the low hill where the Fort William Hotel now stands and its entire front facing virgin forest. Supplies and the bateaux that were to bear the army on toward Crown Point came in slowly, for the teamsters were even less contented than the troops who, between sermons, continued to grumble and curse. They glowered suspiciously at the additional Mohawk who straggled in, until 300 were present. On September 7, which was Sunday, the Indians proved their worth.

A scouting party sent out by Johnson returned in haste toward sunset time to report that it had found the trail of a large body of men moving apparently from South Bay toward Fort Lyman.

New France had been preparing an attack upon the British fortified trading post at Oswego. When Canada's governor, Pierre François, Marquis de Vaudreuil-Cavagnal, heard of Johnson's movement toward Fort St. Frédéric, he reoriented the expedition. Dieskau with 3,500 regulars, Canadian militia and Indians—many of the last converted Iroquois from the Caughnawaga Mission—went up Champlain.

The elderly baron, whose military training under the great Marshal Saxe had done little to equip him for wilderness fighting, paused at Crown Point, increased the garrison there and then moved on to that strategic headland on the upper lake that the Indians called "Ticonderoga" and the French, "Carillon." Here he paused, uncertain whether Johnson would advance by South Bay or St. Sacrement, until a patriotically untruthful prisoner deceived him.

Indians on September 4 brought in an English captive who told the baron that the colonial army had retreated to Albany, leaving only a small garrison at indefensible Fort Lyman. Dieskau moved at once against this reputedly unprotected post, leaving another portion of his force at Ticonderoga and leading a canoe flotilla that bore 216 Languedoc and La Reine regulars, 684 Canadians and some 600 Indians up the southern extension of Champlain.

The baron willingly would have left his red allies behind, for their gluttony and general unreliability offended his soldierly standards and even their leader, LeGardeur de St. Pierre, veteran of almost a lifetime of service on the French-Indian frontier, had no firm control over them.

The party threaded its way up the sluggish stream that twisted among swamps, beached its canoes at the head of South Bay and followed Indian guides through deep woods toward Fort Lyman. It paused in the wilderness to hear Mass and reached the new road from the fort to Lake George on the evening of September 7.

Johnson seems to have felt no great alarm at his Mohawk's tidings, but he did send a mounted messenger toward Lyman with a note of warning to Blanchard. Dieskau's Indians shot the courier out of the saddle and bore his dispatch to the baron, who shortly thereafter received still more complete enlightenment.

That evening, a dozen teamsters in Johnson's camp resolved to serve no further and mutinously drove away for Fort Lyman. Dieskau's force killed two, captured several. A few got clear and fled back to the camp they lately had deserted. The baron learned from his new prisoners how thoroughly his earlier captive had deceived him.

Dieskau was additionally irked by the fashion in which his Indians arranged his plans for him. They now refused to advance against Lyman, telling their apoplectic commander that they feared the cannon at the fort. They were willing to attack the English camp for they believed it destitute of artillery.

Dieskau advanced toward the lake on the morning of September 8. The regulars marched along the road while the Canadians and Indians scouted ahead and on either flank. Three miles from the camp, the advance guard fell back, unseen, before an approaching English column.

The fugitive teamsters had got back to Johnson by midnight, but the amateur general had not deemed the fact that an enemy force was astride his supply line cause for alarm or haste. He waited till morning to call a council of war and with him, as with Dieskau, Indian influence shaped events.

Hendrick, when the officers agreed to send 500 men down the road and 500 more by a hill trail to South Bay to destroy the enemies' canoes, held out a single stick before him and broke it. He gathered several together, tried to snap them and failed. Johnson and his officers understood the parable and resolved to march the entire thousand under Williams, with Lieutenant Colonel Nathan Whiting of Connecticut as second in command, along the road to Lyman.

Again Hendrick demurred, holding that 1,000 were too many to be sent to slaughter and too few to fight successfully, but Johnson prevailed on him and lent him a horse since he was old and feeble. The chief and his warriors joined the column.

The road led between lately felled trees and recently overturned stumps into a deep and narrow defile. On the English left, French Mountain loomed and, on the right, rose the lesser West Mountain. The way passed narrowly between them and here Dieskau had set his trap.

The French regulars waited at the column's far end and, on its either side, Canadians and Indians lay hidden in the forest. The English advanced stupidly, with no scouts before them. A musket shot—legend says it was fired by a converted Mohawk to warn his ancient brethren—saved them from entire destruction.

The single report released a great crash of firing. The forest sparkled; smoke rolled into the road where men went down and screeching Indians leaped upon them. Hendrick was among the first to die. His horse was shot and a regular's bayonet finished him.

The front of the English column had blown away. Its remainder writhed and shuddered. Many broke from it and ran. Colonel Williams rallied the stouter-hearted and led them up the steep pitch of West Mountain from which the heaviest firing came. He fell, shot through the head, near where the marble marker stands, downhill and east of Highway 9.

French muskets continued to hammer at the fraying column, from which more men were fleeing, but Lieutenant Colonel Whiting kept firm hold on Williams' own regiment. It gave way slowly, retiring from tree to tree and steadily firing.

A south wind bore the uproar to the lakeside camp and the swiftest fugitives came in, yowling that all was lost. Johnson, rousing belatedly to the peril, sent Lieutenant Colonel Cole forward with 300 men to stiffen Whiting's defense and prepared at this last moment to fortify his position. He might have been swept into the lake if the French could have pressed their attack but Dieskau's force had got out of hand. St. Pierre and many more had been knocked over by New England bullets; the Canadians and Indians had scattered. The baron was forced to pause and reform.

Whiting was entirely willing to disengage. He fell back upon the camp where frantic men were dropping trees into a rough breastworks and cannoneers rolled the guns into line. A barricade of sorts had been completed before Dieskau advanced again. At the first explosion of cannon fire, the attack stumbled and halted. Neither the Indians nor the Canadians had expected to face artillery. They drew back and limited their further share in the fight to yelling and long-range shooting. Dieskau, with more valor than sense, elected to lead his regulars against a fortified and cannon-supported position manned by ten times their number.

The white-uniformed little column advanced upon the center of the barricade, which was held by Connecticut's men. Musket and artillery fire broke the assault. A bullet struck Johnson in the thigh. He retired to his tent and left the rest of the battle in Lyman's competent hands.

Dieskau reformed in the forest and came again, charging the English left which Massachusetts kept. Once more, the artillery broke the attack. Surgeon Thomas Williams, brother to the dead Ephraim, wrote:

"Our cannon which under God it appears to me saved us, were heard down as low as Saratoga, notwithstanding the wind was in the south & something considerable & which by the way was a great disadvantage to our troops as the smoke was drove in our faces."[3]

Dieskau was down, shot first through the lower leg and, later as his adjutant bound the wound, in the knee and thigh. The wind, shredding the smoke away, revealed to incredulous Yankee eyes a disorderly French retreat. Lyman, mounting the barricade, howled the order to charge.

Powder-blackened men swarmed out to beat apart with hatchets and musket butts the few still cohering elements of Dieskau's command. The French retirement changed into a stampede and, in the confusion, their prostrate commander was shot again through both thighs. He was carried to Johnson's tent and cared for by his captor's own surgeon.

It was five o'clock now. The immediate battle was over. Before the barricade, the wounded wailed and Mohawk warriors prowled among the white-uniformed dead. The south wind brought from a distance a renewed outburst of firing.

Earlier, while Dieskau's regulars still fought, many of the more thrifty Canadians and Indians sought profit from an otherwise unremunerative battle by sneaking through the forest to strip those who had fallen in the morning's fight. Here, a scouting party under Captains McGinnis and Folsom, which Blanchard had sent out from Fort Lyman toward the sound of the guns, fell upon the plunderers hard by a circular pool spattered with lily pads. Its brown water was red that day. Men called it henceforth "Bloody Pond."

McGinnis, grievously wounded, was brought by horse into Johnson's camp, where he died. In this fight, Robert Rogers, a private in the New Hampshire militia, first tasted combat for which he later developed so large an appetite.

The English had lost 262 in killed, wounded and missing. French casualties of 228 were limited largely to the regular troops. All the officers and half the men of the Languedoc and La Reine detachments were either slain or wounded. The victory was emphatic but Johnson ordered no movement to make it absolute. He preferred to stay where he was and risk nothing.

He made no effort to get across the mountains to South Bay and cut off the defeated French but employed his battered army somewhat belatedly in raising a solid entrenchment about his camp and in beginning a fort on the hill above it. Williams and his regiment already had cleared the ground for this structure.

Scouts came in from the north with word that the French were building a stronghold at Ticonderoga. Reinforcements plodded in from the south to Johnson's army but it waited while cold winds whipped the last bright foliage from the hills and ice began to skim the shallows of the lake. On November 27, Johnson broke camp and led his command back to Albany.

He had fought a purely defensive battle and had made no material gain for his cause. His most important if immediately unapparent accomplishment had been to convince provincials that they, of themselves without professional stiffening, could stand up to regular troops and win a victory. Seeds sown on the shore of Lake George were to blossom in 1775.

Few generals other than Johnson have done less toward the accomplishment of their assigned mission with greater consequent award. The ambitious Irishman bent the fight's aftermath to his own best interests. In his dispatches he made no mention of Lyman on whom had fallen the brunt of the battle. He even removed the Connecticut colonel's name from the storehouse on the Hudson and called it "Fort Edward," in honor of one grandson of the king.

Johnson named the stronghold his army built at the lake's edge

"Fort William Henry," after another royal grandson. Already he had erased the singing name the water itself bore and had rechristened it for his monarch.

His assiduity was profitable. Parliament gave him 5,000 pounds and King George made him a baronet.

---

[1] Papers of Colonel Ephraim Williams, quoted by Francis Parkman, *Wolfe and Montcalm* (Boston, 1909), I, 103.

[2] *Ibid.*, p. 104.

[3] Correspondence of Dr. Thomas Williams, in *Historical Magazine*, VII, No. 4 (April 1870).

Chapter 7

Massacre

THE war in which many British and French colonials had died, though their parent governments still remained ostensibly at peace, dwindled during the winter of 1755-1756 into the usual wretched sequence of frontier murderings and burnings. The semitruce was established by the season. Signs were plentiful that in the spring the antagonists would resume more vigorously the continent's first international conflict of native invention.

The wilderness that had intervened between the enemies was wearing thin. Iroquois, plodding on snowshoes up and down the George-Champlain Valley, had only some thirty miles to travel now between the new British fort at the head of the lesser lake to the incompleted French stronghold beside its outlet.

The Iroquois were finding this war more to their liking than the earlier in which with high courage and a higher mortality rate they had upheld the British cause. It was better, they were learning, to be coy than loyal. Both nations wooed the reluctant warriors. It was profitable to spy upon the French for the British and then, turn about, to spy upon the British for the French. Each army still feared too greatly the might of the Long House to dare to offend it by the justified execution of red tattletales.

The French, the Indians told the British, would press the construction of the Ticonderoga fort in the spring. It was little more than a dirt and oak mound now, but when it was finished it would bring the Canadian frontier sixteen miles farther up Champlain than the earlier Fort St. Frédéric had placed it.

The British colonies, the Indians informed the French, were designing a multiple attack during the coming summer. One column would be aimed at the forts on Lake Ontario, a second at

Duquesne, a third at Ticonderoga and Crown Point. In addition, and forecasting the march of Arnold and his starvelings through the Maine wilderness nineteen years later, a diversion was to be made toward Quebec by way of the Kennebec and Chaudière Rivers.

This complexity was fathered by William Shirley, still titular commander of the colonial forces, whose martial ambition had survived the virtual collapse of the previous year's campaign. By the time the ice was out of the lakes, levies from Massachusetts, Rhode Island, Connecticut, New Hampshire and New York had begun to gather at Albany. Shirley had commissioned John Winslow of Plymouth to lead this expedition and Winslow, like Johnson before him, had saved himself subsequent argument with his disorderly followers by having the governor of each additional province represented in the force reappoint him.

His Majesty's government at this point began to suffer qualms lest the impending campaign of the still undeclared war should be mismanaged by mere colonials and notified Shirley that he and his provincial generals were to be replaced in the field by three Englishmen—Daniel Webb, James Abercromby and John Campbell, Earl of Loudon. These in irresolution and ineptitude surpassed all the rest of the unique sequence of blundering British commanders who, first and last, fought on American soil.

This stroke of good fortune for the French was followed by another when on May 11, Louis Joseph, Marquis de Montcalm-Gozon de St. Véran, a small, dark-browed, hooknosed soldier of quick intelligence and temper, arrived at Quebec to command all the troops in Canada. Twelve hundred men of La Sarre and the Royal Rousillon Regiment disembarked with him. They were worth less to New France than the members of the staff that accompanied Montcalm—François Charles de Bourlamaque, the able engineer, Louis Antoine de Bougainville who later was to win renown as a navigator and François Gaston de Lévis who was to die a duke and a marshal of France.

The Marquis de Vaudreuil-Cavagnal, Canadian-born governor of Canada, welcomed the newcomers with a moderate enthusiasm that was to cool rapidly. Throughout the looming climactic struggle, Vaudreuil and Montcalm were to be perpetually at odds and their enmity was to be a prime cause of New France's downfall.

Now that professionals had been selected to lead the colonial armies, Britain and France on May 18, and after a year of slaughter in America, formally declared war.

The ambivalent Iroquois already had brought to Canada tidings of the army marshaling at Albany to move down the lakes and one of Montcalm's first acts was to lead reinforcements to the still incomplete stronghold at Ticonderoga that Michel Chartier de Lotbinière, the governor's protégé, had named Fort de Vaudreuil, but which the French in general for the sake of the clangorous rapids near by called "Fort Carillon."

If the British could be held back till fall, Lotbinière was sure that the stone edifice he and his sappers were raising would be difficult to take. It was to be larger than St. Frédéric at Crown Point but built in the same star-shaped form, stout-walled, heavily gunned and commanding from its hilltop both the narrow breadth of Lake Champlain and the outlet of Lake George. In defense of the still indefensible Fort Carillon and the valley it controlled, Montcalm attacked elsewhere.

The British commanders who had been imposed upon the colonial troops did nothing whatever to hamper the French general's plans. Webb and Abercromby with 900 regulars arrived at Albany in June; Loudon appeared in late July but displayed aggression only in quarreling with the provincial authorities.

Winslow's expedition, brawling, insubordinate and dirty, straggled up the Hudson to the Great Carrying Place and crept toward Lake George, building stockades on the way to protect its line of supply. At the lake itself, Colonel Jonathan Bagley, a vigorous intemperate man, held Fort William Henry and drove his men to building sloops and whaleboats to carry the army down the lake, meanwhile sending out repeated scouting parties to gain intelligence of the French.

"Every party," he wrote Winslow, "brings abundance but all different."[1]

Canadian Indians prowled about William Henry and the road to the Hudson, subjecting the British to the same routine of petty ambushes and isolated killings that the now reluctant Iroquois once had inflicted upon the French.

"What vexes me most," Bagley informed his commander, "we can't catch one of the sons of bitches. I have sent out skulking parties some distance from the sentries in the night to intercept them but the flies are so plenty our people can't bear them."[2]

Meanwhile, Montcalm had unobtrusively slipped away from Ticonderoga, leaving the garrison under Lévis, and was mounting an expedition aimed at Lake Ontario.

The summer ripened while the British force that was to clear the lakes crept forward, continually pestered by Indians and half-paralyzed by Loudon's contagious indecision. Winslow and 3,000 provincials arrived at William Henry where they promptly contracted all the diseases to which slovenly men are heir.

Word came in late August that Montcalm, striking swiftly and unexpectedly, had overwhelmed the British post at Oswego. The tidings blighted whatever energy remained among the 10,000 men who now were scattered between Albany and Lake George. Loudon and Shirley blamed each other for the defeat. All forward movement ceased. Winslow entrenched his force and limited his activity to felling the trees about the fort as a haphazard abatis. Montcalm who had returned to the now completed stronghold at Ticonderoga waited, too. So the campaign of 1756 ended.

In November came word that the main French body had retired from Ticonderoga toward Canada. Major Eyre with 400 regulars arrived to garrison Fort William Henry, and the provincials, depleted by Indian depredation and disease, went disconsolately homeward. The cold and the snow forbade movement of large forces, but the winter was filled with small raids, bushwhackings and skirmishes between French scouting parties, red and white, and provincial woodsmen who were being disciplined, drilled in forest fighting and organized into companies of rangers.

These men, who became the eyes and the ears of the British, took the place of the Indians of whom the French now had an abundance and their foe, since Oswego's fall, almost none at all. The rangers were also the direct ancestors of the raiding organizations in the most recent war—tough, active, resourceful veterans. Israel Putnam and John Stark were among their leaders and Robert Rogers of New Hampshire was their chief.

The rangers' commander had first tasted strife in the fight at Bloody Pond during the battle of Lake George. He was most admirable when danger lay all about him—clearheaded and bold, crafty and ruthless—and yet in all but his most sublime moments continually accompanied by a faintly sour spiritual smell.

By boat until the lakes froze over, on skates or snowshoes thereafter, Rogers and his hard-bitten men ranged through the debatable ground between British and French outposts, making life miserable for the garrison at Ticonderoga and warring upon the scouting parties sent out from the fort. One foray is typical of the many the rangers conducted:

Rogers, in the summer of 1756, with fifty men in five whaleboats, rowed by night down Lake George to the foot of the dim trail that led over hills to Champlain's South Bay.

They hauled their heavy craft across the difficult track, launched them at the head of the larger lake and, rowing by night and hiding by day, got past Ticonderoga and lay concealed for twenty-four hours until a cloudy night enabled them to slip through the strait at Crown Point, unperceived.

Ten miles farther down the lake, they laid an ambush and issued from it to capture two French sloops laden with brandy, wine and flour for the forts. Three Frenchmen were killed. The rest surrendered. One of the prisoners was so severely wounded that he could not walk. Rogers killed him and returned by land to William Henry with his other captives.

All the winter of 1756-1757, raid and counterraid continued. There were savage little battles in the snow-smothered forest where French and British scouting parties collided and several times the rangers stole so close to the walls of Ticonderoga that they kidnaped members of the garrison.

On January 21, Rogers with his lieutenant, John Stark, and seventy-three men, driving deep into French territory, fought amid dripping trees and slushy snow what romance has magnified into "The Battle of the Snowshoes."

The ranger leader came down to Fort William Henry from Fort Edward in mid-January and tarried there several days while his followers fashioned snowshoes for their scout. Two days' march took them far down Lake George and on January 19 they turned into the woods, circled wide about Ticonderoga and two days later slopped through rain to the Champlain shore at Five-Mile Point, down lake from the fort.

A line of horse-drawn sleds was moving over the ice, bound for Crown Point. The rangers gave chase and captured three, but the other teamsters whirled about and lashed their horses back to Carillon. Rogers and his men built a fire, dried and reloaded their guns and retreated through the wet snow. Canadians and Indians, sent out from Ticonderoga, ambushed the rangers and brought them to bay.

All afternoon, guns thumped in the rain and, when they lagged, French voices cried out, urging the outnumbered force to surrender. The rangers were still holding their line on a forest ridge when darkness fell. Thereafter, Rogers, though shot through the wrist, led the fifty-four survivors of his command, six of whom were wounded, through the dark woods all night and emerged in the morning on Lake George, a half-dozen miles from its outlet. Stark, the tireless, was sent on to William Henry to get sleds for the wounded. These arrived on the morrow and the raiders returned to the fort on January 23.

Rogers' men's continual irritation of the French may have been responsible for the wintry expedition that Canada launched against Fort William Henry.

Rigaud de Vaudreuil, brother to the governor, was placed in command of the force of Canadians and Indians that, in early March, plodded on snowshoes up Champlain to Ticonderoga. Here they were joined by a detail from the garrison, were equipped with scaling ladders and, 1,600 strong, marched up Lake George.

Surprise was the one potent weapon of men who otherwise had only small arms. Vaudreuil idiotically threw it away.

Sentries at William Henry on the night of March 18 saw camp-fires blinking on the ice within cannon range. A salvo from the fort's guns scattered Vaudreuil's men and so thoroughly blew away their valor that, when day broke, they refused to do anything more aggressive than to subject the stronghold to a futile, long-range musket fire.

Their martial ambition could be raised no higher than arson. Vaudreuil, that night, wheedled them into advancing toward the fort but the attack broke up at the first cannon fire though a few of the more valiant managed to burn two of Bagley's icebound sloops and a number of bateaux.

On the following day, Sunday, March 20, Vaudreuil paraded his force, equipped with scaling ladders, on the ice and sent one Le Mercier forward, anticlimactically, with a flag of truce. The hope-ful emissary informed the fort's commandant, Major Eyre, that he must surrender at once or else endure immediate defeat and massa-cre. Unimpressed by the enemy's earlier performance, Eyre re-fused.

Vaudreuil's men spent the rest of the day shooting off their muskets. Eyre was certain that when darkness came his works would be stormed, particularly since snow had begun to fall and had blindfolded his gunners, but the French limited their aggres-sion to additional burnings. Buildings outside William Henry's walls—hospital, storehouses and ranger cabins—were set ablaze, together with lumber and the fort's supply of firewood. The snow, falling more furiously now, protected the stronghold against flying embers.

It was still snowing on the morrow and under cover of the storm the French burned a third, half-completed sloop. On March 23, Vaudreuil's men shouldered the unused scaling ladders and re-treated to Ticonderoga.

The summer of 1757 was to see the high tide of French aggres-sion. Loudon set the pitch for all that followed by withdrawing his best troops from the frontier for an attack on Louisbourg.

He sailed from New York after infinite delay, found the fortress too strong to be assaulted and, late in the summer, sailed ignominiously back again. Meanwhile Montcalm, the alert opportunist, had dealt a still heavier blow to British arms and morale.

When Loudon embarked, the French general moved. Scouts brought tidings to General Webb, who sedentarily guarded the New York frontier from Fort Edward, of increasing activity at Ticonderoga. Barges filled with supplies, rafts with cannon lashed upon them, crowded the outlet. Horses and men labored day and night, dragging the boats and their cargoes up the road the French had built around the rapids, launching them in quieter water above. Bateaux were moving up Champlain, deep laden with white-uniformed regulars. Prisoners taken by the rangers reported that the battalions of Béarn, Royal Roussillon, La Reine, La Sarre, Languedoc and Guienne now were at Fort Carillon, with a growing horde of Canadian militia and a swarm of Indians.

These last, led by St. Luc de la Corne, Rigaud de Vaudreuil, Corbière and other experienced bushfighters, spread south along both shores of Lake George, slipping through the forest, watching from hilltops, screening the force at Ticonderoga so thoroughly that intelligence each day became harder to get.

Tumult boiled up on July 18 from the lately toiling thousands. The hills about the fort threw back the cheers of Frenchmen and the Indians' fierce screaming. The uproar endured while a quick little man in the scarlet uniform of a French general stepped from a bateau and smiled in delight at the frantic faces about him. Scouts brought word to Webb that the marquis had arrived at Carillon. The place where he came ashore still is called "Montcalm's Landing."

The storm was lowering, but the British general did little to prepare for it and what he attempted was disastrous. Webb demanded further sure intelligence of the French force and ordered a reconnaissance in force. Colonel John Parker with some 300 provincials, mainly New Jersey militiamen, was sent down Lake George to feel out the enemy.

French scouts saw the flotilla of whaleboats soon after it was

Courtesy of the Fort Ticonderoga Museum

AMERICAN VESSELS AT VALCOUR BAY

LAKE CHAMPLAIN FROM PORT HENRY

ROUSES POINT BRIDGE

launched and laid an aquatic ambush. As the craft oared their way through the crooked channel among the Harbor Islands, canoes propelled by Corbière's screeching Indians darted out of hiding and swarmed about the whaleboats, firing into their crews, stabbing at them with lances. Dazed and overwhelmed by the sudden attack, many of Parker's novices screamed for quarter. Some leaped into the lake and died in a welter of bloody spray as the Indians harpooned them. Those who still fought were shot down.

Twelve men escaped and 131 died in the brief fury. Bodies floated in the lake's slow current for days thereafter. Three of the many less fortunate who were taken prisoner were killed and eaten at once. The rest were reserved for more leisurely torture or possible ransom.

Webb received soon afterward a clear indication of French intentions when Indians and Canadians raided up to the walls of Fort Edward, returning with a prisoner and thirty-two scalps to Ticonderoga where Montcalm, on the eve of launching his campaign, held a council with his painted and befeathered red followers.

The Gallic charm that had endeared Frontenac to the Indians drew the tribesmen to this more polished leader. Montcalm's victory at Oswego furthermore had quickened savage enthusiasm. Forty-one nations were represented among the 1,600 red men at Fort Carillon. One war party, the Iowa, had come from so far away that no one else present understood their language.

Compared to the wild, western warriors, the Canadian Indians, accompanied by their priests, seemed a docile crew, but Montcalm, like all French leaders before him, found his dark allies gluttonous and profoundly unreliable. His control over them was only nominal, despite the solemn pledges of obedience the conference brought forth.

On July 31, the day following the council, the army of 6,000 regulars and Canadians began to move out with its Indian allies. Since there were not enough boats to carry them all, Lévis with 2,500 forced his way over the crooked, up-and-down trail along Lake George's west shore. Montcalm, with his troop-laden bateaux, his raft-borne siege guns and a canopied boat for the priests, started up lake with Indian canoes darting about the heavier craft.

Black Mountain on the left, Tongue on the right seemed to creep with each stroke of the oars imperceptibly higher into the summer sky, through which by afternoon storm clouds reached up to take away the sun. Rain hurried nightfall along. Lightning shone briefly on sodden men and gleaming oar blades as the expedition groped forward. It rounded that point of Tongue Mountain which now bears Montcalm's name and, entering the quieter water of Northwest Bay, steered toward fires that burned in triangle formation on the blacker bosom of a western hill. This was Lévis' signal.

The reunited army breakfasted ashore in what is now the town of Bolton. At 10:00 A.M., Lévis resumed his march. Montcalm re-embarked at noon and, hugging the deeply wooded western shore, landed that night in a little bay, hidden from Fort William Henry by its promontory. Here Lévis already was in bivouac, and here on the morrow the guns were to be landed, giving the place its name—Artillery Cove. The tall pines that still stand close to its shore must have witnessed that disembarkation. A tree surgeon recently cut from the heart of one a handful of grapeshot.

Montcalm's arrival was stealthy but not wholly peaceful. Patrol boats sent out from the fort were puzzled by a looming blackness on the water, and, venturing near, almost rammed the priests' canopied craft. Canoes pursued the intruders and musket balls splashed about them. Several were killed, the rest reached shore where the Indians captured three more. The prisoners were taken to Montcalm. The information they gave him was heartening.

From the curved, sandy beach at the head of Lake George, a pine-clad slope goes up to an uneven tableland and beyond this is rolling and mounded forest. The erosion and the filling of almost two centuries have changed minor features of the terrain but its general aspect is unaltered.

Fort William Henry stood a little to the east of the hotel that now bears its name. It was a square stronghold of timber and earth, with a bastion at each corner, and mounted seventeen cannon and several mortars. East of the fort lay marshy land through which a small stream wound and, still easterly of that, the military road ran sixteen miles to Fort Edward. A knoll on the farther side of the way had been fortified during Sir William Johnson's time by a strong intrenchment and now was occupied by the overflow of the garrison. Fort William Henry was too small to house even the scanty force assembled to defend it.

Yet it was the strongest post between the lake and Albany. Fort Edward, where General Webb twitched and twittered, was only a fortified storehouse and, beyond, it, a few inconsiderable stockades barred the way to the provincial capital. If Fort William Henry fell, the road lay practically clear to the Hudson, yet Webb who was committed to doing things by halves shied away from an all-out defense of the stronghold.

Until the day Montcalm moved south from Ticonderoga, William Henry and the entrenched camp beyond the marsh had contained 1,200 persons—soldiers, sailors and civilian employees, with some women and children. Many of the garrison were unfit for duty for smallpox burned among them and the hospital was filling.

Lieutenant Colonel George Munro of the 35th Foot was in command. On August 1, Webb, who had 2,600 men at Edward, sent a reinforcement of 200 regulars and 800 Massachusetts militia to Lake George. Already, he had written to Loudon promising to defend the post personally with his entire force should Montcalm attack, but when the mutter of cannon fire came down from the north the general revised his intention and, laying a still firmer hold on his pen, sent fresh appeals for militia to the provincial governors and long-distance advice to Munro.

White lines of French tents mushroomed up in what is now the north end of Lake George village on the bright morning of August 3 and in the shallows of Artillery Cove cannoneers splashed and swore as they got the siege guns ashore. Montcalm, conforming to military propriety, sent Bougainville to Munro with a polite invitation to surrender which the fort's commander, equally correctly, rejected. Indians, with cheerful howling, settled themselves among the carcasses of the trees Winslow had felled the year before and began an ineffectual shooting in the direction of the fort.

Tribesmen and Canadians under La Corne worked around through standing timber to the south of William Henry and cut the road to Fort Edward. Lévis followed with his command and the stronghold was encircled. Montcalm, from a distance, inspected the entrenched camp, doubtless recalled how Dieskau's force had broken its back against similar fortification, and began to get his siege guns into battery.

That night, a ranger worked through the French lines and bore to Webb from Munro a last appeal for aid. Thenceforth the sole tidings that came from the north was the growing sound of guns.

The fort smoked and thundered, blasting back into the trenches earth the French sappers had heaved out, but the British cannon did little further damage and presently, to the rapture of the Indians, Montcalm's first battery of eight guns and, soon, another of eleven opened. The tribesmen were so fascinated by the artillery that they crowded about the gunners and could not be induced to undertake any of the scouting for which they had been included in the army.

Montcalm's trenches drew nearer the fort; cannon mounted at only 200 yards' distance more rapidly blew it apart, dismounting British guns, tearing out the ramparts. The French fire slew many of the defenders and, daily, smallpox was killing more. While William Henry crumbled, Webb wrote more dispatches.

Others who listened at Fort Edward to the distant cannonade were less inert. Sir William Johnson had brought in the armed tenants of his estate and what loyal Mohawk he could find. He begged Webb for permission to move out toward the fort with his own people, the rangers and a number of eager volunteers. The general allowed him to march but Johnson was scarcely out of sight when a messenger was sent to recall him.

Webb thereupon resumed his pen and wrote another letter to Munro, informing him that the fort could not be relieved and advising him to make whatever terms he might with his besiegers.

La Corne's men killed the messenger, found the dispatch and took it to Montcalm.

Days later, after a terrific burst of fire, the French guns ceased suddenly and through the drifting smoke Bougainville under a white flag bore Webb's letter to the smashed fort. Munro was polite but noncommital. During the following night, the few light guns that still remained to him were active but on the morning of August 9, with 300 of his force killed or wounded and smallpox raging, he sent the wounded Lieutenant Colonel Young on horseback to ask Montcalm for terms.

The marquis's stipulations were generous. The garrisons of the fort and entrenched camp were to march out with the honors of war and to be escorted by a French detail to Fort Edward. They were to pledge themselves not to serve again in the war for eighteen months and all prisoners the British had taken in America were to be surrendered in three.

Munro agreed, but there was another element in the situation that required consideration. Montcalm's Indians had served chiefly as spectators to the siege. Their infatuation with the French artillery had kept most of them idle and now, suddenly, the conflict was over.

The tribesmen thus far had acquired neither scalps nor negotiable prisoners. The marquis summoned the chiefs and impressed upon them the sanctity of the surrender terms. All promised to observe them and then, as soon as the garrison had been marched away to join its comrades in the entrenched camp, led whooping warriors into the fort.

The British, on Montcalm's advice, had broken in the heads of all their rum casks before they had withdrawn. Thwarted in their search for liquor, the intruders turned to murder. There was brief screaming and, before the French could intervene, the many ill left in the fort had been hacked to death.

Indians also followed the British column into the entrenched camp and stalked among the beaten men, jostling them, snatching at their belongings, filling the precinct with a snarling sound. Outbreak was averted by the intervention of Montcalm and other officers who at last got the precinct clear. Warriors prowled about the camp all night with so plain a malevolence that the nervous prisoners rose early and were so eager to move along the road to Fort Edward and out of danger that they formed their column before the French escort arrived.

While they waited, unprotected, Indians pressed in upon them again and, when the escort finally appeared, refused to disperse. The tension mounted. Painted faces leered at the captives; dark hands began to snatch at their belongings. Somewhere along the wavering files, above the wicked hum of voices, the war yell rose and hatchets flashed white, then red.

The men of the escort made a not-too-creditable effort to hold off the savages. The tormented column lurched forward with Indians worrying its flanks, buckled and broke apart and the howling warriors raged through it. Some prisoners stood stiff with terror while their clothing was torn away; some ran and were struck down from behind; others were snatched away bodily and pulled here and there as rivals struggled for their possession. A few outdistanced their pursuers and reached the comparative safety of the forest.

Again, Montcalm and his officers plunged into the brawl, commanding, beseeching. Meanwhile, other Indians had burst into the hut where seventeen of the garrison's wounded lay and had butchered them all.

Some 50 bodies, tonsured in shining scarlet, were strewn about the camp when the frenzy ended. Montcalm succeeded in rescuing two-thirds of the 600 whom the Indians had kidnaped. The rest were spirited away by their captors who at once deserted the army and paddled north, taking as a tardy retribution the small-pox epidemic with them. Some of their captives were ransomed by Vaudreuil. Others died less enviably than those who perished in the William Henry massacre.

The prisoners whom the French were able to retrieve were sequestered again in the entrenched camp and this time were heavily guarded. Next day, they were marched to Fort Edward. Guns thereafter were fired at intervals from that post to guide the fugitives who had plunged into the woods.

While the frontier quaked and alarm spread through the northern provinces and Webb, presumably, continued to write letters, Montcalm made no attempt to advance farther by the gap he had burst in the British defense, or even to hold the entire valley that momentarily he controlled. He was less ambitious, or perhaps wiser, than Burgoyne. The marquis had sought no decisive victory; he had conducted a massive raid. Now, having struck, he retired.

There were immediate reasons for his withdrawal. He had promised his militia that they should return to Canada in time for the harvest and his Indians were deserting him wholesale.

The bodies of the British dead were gathered and the wreckage of the fort, which Montcalm pulled down completely, was their funeral pyre. On August 16, the French retired to Ticonderoga.

Webb, shying away from the thought of reprisal or countermove, sent home the militia he so belatedly had summoned. In Captain Lyman's company of Colonel Ebenezer Marsh's Connecticut regiment no one complained more vociferously over an empty errand than a bold and blasphemous youngster, Private Ethan Allen.

---

[1] Bagley to Winslow, July 2, 1756, printed in Francis Parkman, *Wolfe and Montcalm* (Boston, 1909), I, 402.
[2] *Ibid.*

Chapter 8

Fiasco

THE wolves fed well in the winter of 1757-1758, digging the snow away from the charred timbers of the pyre that had been Fort William Henry, following the scalloped tracks of snowshoed scouts who stole through the white, still wilderness between Fort Carillon and Fort Edward and, colliding, slew one another in uncelebrated skirmishes. Most profitably, the wolves attended the forays that Rogers and his rangers carried on in the cold-imposed breathing space while the armies rested.

The wolves had a change of diet one arctic night when the rangers crept close to Carillon, snatched away two soldiers of the garrison and killed fifteen steers. The temper of Captain Hébecourt, the garrison's commander, was not improved the following morning when he found, tied to a horn of one of the half-devoured carcasses, the following acknowledgment from Major Rogers:

"I am obliged to you sir for the rest you have allowed me to take and the fresh meat you have sent me. I shall take good care of my prisoners. My compliments to the Marquis of Montcalm."[1]

Hébecourt, in March, had his revenge. Rogers and two companies of rangers set out on the tenth from Fort Edward. He had been ordered by Colonel William Haviland, commanding, to reconnoiter Carillon and among his 180 followers marched two hitherto extremely bored British officers, Captain Pringle and Lieutenant Roche, who had sought relief from garrison tedium.

Four feet of snow had fallen in the woods. The expedition followed the wind-cleared lake northward, dragging its provision on sleds and keeping a point of skate-shod rangers well in advance. On the thirteenth, Rogers led the column off the ice and, bearing westward with Cooks Mountain between him and the

102

outlet, floundered knee-deep in fluffy snow down the valley through which Bernets—now Trout—Brook flowed. There may have been moments, while the rangers slogged through the forest that covered what is now the golf course of the Ticonderoga Country Club, when Captain Pringle and Lieutenant Roche remembered with genuine longing the warm monotony of the Fort Edward barracks.

The column had reached Trout Brook when the advance guard sighted a force of some 90 Indians moving up the ice of the stream. Rogers prepared an ambush and, when the unsuspecting enemy were abreast, fired into them and killed 40. The rest fled. The rangers pursued and ran, headlong, into a party of 600 Indians and French.

For an hour and a half the forest silence was blasted by musket fire and shouting while the heavier force with snow-clogged deliberation beat the rangers' defense to pieces. Toward dusk, Rogers and those of his men who had not been captured or slain gave way and fled.

Legend of no discernible parentage recites that Rogers, chased by Indians, found himself at last on the peak of the grooved, gray rock face on the lake's west shore that now bears his name, cast his pack down to the ice below, reversed his snowshoes and, retracing his steps, evaded his pursuers who, marking his belongings at the cliff's foot, believed he had slid down.

Since the ranger chief, who was never backward in celebrating his own exploits, makes no mention of this feat in his account of the fight, it is extremely unlikely that it ever happened. Rogers merely says that he reassembled the remnants of his command on the lake shore, sent a runner forward to Fort Edward and was met by a relief party under Stark, 6 miles from the head of George. He had lost in killed and missing 131 of his original 180 followers.

Among the missing were the lately bored Captain Pringle and Lieutenant Roche who ran out of their snowshoes in their flight and found themselves, after hours of wallowing through drifts, on the shores of an unidentifiable lake and entirely alone. They marched farther to keep from freezing and on the morrow, to their great joy, encountered Rogers' orderly, also a fugitive, who promised to lead them to Fort Edward.

For six days they followed their guide, uphill and down, through forest and across ice. During that time a Bologna sausage and some ginger that Pringle had brought with him were their only sustenance. Toward the end of their travail they grew convinced that the orderly was not a wilderness authority but a lunatic. He died of exposure on the last night of their ordeal, and on the morrow Pringle and Roche, looking ahead, discovered that their six days' effort had swung them in a great circle and back to the doorstep of Carillon. They staggered across the ice to the fort and eagerly surrendered.

Spring came at last and with it the British advanced the same, now slightly shopworn, proposal for the conquest of Canada. Louisbourg was to be attacked again; another expedition was to march on Duquesne while, once more, a force was to assemble at the head of Lake George and proceed against Carillon and Fort St. Frédéric. If the plan had a stencil quality, there were power and resolution behind it that, heretofore, its prototypes had lacked.

William Pitt had become Minister of State for Foreign Affairs and the conduct of the war, begun in America but now occupying practically all the so-called civilized world, was placed in his capable hands. Loudon was recalled ignominiously. He had asked the colonies to supply in the previous year 4,000 men. Pitt called for 20,000 and got them.

The provinces, this time, were required to provide their levies only with clothing and pay. Equipment, arms and ammunition were supplied by Britain which further deviated from precedent by sending over an adequate number of regulars for the task at hand. A great new camp was cleared of the wreckage of earlier failures at the head of Lake George and in early summer yet another army that purposed to sweep France from the valley began to assemble there.

James Abercromby was chosen to command it, not because he had shown any marked qualities of leadership but, seemingly, because he alone of the 1757 Loudon-Abercromby-Webb triumvirate so far had revealed no damning disqualifications. He was a portly person whose lethargic qualities of body and mind were incongruously combined with an extreme fussiness that immediately won for him among the less reverent of his command the title of "Aunt Abby Cromby." The corpulent general's deputy was George Augustus, Viscount Howe, whose two younger brothers, Admiral Richard and General William, were to play their parts in the Revolution.

The encomiums bestowed upon Viscount George's military genius, following his untimely death, may have been more eulogistic than accurate but he did possess an adaptability extremely uncommon in British soldiers of his time. From his arrival in America, he studied carefully the equipment and tactics of the troops that, until now, had been most successful in warfare upon the French—the rangers—and modified the stuffy standards of the regulars to conform more nearly with the demands of wilderness campaigning.

Howe not only trimmed his coat into a jacket and had his own hair cut short, but he ordered the British troops to divest their uniforms of the cumbersome and brush-entangling tails; to brown with rust the polished musket barrels that, flashing in the sun, had betrayed their owners to the enemy. He also decreed that each man should carry in his knapsack as a basic ration thirty pounds of corn meal and should burden himself with no other bedding than a bearskin and a blanket.

Abercromby's deputy was concerned not only with his own troops' efficiency but with the welfare of the whole army. He seems to have been the sole British general of whom the colonials were genuinely fond.

The sad-colored provincial levies were tramping into the lake camp now. Many of the officers and men wore the piously patient look of folk who had been through this identical maneuver before and had found that it ended in nothing. Nevertheless, they were gathering in unprecedented strength.

Twelve regiments of colonials at last were camped by the shore—four each from Connecticut and Massachusetts, two from

New York, one each from New Jersey and Rhode Island. Colonel John Bradstreet's ancestor of later amphibious forces was here also, a regiment of boatmen, equally skilled in handling their craft and in fighting ashore. These, with the rangers, brought the provincial strength to more than 9,000 men. They were not to be the main striking force. The regulars were to spearhead the attack that was to drive the French up the valley and there were 6,300 of them.

A silence of desolation and death had dwelt for almost a year about the burned mound by the lake shore. Tumult that daily grew greater supplanted it now. Oxen lowed and teamsters bawled as supply trains from the Hudson rolled off the military road into the camp. Hammers rang as caulkers worked over the 900 bateaux, the 135 whaleboats that were to bear the army down Lake George, and the sounds were echoed from the beach where the sloop *Earl of Halifax* was building. Dust and wood smoke drifted through the company streets. Drums buzzed, fifes squealed and each new day was proclaimed, spaced and ended by the bugles of the regulars.

These composed the heaviest force ever sent by the king to aid his periodically embattled colonial subjects. Militiamen did not weary of watching the bobtailed redcoats move and weave through the precise intricacies of the drill.

Here were His Majesty's 27th, 44th, 46th, 55th, 60th and 80th regiments of Foot, part of the Royal Regiment of Artillery and, blue bonnets slanting, leather sporrans swinging, dark kilts aflutter as they followed their scarlet-tartaned pipers, the 1,000 men of the 42nd Highlanders, "The Black Watch." All the French in America, the armed farmers told each other, could not stand against this host.

Before the army embarked on July 5, other men, beside Abercromby and Howe, whose names were to endure, had gathered at the head of Lake George—Thomas Gage, who was to defend Boston against Washington, John Stark, Robert Rogers, Israel Putnam, Charles Lee, William Franklin—Benjamin's natural son and the last royal governor of New Jersey—Philip Skene and, with his haunted face and gloomy air, Major Duncan Campbell of Inverawe.

Years before, so the legend runs, Campbell had sheltered at his Highland castle a murderer who, after the laird had sworn to protect him, had proved to be the slayer of Campbell's cousin Donald, whose justifiably indignant ghost appeared thrice to reproach Duncan. The specter on its third visitation had moaned:

"Farewell Inverawe: farewell till we meet at Ticonderoga"[2]—a place of which Campbell at that time had never heard. Now, he was about to attack it with the rest of his regiment, the Black Watch, and his eyes were dark with a conviction of imminent death.

The army embarked on the morning of July 4 and the largest flotilla the valley had seen moved down Lake George. Bradstreet's whaleboats, laden with rangers and the light infantry companies of the regular regiments, led the way and behind them in four columns of bateaux came the rest of the host with raft-borne artillery in the rear of the hospital boats and supply craft lagging still farther behind.

Where Sabbath Day Point reaches its long, green arm eastward, bateaux were beached and camp was made to enable the sluggish supply boats to catch up with the advance. Men remembered later that, this evening, Lord Howe lay on a bearskin with John Stark and talked long and earnestly with the grim ranger.

The army set out again at 10:00 p.m., July 5. The French already were aware that it was advancing. Toward sunset of that evening, scouts had reached Carillon with news that they had seen the British flotilla proceeding in splendor down the lake. These tidings resolved one of Montcalm's uncertainties yet left him several still unsettled.

The marquis had arrived at Ticonderoga, June 30. The fort which had served him well as staging area for his 1757 thrust against William Henry seemed less desirable now that the British were assuming the offensive. Deserters fixed Abercromby's force at some 20,000 men and Montcalm had most of his French regulars, some organized Canadian troops, a handful of volunteers and

15 Indians, in all some 3,200 men, with which to defend a fort whose strength, as he considered it, seemed increasingly dubious.

The French commander was handicapped still further by the absence of Lévis. Canada's governor, Vaudreuil, who felt that his military genius outshone Montcalm's, had proposed that a diversionary attack be made against Abercromby's rear by way of the Mohawk Valley—the same move St. Leger was to attempt in the Revolution—and the marquis, to humor his rival, had detached not only his principal subordinate but also 400 regulars to be the backbone of this expedition.

Montcalm, while Abercromby's advance hung fire, recalled Lévis and his troops and sent urgent requests to Vaudreuil for further reinforcement. Meanwhile, he was doubtful whether it were wiser to stand at Carillon or fall back to Fort St. Frédéric. The works that Lotbinière had raised at Ticonderoga were far less defensible than their author deemed them.

The outlet of Lake George flows calmly north, plunges in foam over a series of ledges and, farther on, turns almost at a right angle eastward to go down over a second fall just above the present bridge on Montcalm Street in Ticonderoga village and slips quietly again through marshy lowland into Lake Champlain. Beyond this confluence, toward the tip of Ticonderoga's cape, Lotbinière had built his stout little fort. It crowned a steep hill but Vaudreuil's engineer had overlooked in his paternal enthusiasm weaknesses that worried Montcalm.

Carillon, it was true, would be ruinously expensive to take by frontal assault without artillery support, but it was commanded by the higher eminence of what the French called Rattlesnake Hill and the colonials Sugar Loaf Mountain on the farther side of the outlet's estuary. In addition, the fort did not occupy the loftiest ground in Ticonderoga's own peninsula. A half mile north and west of the stronghold, the cape's forest-clad spine humped itself into a knoll that dominated the fort. The enemy who got guns into battery on this height quite deliberately could beat Carillon to bits.

Lotbinière already felt himself aggrieved by the fact that the Frenchman, Pontleroy, and not he, had been chosen Montcalm's chief engineer. The further suggestion that the fort be abandoned must have thrown him into a Gallic effervescence. He himself asserts that it was only by his most earnest representations that the marquis was induced to defend the stronghold.

The mechanics of that defense must wait upon the disclosure of Abercromby's own plan. The British general might advance directly upon Ticonderoga: he might follow the general route taken by Rogers in his March raid, moving north along the valley of Bernets Brook with the mountains between him and the fort to the wooded plain beyond and, across this, to the narrows at Five-Mile Point. Cannon mounted there could cut Montcalm's supply line and starve his underprovisioned army. The marquis, to determine the British intention, went forth a little way to meet the enemy.

The French had built a portage road across the valley through which Lake George's outlet curved like a misshapen hook. The track's upstream end was at a bridge just above the first rapids; its lower, at another bridge downstream from the chiming falls whose power had been harnessed to a sawmill. Montcalm sent Bourlamaque with the battalions of La Reine, Guienne and Béarn to the upper bridge and occupied the ground about the lower with the Sarre, Royal Rousillon, Languedoc and half the Berry troops.

Vedettes were posted in the Bernets Brook Valley to guard against a flank movement and Captain Trepezec of the Béarn battalion was sent with 350 men, including the handful of Indians, down the west side of Lake George to wait for the approach of the British flotilla. When this was in sight at dawn of July 6, the Indians promptly deserted, leaving Trepezec to stumble back toward Carillon without guides.

The British came steadily on, red coats glowing, oar blades flashing in the early sunlight. Light infantry and rangers scrambled ashore from Bradstreet's whaleboats on the west bank of the outlet and Bourlamaque fell back after setting fire to the upper bridge. By noon, all the infantry had landed. It was clear now to Montcalm that Abercromby intended a direct attack.

The marquis thereupon began an eleventh-hour attempt to dig

trenches and fell trees for an abatiş on the "Height of Carillon" north and west of the fort. Meanwhile, Rogers had led his rangers, who were followed by Lyman's and Fitch's provincials, forward through the woodland on the west side of the outlet and the other columns were forming to grope their way across this wilderness toward the base of Ticonderoga's cape.

It was a difficult route for the provincials and a nightmare for the regulars. In the sweltering forest twilight, the terrain grew continually more broken and the breathless columns straggled and lost contact. There was an endless sound of stumbling feet, an occasional rattling thump as a man tripped and fell, yet no one threading his way through the close-packed trees saw more than a few of his fellows.

The forest hid an army so thoroughly that Trepezec's retiring and bewildered 350 were almost upon Lord Howe's columns before either was aware of the other's presence. A voice cried a challenge. The faltered reply was blown away by the crash of muskets.

For a brief space, the fighting was purblind and desperate. Bullets slashed through foliage and brief flames squirted in the gloom. Then, on the far side of the French line, rose the roar of more guns. Rogers, Lyman and Fitch, marching back toward the sound of firing, had struck the enemy's rear.

It was over quickly. French voices beseeching quarter silenced the tumult. Smoke drifted and thinned above the fallen men. Trepezec was among these, and on a ridge a quarter-mile south of the Catholic cemetery in the present village of Ticonderoga lay the body of Howe, shot through the breast. One hundred and forty-eight of Trepezec's men surrendered, some fifty escaped. The rest had been killed.

The dim conflict had entangled the army beyond hope of immediate reordering. The advance was halted and most of the units returned to the landing place. Here, the news of Howe's death dragged morale so low that Abercromby, lacking better qualities of leadership, strove to restore confidence by falsehood. Captain Moneypenny noted in his orderly book that the troops had been instructed "to fire a Rejoicing Fire for the good news the general has had from Louisbourg."[3]

There had been no news worthy of "rejoicing" from Louisbourg, which did not fall till twenty days later. The general's lie could not entirely accomplish its purpose. The army made no further determined advance upon Carillon until July 8. This was a heaven-sent opportunity for Montcalm.

The marquis, who had so tardily begun to protect the fort's most vulnerable side, now roused in his troops a fervor that Abercromby could not kindle in his own. Day and night, officers and men alike labored in the growing entrenchments. Breastworks rose higher, axes rang and with a swish and a crash tree after tree went down. By nightfall of July 7, the new barrier was completed—a tall earthwork and, before it, an abatis of treetops, with each limb sharpened to a point. Beyond the actual fortification more trees had been dropped, haphazardly, to open a field of fire and to break the integrity of infantry attack by their tangle of trunks and branches.

Early that evening 300 regulars under the command of Lévis reached Carillon. Their leader and an additional 100 appeared before morning and marveled to see what had been accomplished in 36 hours.

The entrenchments were proof against infantry. Artillery, properly served, would blow them away in a few hours. Abercromby was plentifully equipped with cannon. He left them on the outlet's shore and elected to storm the barricade. The general remained well in the rear and sent his regulars forward. The disparaged provincials played only a minor part in the ensuing shambles.

By the time Abercromby brought his troops to battle, the French works were completed—a salient-studded semicircle of damp earth and prostrate trees behind which the white-uniformed battalions waited. Bourlamaque with Sarre and Languedoc held the left; Montcalm, with Berry and Royal Rousillon, the center. Lévis commanded La Reine, Béarn and Guienne on the right and this flank was farther extended downhill by another trench, dug at an angle to enfilade the French front and manned by the organized

Canadian troops and the volunteers. The grenadier companies of each battalion were held in reserve.

It was 12:30 when massed redcoats glowed in the woods, then blazed as the regiments moved forward into sunlight. A neighing sound wove through British and French cheering as the pipers played the Black Watch into action. Abercromby from his post at the sawmill, a mile and a half in the rear, had decreed that human courage, unsupported by guns, was to carry the works.

Four solid columns of infantry launched the assault. These broke apart as men waded through or climbed over the appalling tangle before the French position. French volleys smashed the elements into smaller fragments. Still, the troops advanced into the gushing smoke. Two columns tried to claw their way through the abatis before Bourlamaque's position, a third attacked the center, while yelling Highlanders and grenadiers attempted to overwhelm the French right.

The attack reeled, dwindled and withdrew, save for the bright effigies that lay oddly across the trunks or among the branches of the felled trees. The French cheering was premature. Out of range, the red columns were reforming and the pipes were calling. Abercromby had sent forward orders to press the attack. Meanwhile, rangers had worked their way into the mass of prostrate boughs and wilting leaves and from this concealment had opened a murderous fire.

Five times more during the long summer afternoon, the British stormed the works, stumbling forward until bravery could bear them no farther, pausing to fire into the sparkling cloud that enveloped the French and falling back, to leave new scarlet patches glowing like tropic flowers among the fallen trees.

Abercromby deviated only once from suicidal frontal assault. Twenty troop-laden bateaux were sent down the outlet in an effort to turn the French left. Plunging cannon fire from Fort Carillon sank two craft and sent the others scuttling back to safety. Abercromby ordered his bleeding columns forward once more.

The final and fiercest assault came late in the afternoon. The Highlanders led it, sweeping forward so furiously that they hacked a way through the abatis before the French right and drove in almost under the muskets of Guienne. These struck down the front of the attack but the blue bonnets still swarmed through the smoke and were driven back only when the cross fire of the Canadian French tore through the column. It was here that Major Campbell was wounded in the right arm—not killed, as the ghost had foretold. The battle dwindled, though ambushed rangers kept up a sniping fire until dark.

Montcalm, moving through his cheering troops, felt something less than their exultation. His own losses had been small, Bourlamaque had been severely wounded, Bougainville slightly and some 350 others killed or injured. The marquis had repulsed the British but he had not broken their army and on the morrow Abercromby doubtless would employ his hitherto idle artillery. The French devoted most of the night of July 8 to enlarging and strengthening their entrenchments. It was needless effort. Abercromby would not try again.

Aunt Abby's force had been badly mauled. Out of some 6,000 regulars, 1,610 had been killed, wounded or were missing. No other regiment had suffered as severely as the Black Watch which had lost 490 of its 1,000 men. The total provincial casualties were 357.

Abercromby still had more than 13,000 men fit for duty, and also his hitherto unemployed guns, but while Montcalm labored to prepare for a renewed attack, panic seems to have swept through the British army and to have laid hold most severely upon its commander. Dawn of July 9 revealed to the French no sign of their enemies. Scouts sent out by Montcalm brought back the incredible report that the enemy had fled. Lévis with a strong force moved out on July 10 to make sure.

He found some wounded left behind by the British in their haste, as well as tons of supplies and an infinite amount of cast-away equipment. Most eloquent testimony of the dread that had overwhelmed the army was discovered in a marshy space. Here were mired dozens of shoes, out of which their fugitive owners had run.

Abercromby, having led his host back to its starting place,

abandoned whatever original initiative had been his. He began to entrench. He is said to have buried a treasure on little Tea Island, near the head of Lake George. So legend recites and the island in subsequent years was thoroughly and entirely unprofitably excavated by the credulous.

The British wounded were sent on to Fort Edward. There, on July 17, the haunted Major Duncan Campbell died, thoroughly refuting the spectral prediction that he was to meet his end at Ticonderoga and, since his wound was not mortal by modern medical standards, probably perishing, not in compliance with a ghostly doom, but from infection. His bones now rest in the Union Cemetery between Hudson Falls and Fort Edward, under the ancient brown stone that recites:

> Here Lyes The Body of Duncan
> Campbell of Inverawe, Esq.
> Major To The Old Highland
> R'g't aged 55 Years Who Died
> the 17th of July, 1758 of The Wounds
> He Received in The Attack
> of the Retrenchments of
> Ticonderoga or Carillon the 8th July 1758

The post-mortem fate of Lord Howe's body has been more debated. Few historical matters are better attested by the writings of all parties concerned, save the principal, than the allegation that the body, after hasty embalming by an army surgeon, was taken to Albany for further preparation before shipment home. At Albany it was deemed advisable to bury it at once and it was interred beneath the Episcopal edifice, then called "The English Church," and later renamed "St. Peter's."

These are facts, if documentary testimony can make them so. It is inadvisable to voice them too loudly in the village of Ticonderoga which deems itself the possessor of Lord Howe's authentic remains and has set up a boulder-embedded plaque on the edge of the park before the brick public school to proclaim its proprietorship.

Peter Duchane, an illiterate laborer, while digging a sewer ditch on October 3, 1889, drove his pick into a pine coffin that lay some four feet underground and directly across the street from the present marker. There was a clay-encrusted stone at the coffin's head and within it, among the bones of an apparently young man, some buttons and a bullet.

Duchane took the stone to the then town clerk, John C. Fenton, who, after repeated scrapings and washings, excitedly summoned his friends and showed them, scratched upon the stone's face with a knife or bayonet point, the following:

MEM OF
Lo HOWE
KILLED
TROUT
BROOK

The exhumed bones lie beneath the boulder in the school park but the controversy, despite its age, goes marching on. Skeptics, of whom Ticonderoga harbors few, hold that "Lo HOWE" was not the British general but some obscure person whose first name may have been Lorenzo. They also offer more damaging testimony by pointing out that what the later settlers renamed "Trout Brook," at the time of Howe's death was called "Bernets Brook" or "Bernes Brook."

Contemporary reports, letters and records—and there are a mass of them—insist that Howe was buried beneath the English Church in Albany, but this does not entirely dispel the mystery. A body said to be the nobleman's was dug up when a new St. Peter's was built in 1802. It was reburied in the crypt: re-exhumed and re-interred when another St. Peter's was erected in 1859. In the coffin, at the time of the second exposure, were found bits of what indubitably had been a hair ribbon. Lord Howe had cropped his hair short for the Ticonderoga campaign. There are agnostics who hold that no one knows precisely where the general's bones now lie.

Abercromby's battered army, lurking behind its hastily raised entrenchments at the head of Lake George, fought nothing for the rest of the summer of 1758 but the camp diseases that flourished among the idle troops, though the rangers were continually employed in warding off raiding parties under La Corne and other partisans that, launched from Carillon, struck at the army's supply lines.

In one such skirmish between Fort Ann and Fort Edward, Israel Putnam's musket missed fire. A French Indian captured him, trussed him to a tree for safekeeping and then plunged back into the fight. Bullets whizzed about the helpless Putnam but his position was more comfortable than it became later when, with the skirmish over, the Indians prepared to burn him. Marin, their leader, intervened and the prisoner was taken intact to Ticonderoga.

At the fort, Montcalm was willing to remain as inactive as his adversary. He was too keen a general not to feel that the sands were running out. As the enemy's blows grew heavier elsewhere, he relied more on defense than attack. To him and the pest-ridden British at Lake George's far end, news came in August of Louisbourg's fall on July 26. It would be interesting to know how Abercromby, having once fraudulently announced it, proclaimed the authentic capitulation to his troops.

The summer waned, with only the barbarities of bush warfare to break the monotony. Abercromby roused from his lethargy sufficiently to permit Bradstreet with 3,000 provincials to move against Fort Frontenac, where Kingston, Ontario, now stands. Its capture cheered the army. The arrival of General Jeffrey Amherst with several regiments of Louisbourg veterans encouraged it further, but it was October now and too late for the mounting of another campaign.

Toward the month's end, a deserter reported that Montcalm was leaving Carillon with all his troops but the usual garrison. The British army, which found itself precisely where former expeditions had been at a summer's end, buried its heavy artillery, sank the lately launched sloop, *Earl of Halifax,* and broke camp.

Still another effort to drive the French from the George-Champlain Valley had accomplished nothing, but the time of humiliation and defeat was near its end. Before a memorably bitter winter closed down, Fort Duquesne was taken. One by one, New France's defenses were being burst in. Another summer would see the fulfillment of a purpose that had been cherished unavailingly since the first Winslow fiasco, sixty-eight years before.[3]

1 Fort Ticonderoga Museum *Bulletin,* VI, 2.
2 Francis Parkman, *Wolfe and Montcalm* (Boston, 1909), II, 450.
3 Captain A. Moneypenny, Orderly Book in Fort Ticonderoga Museum Library.

Chapter 9

Decline and Fall

SPRING came tardily in 1759. Among its harbingers was still another army, marshaling at Albany to move, like its predecessors, along a way that hitherto had led only to anticlimax or defeat. It was a different host from its forerunners: smaller than the expedition commanded by Abercromby, who had retired into the limbo that had enfolded Loudon, Webb and earlier inefficients, but harder, with a hard leader.

The regulars—the 1st, 17th, 27th, 55th and 80th Foot, the 42nd and 77th Highlanders and a battalion of Royal Artillery—had learned American warfare in the battles of the preceding year. Most of the provincial regiments also had seen service. Connecticut sent four; Massachusetts, two, and New Hampshire, Rhode Island and New Jersey, one each. This army had for commander Jeffrey Amherst, conqueror of Louisbourg.

The general, a large-eyed, large-nosed man with a low forehead between a shock of wavy hair and thick brows, was deliberate, careful and stern, as his troops soon learned. The sword was the prime tool of Amherst's trade but the shovel was equally dear to him. He had a hunger for new fortifications and seems to have tarried nowhere for any length of time without appeasing it. He was also the apostle of a discipline more rigorous than colonial levies until now had endured. He spared neither the rod nor, when he deemed it necessary, the firing squad in stamping out insubordination.

Robert Webster, a recruit in Colonel Eleazer Fitch's Connecticut Regiment, wrote in his diary, May 29:

"We march over the wast sid of the Cyty and joyned the Regiment this Day there was one of the Rodisland solgers shot for Desertion."[1]

118

Captain Moneypenny entered in his orderly book on **July 18:**

"Thomas Bourke Waggoner try'd by a Court Martial of the Line for abusing and threatening to strike his officer at Half way Brook is found guilty of the Crime laid to his Charge and is sentenc'd to 400 lashes." [2]

Similar punishments were frequent. None of his subordinates was likely to prefix Jeffrey Amherst's name with "Aunt."

Eleven thousand men moved deliberately from Albany to the calamity-haunted camping place at the head of George. During their progress Amherst gave way to his passion and studded the Military Road from the Hudson to the lake with stockades and blockhouses. He also took grim good care of his men. Drills were long. Regulars and colonials alike were instructed in marksmanship and the ailing were promptly marched to their regimental surgeons and copiously dosed.

The hale, beside their other duties, dug up the artillery "Aunt Abby" had buried the year before and raised the sloop *Earl of Halifax,* which he had scuttled. Before the army embarked, Amherst had begun work on an ambitious stone stronghold which, though only a single bastion was completed, he named "Fort George." It still stands among the tall trees above the lake. On July 21, a new flotilla moved toward Carillon, the only British force in the present campaign to retrace its steps of the previous year.

New France was beginning to bend and buckle. Montcalm and Vaudreuil were bombarding Versailles with mutually recriminatory letters, but they both were aware of the structure's ominous creaking. Louisbourg, Duquesne and Frontenac were in enemy hands and British frigates, cruising off the mouth of the St. Lawrence all winter, had cut off supplies sent to a colony impoverished by war.

Bougainville had got through the loose blockade and had carried to the dissolute French court a tale of privation and impending defeat. He begged for reinforcements and got less than four hundred recruits and some munitions, though it was clear that New France must endure in 1759 heavier pressure than in the preceding year.

Vaudreuil turned away from his unending squabble with Montcalm long enough to conduct a military census of his province. This revealed that in all eastern Canada there were scarcely 3,500 regulars and 1,500 colony troops. Civilian males capable of bearing arms amounted to only 13,000 more. Less than 20,000 men, 5,000 of whom were soldiers, must oppose the 5,000 provincials and regulars that Brigadier General John Prideaux was leading against Niagara, the strong fleet and 8,500 troops under Major General James Wolfe that were sailing toward Quebec and the trained army of 11,000 that Amherst was bringing down the lakes.

Outer defenses, Montcalm resolved, must be abandoned as deliberately as possible. The French, when hard-pressed, must fall back and make their final stand at the natural protections of the colony's heart—Quebec, where the marquis commanded in person: the rapids of the St. Lawrence and the fortified Isle aux Noix in the Richelieu River—until winter came to the rescue. Time was New France's greatest need.

The British fleet appeared before Quebec on June 26. On July 22 Amherst's army got ashore at the outlet of Lake George. It drove a thin screen of French skirmishers down the portage road and that night camped at the sawmill below the last rapids. Bourlamaque, obedient to his orders, immediately evacuated all the garrison of 3,000, save 400 men whom he left with Hébecourt to fight a delaying action.

The force was too small to defend the entrenchment Montcalm had held the year before. It clung only to the fort itself. The British manned the outer works in reverse while Amherst with methodical deliberation prepared to take the stronghold, not by headlong infantry attack but by blowing it apart with the cannon he was placing.

Hébecourt, meanwhile, deemed it more praiseworthy to shoot his ammunition at the British than to use it later to blow up Carillon. He poured a continual, spectacular if generally ineffective fire upon the besieger's lines. It astonished the veteran Captain James Murray of the Black Watch, who wrote home:

"During the time the enemy remained they could not keep a hotter fire for I dare say they fired ten thousand cannon shot and five hundred bombs and I don't believe there has been forty men killed and wounded during the hott fire."[3]

By July 26 Amherst's batteries were ready to open. That evening deserters reported that the garrison had left the fort and was rowing toward Crown Point. A little later a great red flame and a thunderous sound proclaimed that Hébecourt before evacuating Carillon had set a match to its magazine.

Amherst made no hasty attempt to pursue. He inspected the damage on the morrow, found that one bastion had been destroyed and the barracks burned and immediately began to repair and improve the stronghold that henceforth was to be called "Fort Ticonderoga." He did not stir till August 1 when, scouts having discovered that the French had left Crown Point, he and his army advanced to this post.

Fort St. Frédéric also had been partly blown up and across the narrow strait the little cottages—France's farthest settlement in the valley she had claimed for 150 years—were deserted. Before Quebec, Wolfe was in difficulty but Amherst did not hasten. The enemy still had four armed vessels loose on lower Champlain. Amherst stayed at Crown Point and embarked upon an orgy of building.

The general began another and larger fort behind the damaged St. Frédéric and on higher ground, cutting most of his timber within what is now the village of Port Henry. He started to add to his own navy—which had consisted only of whaleboats, bateaux and, on Lake George, the sloop *Earl of Halifax*—laying down a brigantine, a floating battery and another sloop. He decreed the construction of a military road clear across the mountainous breadth of what would one day be Vermont from Fort Number Four, now Charlestown, New Hampshire, to the shore opposite Crown Point.

Amherst sent exploring parties to seek the source of the Hudson and Otter Creek and, almost as an afterthought, despatched Ensign Hutchins of the rangers with an encouraging letter to Wolfe. Hutchins cut through the Vermont, New Hampshire and Maine wilderness and delivered the message in a month.

Word reached Amherst that Sir William Johnson, replacing Prideaux who had been killed in the attack, had captured the French fort at Niagara. Tidings also came up Champlain that Bourlamaque, having fallen back to Isle aux Noix, just below the entrance to the lake's outlet, was fortifying and obviously intended to make his stand there. Amherst in a wily attempt to get further word to Wolfe, sent Captains Kennedy and Hamilton with a flag of truce to the St. Francis Indians.

St. Francis, a mission village on the south shore of the St. Lawrence midway between Montreal and Quebec, had long been a catchall for fragments of a number of tribes that had no cause to love the British, and a major affliction to the New England frontier. Raid after raid had gone south from the place to massacre settlers and burn the beginnings of villages.

Earlier British commanders had endured the slaughter of insignificants with manful composure and Amherst had displayed like fortitude until the enormity now inflicted by the inhabitants of St. Francis upon his emissaries enraged him. The Indians not only refused to recognize his flag of truce; they also made prisoners of Captains Kennedy and Hamilton and carried them to Montcalm. The righteously furious British general immediately embarked upon reprisal. He ordered Major Robert Rogers and his rangers to destroy the village.

Rogers set out upon this, the climactic foray of his career, in September. It took him and his 200 followers ten days to row from Crown Point to the upper end of Missisquoi Bay, for armed French vessels still were abroad on Champlain and the rangers hid during each day and advanced only at night.

The expedition concealed its boats, left two Indians on guard and made their first march toward St. Francis. Before it was completed, the Indians overtook the column with the tidings that the French had discovered the craft and were in pursuit. Rogers already was deep in hostile territory. If he stood to fight, he would bring enemies down upon his command from all sides. He struck across country by forced marches, first sending Lieutenant Mc-Mullen back to Amherst with a mesasge.

This dispatch explained that Rogers, after striking St. Francis, could not possibly retrace his way through an aroused countryside but would push farther through wilderness toward the Connecticut River, aiming for the mouth of the Ammonoosuc that empties into the larger stream opposite where Guildhall, Vermont, now stands. He begged Amherst to send supplies to that point and the general immediately named a detail under Lieutenant Stephen to bear them thither.

Nine days further marching through forest and swamp—an ordeal so brutal that 60 of the tough rangers succumbed and were left behind—brought Rogers to St. Francis. He attacked at dawn, released 5 English prisoners, killed 200 Indians and burned the scalp-adorned buildings. Thereafter the rangers, already spent, were forced to outrun the retaliatory Canadians and Indians.

The fugitives subsisted for a time on corn they had taken from St. Francis. When this failed, the command broke up into smaller groups to baffle pursuit and for better foraging. They staggered on toward the rendezvous. Many were overtaken and killed by the French. Less than a hundred finally reached the Ammonoosuc's mouth, exhausted and starving, to find that Lieutenant Stephen, grown weary of waiting, had departed. There were live coals still in his campfires. Stephen heard the signals fired by the desperate men but believed the French were after him and made more haste downstream.

Of the few who did not collapse in despair, Rogers was the most vigorous of heart and enterprise. He fashioned a log raft and with Captain Ogden, another ranger and an Indian boy captured at St. Francis, drifted down the Connecticut. The raft broke apart in rapids. Too weak to swing an ax, her crew burned down trees, got another raft together and floated farther to Fort Number Four, from which relief immediately was sent upstream to the remnants of Rogers' command. The timid Lieutenant Stephen was cashiered from the service.

Quebec fell, September 17. Wolfe died in the assault and the wounded Montcalm soon afterward. The British under Brigadier General James Murray occupied the town and found themselves cooped up by the reinforced French. At Crown Point Amherst continued to indulge himself in fort-building until, on October 11, his new little navy was ready to sail. The brigantine, sloop and floating battery under the command of Captain Loring stood out so imposingly that the French armed vessels fled in panic. One finally reached the protection of Bourlamaque's cannon on Isle aux Noix, one ran aground. The other two were scuttled by their crews.

Amherst loaded his regulars into 160 bateaux and started down the lake in the wake of his fleet. He had delayed too long and the yelping winds of autumnal Champlain opposed him. A gale from the north on the evening of October 12, drove the half-swamped bateaux into Ligonier Bay on Willsboro Point and held them there throughout the morrow. On the fourteenth, cold rain was added to the blast. The storm endured all next day and, though the downpour ended that night, the persistent wind brought freezing temperatures. On the seventeenth, the blast switched round briefly to the south, changed its mind and blew fiercely from the north again.

The bateaux made good time back to Crown Point over the white-capped rollers. It was too late, Amherst had decided, to try to relieve the British garrison at Quebec. The general spent the remnant of the season in further work on his fort, which he named after himself, and left a garrison there when he and the rest of his army retired for the winter. The war had still another ten months to run before final, complete surrender of the French.

Lévis, in April 1760, laid active siege to Quebec but fell back when, on May 9, the first frigate of the rescuing fleet arrived. Amherst, now at Oswego with 10,000 men, organized the final ponderous campaign. He, himself, would advance by way of Lake Ontario and the St. Lawrence River. Murray, with the Quebec garrison and units of the British fleet, would sail upstream. Brigadier General William Haviland, moving north from Crown Point with 3,500 provincials and regulars, would take fortified Isle aux Noix, where Bougainville now commanded, and break into the St. Lawrence Valley from the south. Midsummer had passed before the three-pronged attack was in complete motion.

Haviland's expedition rowed into the breadth of lower Lake Champlain in late August and, entering the Richelieu, made landing on the swampy tip of Isle aux Noix to begin a cannonade. Bougainville's 1,700 men clung to their intrenchments. French *élan* had dropped so low that Majors Darby of the regulars and Rogers of the rangers were able to drag three fieldpieces through the mainland forest to the river bank below the fortification. Here, the remnant of the French fleet had sought protection—3 armed vessels and several gunboats.

The anchor cable of the largest craft was cut by the first fire and it drifted ashore under the British guns to surrender. The others, while cannon balls plunged about them, made sail and went down-river in such haste that, at a bend in the Richelieu, all drove aground. Rangers with knives or hatchets in their teeth swam out and swarmed aboard to capture the second vessel. The third surrendered immediately.

Rogers' and Darby's fieldpieces had cut off Bougainville from contact by water with downstream St. Johns where Roquemaure had a garrison of 1,200. That night, August 27, Isle aux Noix's commander got his men ashore and led them 12 miles to St. Johns. With Haviland treading on their heels, Roquemaure and Bougainville fell back to the St. Lawrence. Murray waited below Montreal for the other British forces to arrive and Haviland made contact with him.

The power and will of New France were dwindling together. Even among the regulars, desertions were frequent; the militia were quitting the war and the Indians already had abandoned it. On September 6, Amherst's 10,000, less some eighty drowned in passage of the rapids, appeared above Montreal, beached their battered boats and, in concert with Haviland's and Murray's men, invested the town which Vaudreuil and Lévis held with the dregs of French colonial might—barely 2,400 men.

New France was surrendered to Britain on September 8. The war that had begun seventy-one years before had ended.

It had been, for American participants, a needless ordeal. Land and resources were plentiful enough to have kept many times the continent's thin population in prosperous peace. Yet it had not been entirely unprofitable strife.

The conflict that had swayed back and forth through the Champlain-George valley had schooled a most unmartial people in the arts of war. The generals sent from England to serve as instructors had done little to rouse in colonists any extensive respect for British arms. Seeds of revolution already had been planted when the canoes of the first expresses hastened up the lakes to bear tidings to Albany of the French surrender.

The messengers passed through a wilderness as unmarred and, save for the forts and the ruins of a few incautiously begun settlements, as absolute as it had been when the first white man had entered the lovely valley, a century and a half before. Now that the war was ended, a restless people would begin to move in upon this empty region.

[1] Robert Webster's Diary, in Fort Ticonderoga Museum Library.
[2] Captain A. Moneypenny, Orderly Book, in Fort Ticonderoga Museum Library.
[3] Frederick B. Richards, *The Black Watch at Ticonderoga* (n.d.), p. 31.

"COMMODORE THOMAS MACDONOUGH" BY GILBERT STUART

BATTLE FLAG OF H.M.S. *Confiance*

LONG 24 FROM H.M.S. *Confiance*

This long 24, dismounted by an American cannon ball, killed Captain Downie.
Note the dent in the muzzle.

Chapter 10

Settlements and Shares

HE terror by day and the arrow by night that long had harried the George-Champlain Valley had been abolished by a final paroxysm of war. Before the ink was dry on the Treaty of Paris which transferred all of what had been New France to Britain, men were reaching out for a lately perilous, now greatly promising region.

Geography decreed that the earliest settlements should be on Champlain. Here navigable water ran clear from South Bay to St. Johns on the Richelieu. For long stretches, the mountains stood back from the larger lake's shore and at their feet, particularly on the east side, the deep, dark forest loam was astoundingly fertile. There were streams here too, long and swift, to empower the mills an ingenious people planned.

Against these allurements, Lake George could offer little beyond scenery and seclusion, for either of which men who sought profitable farms had scant respect. On the banks of the lesser lake, the mountains stood with their feet in the water and through pinched, intervening valleys flowed only piddling brooks.

Champlain settlers were in sight of Canada before pioneers had advanced from Fort Edward to Lake George and those who came thither before the Revolution were employed at the never completed Fort George, or else were folk of the true wilderness breed, like the Harris clan, who welcomed hardship and lived their isolated lives as hunters and fishermen.

The system whereby new land finally got into the hands of an actual occupant was complex, often nefarious and prevailed with only minor variations throughout all the colonies.

The provinces themselves were chartered to corporations or individuals by their owner, His British Majesty, who prescribed territorial limits with a lavish disregard for actual geography. The governors of the colonies, acting as the·king's agents, bestowed upon the monarch's allegedly deserving subjects grants or patents to tracts of land. Fees for this service differed from colony to colony. Patent fees in New York were £14 sterling per 1,000 acres; in New Hampshire, £20 sterling per 15,000.

The grantees, once in possession, were expected to fulfill a number of obligations, including settlement and cultivation of their holdings. The only one strictly enforced was the rule requiring payment of quitrent. This annual tribute was made, in theory, directly to the Crown. New Hampshire's quitrent per 1000 acres was one shilling, six pence; New York's, two shillings, six pence.

Few of the proprietors made any personal attempt to settle the territory they had obtained. Many never laid eyes on their property. Most of them were capitalists who sponsored the first extensive American industry—the land business. These magnates in an era of small enterprises issued rights entitling the purchasers thereof to a certain number of acres of territory and entrusted these shares to jobbers who went up and down the colonies, selling them to the land-hungry and to folk with a taste for gambling.

An enormous number of such shares were floating about the provinces, rising or falling in price as the informal market changed, bought and sold by speculators and serving in a time of currency shortage as more or less legal tender.

Greed and chicanery and downright crookedness stimulated trading. The basic craving of Anglo-Saxons for land of their own poured money into a market which was stimulated and expanded by the opening-up of the Champlain-George Valley and near-by territory. The governors of New York and New Hampshire industriously issued patents and grants. In addition, an inflationary number of "military rights" came into being.

The veterans of the French wars had received a bonus, not in cash but in warrants for land. Each field officer was entitled to 5,000 acres; captains 3,000; subalterns, 2,000; sergeants and corporals, 200; and privates, 100. Many of these immediately sold out to speculators. One of the original recipients, Major Philip Skene, determined to establish a baronial demesne on Lake Champlain. William Gilliland, a businessman, industriously bought up rights to found his own colony on the lake. The Revolutionary War broke them both, as it did similarly hopeful lesser men.

Skene was a person of vision and energy with a willful mouth, a pleasant manner and the high intention of becoming a landed proprietor. He was born in 1723 in Hollyards, Fifeshire, Scotland, became an ensign in the 27th Foot at sixteen, fought at Cartagena, Porto Bello, Fontenoy and Culloden Moor and was wounded in Abercromby's assault on Montcalm's entrenchments. He served with Amherst in the following year and was appointed brigade major in charge of the Ticonderoga and Crown Point garrisons.

By the war's end, he had determined to settle in the region he had inspected thoroughly during two years of campaigning. Amherst endorsed his major's application for a large grant, over and above his military rights, and Skene sent it to Parliament. His petition asked for the territory at the head of Champlain where Wood Creek pours its murky water into South Bay and he must have been assured that it would be granted for he settled thirty families on the property before he was off again to the wars. He served under the Earl of Albemarle in the West Indies, whence he brought several slaves to the lake settlement which still did not belong to him.

He was in London in 1764 and argued his claim so eloquently before the Lords of Trade that they granted him a large tract, to which he himself added more, and he called the whole 29,000 acres Skenesborough. Whitehall stands on the site today, but no material remnant can be found there of the dream that Major Skene, having sold his commission, set out to realize.

His was no small ambition. He purposed to make himself and his family great in this wilderness. The stone mansion he built was 130 feet long—a manor for future generations of Skenes and a lordly present habitation for the major and his wife, their son and two daughters. The community that grew up through the pre-Revolutionary years far outstripped any other lake settlement. Here were barns for the major's crops and cattle, and for the horses he had begun to raise for export. Meadows were cleared and fenced, and Skene built sawmills, an iron forge and a store.

The riverlike extremity of Champlain ran unimpeded from his premises into Canada. Skene obtained title to 600 acres of land rich in iron ore in the hills behind what is now Port Henry.

"I am very busy," he wrote Lieutenant Thomas Gamble, April 26, 1771, "and shall have a sloop on the lake by the Month of Aug't to convey horses over for the West Indies that are much demanded and carry the produce of Staves, boards, etc. to Canada from hence. . . . I have made her of a compleat Model and most of her works that can be will be of red cedar."[1]

Skene built barges of the same wood to carry his produce north. He constructed a road from Skenesborough to Salem to move farther southward what goods he had imported from Montreal. Benjamin Franklin and John Foxcroft, Postmasters General, established the first post office on either lake at Skenesborough.

The major was continually in need of money, not through great extravagance but because his purpose outran his income. He sent his son to Kings College, now Columbia, with the earnest hope that "the Corruption of the Moral Charracters of the Youth of York will not enfect him,"[2] and worried much thereafter over Andrew's progress, which could not have been entirely decorous since the boy wrote him:

"A man has informed against Me for shooting a gun off in the Colledge yard and am sued and obliged to pay eight shillings as a fine for shooting within the town."[3]

When the crisis came in 1775, Skene remained loyal to the uniform he had worn and thus became an abhorred and profusely slandered person, but what can still be seen of him down a perspective of a hundred and seventy years reveals a man not only energetic but kindly and gracious. He impressed no less violent a rebel than Ethan Allen, who wrote him in 1772:

"Your Generous & Social Treatment to me when at Your house prompts me to write to You Tho Your Station in Life is Honourable and Commands submition from Those of an Inferior rank Yet it is Your Personal Merit that Demands Esteam. Ever since my

Small Acquaintance with You I Have Retained the most honourable Sentiments Toward You Not onely as the Most Consummate politician whose Eye pierces through Humane Nature but also as one who acts from Generous and brave principles——"[4]

Allen's tribute to the major's acumen probably was the echo of a project on which they seem to have worked together. The struggle of what is now Vermont against the New York authorities and the persons to whom they had granted land patents had roused in the insurgents a hope that the territory on both lakes' shores and the land beyond them might be set off and organized as a separate province, with Crown Point as its capital.

Skene favored the scheme and, early in 1775, arrived in London to lay it before the authorities there. He got no final decision but received the post of Lieutenant Governor of Ticonderoga and Crown Point from Lord Dartmouth. When the ship on which he returned to America in June 1775 set him ashore at Philadelphia, misfortunes as conglomerate as Job's fell upon him.

The lake forts that were to have been his charge had been captured by rebels, who also had occupied Skenesborough. The major's son and daughters had been made prisoners. His brand-new trading schooner *Liberty* had been confiscated and added to the patriot fleet. As climax to his monumental woes, Skene was arrested and jailed as a British official.

Though Britain belatedly granted the major partial compensation for his losses, he never recovered his property. In 1779 he was declared attainted and Skenesborough was forfeited to New York. Its name was changed to Whitehall in 1788. Its founder died in England in 1810.

William Gilliland's dream was less grandiose than Skene's but it fell apart still more tragically. He was born in 1734 at Caddy, near Armagh, Ireland, and an agreeable tradition holds that he took the king's shilling because he loved above his station.

In 1758 he was discharged at Philadelphia from the 35th Regiment of Foot, in which he had served four years. Gilliland went to New York, prospered in business there and married Elizabeth, daughter of his partner, one Phagan. At some time during his mercantile career, he explored the shores of Lake Champlain, probably to determine what sort of land he could obtain with his military warrant for 100 acres and, like Major Skene, fell in love with the region. The devotion of both men was of that ardent variety in which the devotee sees future profit.

Gilliland apparently bought largely in the informal land-rights market, for when he led an expedition consisting of thirteen men, three women, twenty oxen, twenty cows and one bull to the head of Lake George in 1765, he already owned several thousand acres about the mouth of the Boquet River in the present town of Willsboro on Champlain's west shore. He continued to increase his holdings at every opportunity. The expedition in four bateaux arrived at the Boquet on June 8. Gilliland named his settlement Milltown.

By winter, a wing dam, flume and sawmill had been erected at the falls of the Boquet and a communal log house, forty-four feet by twenty-two, had been completed. Beside superintending this work, Gilliland had explored the region, ranging as far as Cumberland Head to the north and writing the earliest account extant of Ausable Chasm. Meanwhile, he continued to buy land and, that fall, laid out sites for future towns.

He had no gift for vivid nomenclature but called his property about the mouth of Salmon River "Janesboro" for one daughter; 4,500 acres in the present town of Westport, "Bessboro" for another; and land on Cumberland Head, "Charlottesboro" for a third. Elizabeth, now Essex, was named for his wife. Major Skene's ambition had reached no farther than a manor; Gilliland was laying the foundations for a county.

The wilderness magnate brought his family north to the settlement in the spring of 1766 and was smitten, during the journey, by the first of the many misfortunes in store for him. A bateau overturned near Fort Edward and his little daughter Jane was drowned. In his diary, Gilliland inscribed this threnody for her:

"Six years old lacking twelve days and the wonder of her age for beauty, stature, politeness, discretion, education, propriety of language, sweetness of temper, gracefulness of address, strength of genius and memory and, above all, of charity."[5]

Despite this bereavement, he made his properties flourish in the subsequent years. Gilliland's repute increased. He was one of the party that Governor Henry Moore led down the lake in 1766 to find the 48th parallel of latitude, which the British already had established as the boundary between New York and Canada. The survey sowed seeds of future difficulty by running the line three-fourths of a mile too far north.

The plan to set off the lake country into a separate province with Major Skene as governor was abetted by Gilliland. Thus far, the retired officer and the discharged private were in agreement, but Gilliland's enterprise had radical extensions that were shocking to Skene.

The major had established on upper Champlain a feudal manor. The Milltown settlement was moving toward what Skene would have considered dangerous democracy. On March 17, 1767, the settlers held a town meeting and signed an instrument for local government. The law and the agents of New York were too far away to serve them, so they set up their own system. It was simple. The articles provided for the election annually of a moderator, two superintendents of roads and bridges and three appraisers. Taxes were to be paid in labor for the community. The mind of William Gilliland was advancing still farther toward republicanism.

While his properties grew and more settlers joined him; while additional land was cleared yearly and new houses were raised and his saw and his gristmills sang all day long, the Irish idealism of the proprietor was leading him along an increasingly perilous road. Here, on the doorstep of Canada, he was establishing himself as an outspoken exponent of the rights of the American colonies.

Gilliland, moreover, seems to have been intelligently and patriotically active in preparing the region for war. The pretext is dim whereby he persuaded the British to sanction, and perhaps co-operate in, the erection of a fortified stone building on the solid tip of marshy Point au Fer, but it is certain that the structure was raised there in the early 1770's.

Point au Fer—possibly an abbreviation of the French "Point au Fer de Cheval" or "Horseshoe Point"—hooks south and east from the New York shore, hardly a mile south of the village of Rouses Point. "The White House," a whitewashed garrison building of strength, was a British or American military post during the Revolution and, at the war's end, a thorn in the side of the young republic since a company of redcoats continued to occupy it until 1795. The White House burned down in 1805.

Gilliland in Milltown and Moses Pierson, founder of Shelburne on the lake's opposite shore, jointly organized a company of minute men. The proprietor in a memorial to the New York legislature in 1777 sets forth:

"That your memorialist has reason to think that he was the first person who laid a plan for & determined upon seizing Ticonderoga, C. Point and the King's armed vessel & therewith the entire command of Lakes George & Champlain."[6]

He must have been at Ticonderoga, during or immediately after its taking by the Green Mountain Boys, for his memorial pursues:

"That by means of your memorialist an unhappy dispute between Mr. Allen and Mr. Arnold (the then rival heads of our handful of people on L Champlain) was composed."[7]

It may have been then that he won Arnold's lavish and enduring enmity. Gilliland's activities in the immediately pre-Revolutionary time earned him other animosities. General Guy Carleton, governor of Canada, proscribed him and offered £100 for his capture.

When the war began and weaker spirits were withdrawing from the exposed region of the lakes, Gilliland held his ground, hospitably caring for members of the Canadian expedition "from the Gen'l down to the centenel,"[8] selling cattle and farm produce to the army on promises to pay that generally went unfulfilled. Then Arnold and he clashed and the era of Gilliland's prosperity was over.

In August 1776 men from Arnold's fleet, whether or not incited by him, requited Gilliland for a recent gift of seventy-five salmon by raiding his settlement, ravishing two fields of potatoes, an acre of peas and five or six acres of corn. They also bore away, according to the victim's letter of September 1 to their commander, such un-naval plunder as "about ten dollars' worth of smith's tools and a multitude of other irons, two pleasure sleighs, five new sash windows, a new bedstead and bedcord, several chairs."[9]

Arnold's response to this complaint and its implied criticism of him was characteristic. He straightway branded the aggrieved man a liar and a scoundrel, accused him of being in British pay, arrested him and sent him on to Gates at Ticonderoga.

There is no record of how Gates dealt with this prisoner, against whom Arnold's reckless ill temper was the principal evidence, but the general apparently set Gilliland free, for the unhappy man wrote to Schuyler in a letter that bears no date other than "Fort Edward Sunday afternoon":

"I am thus far on the way with the whole of my family & some necessary articles of furniture toward some safe retreat & have it not in my power to proceed for want of Boats or Carriages."[10]

He begs Schuyler to lend him two craft in which to go down the Hudson, and thereafter for two years drops from sight.

The ill repute that Arnold had fastened upon Gilliland still clung. He was jailed in 1778 at Albany, charged, once again, with being a British sympathizer.

Meanwhile, Carleton's advance up the lake had ruined the Milltown settlement and what destruction this expedition left undone Burgoyne in the following year completed. The British were not kind to their alleged agent, for Gilliland lists among the losses they inflicted twenty-eight dwellings, forty other buildings, two gristmills, two sawmills, many gardens and orchards.

When the war ended, he suffered further deprivation. He had neglected to patent 8,500 acres of his holdings and New York confiscated them. The stars were against him now. He risked what remained of his fortune in rafting white oak to Canada and was ruined by his partner. He was clapped into debtors' prison in New York where he lay from September 21, 1786, to December 2, 1791.

Upon his release Gilliland returned to the desolation that had been his settlement. He lived with his son-in-law, Daniel Ross, in Essex and, with what energy remained to him, embarked again on a new real-estate venture with Platt Rogers as partner. The aging man was physically ailing now and his mind had begun to crack. On February 1, 1796, William Gilliland went from his son-in-law's home to confer with Rogers and did not return. They found his body later, lying frozen in the woods. The state of his hands and knees showed that after a seizure had overthrown him, he had crawled a long way.

The destruction of the Skene and Gilliland enterprises were spectacular instances of the general ruination settlers endured when the tide of war, after fifteen years' quiescence, rose to move again through the valley. By the time the Revolution broke in the region, a smaller, more tangled conflict already had begun.

The forces that brought about this peculiar, semicomic struggle themselves were complicated. The greed of royal governors that thwarted a stubborn people's intense desire to possess in freedom land of their own was the principal provocation. Other, less obvious incitations included the indifference of the British colonial office to frontier squabbles, His Majesty's spectacular ignorance of American geography as betrayed in the charters he had granted his several colonies and, not the least of these, the slow-kindling, long-burning Yankee anger.

The spark that set the strife ablaze was struck by Benning Wentworth, governor of New Hampshire, in 1749, but the fire already had been laid by the fantastically conflicting geographical provisions in the charters themselves. The document that created Massachusetts established the Pacific Ocean as the colony's western boundary. Connecticut, by charter provision, ran to the same water. But Charles II when, in 1664, he bestowed New York upon his brother, provided that this province, standing directly in the authorized western course of its New England neighbors, should extend easterly to the Connecticut River.

By the time Wentworth, a high-living, high-colored personage, began to consider the western limits of his own New Hampshire, the chaos the charters had wrought was beginning to be solved by compromise. New York and Connecticut had agreed that the latter colony should extend far across the Connecticut River to within twenty miles of the Hudson and then, leapfrogging over New York territory, continue its march to the Pacific.

Massachusetts was settling far west of the Connecticut too. It was evident that the Bay State would work out some such compromise with New York as Connecticut already had established. If the west boundary of both her neighbors should stretch so far, why should not New Hampshire's be considered to reach an equal distance, particularly since, by her governor's commission, her extent in that direction was to continue "untill it meets with our Other Governments?"[11]

This seems to have been the argument by which Wentworth converted himself. Two factors supported it. A frontier fort built by Massachusetts on the Connecticut's west bank where Brattleboro, Vermont, now stands, lately had been declared by George II to be in New Hampshire. Furthermore, if the French wars ever were to end, the rich, well-watered forest soil of what is now Vermont would bring the person qualified to grant the land a fortune in fees. Wentworth took a deep breath and proceeded to go into the real-estate business after the fashion of all royal governors of his time. He was to deal in land that he didn't know belonged to his province. On the other hand, he couldn't be quite sure it did not.

The governor of New Hampshire began his operations cautiously. He established a test case over which he doubtless hoped he might argue with George Clinton, governor of New York, and come to some compromise profitable to Benning Wentworth. On January 11, 1749, he granted the town of Bennington and waited for New York's protest.

Wentworth waited eleven months and then, apparently able to stand Clinton's disregard no longer, prodded New York's governor with a letter. In this missive, New Hampshire's chief executive professed himself deeply puzzled as to the exact location of the west boundary of New York and begged Clinton for enlightenment. It was not until June 6, 1750, that New York's governor got around to answering his colleague's inquiry and then his response was brusque. If Wentworth, the letter said in essence, didn't know where New York began, why had he granted a town in what was obviously New York territory? Clinton advised his fellow governor to recall the grant at once, promising that otherwise he would "Send a Representative of the Matter to be laid before his Majesty."[12]

After further exchange, both governors agreed to let the king referee the dispute. Clinton waited for the royal judgment. Wentworth went on granting towns, though he now was aware that he was dealing in clouded titles. The real-estate market boomed tremendously after the fall of Quebec.

While a whole series of New York governors uttered shouts of "Trespass!" and made appeals to the king, Wentworth continued busily to create towns. He bestowed 131 in what is now Vermont before he retired in 1766, full of years and fees, having very thoroughly sown a wind that already was beginning to rise.

New York had become alarmed at its rival colony's encroachments. Men were beginning to refer to territory that, by charter, was New York's as the "New Hampshire Grants." New York's governors, tardily aware of the fees that might have been theirs which Wentworth already had scooped in, started furiously to issue patents of their own.

Many of these granted to a new set of proprietors territory already bestowed on an earlier group by Wentworth. Furthermore, by now, some of the land had been cleared after months of toil and had been settled by the humble folk, the ultimate consumers, the land-hungry hitherto landless men who had bought in good faith rights to the "pitches" they had made.

New York's governors began to nullify the titles bought by these hard, frugal people. New York, by issuing patents to territory already granted by New Hampshire indirectly was evicting men who already possessed the soil.

The strife that lowered over "The Grants" was not a conflict between New Hampshire and New York but between the latter province and Wentworth's innocent dupes. Strange consequences

were to come from it. The struggle was to influence radically the
course of the Revolutionary War. It was to create the brief-lived
Vermont Republic and, finally, was to bring the fourteenth state
into the new-born Union. The tale of this complex, vehement and
highly improbable travail began when the French wars ended
and the first settlers came into Champlain's valley. Subsequent
chapters will trace the progress.

---

[1] Skene Papers, in Fort Ticonderoga Museum Library.
[2] *Ibid.*
[3] *Ibid.*
[4] *Ibid.*
[5] William Gilliland, Diary, May 13, 1766, quoted in Winslow S. Watson, *Pioneer History of the Champlain Valley* (Albany, 1863).
[6] William Gilliland, to the New York Legislature, quoted in Watson, *History of the Champlain Valley.*
[7] *Ibid.*
[8] *Ibid.*
[9] William Gilliland, to Benedict Arnold, quoted in Watson, *History of the Champlain Valley.*
[10] Schuyler Papers, in New York Public Library.
[11] E. B. O'Callaghan (ed.), *Documentary History of New York,* IV (1851), 332.
[12] *Ibid.,* p. 333.

Chapter 11

Allen's Men

THE French wars that had kept the Champlain-George basin a wilderness paradoxically had gained for it widespread publicity as an area for settlement. Agents for this impromptu advertising campaign were the regulars of a dozen British regiments and thousands of militia veterans, chiefly from New England.

The troops had marched, camped and fought up and down the valley and had looked covetously upon the unexploited wealth of virgin timber. Farmers among them saw in the dark deep forest loam sustenance for prodigious crops.

After each campaign, veterans carried back to the lean soil of Massachusetts and Connecticut accounts of the region's excellence. Highlanders bore to the pinched farmsteads of Scotland tales of a rich, unoccupied territory, augustly watered and wooded like the garden of the Lord. It would be a land of great reward, if ever peace should come.

Thus, the story spread through the colonies and traveled overseas. Then, suddenly, the obstructive French and Indians were gone. Peace came to a valley long unaccustomed to her presence and established herself there with an air of permanence. Actually, peace resided in the region, with increasing difficulty, for less than fifteen years but, in the millennial false dawn, men rose eagerly and came up to possess the land.

Most of them were farmers, seeking fertile soil, and they reached first for the heavily wooded rolling plain that ran far back to the tall hills guarding Lake Champlain on the east. The way had been prepared for them. They themselves had seen or else, from returning soldiers, had learned of the area's virtues.

In Portsmouth, New Hampshire, Governor Wentworth was

furiously issuing grants to the territory, over New York's protest. The proprietors whom he had favored were in haste to get their properties settled before George III got around to deciding which of the two disputing provinces owned the land. Clearings in the forest and folk in residence there might be, the proprietors thought uneasily, the best endorsements to decidedly shaky titles. They were as anxious to sell lots to actual settlers as men were now to buy.

The folk who began to move into the New Hampshire Grants were a special and homogeneous people. Poverty distinguished most of them. Aside from Gilliland and Skene with their spacious dreams and affluence few of the early settlers of the Champlain Valley brought more into the wilderness than themselves and their small ambitions.

The human tide that came up from the south was not spectacular or dramatic. The men who composed it were neither adventurers nor tenderfeet. They were lank, durable, experienced, with muskets in their fists and axes strapped to the packs between their shoulders, pioneers and the sons of pioneers. They sought, unlike participants in later oil and gold stampedes, not easy wealth but farms that could be won from the wilderness only by incredible toil. They also were in search, whether they immediately were aware of it or not, of freedom.

Among the short-spoken, hard-bitten persons who plodded north was a sprinkling of Scots. Otherwise the immigration was almost entirely Anglo-Saxon and came chiefly from Connecticut. Most of the Grants' settlers already had served an apprenticeship in privation.

Many were implicit revolutionaries. The wilderness and the ordeal of subduing it did not lure the established or the wealthy. These men who tramped through the forest to locate and establish their "pitches" were younger sons, dissenters, freethinkers, insurgents who had not found places for themselves in the solidified theocracies of lower New England and were determined to discover in this severe north country not only physical but mental and moral elbowroom.

There was an original identity of purpose and temper about these immigrants that the land itself intensified. Most of the new-comers opposed and subdued the forest with no other resources than an ax, a few other elemental tools and the amazing skill and strength of their own bodies. Labor beyond the utmost abilities of men today was the lot of them all.

The task of "making a pitch" or "commencing a betterment" was usually an individual enterprise and not accomplished in a single year. Men came up in the spring singly from the established settlements, found the lots they had purchased and, alone and un-aided, began the colossal task of clearing them.

Lean-tos were their shelters and their food, apart from imported salt and meal, whatever the forest and its streams furnished. Day after day "from can to can't," from dawn to dusk, the ax of the settler-to-be rang and trees went down. Logs that could be used were immediately notched and fitted into the beginning of a cabin. The rest of the wood was left for later burning. Week by week, the area in which sunlight shone on raw new stumps dilated. No single man could complete his clearing and his cabin in one summer. When the nights grew frosty, the pioneers trudged back to civilization to wait there impatiently the coming of an-other spring.

Two years and often three passed before the new property was ready for family habitation. When that time arrived, the house-hold moved north. The wife, if they were sufficiently prosperous folk, rode a horse. The husband and the children, each burdened according to his ability, walked, driving the cow before them.

No farmer today would house his stock in a dwelling such as the family found at its journey's end. The log-walled, bark-roofed structure had no windows and frequently a deerskin in lieu of a door. The floor generally was only packed earth. A fireplace of wattled clay, an ax-hewn table and settle and rough bedsteads, knocked together with the same implement, were commonly the sole furnishings.

The family occupied this hovel and immediately went to work. It was always questionable during pioneer days whether a house-hold could labor hard and profitably enough during spring, summer and fall to keep starvation at bay during the winter.

Thus, the original human type was firmly fixed by rigorous frontier existence. The wilderness weeded out the weak of body or character, killing the former, driving away the latter. The men left in possession of the land, the original Vermonters, were strong, obstinate, adept, at once bold and prudent, unlettered yet resourceful, with few of New England's traditional repressions and more than normal Yankee guile.

One resolution possessed them all. The bitter toil of wresting their pitches from the wilderness had, almost mystically, wedded them to the land. They had gained it through travail, long and extreme. It was theirs as their wives were their own and it could be taken from them no more easily. Vermont's history, during its formative years, is most simply the tale of a stubborn people's determination, whatever the cost, to hold fast to their properties.

Such were the folk who already were settling many of the 131 towns the enterprising if unscrupulous Benning Wentworth had granted. On July 20, 1764, His Majesty finally made up his mind and proclaimed "The western banks of the river Connecticut from where it enters the province of Massachusetts Bay, as far north as the 45th degree of north latitude to be the boundary line between the said two provinces of New Hampshire and New York."[1]

The decision filled New York's authorities with self-justified glee, even though the king directed that actual settlers under the Wentworth grants should not be molested until his later will should be known. It brought an abrupt end to the real-estate activities of New Hampshire's governor who, shortly thereafter, retired. It theoretically impoverished the Grants proprietors and their associate gamblers, who, in desperation, grasped at a single straw in the royal verbiage—the infinitive "to be."

"To be," the disconcerted gentry announced so often that they began to believe it themselves, obviously referred to the future. The eastern boundary of New York was to be the Connecticut River— hereafter. Surely it could not mean that all the towns granted by

Wentworth were to be abolished. Nevertheless there was a sharp drop in the market for New Hampshire Grants shares.

The persons most nearly unmoved by the king's decision were the gaunt, grimed men in the clearings. News traveled slowly to the new settlements and was not greatly heeded by folk who had bought and had occupied and were improving their land. Their properties were too clearly their own for provincial squabbles to disturb them.

Through the subsequent years of dispute, the pioneers continued to hack at the forest, grub out stumps and plant increasingly large fields. Settlers, still believing in the validity of their titles, plodded north to occupy more of the fertile forest soil on Champlain's east shore. Moses Pierson, in 1769, built himself a home in Shelburne, just across the lake from the Gilliland development, and other immigrants were pressing behind him, oblivious to the mounting heat of the dispute between New York authorities and the Grants proprietors.

From 1764 to 1770, the issue was pulled back and forth, neither side permanently yielding anything and each party repeatedly begging the king for a final decision as to the ownership of already settled Grants territory, which George III still withheld. Those settlers nearest to the disturbance, which appropriately enough was centering more and more in Bennington, first of the Wentworth-granted towns, were becoming aroused and among them leaders were developing.

One man of the many learning to rear an infant colony whose legal parentage was still in doubt surpassed all his associates in stature, in violent behavior, in blustering resolution. He was a physical giant with a voice like a trumpet and so inclusive a scorn of arbitrary authority that he professed himself an atheist, insofar as the Biblical deity was concerned.

He was the eldest of the six Allen brothers who had been reared in Salisbury, Connecticut, and his name was Ethan. To him and his clan—Brothers Heman, Heber, Levi, Zimri and Ira; Cousins Seth Warner, Remember Baker and Ebenezer Allen—Vermont largely owes her existence as an entity.

Now, in the spring of 1770, as the times grew darker, the leadership that assembled in Stephen Fay's hip-roofed tavern on Bennington Hill turned more and more to Ethan Allen. His was a spirit that soared in times of crisis, and crisis was at hand.

New York, in defiance of the king's command, was issuing patents to land already occupied by holders of Grants titles. In June, the New York Supreme Court, sitting in Albany, heard the case of Isaiah Carpenter, farmer in Shaftsbury since 1765 under title granted by New Hampshire, against Captain John Small of the Black Watch who in 1769 had been awarded a military patent to the same property by New York. The court directed a verdict for Small and, by this act, implicitly nullified all Wentworth grants.

There may have been gloating among the patent holders in Albany. There was graver debate in the upstairs room at Fay's tavern that men had begun to call the "Council Chamber." The Grants leaders had been defeated under the law. They determined now to go beyond the law, with Ethan Allen as their leader.

The giant from Salisbury was chosen colonel commandant of the fighting force the Grants would raise. He devised for himself a uniform, immediately. It was characteristic of the eternally adolescent half of a strange character that this should be Ethan Allen's first step toward the protection of his people. It is a tribute to the man's intelligence, of which he had an abundance when he thought to use it, that the troops he enlisted and named the "Green Mountain Boys" were so unprecedented and successful a battalion.

The actual aspect and conduct of Allen's legion has been pulled out of shape and fantastically repainted by romanticists. The war they and their leader conducted against New York with a satanic skill and a fine sense of timing has been mispictured as conventional frontier skirmishing.

The Green Mountain Boys were not soldiers in the word's accepted sense. Despite their colonel's love of pomp, their appearance was anything but military. When raiding, they wore a variety of disguises from blackface to women's raiment. The strategy they employed was prescribed by no martial treatise of that era.

Allen's unusual mind had laid hold, before he organized his men, upon truths more familiar today than in his time. He was aware that open battle against a stronger foe could result in nothing but the downfall of Grants pretensions. He saw that dead Yorkers in strife such as lay before the Green Mountain Boys inevitably would be martyrs. He knew too that a person maimed or killed was tragic but a man frightened and humiliated was likely to spread his affliction.

The colonel commandant bent his Boys to these beliefs. They held York at bay for five years. They dealt violently with many persons. They never killed anyone and they devoted themselves to making unlimited nuisances of themselves, without serious personal hurt to any man.

They bullied York settlers; they threatened York officials; they made life miserable for all adherents to the cause of New York.

John Munro was a York-appointed justice of the peace in the town of Shaftsbury and he whiled away his time when not exercising his formal office by acting as a stool pigeon for Sheriff Henry Ten Eyck of Albany. He had this to write of the Green Mountain Boys' tactics:

"They assemble themselves together in the night time and throws down all the Yorkers Fences etc as we are called and Drives the cattle into the Fields and meadows and destroys both Grass and corn and do every mischief they can think of. Pardon the imperfection of this and the other papers herewith sent you as I am in confution my House being full of Rioters and the Felon that shot the Horse going to Goal with the Constable secured and by his confession two more are concerned but I doubt whether we can secure them."[2]

Allen bawled and blustered and uttered hair-raising imprecations. His Green Mountain Boys imitated their leader but, though they intimidated York settlers, distracted York sheriffs, justices and constable and drove successive governors of New York frantic, the most severe vengeance they ever executed upon their enemies was not specially severe whippings. This punishment their flamboyant leader styled the "beech seal of the wilderness." It was applied infrequently.

Yorkers who were unable to understand what was happening to them termed the raids by Allen's men "riots," and the organization itself the "Bennington mob." There was excuse for this inaccurate epithet: the general appearance of the Green Mountain Boys in action was more moblike than soldierly.

The men who rode in Allen's band—and his followers more often traveled ahorse than on foot—were usually, in their sudden public appearances, a most reprehensible-looking company. The "rioters" who called on Samuel Gardner, holder of land near Bennington under a York title, were, Gardner declared in the affidavit he executed as soon as he had sufficiently recovered from his fright, "disfigured with Black, others with wigs and Horse Tails and Women's caps and other disguises."[3]

Rioters, however, are frenzied. Mobs get out of hand and commit atrocities from which their members shrink, in thought, thereafter. The Green Mountain Boys, apparently so wholly undisciplined, limited their terrorizing to the destruction of property and filling the souls of their victims with dread. Only men carefully schooled by an inspired leader could have been brought to the edge of infamy without ever overstepping it by actually accomplishing any of the threats they roared at Yorkers.

Gardner emerged from his ordeal intact but his affidavit recites that the "rioters" promised that "he would be cropt, gelt and whipped by the said Rioters and tied up to a tree with a gag in his mouth and so starved to Death."[4]

During the years of the Green Mountain Boys' activity, the unfortunate men who governed New York—Colden, Dunmore, Tryon—were afflicted by a continual train of Job's messengers from the Grants most of whom reported moderate outrages upon themselves and demanded, since New York had issued the titles to the lands they had tried to hold, that the province immediately suppress Allen and his men.

The affidavit of Alexander McNaughton recited for Governor

Tryon's benefit that he had attempted to settle and build under York title in the Grants town of Rupert, but that Ethan Allen and his horsemen had swept down upon him, pushed him about, burned his cabin, bawled ear-burning threats, and that Allen in farewell had shouted:

"Go now and complain to that damn scoundrel, your governor, God damn your governor, laws, king, council and assembly."[5]

Tryon issued placards offering £20 reward for the capture of the three leaders of the "rioters"—Ethan Allen, Remember Baker and Robert Cochran, who immediately offered similar rewards for James Duane and John Kempe, notorious gamblers in New York patents.

The governor's expedient brought him only further distress in an affidavit from one Benjamin Buck of Albany who, traveling through the Grants, was incautious enough to pause at Fay's tavern in Bennington where, he deposed, Ethan Allen demanded his politics. Buck's affidavit says that when he admitted he was for York, Allen cuffed him thrice and bawled:

"You are a damn bastard of old Munro's. We shall make a hell of his house and burn him in it and every son of a bitch who takes his part."[6]

Squire Munro himself was getting ready to quit. Popular feeling against all Yorkers, and himself in particular, was becoming so intense and intemperate that he felt he had outlived his usefulness in the Grants and might not, if he tarried there, exist much longer. He wrote to Sheriff Ten Eyck:

"It's got so no man durst Speake one word in favour of this Government without being in danger of life and property—for they declare themselves not afraid of all the Force that the Government can send against them and they will hold the land in Defyance of His Majesty's shold he go contrary to what they think is right."[7]

Other and weightier complaints were reaching the governor. Colonel John Reid, late of the Black Watch, was proprietor, through a fortunate marriage, of 35,000 acres of land on either side of Champlain, including the site of what is now the little city of Vergennes. Where the falls of Otter Creek promised unlimited power, Reid was attempting to establish a settlement, complete with saw and gristmills. He protested to Tryon that "rioters" continually were chasing away the tenants he placed on his property.

Nothing like this had ever happened to New York's then chief executive. Tryon, while governor of North Carolina, had bloodedly suppressed an insurrection there but New York's law officers seemed entirely unable to cope with the hit-and-run tactics of Allen's riders. The governor appealed to General Frederick Haldimand, commanding in Boston, for troops to deal with the rebels and his request was bluntly denied.

In May of 1772 Tryon took firm hold upon his temper and addressed a letter to the "Bennington mob" in which he offered pardon to all offenders—except Ethan Allen, Seth Warner, Remember Baker and Robert Cochran, chief officers of the Green Mountain Boys—and asked that delegates be sent to confer with him on a truce. Landlord Fay and his physician son, Dr. Jonas Fay, met with Tryon in New York, and brought back to Bennington the terms of the armistice. Tryon and the Fays had pledged their parties to maintain the *status quo,* and to commit no more overt acts until the dilatory king decided the controversy.

There was a celebration in Bennington when the Fays returned, but whatever satisfaction Tryon may have felt at temporarily settling his most troublesome problem was blasted almost at once by another complaint from Colonel Reid. Raiders, led by Seth Warner and Remember Baker, had descended again upon the falls of Otter and had chased out the settlers once more.

The peace that was to have endured until His Majesty's will became known crumbled rapidly after this. When certain events at Concord, Ticonderoga and Bunker Hill deposed George III as supreme judge of colonial affairs, he still had not uttered his decision in the Grants-York controversy.

On May 12, 1773, New York's boundary dispute with Massachusetts was settled identically as the Connecticut-New York trouble had been, earlier. It was agreed that Massachusetts' western

line was to run parallel to the Hudson and twenty miles east of the
stream. New York, in two instances, had abandoned her contention that her territory extended to the Connecticut River, but she
still held to it in dealings with the Grants.

This obstinacy did nothing to reassure the holders of New
Hampshire titles. Tryon's truce collapsed into violence more
vigorous and persistent than that which it was supposed to have
ended. The increased hounding of Yorkers by the Green Mountain Boys may have been due in part to the fact that their commander and his brother Ira had purchased 45,000 acres of land in
the Onion River—now the Winooski—region, had established the
Onion River Land Company and inevitably would lose their investment, if New York were to gain control of the Grants.

Whatever the impulse, when Allen on August 11, 1773, struck
at the community the obstinate Colonel Reid had established once
more at the Otter Creek falls, he hit so hard that he destroyed it
completely and finally.

More than a hundred horsemen followed the colonel commandant, Seth Warner and Remember Baker out of the woods
and charged, screeching, down upon the hapless settlement.
Its inhabitants surrendered. One of them, James Henderson,
afterward wrote to his principal:

"Our Houses were All Brunt Down The Gristmill is All Put
Down The Millstones Brock and Throne into the Crick The
Corn is all Destroed by There Horses and When it was Proposed
That We Should build homes and Keep Possion They Threat-
ened to Bind some of us to a Tree and Skin us Alive. Therefore
we think it Impossible To us To live hear in peace."[8]

The broken millstones and other debris were used as material
for the blockhouse the Green Mountain Boys raised here to keep
Yorkers away thereafter.

Tryon's response to this and similar violences was to wring a
law from the New York legislature, condemning to death without
trial anyone hereafter opposing the province's authority. In retaliation, Allen and his men drove the last of York officials from
Grants' territory by exiling the Reverend Benjamin Hough, Ana-

baptist minister and justice of the peace, with the following safe conduct:

"Sunderland January the 30th day, 1775.

"This may certify the inhabitants of the New Hampshire Grants that Benjamin Hough hath this day r'cd a full punishment for his crimes committed heretofore against this Country and our inhabitants are ordered to give the sd Huff free and unmolested Pasport toward the City of New York or to the Westward of our Grants he behaving himself as becometh Given under our hands this day and date aforesaid.

"Ethan Allen
"Seth·Warner."[9]

Hough was flogged before he was permitted to depart but not so heavily that he was unable to travel immediately afterward. His was the most grievous personal hurt the Green Mountain Boys inflicted upon anyone during the Yorker troubles.

The manifold, cannily controlled disturbances by Allen's band were only dramatic evidences of a general revolt. It expressed the feelings of a host of obscure but increasingly angry men. Among the folk in the clearings that multiplied along Champlain's east shore and elsewhere throughout the Grants, the slow-kindling, long-burning wrath that was to distinguish Vermonters was ablaze.

Concern for the safety of their own properties had lighted the fire; winds of calamity that ranged through all the colonies in the early 1770's fanned it. Rebellion was in the air and Freedom, then as now, was a slogan to inspire the people of Vermont.

The Grants settlers had no possible grievance against George III, except for his extreme deliberation in deciding their fate, but it was easy in a time of stress to misidentify oppressions by York officials as acts of the king. Back of the disorders caused by the Green Mountain Boys, stood a solid mass of popular approval. This was expressed more frequently as the decade advanced by sundry meetings and conventions of the people, each more antagonistic to Yorker and royal authority than the last.

Before musket smoke rolled across Lexington Green the Grants inhabitants were implicit revolutionaries. A people adept in dickering and trading blinded themselves to advantages to be won by bartering their neutrality in the looming conflict. Disregarding their own obvious interests, because they were infatuated with Freedom's very name, they already were planning a blow against Britain. The man who would lead them in the crazily valiant enterprise was risking most.

War, if it were unloosed against the Grants, would come down upon them out of Canada, and close to the border lay the properties of the Onion River Land Company in which Ethan Allen had invested his fortune.

---

[1] E. B. O'Callaghan (ed.), *Documentary History of the State of New York* (Albany, 1851), IV, 332.
[2] *Ibid.*, p. 433
[3] *Ibid.*, p. 443
[4] *Ibid.*, p. 444
[5] *Ibid.*, p. 454
[6] *Ibid.*, p. 464
[7] *Ibid.*, p. 453
[8] *Ibid.*, p. 510
[9] *Ibid.*, p. 541

Chapter 12

Ticonderoga

THE taking of the lake forts by His British Majesty's insurgent subjects was an enterprise which many persons urged before its accomplishment and in which divers elements shared. Probably no one considered the project more intensely than did Ethan Allen. This was the rash yet promising sort of adventure in which his peculiar spirit delighted.

In a winter dark with omens of conflict, it was natural for men of military training or instinct to brood on the strategical importance of the strongholds that guarded the ancient waterway to war—Fort George at the head of the upper lake, Crown Point, commanding the narrows of Champlain and, greatest name of the three, Ticonderoga. If the colonies held these, one broad road of attack was blocked. In British hands the lakes were, as always they had been when enemies possessed them, a bayonet pressed against the colonies' spine.

It was the fate of Ticonderoga to be captured by British from French, Colonials from British and by British from Americans again in atmospheres of anticlimax and with a minimum of bloodshed. The fort, nevertheless, loomed in the New England mind as mate in power and importance to Gibraltar itself. There would be a splendor in wresting it from the minions of King George that set the effervescent spirit of Ethan Allen to seething.

No doubt the colonel commandant of the Green Mountain Boys thundered his intentions in the "Council Chamber" of Landlord Fay's Bennington tavern. There is evidence that, before the enterprise actually was launched, he had progressed farther in his plans than mere fulminating talk.

John Brown, of Pittsfield, Massachusetts, an agent of the insurgent colonies, was sent in March 1775 on a mission to Canada, and plodded across the ice and slush of Champlain with Peleg Sunderland of the Green Mountain Boys and Winthrop Hoyt, lately a Caughnawaga Indian captive, for guides. Brown, who was a lawyer and a former student at Yale—where spelling apparently had not been one of his courses—wrote to Samuel Adams from Montreal, March 24:

"The fort at Tyconderogo must be seised as soon as possible should hostilities be committed by the Kings' Troops. The people on N. Hampshire Grants have ingaged to do this Business and in my opinion they are the proper Persons for the jobb."[1]

In this one may detect a faint echo of Ethan Allen's own vainglorious bellowings. He who already had dared to disparage pious New England's Jehovah was not to be daunted by the power of Ticonderoga.

Most of the fort's strength lay, as a matter of record, in its name alone. Neither Ticonderoga nor Crown Point possessed in their curent state any great material might. The dreariness of decay brooded over both and seeped into the minds of their unhappy garrisons.

In 1773 the crumbling barracks of Crown Point had caught fire while soldiers' wives were boiling soap. The fort had blown up with a thunderclap that had shaken the earth for ten miles around. It had been, until the explosion, headquarters of Captain William Anstruther, 27th Foot, commanding the Crown Point and Ticonderoga garrisons. Now, in what shelters they could contrive from the ruins, Sergeant Alexander Nairns and nine other members of the 26th Regiment found the monotony of existence disturbed only by occasional forays against Grants folk who sneaked across the lake to steal iron nails from the charred ruins.

At Ticonderoga, the garrison's life was little more cheerful or martial. Here dwelt forty-three aged or infirm members of the 26th and, commanding them, two thoroughly bored and homesick officers, Captain William Delaplace and Lieutenant Jocelyn Feltham. The latter was waiting hopefully for the arrival of Lieutenant Wadman who was to relieve him; the captain spent most of his time in writing doleful letters to his superiors, concerning the increasing decrepitude of the fort, and in managing the farm he had established as a diversion from soldiering. Forty-five sheep, eleven cows, a wife and two children shared with him what amounted to exile.

Fort George at the head of the lesser lake was decaying more deliberately. John Nordberg, a retired officer of Swedish birth presided here as "governor," which seems to have been a more august synonym for "janitor." He had three or four assistants whose chief duty was to expedite expresses to or from Canada.

This was the total force the British had thought it worth while to maintain on the lakes in a time of waxing peril, but Captain Delaplace's disconsolate letters had begun to have some effect. Engineers had made a survey of the two Champlain forts and had recommended that Crown Point be rebuilt and Ticonderoga permitted to slide down the brief remaining way to complete ruin. At about this time, Delaplace reported that the roof of the commissary room had fallen in. General Thomas Gage in Boston and General Guy Carleton, governor of Quebec, were conducting a desultory correspondence concerning reinforcement of the posts with a regiment or so. This came to nothing because Ethan Allen got there first.

The thoughts, vague or purposeful, of many rebellious minds met, merged and produced action. A dark intemperate little man, Captain Benedict Arnold, while leading his company of Connecticut Foot Guards toward beleaguered Boston, encountered Colonel Samuel H. Parsons, a member of the Connecticut Assembly, in Hartford on April 26 and spoke so fiercely of the necessity of capturing Ticonderoga that Parsons on the following day met with other influential citizens, discussed the project and decided to sponsor it. These men drew, with no further warrant than their personal I O U's, £300 from the provincial treasury and on Friday, April 28, started Noah Phelps and Bernard Romans, an engineer, on horseback for the New Hampshire Grants.

On the following morning, six other enthusiasts, headed by Captain Edward Mott, rode away and made such haste on the muddy roads that they overtook Phelps and Romans at Salisbury, Connecticut, home town of the Allen tribe where Heman then was in residence. Romans sent him galloping ahead to the Grants to find Ethan Allen. The rest of the party followed more deliberately to Pittsfield, condoning their violation of the law against Sabbath travel by the urgency of their mission.

Other men whose thoughts had marched with the travelers accompanied them when they rode out of Pittsfield, May 1. John Brown, the emissary to Canada, was among them and so was James Easton, a colonel of Massachusetts militia.

Meanwhile, in Bennington, the mud-spattered Heman was babbling to his gigantic brother a tale that fired Ethan more thoroughly than the vastest bowl of punch. Connecticut had ordered that the forts were to be taken.

Men with their ears still buzzing from the power of the colonel commandant's voice rode north from Bennington that day to rouse the Green Mountain Boys. Castleton and Shoreham were to be the rallying places. Allen, fretting and fuming, waited at Bennington for the Connecticut emissaries to arrive.

In Cambridge, Massachusetts, the voluble and persuasive captain who had fired Parsons with his enthusiasm for taking Ticonderoga and its cannon that were so sorely needed by the colonies' forces was subjecting the Massachusetts Committee of Safety to similar infectious arguments. On May 2, Benedict Arnold was commissioned a colonel by Massachusetts, supplied with funds, empowered to attack Ticonderoga and authorized to raise not more than 400 men for that purpose. He started north, with Allenlike precipitation, leaving the recruiting of a force to subordinates, Captains Brown and Oswald. At about this time, the Connecticut column arrived at Bennington.

Its numbers had been materially increased during the journey from Pittsfield. Colonel Easton had tarried by the way to enlist twenty-four farmers in Hancock Valley, fifteen more in Williamstown. The column halted at Fay's tavern, while its leaders entered to confer with an impatient, astonishingly uniformed giant within.

The party held counsel, belatedly imparting to the enterprise what legality or sanction it could summon. Captain Edward Mott was elected chairman of an impromptu general staff, styled a "Board of War," and Ethan Allen was chosen field commander. The board commissioned Bernard Romans to capture Fort George and he rode away with two others toward Albany, apparently to the great relief of Mott who entered in his diary:

"Mr. Romans left us and joined us no more; we were glad, as he had been a trouble to us all the while he was with us."[2]

It is not clear how long the Board of War sat in Bennington, but as soon as he could tear himself free from its debates, Ethan Allen also departed, galloping furiously northward. The rest of the expedition followed more deliberately.

By desecrating another Sabbath the Connecticut and Massachusetts men on Sunday evening, May 7, reached the raw little settlement of Castleton. A hundred-odd hard and dingy persons milled about Zadock Remington's tavern and filled the taproom where Colonel Commandant Ethan Allen had set up headquarters.

Legend supplies most of the available information concerning the events of the days between May 2 and 7. It is said that Noah Phelps and one Ezra Hickok were sent to Ticonderoga as spies. The tale then forks. One version holds that Phelps gained entrance to the fort by pretending to be a half-wit; the other, that he posed as a traveler. Both agree that he was shaved by the post's barber. Nothing has survived concerning Hickok's accomplishment.

The mythical prowess of Gershom Beach, blacksmith of Castleton, has been enshrined in balladry. Folklore recites that when the alarm reached him, he straightway dropped his tools and ran sixty miles in twenty-four hours to rouse the folk of Shoreham, Rutland, Pittsford, Brandon, Middlebury and Whiting. Mrs. Julia C. R. Dorr, the Vermont poetess, describes the race in her verses "The Armorer's Errand":

> "He threaded the valleys, he climbed the hills,
> He forded the rivers, he leaped the rills,
> While still at his call, like minute-men
> Booted and spurred, from mount and glen,
> The settlers rallied.—"

Since Mrs. Dorr equips her settlers with spurs and boots and since, more veritably, Beach was a blacksmith by trade, it is difficult to understand why, in a region evidently well supplied with horses, the messenger should have elected to make his journey on foot.

When Captain Mott and his associates reached Castleton, this much had been done: One group of Green Mountain Boys had gathered at the village, noisy, irreverent frontiersmen, deplorably clothed but with well-cared-for weapons. Another company was assembling at Shoreham. Patrols had been posted on all roads and trails with orders to permit none to pass toward the forts.

By Monday, May 8, 160 of Allen's men were crowded about Remington's tavern. They were so loud in their enthusiasm for their commander and the purpose for which they had been summoned that Allen and the Board of War found it advisable to transfer their meeting from the inn to the home of Richard Bentley.

Here, with Mott presiding, final preparations were made. The assault upon Ticonderoga was set for early morning, May 10. Allen was reconfirmed as chief of the expedition; Colonel Easton was chosen second in command and Seth Warner, third.

Some methodical person brought up the question of how a couple of hundred men were to get themselves across the better part of a mile of water separating Ticonderoga from the Shoreham beaches. The Board of War belatedly weighed this problem.

It was resolved that Captain Asa Douglass go over at once to Crown Point with the artless request that the garrison there rent him its boats. It was further resolved that Captain Samuel Herrick and thirty men move immediately upon Skenesborough, capture the manor and bring back all the craft they could find.

The meeting finally adjourned; Allen rode off to Shoreham to meet those of his men who were gathering there. Captain Herrick's detail shouldered firelocks and headed out for Skenesborough. Captain Mott accompanied them. The Green Mountain Boys in Castleton still swarmed about Remington's tavern, since they were

BATTLE OF PLATTSBURG, SEPTEMBER 11, 1814

This battle between the American fleet under Commodore Macdonough and the British fleet under Captain Downie was the last naval engagement between the two countries.

not to move to Shoreham till the morrow. The enterprise, to this moment, had progressed with a minimum of friction.

Troubles now arrived in the person of a haughtily scowling mounted officer. A respectful orderly followed him, which was bad enough. The stranger wore the red and gold uniform of the Connecticut Foot Guards, which was worse, and he completed his immediate unpopularity by announcing to all those present that he was Colonel Benedict Arnold and henceforth in command.

Immediately, there arose one of the brawls that commonly followed Arnold's intrusion on any situation. The suggestions, the sounds, the gestures with which the rabble received their self-proclaimed commander were progressively insubordinate, insurgent and downright insulting. Arnold's hair-trigger temper exploded. It seemed probable, as the tumult waxed, that presently his adversaries would set down their tankards and pick up their guns.

Some peacemaker hurried off after the Skenesborough expedition and returned with the breathless Captain Mott, who drew the infuriated Arnold out of range and asked for his credentials. The newcomer produced them. They were wholly in order, except for the fact that the army they empowered him to raise was absent.

Arnold explained to the now reassembled and not-to-cordial majority of the Board of War that his own men were being recruited and that he himself, hearing that another expedition was forming, had ridden on ahead to lead it. He stressed the fact that he alone of all engaged in this impromptu enterprise had a colony commission. The Board demurred. John Brown knew and detested Arnold. A milder version of the earlier quarrel ensued and on the morrow the still thwarted man rode ahead of the column that moved from Castleton to Shoreham. Arnold was determined to find and browbeat Ethan Allen into relinquishing the command.

There was another noteworthy explosion when the two egotists met, head on. Neither prevailed. It was the Green Mountain Boys who decided the dispute. Allen's men announced in lurid terms that they would serve under no one but him; that if Arnold took command, they would all go home. This seems temporarily to have settled the matter.

It was Allen who led the force of some 230 from Wessel's farm in Shoreham, where they had assembled, to the embarkation point at Hands Cove. The discomfited man in the red uniform went along apparently as an observer. He must have derived some satisfaction from contemplating Allen's plight when the expedition arrived at the cove. Before them was the lake; beyond it, Ticonderoga, and there were no boats to ferry the force.

No tidings, let alone craft, had come from the Skenesborough expedition. Captain Douglass had returned from Crown Point with news that the unreasonable British there had refused to let him have a single skiff. Someone told him that there was a scow in Bridport and he hurried off to find it. While the night moved on and the moon went down and Arnold probably grinned malevolently, Allen's command waited, stranded on the beach.

It was perilously late when relief arrived. Douglass came back with the scow. James Wilcox and Joseph Tyler of Bridport, learning of his mission, had hastened to Willow Point in northwest Bridport, where a galley belonging to Colonel Skene was anchored. By plying a jug of rum they had taken with them, they persuaded the Negro in charge of the craft to lend it to them.

Galley and scow together would hold no more than eighty-five men. With only a third of his force, and the insistent Benedict Arnold, Allen set out to take Ticonderoga. The darkness before dawn was made still more impenetrable by wind-driven gusts of rain. They landed at last on a point from which a wood road ran the better part of a mile to a "covered way." That path, guarded on either side by a stone wall, slanted up into the fort which loomed black and portentous against a paling sky. There was need for haste, but Ethan Allen never let urgency deprive any moment of its ultimate melodrama. While his men stumbled about in the gloom, he assembled his oration and when they at last stood silent, delivered it:

"Friends and fellow soldiers, you have, for a number of years past, been a scourge and terror to arbitrary power. Your valor has been famed abroad and acknowledged, as appears by the advice and orders to me (from the general assembly of Connecticut) to surprise and take the garrison now before us. I now propose to advance before you and in person conduct you through the wicket gate; for we must this morning either quit our pretensions to valor or possess ourselves of this fortress in a few minutes; and in as much as it is a desperate attempt (which none but the bravest men dare undertake) I do not urge it on any contrary to his will. You that will undertake voluntarily, poise your firelocks."[3]

So he quoted himself in his *Narrative* published four years later and no competent authority contradicted him; therefore it is probable that he delivered some approximation of this address, though why he should have waited until he had got his storming force across the lake to ascertain whether they were willing to attack is a problem beyond the reach of modern minds.

From the poised firelocks, it appeared that the men had made the trip for the exact purpose their leader had explained to them. The uphill march began. The ensuing farce has detracted unfairly from the fine courage of that ascent against a fortress manned by regulars and profusely equipped with cannon. If the slipshod garrison had not been so deep in slumber, the ensuing victory might easily have been turned to butchery.

The men plodded along with Allen and Arnold in unbrotherly association at the head of the groping, stumbling files. They entered and passed up the covered way. The slumbers of Ticonderoga's garrison, including the sentries' were sound. The attackers mounted the ramparts and reached the iron-studded wooden portal that gave access to the parade ground and surrounding barracks and storehouses. The great door was shut, but let into its expanse was a smaller open entrance, the "wicket gate." Before this, a sentry dozed until the advance was almost upon him.

Rousing belatedly, the unhappy man stared with horror at the advancing host, tried vainly to fire his musket, then wheeled and fled while a most atrocious yelling and a giant's sword threatened his ears. The attackers cast away what small military discipline had been imposed on them and poured in a mob after Allen through the wicket gate and out onto the parade.

Another sentry made feeble jabs with his bayonet at the demoniac invaders whose leader clouted him across the skull and, when he surrendered, bellowed to be shown where the troops were lodged. The captive pointed out the buildings. Part of the rabble ran after Allen and Arnold toward the officers' quarters. The rest beat in the barracks' door and captured the dazed and profoundly shocked garrison.

There were no inside stairs to the Ticonderoga buildings but wooden steps slanted up the exterior walls to landings before doors on the second floor. The outrageous racket on the parade woke Lieutenant Feltham who seems to have had a brief struggle between propriety and panic before his self-possession deserted him entirely.

While the uproar increased below and cries of "No quarter!" were interspersed with Indian yells, Feltham rushed from his room, beat upon Captain Delaplace's door and, returning to his own chamber, hustled himself into his uniform waistcoat and coat, before emerging again to open the portal that gave upon the exterior landing and stare down at the mob below.

An enormous man in a uniform strange to the lieutenant and a smaller individual in a comfortingly red coat who had been charging up the stair paused in mid-career and gaped at the spectacle of Lieutenant Jocelyn Feltham, clothed from the waist up in the yellow-faced scarlet coat, the white waistcoat and silver gorget of His British Majesty's 26th Regiment of Foot and, below these, wearing nothing at all but his own original covering.

The paralysis of amazement passed. Tradition says that the uniformed giant pounded the rest of the way up the stair, shook his sword under Feltham's nose and bawled, unnecessarily, "Come out of that, you goddamned old rat!" (Other variations substitute "skunk" or "bastard".) Thereafter he bellowed, according to Feltham's subsequent report to his superiors, a demand for the "immediate possession of the fort and all the effects of George the Third (these were his words.)"[4]

Captain Delaplace, at this moment, issued from his own quarters. He had had the forethought to put on his breeches. Allen again demanded the fort's surrender and when its dazed commander inquired in whose name, thundered:

"In the name of the Great Jehovah [a personage with whom he was never on cordial terms] and the Continental Congress."[5]

A hundred and seventy years of debate over the authenticity of that utterance have proved nothing. It is best dismissed by the factual statement that Ethan Allen himself insists that he said it and that, during his lifetime, none of those who had been present ever denied it.

Meanwhile, the boats had gone back to Shoreham for another load of invaders. The behavior of the Green Mountain Boys was equally offensive to Delaplace, Feltham and Arnold. The men cavorted about the parade, whooping with equal vehemence for battle, liquor and plunder.

Allen supplied the second demand by confiscating ninety gallons of King George's rum. The Boys, Delaplace complains, appeased their hunger for loot by wholly ravishing his farm, taking among other things his forty-five sheep and eleven cattle. By daybreak the entire force that had gathered at Hands Cove had been ferried over to Ticonderoga, which only made the uproar within its walls thrice as violent. Allen wrote of this happy moment:

"The sun seemed to rise that morning with a superior lustre and Ticonderoga and its dependencies smiled on its conquerors who tossed about the flowing bowl and wished success to Congress and the liberty and freedom of America."[6]

There was a dissenting voice. Lieutenant Feltham noted in his report:

"This person, Ethan Allen, and Seth Warner are as great villians as any on earth."[7]

Seth Warner had been marooned at Hands Cove while Ticonderoga had been taken. Now he demanded the privilege of capturing the ruin that had been Crown Point and Allen sent him and Peleg Sunderland and an expeditionary force thither. Warner encountered Captain Remember Baker and another company of Green Mountain Boys on the same errand. Sergeant Nairns surrendered his ruin without a struggle.

Word came from Skenesborough that Sam Herrick had captured Major Skene's son, Andrew Philip Skene, Major Skene's two daughters, fifty tenants, twelve slaves and one brand-new schooner that its owner prophetically had christened *Liberty*.

Tidings arrived forty-eight hours later from the head of Lake George. The objectionable Mr. Romans had enlisted sixteen patriots in the Fort Edward area and had captured the fort there. This was only the single moldering bastion of the never completed edifice Amherst had begun. Romans also gathered in two fort employes and Captain Nordstrom, late of the 60th Foot, "The Royal Americans."

The titular governor of the fort was living "in a little cottage as an Hermit, where I was very happy" and, though evicted by Romans, found him "very genteel and civil."[8]

Lieutenant Wadman, journeying down Lake George to relieve Lieutenant Feltham, also was taken.

There were further, more important spoils of war. Ticonderoga and Crown Point yielded 120 iron cannon, 6 of them 24-pounders, 50 swivels of various calibers, 2 ten-inch mortars, 1 howitzer, 1 coehorn, 2 brass cannon, 10 tons of musket balls, 3 carloads of flints, 30 new gun carriages, 1 warehouse filled with boatbuilding material, 30 barrels of flour, 18 barrels of pork and 10 casks of poor powder. Almost all of the armament, eventually, was employed in the patriot cause.

The victory was complete, entirely bloodless and, immediately after its achievement, complicated and curdled by a revival of the Arnold-Allen feud, into which practically all present were drawn.

Echoes of the brawl still resound in letters most of the participants wrote on May 11. Mott informed the Massachusetts General Congress how thoroughly he and his associates had been "shockingly surprised when Col. Arnold presumed to contend for the command." He with Easton, Bull and Phelps on the same day prepared a more formal protest to the same body, complaining "Col. Arnold refuses to give up his Command which causes much Difficulty" and terming his conduct "highly inexpedient."[9]

The chief antagonists were writing, also. They never were too busy to dash off fulminating letters. Allen announced the fort's capture to the Massachusetts legislature, praising Easton and Brown but not even mentioning Arnold's presence, while his rival, addressing the same body, proclaimed himself to have been "the first person who entered and took possession of the fort" and asking immediate aid for the suppression of "confusion and anarchy"[10] reputedly raging at Ticonderoga.

The grievous lack of discipline among the Green Mountain Boys, their looting, tippling and general misbehavior roused the scorn and released the never long dormant temper of the Massachusetts colonel. Arnold again advanced his claim to the command and once more subsided only when mutiny seemed imminent.

Captain Herrick created a diversion by arriving at the fort with his captured schooner and his prisoners. The Massachusetts recruiting officers, Brown and Oswald, who had raised 50 men, accompanied him. This force seems to have given Arnold renewed confidence, for now he so vigorously insisted that his commission from Massachusetts gave him supreme authority at Ticonderoga that Mott was compelled to write out a formal commission for Ethan Allen. This document or else the disapproval of the Green Mountain Boys, who twice during the dispute took snap shots at Arnold, hushed him, again only briefly. His restless spirit momentarily was distracted by another enterprise.

Whether it were he or Ethan Allen who conceived it, no one knows. On May 13 Arnold and his Massachusetts men went aboard the Skene schooner *Liberty,* and stood out from Ticonderoga for St. Johns, beyond Champlain's outlet. This was the home port of a British armed sloop, *Enterprise,* whose capture would give the patriots complete control of the lake.

Arnold was in great haste but a north wind blew and, for all his considerable seamanship, twenty-four hours of constant tacking found him no farther along than Crown Point. He left the schooner there, put thirty men into a bateau and went on with them down the lake. The perverse wind changed. *Liberty* overhauled him, took him and his weary sweep-swingers aboard, bore them almost to the promontory that later was to be called Rouses Point—and there was becalmed.

Arnold hustled his men into the bateau again. He drove them hard. Somewhere behind him, he knew, Ethan Allen and eighty of his rascals in four bateaux were rowing north on the same errand.

Arnold won his race. He captured the King's sloop and her crew of seven, made prisoners of the sergeant and twelve men who comprised St. Johns' garrison, burned five bateaux, appropriated four and, sailing victoriously back up Champlain, met Ethan Allen and his sweating oarsmen.

It was easy to be generous now. It was pleasant to welcome the defeated man aboard the captured sloop and to drink his health. It must have been less agreeable to Allen. He proclaimed his intention to row on to St. Johns, capture the town and hold it with his handful for Jehovah and the Continental Congress. Arnold's dissuasions were vain. The tiny fleets parted. St. Johns, when Allen landed, offered no objection to being taken again.

Spacious plans were developing in the mind of Ticonderoga's captor. He resolved not only to occupy the little river town but to advance farther into Canada. James Morrison, a sympathizer with the patriot cause, lived in Montreal. Allen dispatched a trader, one Bindon, with a letter begging Morrison for reinforcements and supplies. Bindon returned more rapidly than he had left and reported that 200 British regulars and a field battery were advancing to retake St. Johns.

The tidings did not interfere with the subsequent slumbers of Colonel Allen and his command. They bivouacked on the riverbank and slept until the British guns opened on them from the Richelieu's farther shore.

The Ethan Allen invasion of Canada collapsed in a shower of grapeshot. Leader and followers scuttled to their bateaux and rowed out of range with such haste that they left three of their party, whom cannon fire had not disturbed, still slumbering on the beach.

Arnold was at Crown Point when Allen's expedition came oaring wearily up the lake. It did not halt but limped on to Ticonderoga. At the moment, the colonel commandant was quite willing not to face his rival.

They were to meet again shortly and resume the old quarrel. The balance of power was shifting at Ticonderoga. The Green Mountain Boys were departing by platoons. The liquor supply was dwindling; there was no further fighting in immediate prospect and the spring planting had to be done. Strife for command of the post was renewed and Arnold obtained it.

Ethan Allen submitted. Again, he had larger plans. On May 29 he wrote Congress guaranteeing, on receipt of 500 troops from that body, to capture Montreal. A little later he revised his estimate and asked for 1,500 infantry and "a proper artillery."

Congress paid no heed to his letter. Congress had been profoundly embarrassed by the capture of Ticonderoga. That body's sensations, when John Brown bore the victorious tidings to Philadelphia, were like those of a householder who has been presented with an elephant by a too-zealous well-wisher. Resisting unjust taxation, with a little shooting of redcoats, was one thing; taking his British Majesty's forts by force was another and much more revolutionary.

Actually, thanks to long-time British neglect, the lake forts were, of themselves, not the important prizes that uninformed persons deemed them. Silas Deane, member of the Continental Congress from Connecticut, inspected them that spring and wrote, thereafter, from Albany:

"Everything is in the utmost decay at Ticonderoga and Crown Point. It struck me with horror to see such grand fortifications in ruins. Crown Point is one heap of rubbish and the woodwork of Ticonderoga not much better. Fort George is a small stone fort and secure against small arms but would not bear cannonading."[11]

Congress directed that a careful inventory of the forts' contents be compiled at once, so that these might be returned intact to King George with suitable apologies when the current difficulty was over. Later, the amateur strategists in Philadelphia directed that Crown Point and Ticonderoga be evacuated and all munitions be moved to the head of Lake George.

Withdrawal from the lakes, after the patriots had won control of them, would have been a military insanity, baring all northern New England to invasion. The howl that rose from soldiers and civilians made the nervous gentlemen in Philadelphia hurriedly change their minds again and rescind the order.

At Ticonderoga, strife for command of the fort had been resumed and now became so vociferous that Massachusetts appointed a committee, headed by Walter Spooner, to abate it. The arrival of the body at the fort only increased the tumult. The slightly deafened committee learned that Benjamin Hinman, commissioned colonel by Connecticut, lately had led a regiment to Ticonderoga with Governor Trumbull's instructions to take command. Arnold had refused to recognize his authority and the place now tottered on the verge of civil war.

Spooner and his committee strove to reason with the rebellious officer, and told him it was his duty to serve under Hinman, "but," Spooner reported, "he declined it, declared he would not be second to any man, disbanded his forces and resigned his commission."[12]

There were rumors that Arnold's men intended mutiny and there was some difficulty in persuading the crews of the schooner and sloop to surrender the craft, but the crisis passed without bloodshed. Arnold stormed back to Cambridge and Hinman remained in command at the lakes.

Ethan Allen, meanwhile, assiduously continued to write letters. He appealed for sympathy and aid to the French people of Canada. He sent to the Provincial Congress of Massachusetts an unsolicited promise to capture Canada if the body would supply the troops— and asked now for 3,000 men. He even so far abandoned pride as to write to the New York Provincial Congress, begging it to commission him to raise a regiment of Green Mountain Boys. There is no record of how this proposal was received by the Yorkers since, in their eyes, Allen still was an outlaw with a price on his head.

The fretting giant was comic and at times ridiculous but in essence he was sound. Guy Carleton, a professional soldier, saw what Allen by instinct had grasped. The lakes in rebel hands were a menace to Canada and Quebec's governor had barely 700 regulars with whom to meet invasion.

Carleton strove with scant success to enlist the loyalty and the persons of the habitants. He labored prodigiously to fortify St. Johns. He was able, active and overapprehensive.

Arnold had been dismissed. No one paid much heed to Ethan Allen's fulminating letters. Congress vacillated, ambitious officers strove against one another and the dry, bright summer went by while the lakes' slow current ran, indicatively but emptily, north into Canada.

---

[1] John Brown to Samuel Adams, quoted in Lucius E. Chittenden, *The Capture of Ticonderoga* (Rutland, 1872).

[2] *Connecticut Historical Society Collection*, I, 169.

[3] Ethan Allen, *Narrative,* (Fort Ticonderoga, 1930), pp. 6-7.

[4] Allen French, *The Taking of Ticonderoga,* (Cambridge, 1928), ₌. 49.

[5] *Ethan* Allen, Narrative, p. 8.

[6] *Ibid.,* p. 9.

[7] Allen French, *The Taking of Ticonderoga,* p. 51.

[8] *New York Revolutionary Papers,* (Albany, n.d.), I, 206.

[9] *Fort Ticonderoga Museum Bulletin,* IV, 60.

[10] *Ibid.,* p. 62.

[11] *Connecticut Historical Society Collection,* I, 248-249.

[12] Walter Spooner to Governor Trumbull, in *Fort Ticonderoga Museum Bulletin,* IV, 83.

Chapter 13

Calamity

THE drought that baked the valley and shrank the lakes in the summer of 1775 was attended by unrelated but even more remarkable phenomena. Reconciliation suspended the strife between the settlers on the Grants and the people of New York. Ethan Allen and Seth Warner appeared before the New York Provincial Assembly, not with gyves on their wrists or halters about their necks, but as respected emissaries. Common peril ordains stranger bedfellowships than politics.

Officers who had girded against the anarchy that possessed Ticonderoga and Crown Point held a caucus at the latter fort on June 10 and chose Allen and Warner to present their case to Congress in Philadelphia. The highly insubordinate expedient drew no reproof from Hinman, and the emissaries delivered a round-robin letter to Congress on June 23. Later, they appeared before the body and pleaded their own cause.

The legislators on June 15 had adopted the army about Boston as a continental force and had named George Washington commander in chief. Congress called upon him now to remedy the chaos at the forts, and Washington referred the appeal to one of the newly appointed major generals, Philip Schuyler, who had just received command of the so-called "army" in the North.

As for the lately proscribed Grants leaders, Congress was willing to let bygones be bygones and to welcome into the service a regiment of Green Mountain Boys that the outlaws, Allen and Warner—Congress blandly overlooked their legal status—wished to raise.

A copy of the resolution was sent to the New York Provincial Assembly, in session at New York City, with a covering letter from John Hancock, urging the members to emulate Congress in broadmindedness. Allen and Warner presented themselves before the Assembly, minus the horns and tails with which the imaginations of a number of New Yorkers had endowed them. They were received with at least surface cordiality and the right of the Grants people to raise a regiment was confirmed.

"Respectable Gentlemen," Allen wrote to the Assembly after his return to Ticonderoga: "When I reflect on the unhappy controversy which hath many years subsisted between the government of New York and the settlers of the New Hampshire Grants, and also contemplate on the friendship and union that hath lately taken place between the government and those of its former discontented subjects, in making a united resistance against ministerial vengeance and slavery, I cannot but indulge fond hopes of reconciliation. To promote this salutary end, I shall contribute my influence, assuring your Honours that your respectful treatment not only to Mr. Warner and myself, but to the Green Mountain Boys in general are by them duly regarded and I will be responsible that they will retaliate this favour by wholly hazarding their lives, if needs be, in the common cause of America."[1]

Righteousness and Peace had kissed each other.

The millenium was not to be of long duration and another of the abnormal summer's aberrations marred it badly soon after Allen's letter was written. The people of the Grants assembled in Dorset, to choose officers for the new regiment. Seth Warner was elected Lieutenant Colonel Commanding. Ethan Allen, the leader of the revolt against New York, the apparent embodiment of his people, did not get a single recorded vote.

No clear explanation has come down to us why the Grants disavowed their erstwhile leader in conflict and chose as their first soldier Allen's solid cousin. The most pertinent comment was made in a letter written to Governor Trumbull of Connecticut by the defeated man himself.

"I find myself in favour of the Officers of the army and the young Green Mountain Boys how the old men came to reject me I cannot conceive inasmuch as I saved them from the encroachments of New York."[2]

He blamed it on the old men, who probably disapproved of his loud violence and agnosticism. Many resented the election's result almost as vehemently as Allen himself. Warner had extreme difficulty in raising his regiment and never recruited it to full strength.

The captor of Ticonderoga found himself suddenly out of the war yet he could not stay away from it and returned, a mere civilian now, to Champlain. There, the summer dragged on and the rain still withheld itself, and the frowzy Massachusetts and Connecticut men who garrisoned the forts seemed more inclined to fight one another than to move down the lake toward Canada.

The conditions that had affronted Allen and other patriotic officers five weeks earlier profoundly scandalized Schuyler when he arrived at Ticonderoga, July 18. He was introduced to the fashion in which Colonel Hinman of Connecticut and his fellow incompetents carried on a war when he arrived at the north end of Lake George at ten o'clock at night. At the post there, Schuyler found everyone, including sentries, sound asleep. Worse was to be revealed to him on the morrow.

The troops were underequipped, undisciplined, dirty. The barracks were pigsties. Sickness was prevalent. Almost nothing had been done toward creating a fleet with which to hold the lakes, though the sawmills still stood at Skenesborough and on the Lake George outlet and there was an endless supply of timber, besides boatbuilding materials captured at Ticonderoga.

Schuyler was aghast at the waste of munitions and time. He was particularly scandalized by the herd of fifty cows the thoughtful people of Connecticut had sent to the fort so that their regiment could have fresh milk with its meals. These animals fed on the best of the scant grazing the drought had left. In consequence, beef cattle for the rest of the army were starving and draught oxen few and weak.

The general had expected to use the forts as a base for an attack upon Canada. What he found made him suddenly fearful of an assault by the British. He sent John Brown north to find out what Carleton was doing. He employed Remember Baker also as a scout. The two brought reassuring tidings back up Champlain. The British were on the defensive. They had mounted 12 cannon on the St. Johns fortification and had there quartered 450 regulars, more than half of all the troops in the province. Canadians in general were taking little interest in the war.

Schuyler left for Albany on August 17 to attend a conference with the Iroquois, at which he hoped to attach them to the colonies' cause or, at worst, hold them neutral. Baker, prowling north again apparently on his own initiative, did his unwilling best to nullify the general's efforts.

The scout and four or five other restless spirits borrowed a boat from the army, rowed north to Champlain's outlet and dropped by night down the Richelieu. Toward dawn, they hid their craft in a cove, some four miles below Isle aux Noix on the river's east shore, and were moving on foot along the water's edge toward St. Johns when Indians in the lately hidden boat came paddling downstream.

The scouts, according to the survivors' tale, got behind trees and Baker hailed the Indians in a pacific tone, saying that no war existed between the red men and the colonials and asking for the return of his boat. One of the Indians raised his musket and Baker tried to shoot first. The flint missed fire and Baker, peering incautiously out to see what ailed it, took an Indian bullet through the skull. The other white men wounded two of the boat's occupants and fled.

Baker's head was cut off and carried to St. Johns. The Grants people mourned him, as the first man to fall in the lakes campaign, but Schuyler grieved more over this provocation to Indian war than for his enterprising scout.

It may have been Baker's insurgence that led the general to take immediate steps to prevent any further rash upsetting of his plans by the Allen clan. Remember's cousin, Ethan, still was at the fort and still a civilian. Schuyler, before he would permit him to join the Canadian expedition that the general distractedly was trying to marshal, insisted on pledges and guarantees of Allen's good behavior.

"I always dreaded," the general wrote to John Hancock later, "his impatience of subordination and it was not until after solemn promise made me in the presence of several officers that he would demean himself properly that I would permit him to attend the army; nor would I have consented then, had not his solicitations been backed by several officers."

The epidemic slackness and insubordination of the men he was trying to mold into the semblance of an army drove Schuyler frantic and undermined his health. Gradually, with tormenting deliberation, the expeditionary force got itself together but it did not move until the summer was almost spent.

On August 30, the first slow wave of the invasion moved north. Richard Montgomery, a transplanted Irishman who had served under Wolfe, led it pending his superior's return from Albany whither he had gone to attend an Indian Council. There was splashing and a deal of swearing at Crown Point as the boats Schuyler had knocked together got under way. The clumsy, flat-bottomed craft, packed with soldiers, moved in ragged procession through the narrow water into the wider reaches of the upper lake. The advance was as deliberate as the preparations had been.

Twelve hundred untried men bivouacked that night on the Champlain's west shore, near the frontier settlement of Westport that William Gilliland had founded ten years earlier. Their camp-fires shone on the rocks and trees of Four Brothers Islands twelve miles farther on, the following night, and on September 2 they drew up their boats on a gravel beach at Isle La Motte and waited for Schuyler.

The general was an ill man when he arrived, September 4. Rheumatic fever, biliousness and anxiety had laid him low, but he ordered immediate advance. Scarlet shone like danger signals on the maples as the boats oared past Rouses Point and the Richelieu's slow current grasped and bore them. The army camped that night on Isle aux Noix. The invasion of Canada that Allen had urged four months earlier at last had begun.

In Cambridge, Washington was detaching New England infantry, Pennsylvania sharpshooters and Daniel Morgan's Virginia riflemen, 1,100 in all, from the army besieging Boston. The force was to form the second prong of the double attack on Canada, pressing up the Kennebec into the maze of lakes, swamps and forest of interior Maine, descending by the Chaudière to the St. Lawrence opposite Quebec. This was a revived item from the plan for reducing Canada that Governor Shirley of Massachusetts had prepared in the early days of the French and Indian War.

Only a man with Benedict Arnold's infectious resolution could have persuaded the commander in chief to approve the wild scheme. No one but him could have wished to lead it. He moved his troops into the wilderness, September 12.

By then, Schuyler's command, feeling its way down the Richelieu, had learned the strength of St. John's fortifications and had fallen back on Isle aux Noix to wait for artillery. Ethan Allen had been sent out to roam the region and preach the gospel of liberty to the indifferent habitants and the suspicious Indians. He returned to Isle aux Noix, well pleased with himself, just before the now prostrate Schuyler surrendered command to Montgomery on September 16.

The general was borne back to Ticonderoga where, recovering, he devoted himself to the maddening task of trying to assemble and forward supplies and reinforcements to Canada.

His endurance was to be tried severely as food, munitions and men dribbled fitfully into Ticonderoga, autumn's fires burned themselves out on Champlain's hills, and tidings from the north that had been heartening at first grew progressively worse.

Besieged St. Johns fell on November 3. Most of General Carleton's professional troops had been taken or destroyed. Canada, it appeared, lay prostrate. Montreal was captured November 12. The tidings must have dissipated whatever regret Schuyler felt over news that Ethan Allen had been taken by the British.

The erstwhile leader of the Green Mountain Boys had received a roving commission. Part forager, part missionary, he traveled through the habitant settlements, occasionally forwarding needed supplies and less welcome advice to Montgomery and, in the course of his roaming, raising a personal force of more than a hundred men.

Allen says in his *Narrative* that he was encouraged by John Brown, now a colonel and also roaming the countryside, to join him in an attack on Montreal. There is no other evidence that Brown was involved in the harebrained scheme. On September 25, Allen advanced against the town, found himself more attacked than attacking and, after being chased a considerable distance by a British officer, surrendered. He was sent eventually to prison in England. George Washington chose his disastrous exploit as text for a sermon on army discipline. The Grants were more peaceful, if less colorful, for Ethan Allen's absence.

November 13, the day after Montgomery captured Montreal, 700 gaunt and hungry men emerged from the mouth of the Chaudière, rowed across the St. Lawrence and crawled by the path Wolfe had taken to Abraham Martin's field before Quebec. There, while the rabble ordered themselves for battle, their haggard leader dared the garrison to come out and fight.

For thirty-three days, Arnold's band had forced its way through the ghastly wilderness. Two hundred of his men had died of fatigue and starvation. Two hundred more had turned back. Now, with the remnant, the leader invited the troops in Quebec to battle or surrender. Their commander ignored both proposals. He manned the fortifications and Arnold, knowing the weakness of his troops, could only wait for Montgomery to arrive.

The hills were frosty blue and ice ledges were thrusting out from the lakes' shores when Seth Warner and his men returned from the Canadian campaign. They had beaten back an attack that Carleton and the partisan, St. Luc de la Corne, had launched across the St. Lawrence on October 30, in the hope of raising the siege of St. Johns. It had been a smart, well-conducted action but thereafter Warner and Montgomery had quarreled and on November 20, the Vermont regiment had been discharged from the service, ostensibly because it was not equipped for winter campaigning.

More human drainage from the army came up the lake before the early and bitter winter shut down—men whose time of enlistment had expired, invalids, wounded, malingerers. Montgomery's command was dwindling. He joined Arnold at Quebec with barely 500 troops. The combined force invested the town but Carleton cannily made no sortie. It was better to wait and let winter do the killing.

Colonel Henry Knox, the former bookseller, a fat and cheerful man, came to Ticonderoga in December with a preposterous plan that his energy straightway made practical. His enthusiasm put disbelieving men to work stripping the fort's battlements of their inordinate supply of cannon. Knox acquired ox teams, loaded the guns on sledges and moved up frozen Lake George, bound for the Continental army at Cambridge 300 miles away over snow-smothered roads.

In a hut at the lake's head, the cheery colonel spent a night with a subaltern of the 7th Royal Fusiliers, captured at St. Johns and now on his way to a prison camp in Lancaster, Pennsylvania, a pleasant young man named John André.

Forty-two sleds were laden with forty-five pieces of artillery. The eighty yoke of oxen that drew them plodded through the woods to Fort Edward, and then to Albany. From there the train slanted more easterly to Springfield and on to Boston. The cannon that Allen had taken at Ticonderoga, to the scandal of Congress, hammered the British out of the town the following spring.

The army, clinging to its lines before Quebec, was increasingly tormented by privation and disease. It wasted away with, to Carleton, gratifying rapidity. What December left of it, January and February would abolish. At two in the morning of the last day of the year, the Americans launched in tempest and snow an attack that was like the final frenzy of a dying creature. Montgomery and Arnold threw their starvelings against the fortifications from either side of the town.

In the desperate and doomed assault, Arnold dropped, grievously wounded; Montgomery died in the arms of an aide, Captain Aaron Burr. Morgan and his men fought their way into the town, were surrounded and captured. Brigadier General David Wooster, who succeeded to the command, abandoned the siege, led what was left of the besiegers three miles upstream and went into winter quarters there.

The lake forts and the land beyond them learned of the army's progressive dissolution from the new commander's frequent and frantic appeals for men and supplies. Recruits were assembled at Ticonderoga and Crown Point and sent north over the ice. Warner, besought by Wooster, came out of his sulks and joined the army with 400 men. The reinforcements accomplished little more than to increase the sick list and to enlarge the burying ground. In addition to scurvy, dysentery and typhus, smallpox now kindled and spread through the camp.

So dire was the tale Wooster's letters recited that in March Congress sent Benjamin Franklin, Samuel Chase, Charles Carroll and his brother, Father John Carroll, to estimate the situation and, if possible, wheedle the Canadians into alliance.

The dignified gentlemen had a wretched time during their northward journey and a wholly unprofitable negotiation afterward. A series of spring tempests roared up the lake and drove them ashore, in succession, at Crown Point, Panton and Essex.

The deputation arrived at Montreal April 29, but it was too late for diplomacy then. The provident Canadians had no intention of allying themselves with an army that was visibly rotting to pieces—pest-ridden, starving and half naked. Furthermore, word sped through the province that a mighty host was coming from Europe to Carleton's aid—crack British regiments under John Burgoyne and a host of German mercenaries.

The first of the redcoats already were arriving, advance guard of a force that would number more than 10,000. Brigadier General John Thomas, when he succeeded Wooster as commander of the American expeditionary force, found he had under him no more than 1,000 reasonably well men and 2,000 ill.

Thomas immediately ordered retreat, and Carleton, with a force that each day grew larger, let him go. Thomas died of smallpox, and command of the ambulating pesthouse devolved upon Brig-

adier General John Sullivan. The groaning army crept southward
with Arnold, now convalescent, directing the rear guard. Carleton
was strong enough to strike and destroy, but he followed the retreat, gathered in prisoners, and withheld the blow.

Much that happened later in the Champlain-George Valley
seems less irrational if you consider the character and the convic-
tions of Major General Guy Carleton who, on July 6 of this year,
was to become a Knight of the Bath.

Though by profession a soldier, the governor general of Canada
was also a statesman with theories of his own. He was generous
and kindly toward his inferiors, contentious with his superiors, and
he clung to the belief that peace could be most effectively regained,
not by battle but by temporizing and appeasing. He thought he
could kill a rebellion with kindness. The idea was lodged so
solidly in his mind that it swayed all his actions during the fate-
ful year of 1776.

The remnant of the American army crept through St. Johns,
June 17, and burned the fort and barracks before it stumbled on
to Isle aux Noix where it paused to bury its latest increment of
dead and then embarked for the journey up Champlain. At least
twice during the clumsy retreat, Carleton had it in his power to
abolish the ailing little host and refrained. The hale prisoners that
he took were fed and clothed; the ill were hospitalized. Later,
they were returned to their own country on parole. All this was
part of the British general's strategy. He explained its purpose in
a letter to General William Howe, August 8.

"It appears that this Congress is intent upon exciting the people
of America to acts of blood. Probably the sending back their
prisoners, notwithstanding this, loaded with every favor which
was in my power to confer upon them, will be such testimony to
the thinking people among them of the humanity and forebear-
ance with which His Majesty's just resentment toward his revolted
subjects is tempered as may serve effectually to counteract the
dangerous designs of those desperate people."[3]

The rabble that, thanks to Carleton's forbearance, arrived at
Crown Point, July 3, was a destitute, diseased, semimutinous mob

that showed more animosity toward one another than to the British.

"The most descriptive pen," Schuyler wrote to Washington, July 12, "cannot describe the condition of our army. Sickness, disorder and discord reign triumphant, the latter occasioned by an illiberal destructive jealousy which unhappily subsists between the troops raised in different colonies."[4]

Three hundred more men died during the ten days' sojourn at Crown Point. The remaining whole then were removed to Ticonderoga; the ill were borne up Lake George to a hurriedly built hospital at its head.

Not even the evacuation of Boston by the British could atone for the bitterness and shame of this defeat. It spread through the countryside even more rapidly than the diseases imported from Canada and dragged patriot morale to nadir.

Militia, summoned to defend Ticonderoga against probable attack by Carleton, refused to report, dreading the epidemics that still blazed at the fort. Even when Schuyler promised to quarter newly arrived troops on the opposite side of the lake from Ticonderoga, many still hung back and some of those who did appear already had inoculated themselves with smallpox to ensure their prompt discharge.

The Canadian winter, as Carleton had foreseen, had been a terrible ally. Now, the rumor came up Champlain, the governor general was staging an invasion of his own. The northern frontier had been bared by the blasted army's retreat, and at Ticonderoga and Crown Point there were only broken works and broken men to oppose the British advance.

---

[1] E. B. O'Callaghan (ed.), *Documentary History of the State of New York,* IV, 554.

[2] Trumbull Papers iv, 144 a-d, in Connecticut State Library, Hartford.

[3] Canadian Archives B, XXXIX, 93-94.

[4] Schuyler's Letter Book, in New York Public Library.

Chapter 14

Storm Clouds

BRIGADIER GENERAL HORATIO GATES was in command at Ticonderoga when the remnants of the Canadian expedition reached the fort. The general, a flabby and ornate person who was deft in the art of self-advancement, had become chief of the northern army. Sullivan, whom he superseded, stormed off in a temper to tell his troubles to Congress. The problems he left in Gates's lap were more than ample retaliation.

The never overdisciplined Canadian expedition had collapsed into a pest-ridden mob. The lake forts were crumbling closer to absolute ruin. Dire tidings came from the north and news, equally fell, from the south.

General William Howe's transports, escorted by Admiral Richard Howe's warships, had sailed southward from Halifax. Redcoats and German hireling troops were pouring from overseas into Canada.

The familiar shadow of peril was stretching again over the lakes. The new war was picking up the old thrust and counter-thrust rhythm. The recently assailed enemy in the north was about to mount its own invasion, according to the pattern first established in Frontenac's day.

Spies, scouts and less-accredited informants brought increasingly alarming versions of the same tale to Ticonderoga.

General Guy Carleton was coming. The Fabian soldier whose caution and delay had saved Canada for his King the previous winter was preparing an armada to sweep Champlain. An army would follow at the sterns of the war fleet and, crossing from the head of Lake George to the Hudson, unite with Howe advancing up-river, crush New York and cut the new nation in halves.

It was a time of alarm and outcry. Wails of dread came up to the lakes from threatened New England and New York. More piercing yells for aid were uttered by dwellers on Champlain's shore. There, cabins and the brave small beginnings of towns had been left defenseless and increasingly frightened by the collapse of the Canadian invasion. From the settlement on the Onion River, from Panton, Poultney and Shelburne, appeals for protection were forwarded to Ticonderoga which did not have enough whole soldiers to protect its own moldering walls.

Moses Pierson, a solid man, was the first signer of Shelburne's appeal:

"We, the inhabitants, being but few in number and having considerable large crops of wheat and other grain in the ground, besides stocks of cattle, we hereby beseech that His Excellency would be graciously pleased, if he thinks it consistent with the good of the service, to let some of the men who were there go back again, or some others as a small guard."[1]

Something more expedient than obstinacy or recklessness made the frontiersmen cling to their cabins in the face of danger. The green that spread over the rich soil of the hard-won clearings represented, in many cases, the investment of the settler's entire capital. If the harvest were lost, he was ruined and, in a land where neighbors were far away and food was scant, might starve with his whole family before another spring.

A few details of troops were sent north. The danger, it appeared, was not immediate. The British invasion hung fire. Meanwhile, Gates himself was clamoring to all available authorities for reinforcements to strengthen the decrepit forts. That rehabilitation went forward slowly. So did another construction that was proceeding, without advertisement, in the New Hampshire Grants where a few crafty, farseeing opportunists had begun to build an independent state.

The millennial conciliation between the Grants people and their ancient enemies of New York had endured no longer than most such raptures. The hard men who had cleared their land and built their cabins, the abler who held shares in a score of towns granted by New Hampshire, considered New York with a revived and intensified suspicion.

That province, while displaying a noble air of forgiveness, had actually surrendered nothing. It had permitted the Grants people to raise troops for the cause, but had not that permission, itself, been a reiteration of New York's proprietorship? The Grants already had sacrificed a deal for Liberty, had risked more, and what had they got in return? The belief was stirring among a trading folk that, in some way not yet quite clear, they were being cheated.

Ethan Allen and his Boys had taken the lake forts. Immediately afterward, Congress had tried to abandon the strongholds. There had been rumors aplenty that Yorkers in Congress—James Duane, Robert Livingstone and other land jobbers who still insisted that the Grants people were squatters and should be driven from their farms—had urged that abandonment. Why? So that the Grants frontier might be left unprotected and the British and Indians might extinguish together inhabitants and troublesome titles. The Grants had no representation in Congress. Some of the more acute settlers were beginning to see that the Grants, though they were fighting for freedom, had been allowed to make, so far, no progress whatever toward attaining their own liberty.

The movement for an absolute secession from New York and the establishment of the Grants as an independent entity began in January 1776, when "four of the leading men conferred on measures to be recommended to the people for the establishment of a Civil government which appeared necessary effectively to carry on the war, raise men and money, and to secure the titles of the lands against the latent intentions of the Governor of New York."[2]

Since Ira Allen describes the proceedings of this conference at length, he undoubtedly was one of the four. There never has been a positive identification of the other three but the weight of historical opinion believes they were Heman Allen, Ira's elder brother; Dr. Jonas Fay who was to serve as a talented accoucheur during the labor attending Vermont's birth; and Thomas Chittenden, a long, taciturn, one-eyed farmer who hid behind a pose of

innocence statecraft that maintained him as governor during thirteen of Vermont's fourteen years as an independent republic.

Toward the foundation of that republic, the quartet now took
the first small, cautious step, resolving:

"That the district of the New Hampshire Grants on revolutionary principles was the *oldest* in America; that the people had
governed themselves by Committees of Safety and Convention
against the oppressions and tyranny of New York, eight years before the colonies of America took similar measure against Great
Britain: of course the people ought to persevere and brave every
danger that might be in the womb of destiny."[3]

"The result of these deliberations," Ira Allen pursues, "was to
establish a new Government; accordingly great care was taken to
prepare the minds of the people for such an event and to effect
the important subject."[4]

The people whose minds were to be prepared were anything
but impressionable folk. The originally tough dissenters had
acquired further obstinacy and truculence during the guerrilla
warfare with New York. Hatred of that province, though abiding,
was a lesser emotion than their passion for liberty and the colonies'
cause. They were men difficult to lead, impossible to drive, yielding
best to that insidious persuasion whereby one is made to believe
that his conversion has been his own idea. The uncertainly identified quartet and their even more obscure associates moved unobtrusively through the Grants, sowing their seed.

Either by reiterated fortunate accident or through the veritable
intervention of destiny, this seed enjoyed astonishing growing
weather. Henceforth the assorted violences and disasters that were
visited upon the newborn United States always seemed to happen
at the time when they could most benefit the Grants cause.

From the beginning, this mysteriously was so. Thus, when
delegates from the Grants towns met at Cephas Kent's tavern in
Dorset, July 24, 1776, and took another tentative step toward independence, the eyes of America were distracted by looming calamity
elsewhere and its ears were tuned to its thunder.

The thirteen embattled colonies had lately decreed for them-

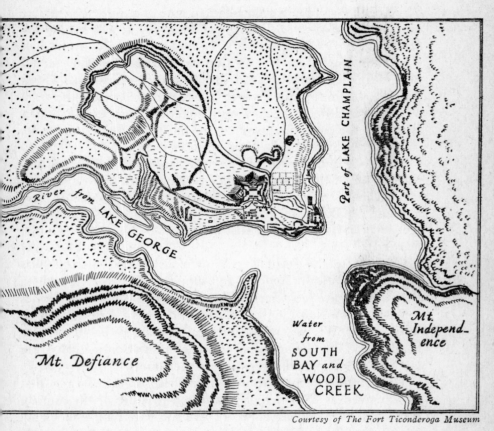

onderoga Terrain with Fort in Center. After a map drawn by General Burgoyne's engineers.

selves the independence the Grants now sought. On July 18,
the Declaration had been read to the tattered and ailing garrison
of Ticonderoga. A salute of thirteen guns had hailed it and in
honor of the occasion a saddle-backed eminence opposite the fort
on Champlain's eastern shore had been christened Mount Independence.

Invasion was assembling in Canada, though Carleton seemed
to be taking his time. Invasion already stood on New York City's
doorstep. Admiral Howe's fleet lay in the harbor and the tents
of General Howe's regulars and mercenaries shone on Staten
Island. In the peril and the tumult, no one paid heed to the Grants
convention which on July 25 proclaimed that:

"The long and spirited conflict which has for many years subsisted between the Colony or State of New York and the inhabitants of land commonly called and known by the name of New
Hampshire Grants, relative to the title of land on said district,
renders it inconvenient in many respects to associate with the
Province or State."[5]

Gates, from the crumbling battlements of Ticonderoga, was
appealing frantically for men and supplies. The former, such as
they were, could be obtained with satisfactory promptitude. Levies
came in from New England, New York, New Jersey, Pennsylvania. Seth Warner, whose original command had been disbanded, had been commissioned colonel in the Continental Army
and was recruiting a line regiment in the Grants.

The reinforcements acquired their share of the diseases that
still lingered at Ticonderoga and also a measure of the original
garrison's insubordination. Work was the only remedy at hand.
It was administered in heroic doses.

The heavy-footed regiments of Howe drove Washington from
Long Island. In the infant villages of the Grants, in the cabins
in the new clearings, men debated whither their convention's
recent defiance of New York would lead. Carleton's expected
invasion still did not come. Meanwhile, the army at Ticonderoga
worked desperately to repair and enlarge the fort.

Schuyler, after inspection, had decided that it would be waste effort to try to revive Crown Point. The post was left as it was though riggers and outfitters worked there all summer on the cockleshell navy that was being assembled. All the army's ingenuity and effort were bent upon making Ticonderoga impregnable. The plans drawn up for its reconstruction were gratifyingly elaborate but difficult to execute, since there was a shortage of tools that compelled the garrison to work in shifts.

Gradually, while Carleton withheld his attack, the outline of a great fortification took form. Ticonderoga was strengthened; the newly christened Mount Independence on the east shore had been shorn of its trees and was being crowned by a hospital, barracks and a new, star-shaped fort. The guns of this and of Ticonderoga would command every foot of the narrow lake between them, as well as the entrance to the upper reaches of Champlain that twisted through swamp some fifteen miles to Skenesborough and South Bay.

This protection seemed not enough. Axes rang all day long and details, marching to the entrenchments, received spades, mattocks and bars warm and moist from the hands of the shift that had proceeded them.

Breastworks were built at the lakeside foot of Mount Independence. The old lines to the west of Ticonderoga that Montcalm had built were revived and a blockhouse was established to strengthen them. A small additional fort was begun on Mount Hope, north and west of the original post. Redoubts and batteries were created upon the lowlands before Ticonderoga. The sawmills above and below the outlet were protected by blockhouses. Still another blockhouse was raised at the head of Lake George.

Nor was this all. The troops in the area had been transformed into an engineer corps. Under the disturbing eye of Colonel Anthony Wayne, they added further embellishments for the confusion of the British who still lingered in Canada. A way was built down the east face of Mount Independence, to connect with the road to Castleton, and a bridge 400 yards long was flung across the water connecting the hill with Ticonderoga. It was a solid structure resting on 22 piers, with pontoons between them and, lest this barrier be not strong enough to repel any ship of His Majesty's lake navy, a boom was laid along the north side of the bridge, and beyond that, a massive iron chain was stretched.

Once all these works were completed, no force, its creators were sure, that Carleton ever might muster could attack successfully. The scope and intricacy of the defenses were sedatives for anxious minds.

Twenty thousand troops, Gates felt certain, never could take Mount Independence. Admiration for the spacious plans, satisfaction in seeing them brought ever closer to completion without British intervention, dazzled the commanding general and other high officers. They persisted in overlooking a weakness in the apparently mighty fortifications, a prime defect that could cancel at a stroke all the labor and the outlay.

South and west of Fort Ticonderoga, opposite Mount Independence and half encircled by Lake George's outlet, rose the bulk of the rugged hill the Americans called "Sugar Loaf Mountain." Its blunt summit was 572 feet above Mount Independence's crest and little more than a mile from that lesser eminence, or from the fort itself, as the plunging cannon ball traveled.

Guns on the peak of Sugar Loaf Mountain, which the British later rechristened "Mount Defiance," would command the entire area. Schuyler and Gates, who fortified Mount Independence so heavily, ignored the greater height and placed no guns there. They were infatuated with their accomplishment in strengthening Ticonderoga and believed the taller peak impassable for guns. The warnings of Arnold and Wayne could not rouse them to the danger. Even a practical demonstration by Colonel John Trumbull, who later became an artist but who now was an officer of engineers, failed to shake their complacency.

Trumbull, after argument with Gates over the peril Sugar Loaf Mountain represented, repaired to Mount Independence and directed that a brass long 12-pounder be elevated and aimed at the crest of the threatening hill. After the discharge, he and the gun crew saw the shot strike halfway up the slope. Trumbull thereupon essayed to prove his contention further.

"I returned to headquarters and made my triumphant report, and after dinner requested the general and the officers who were with him to walk out upon the glacis of the old French fort where I had ordered a common six-pound field piece to be placed in readiness. This was, in their presence, loaded with the ordinary charge, pointed at the top of the hill and, when fired, it was seen that the shot struck near the summit. Thus the truth of the new doctrine was demonstrated but it still was insisted upon that this summit was inaccessible to an enemy.

"This also I denied and again resorted to an experiment. Gen. Arnold, Colonel Wayne and several other active officers accompanied me in the general's barge which landed us at the foot of the hill where it was most precipitous and rocky and we clambered to the summit in a short time. The ascent *was* laborious and difficult but not impracticable, and when we looked down upon the outlet of Lake George it was obvious to all that there could be no difficulty in driving up a loaded carriage."[6]

Gates complacently and stubbornly continued to insist Trumbull was wrong and the hill was too steep for guns to be dragged to its top. He had precedent for his blindness. Neither Abercromby nor Amherst had been able to grasp the importance of the eminence. Montcalm may have appreciated it and, for that reason, may have hesitated to meet Abercromby's 1757 attack at Ticonderoga. Burgoyne's able generals saw at a glance that Mount Defiance, still unfortified, was the key to Ticonderoga.

As 1776 advanced and the works grew stronger, the condition of the garrison also improved. Rations were more plentiful. Beef and mutton supplanted pork and there was a sufficiency of spruce beer. This was an antiscorbutic draught brewed of spruce needles and molasses. The troops were encouraged to drink it instead of water from the lake, which, physicians had proclaimed with no regard for the adjacent marshes and their swarms of mosquitoes, was imbued with a mysterious poison that caused fever and ague.

The might of the fort, the rickety navy that was being assembled as Champlain's first line of defense, and the Grants inclination toward independence all were stronger for the long respite Carleton allowed them in that critical summer.

---

1 Petition to Gates, quoted in Walter Hill Crockett, *History of Vermont* (Burlington, 1938), I, 536.

2 Ira Allen, *The National and Political History of the State of Vermont* (London, 1798), p. 75.

3 *Ibid.*, p. 75.

4 *Ibid.*, p. 75.

5 Walter Hill Crockett, *History of Vermont*, II, 180.

6 John Trumbull, "Autobiography," in *Fort Ticonderoga Museum Bulletin*, III, 8.

Steamer Burlington.

R.W. SHERMAN,

COMMANDER.

LAKE~CHAMPLAIN.

~1837~

CHAMPLAIN TRANSPORTATION COMPANY'S *Burlington*

1844.

STEAM PACKET

Wm. Caldwell,

LAKE GEORGE,

L. C. Larabee, Master,

WILL commence her regular Trips on *TUESDAY*, the fourth day of June next—Leaving J. F. SHERRIL'S *Spacious Lake House* at Caldwell, every Morning, (except Sundays,) at 8 o'clock. The Boat will remain at the foot of the Lake 3 1-2 hours, giving Passengers time to visit

THE RUINS OF FORT TICONDEROGA,

and Dine and return to Caldwell the same Day, leaving Ticonderoga at 3 o'clock, P. M. Should any alteration be made in the Steam Boat Arrangement on Lake Champlain, the above arrangement will be altered so as to conform thereto. And thus

Form a regular Communication between

SARATOGA SPRINGS AND LAKE CHAMPLAIN THROUGH LAKE GEORGE,

☞ Passengers taking or leaving the Champlain Steamers at the Hotel near the Fort, now kept by Mrs. ATHERTON, formerly of the Hotel on the Outlet of Lake George, will find Carriages to convey them from one Lake to the other.

May 1st, 1844.

BLAISDELL'S PRINT, Vergennes, Vt.

EARLY LAKE GEORGE STEAMBOAT COMPANY POSTER

Chapter 15

Britain Sweeps the Lake

GATES wrote to Washington from Ticonderoga: "As soon as all the vessels and gondolas are equipped, General Arnold has offered to go to Crown Point and take command of them. This is exceedingly pleasing to me, as he has a perfect knowledge of maritime affairs and is, besides, a most deserving and gallant officer."

In time, Gates was to alter radically that high opinion but now, in the midsummer of 1776, the presence of the restless, truculent little man was a boon and a comfort.

Hammers banged and saws whined at Skenesborough and Ticonderoga where imported New England shipwrights knocked together the little boats that, with the craft already taken from the British, were to constitute the American fleet. One small schooner was launched at Ticonderoga and named *Revenge*. Otherwise, the builders limited themselves to the more quickly produced two-masted round-bottomed galleys and single-masted flat-bottomed gondolas, clumsy creations with square sails for blowing weather and sweeps for calm.

On the Richelieu River, the appeasing and deliberate Carleton was assembling a British squadron, jigsaw-puzzle fashion. He had no lack of naval stores, trained artificers or experienced seamen, and Captain James Douglas had overcome the great difficulty that the river's falls presented. His craft, built in the St. Lawrence shipyards, were worked up the Richelieu to Chambly. There they were taken apart and carried around the rapids to be reassembled at St. Johns and adjacent settlements.

The precious summer weeks, during which an invasion could be mounted with the best chance of success, were flying, but Carleton still took his time. He was creating a naval force that would be

191

certain to blast away whatever craft the Yankees could put on Champlain to oppose it.

News of the heavy, 16-gun floating battery the British were building and the 18-gun ship that was almost completed, distracted Gates from the intrigue he was fomenting in Congress against his superior, Schuyler. The bungling and delay, the difficulty with which naval supplies were transported through wilderness to Skenesborough, the slowness with which the hulls were launched and towed down the lake to Crown Point for rigging, fitting and arming infuriated Arnold who grasped command of the fleet while it was still uncompleted.

Immediately, another of the brawls that stand like milestones along a traitor's career arose. Authority over the vessels hitherto had been vested in Captain Jacobus Wynkoop who, because he held commission from Schuyler, contested Gates's orders and fought bitterly against yielding his command. Peace was restored only after Wynkoop had been arrested and sent to Albany where he straightway followed the procedure already established by aggrieved officers and began a series of letters to Congress.

The justified Arnold immediately laid energetic hands upon the raggle-taggle American fleet. It would require all his energy and skill if it ever were to become an effective weapon.

Here were the elderly *Enterprise,* the king's sloop that Arnold himself had captured at St. Johns; *Liberty,* that had been Skene's trading schooner; *Royal Savage,* schooner taken at St. Johns by Montgomery's army, and *Revenge,* built at Ticonderoga. They were light craft, armed with 6, 4 and 3-pounders but they and the ten gondolas newly commissioned were all Arnold had with which to hold the lake. The rest of the ships still were slowly building.

The deliberation vanished after a human hornet had buzzed and stung its way through the shipyards. Men rubbed their tingling ears and the rhythm of saw and hammer quickened, but Arnold could not wait. He manned his craft, which never were satisfactorily outfitted, with drafts from the northern army. Its ranks yielded only seventy men with sea experience and he rounded out his complement with what he could get. The crews would need intensive training. It was characteristic of their commander that he chose to conduct it on the enemy's doorstep.

The little squadron yawed and splashed north into the wide blue shining of the lower lake, groped its way past islands whose foliage already was tarnished by approaching autumn and took station in the narrow water below Windmill Point, watching the channel through which the British must advance. Signs were plentiful that Carleton, at last, was moving. Indians prowled on either shore and red coats shone through the foliage.

On September 7, Arnold sent a working party ashore on Isle La Motte to cut saplings with which to fashion fascines for his gondolas' better protection. Indians under Lieutenant Scott of the 47th Foot laid an ambush in the hope of taking prisoners. They failed in this endeavor, though Scott grappled with a sailor whose pouch belt broke and freed him. Five Americans were killed and three wounded before the party got back to the boats and drew out of range.

Gunfire from the fleet scattered the enemy. The sound of cannon, rolling up the lake to Crown Point, spread the rumor that Arnold was in battle with Carleton.

"A party," Arnold reported to Schuyler, "was immediately sent on shore in pursuit of the Savages but were not able to come up with them, they found a Laced Beaver Hatt marked on the button 47th rgt."[2]

Lieutenant Scott must have returned to his commander bareheaded. Arnold was less than satisfied with the behavior of his crews in their first small engagement, for he wrote to Gates that day:

"We have but very indifferent men in general. Great part of those shipped for seamen know very little of the matter. Three or four good gunners are wanted. . . . I wish fifty-eight good seamen could be procured and sent down."[3]

He already had received an additional detail of sailors from Governor Trumbull of Connecticut and another company was on its way to him via Albany.

The cutter *Lee* and a gondola, fresh from the sweating shipwrights and riggers, joined the fleet that evening. Lights gleamed on Isle La Motte during the night and a sound of hammering convinced Arnold that the British were building a battery there to rout him. He moved up the lake and anchored off Cumberland Head, still watching the channel.

A man hailed *Liberty* from the shore and begged to be taken aboard. The schooner put over a boat but its wary crew could not be lured to the beach, though the imploring man waded deep into the water to entice it. When the Americans refused to be decoyed, a volley was fired from the lakeside brush, wounding three men. *Liberty* broke up the ambush with a burst of grapeshot.

There were more prowlers on the beaches now and watchers on the headlands, but though the month waned and color that had smoldered on the islands began to flame, Carleton's fleet still delayed. Those who saw the Americans weigh anchor September 23 and go up the lake must have deemed it retreat but Arnold was taking position at a place where he believed he could sell his squadron at the highest possible price.

Between the oblong bulk of rock-rimmed, tree-crowned Valcour Island and the shore, he had found a roadstead, deep yet so narrow that Carleton would have difficulty in reaching him with more than a few ships at a time. Here Arnold anchored, set out guardboats and waited, enlivening his vigil by pressing his quarrel with William Gilliland and eventually sending him to Ticonderoga, under arrest, by the schooner *Liberty* that went up the lake for supplies.

Nights grew colder and each day trees on either shore dyed the channel's quiet water a fiercer hue. The galleys *Trumbull, Washington* and *Congress* arrived, last reinforcement to reach Arnold. *Washington* brought Brigadier General David Waterbury of Connecticut to be the fleet's second in command. Arnold, for some obscure reason, shifted his flag from *Royal Savage* to *Congress* when at eight on the morning of October 11 a guard boat fired a gun and came scuttling back to shelter. Carleton's fleet at last was in sight.

Even though the season was perilously late, Canada's governor had continued to procrastinate. He had left St. Johns on October 4, had tarried at Point au Fer to re-establish a garrison in "The White House" there and now, a week later, bore up the dark lake with a stiff north breeze behind him.

The swift schooner *Maria* led. Aboard her were Carleton and Captain Thomas Pringle, into whose clumsy hands the governor had placed direction of naval operations. She bore, full sail, past Valcour Island, though all Canada must have been aware by now where the American fleet lay. Behind her, the rest of the squadron followed haphazardly.

Foam rolled beneath the prows of the ship-rigged *Inflexible* and the schooner *Carleton* and burst against the blunter bows of the floating battery *Thunderer* and the gondola *Loyal Convert*. Sunlight flashed from the laboring sweeps of twenty gunboats and dwelt upon the single brass cannon each bore. Four longboats labored, the fieldpieces in their bows curtseying as they pitched. Indian canoes darted in and out among the larger craft. With gleaming sails and white water, the British fleet ran down the outside shore of Valcour Island, as an opening ineptitude, then tried to claw back into the teeth of the wind to get at Arnold.

The American commander had ample time to array his squadron for action and to rouse in the hearts of his men the battle glee he always was able to kindle. They had need of headlong valor. They were outgunned, outweighed, outnumbered—700 British soldiers and sailors against 500 men of varying ability. It was four hours after the British fleet was sighted before the conflict was joined.

Pringle's clumsy handling of his fleet stirred alarm and then contempt in some of his officers. He backed and filled in a go-as-you-please fashion and in consequence his oar-propelled gunboats came into range before his heavier elements. Meanwhile, Indians who had swarmed ashore on the island began a whooping and a long-distance musketry fire equally harmless.

The gunboats, each carrying a heavy bow cannon and a score of soldiers and sailors under a subaltern of the British or the Hesse-Hanau artillery, moved in and spread across the south entrance to the roadstead. Theirs was to be the battle, with sporadic intrusion by wind-buffeted larger craft.

There was confusion when the British *Carleton,* either by design or by the thrust of a sudden gust, ran in through the gunboats' line and dropped anchor before the American fleet that lay in a crescent, facing south. Gondolas and *Royal Savage* advanced to engage the enemy at close range.

Iron poured into *Carleton* and splinters flew. Her captain, Lieutenant Dacres, and his second in command were wounded but her youngest officer, Edward Pellew who was to become Admiral Lord Exmouth, got his battered craft clear, and boats from *Inflexible* towed her out of range. *Royal Savage* attempted to work back upwind but bad seamanship delayed her and, while she hung, *Inflexible* got close enough to throw a broadside into her. Her green crew immediately rammed her into the south tip of Valcour Island and began to drop ashore.

If the general British attack was dilatory, individuals were alert. Lieutenant Edward Longcraft laid *Loyal Convert,* gondola, alongside *Royal Savage* and led a boarding party over her side. They captured some members of the schooner's crew who had been tardy in leaving, and Longcraft held the craft for a space, firing into Arnold's fleet with its late member's guns and signaling frantically for Pringle to come up and draw off the prize. The British commander seemed blind, and Longcraft, when half his boarding party had fallen, was compelled to abandon his capture. Later, Indians plundered *Royal Savage* and set fire to her.

The conflict had settled into an obstinate, hammer-and-tongs contest between Arnold's fleet and the gunboats. While the rest of Pringle's ships hung in the offing, the steady battering continued. Shot after shot crashed into the American craft from well-served British pieces. The gunboats, anchored in line, reared back upon their cables at each explosion. Smoke from their own and the American fire blew over them, and as the crisp ripples roused by the muzzle blasts faded, spongers, loaders and rammers leaped upon their pieces, showered by spray and rocked by close misses from the American line.

All afternoon, the uneven thunder rolled across the lake to the eastern hills while smoke blew southward as though Valcour Island was ablaze. At five o'clock the fight ceased abruptly. The gunboats, having spent their ammunition, drew off to where the rest of Pringle's force lingered, largely as spectators. The craft that had seen action that day, Lieutenant James M. Hadden, of the Royal Artillery and commander of one of the gunboats, noted in his journal, were "little more than ⅓ of the British Fleet."[4]

They had acquitted themselves well. Arnold had only begun to count the damage to his splintered and listing ships when he saw the gondola *Philadelphia* lurch and go under. No American boat had escaped damage. Two other gondolas were swamped and broken. The galley *Washington* could barely keep afloat and General Waterbury was her only surviving officer. *Congress,* Arnold's flagship, had been hulled again and again. There were a dozen holes at the waterline, and her mainmast had been wounded.

Sixty men had been killed or injured, and three-fourths of the American ammunition had been spent, to small effect. Though the anchored gunboats had been stationary targets, Arnold's hobble-dehoys in five hours' shooting had succeeded in sinking only two and blowing up a third. Carleton reported his loss as eight killed and six wounded, which must have been an underestimate.

As darkness came down, the stranded *Royal Savage* was set afire. While the schooner blazed and steamed, Arnold summoned his captains to his flagship. All of them had variations of his own grievous tale—smashed and leaking craft, dismounted guns, scant remaining powder and ball. Their chief's flawless courage which saved his fleet that night was assisted considerably by Captain Pringle's remarkable arrangement of his own ships.

The British naval commander did not closely guard the entrances to the little sound where Arnold lay. He drew off to the south and anchored with one end of his line a mile from the west shore and the other beyond Garden Island, southeast of Valcour. The American commander was unlikely to overlook so Pringle-sent an opportunity, and the north wind still blew.

The galley *Trumbull* led the way, hugging the deeper gloom of the western shore, and the rest of the crippled craft, lightless save for a hooded lantern in each stern, followed. Arnold in *Congress* brought up the rear. When Pringle roused on the morning of the twelfth to destroy the remnants of the Yankee fleet, only empty water shone in the roadstead and on the lake there were no traces of the enemy.

The British did not pursue at once. They dallied twenty-four hours. It may have been Pringle's inertia which granted the Americans this respite; it may have been Carleton's insistence upon his own earlier strategy which had allowed the ruined American army to escape from Canada. His campaign that fall is replete with oddities that are inconsistent with vigorous warfare.

If he had been hard pressed on October 12, Arnold must have been overtaken and captured or abolished. His damaged fleet had crept only eight miles up Champlain and now, in the lee of the wooded Schuyler Island, spent men were working desperately to patch whatever craft still had a likelihood of remaining afloat.

Two of the gondolas were beyond salvage. Arnold sank them and late on the afternoon of the twelfth resumed his retreat but the favoring blast from the north failed. By morning a breeze was rising from the south, while farther down the lake where Pringle stood out from Valcour, a north wind still blew. There is a Champlain legend that the tricky morning light gave a rock off Providence Island the look of a hostile ship and that the British bombarded it heavily before they saw their mistake. That outcropping still bears the derisive label, "Carleton's Prize."

The pursuing fleet had come close enough to see the flash of oars plied by Arnold's weary men before the north wind expired, and the British were forced to tack in the making head breeze. Sound ships and rested men were advantages that Pringle's variety of seamanship could not nullify and he gained on his quarry.

The wounded galley *Washington* came first within range. After a few minutes battering by *Inflexible* and *Maria,* General Waterbury struck his colors. The gondola *New Jersey* likewise was overhauled and taken. Water began to leap about the cutter

Lee, Arnold's *Congress* and the four gondolas that labored in the rear of the flight.

Fifteen miles from Valcour, where Split Rock and Thompson's Point pinch the lake into less than a mile's width, *Lee* had had enough. The men at her sweeps headed her for the west shore, beached her and fled. Arnold's dwindling fleet forced its way through the narrows' rough water to the wider breadth of the lake beyond.

The chase was stretching out now, with the fleetest craft in the fore. *Congress* and four rickety gondolas still clung together in the rear, while about the laboring flagship spray spouted and shot went home. *Congress,* struck again and again by *Inflexible, Maria* and *Carleton,* which were coming up fast, at last turned shoreward.

To the east, beyond Button Island, lay a cove, three-fourths enclosed by land. Arnold headed for it, and the four faithful gondolas followed over the shot-tumbled water. The five craft were beached and set afire in what is now called "Arnold's Bay" before the British came up. Arnold led the surviving members of the crews, most of whom had had little rest and less sleep for three days, through the wooded lowlands to Chimney Point. Thence they were ferried across the narrows to the equivocal safety of Crown Point, where the surviving vessels of the fleet were being laden for further retirement up the lake to Ticonderoga. Arnold had had sixteen craft at the beginning of the Valcour fight. There now remained two galleys, two schooners, one gondola and the sloop *Liberty* which had not been in the action.

The British might have trapped this remnant of the American Navy, but again the knockout blow was withheld. Fugitive craft and fleeing men were permitted ample opportunity to escape.

Carleton sent rangers and Indians ashore at Crown Point, October 14, shortly after the last American had left. He tarried there for a full month and, with his navy controlling the lake and a powerful professional army behind him, did precisely nothing, beyond a belated and feeble attempt to feel out Ticonderoga's defenses.

The invasion that all America dreaded sputtered out like a wet fuse. No sure explanation can be offered for this anticlimax unless it can be found in the character of Carleton himself. The governor still was the philosopher-general, with his theory which held that kindliness would succeed where military vigor might fail.

The prisoners the British had taken were treated, from General Waterbury down, like honored guests. Carleton spent on them much graciousness and generosity, praising their bravery, tending the wounded, plying the whole with food and liquor and high expressions of admiration. After receiving their paroles, he sent them all on to Ticonderoga under the escort of Captain James Craig.

At that fort, where 9,000 Continental troops and militia waited for the blow to fall, Carleton's theory was half justified. The released prisoners were so loud in approval of the British general that Gates, fearing their hallelujahs would sap the garrison's morale, shipped them hastily onward to Skenesborough.

A strong south wind that snored down the lake for a full week may have been responsible in part for the British delay but when they did advance it was only to probe and tap at the outer fortifications. While his ships lay well out of range of the fort cannon, Carleton on October 27 landed rangers, Indians and light infantry. They scouted ineffectually about the defenses and, re-embarking, fell back again to Crown Point.

The British fleet's only other offensive activity during the 1776 campaign added another name to the map of the Champlain area. Tidings came to the thirsty invaders that settlers in the present town of Essex possessed a large store of rum. Legend recites that when a confiscating force approached, the patriots poured all their liquor into the lake at a spot still known as "Grog Harbor."

In mid-November, Carleton and his ships and whatever troops he had brought up to Crown Point abandoned the campaign and retired into Canada. Lieutenant Hadden of the Royal Artillery entered in his journal:

"It appearing too late in the Season for an attack on Tyconderoga 16 miles from hence where report said the Enemy had from 12 to 16000 men, Gen'l Carleton order'd Fascines to be made (4000) for the repair of the old Fort and prepar'd to put the barracks in order. Gen'l Carleton reconnoiter'd the Enemy Works from the Water and the Boats went near enough to be fired at. Altering his determination about repairing the Works etc at Crown Point, the stores were sent back and the whole armament return'd abt the 13th, 14th or 15th Nov, '76, With so favourable a wind that the Radeau"—the floating battery—"a square-built vessel sailed from Crown Point to Isle aux Noix (90 miles) in 9 hours."[5]

The Northern Campaign of 1776 was a moderate success for American arms, thanks not only to the fighting qualities of Benedict Arnold but also to the placating tactics of Sir Guy Carleton. Admiral A. T. Mahan has written:

"That the Americans were strong enough to impose the capitulation of Saratoga was due to the invaluable year secured to them in 1776 by their little navy on Lake Champlain, created by the indomitable energy and handled with the indomitable courage of the traitor, Benedict Arnold."[6]

Others, historians and romance writers alike, have embroidered that theme. In a sentimental effort to give a scoundrel just praise, they have accorded Arnold too much. The Americans' quasi victory was more due to Pringle's blundering and to Carleton's monumental deliberation and his determination to temper warfare with mercy, than to the courage and energy, however high, of Benedict Arnold.

It was the American fleet in being, not in action, that materially delayed the advance from Canada. Its presence on Champlain compelled the British to build ships to meet it. When battle was joined, Arnold's craft were defeated in half a day. His fleet was destroyed in another day of flight. If the British squadron had not been handled with a clumsiness that several of Pringle's officers considered poltroonery's first cousin, the American navy would have been abolished or captured at Valcour Island.

The British, with only a fraction of their fleet brought into action, emphatically beat Arnold on October 11. Pringle could have done more. Three of his chief officers expressed the belief that he could hardly have done less.

Lieutenant John Starke, commanding *Maria,* Lieutenant Edward Longcraft, commanding *Loyal Convert,* and Lieutenant John Schank, commanding *Inflexible,* read the self-congratulatory report their superior sent to the British Admiralty and forthwith prepared an open letter to their commander. Its tone is set by its first paragraph wherein Pringle's three subordinates charge "that in preparing and fitting out the fleet and also in operation afterward, no officer or other person employed therein had so small a share as yourself."

With waxing vehemence the trio then accuse Pringle of making no plan for the attack upon Arnold, of giving no orders when battle had been joined and of permitting the Americans to escape by an idiotic arrangement of his ships on the night after the Valcour fight. The letter also accuses the British commander of cowardice in conducting the pursuit of October 13 and finally berates him for omitting from his report any mention of "the officers of the Artillery who commanded the Gunboats, that did more service in the first day's action than all the rest of the fleet."[7]

No similar attack was launched against Sir Guy Carleton, but his conduct of the campaign from early summer when, with reinforcements sent from overseas, he began to press the invaders out of Canada, is equally vulnerable. It may have been his theory that prevented him from employing effectively the splendid army his king had sent him to use in bursting the northern gateway to the rebellious provinces. There is scant evidence that, in the year 1776, he intended to wield it for that purpose.

Carleton had a professional, highly trained military machine, the British 9th, 20th, 21st, 24th, 29th, 31st, 34th, 47th, 53rd and 62nd Regiments of Foot, a battalion of Royal Highland Immigrants and four companies of Royal Artillery. His British troops numbered, according to the July 1, 1776, return, more than 6,000 men fit for duty. Generals of proved ability were among the governor general's subordinates—John Burgoyne, Simon Fraser and the artillerist, William Phillips.

The first division of German mercenaries, by Carleton's return of July 1, consisted of a dragoon regiment and the Prinz Friedrich,

Riedesel and Grenadier Regiments of Foot and the Hesse-Hanau Regiment of Artillery, totaling 2,800 more. The second German division which arrived in Canada September 15 was composed of the Rhetz and Specht Regiments and a battalion of the Barner Regiment, a total of 1,500. Indians and Canadian militia swelled the governor general's command to at least 12,000 men. There is no indication that he attempted to bring even a majority into action.

Carleton's own returns show that on October 19 while he himself was at Crown Point, the second German division still was at Chambly. He must have ordered not more than a small fraction of his available force up the lake, for on October 30 Schuyler wrote to Robert Gates that Colonel Ogden "brings Intelligence that there are not above two hundred Tents at Crown Point. General Carleton has consequently only part of his army there."

That part could not have numbered much more than one-eighth of his force.

Ill-considered praise has been spent on Benedict Arnold. British procrastination and reluctance to force a decisive battle were the prime reasons why Ticonderoga remained in American hands for another eight months.

---

1 Walter Hill Crockett, *History of Vermont* (Burlington, 1938), II, 8.
2 Schuyler Papers, No. 48, New York Public Library.
3 Jared Sparks (ed.) *Correspondence of the American Revolution* (Boston, 1853), II, 345.
4 Lt. James M. Hadden, *Journal and Orderly Books, A Journal Kept in Canada and Upon Burgoyne's Campaign in 1776 and 1777* (Albany, 1884), p. 18.
5 *Ibid.*, 13.
6 A. T. Mahan, "The Naval Campaign of 1776 on Lake Champlain," in *Scribners Magazine*, Feb., 1898.
7 Manuscript in Fort Ticonderoga Museum Library.

Chapter 16

Burgoyne Invades

Young ice glazed the shallows of upper Champlain when Gates discharged ten militia regiments of the Fort Ticonderoga garrison and moved out with eleven more of the line to join the battered Continental Army in New Jersey. The general himself did not tarry with Washington, though the attack on Trenton was in preparation. Turning his back on warfare, he hurried on to Baltimore.

A timorous Congress had fled thither, and Gates undertook for the winter the job of convincing the honorable gentlemen that he should supersede Schuyler in command of the Northern Department. Horatio Gates was always a better lobbyist than field commander.

At Ticonderoga, six undermanned regiments that had been left in garrison under Colonel Anthony Wayne suffered or died in the arctic cold of an unprecedentedly cruel winter. Colonel Joseph Wood, of the Pennsylvania troops, wrote to Thomas Wharton, Jr., president of the Committee of Safety in Philadelphia, December 4:

"One third at least of the poor wretches is now barefoot and in this condition obliged to do duty. This is shocking to humanity. It cannot be viewed in any milder light than black murder. The poor creatures is now (what's left alive) laying on cold ground, in poor thin tents and some none at all and many down with pleurisy. No barracks, no hospitals to go in. The barracks is at Saratoga. If you was here your heart would melt. I paid a visit to the sick yesterday in a small house called a hospital. The first object presented my eyes, one man laying dead at the door, the inside two more laying dead, two living lying between them the living with the dead has so laid for four and twenty hours."[1]

Snow, ice and cold afflicted also the dwellers in the little farm-

204

houses and rough cabins of the Green Mountain region, yet the brutal season did not abate the immaterial fire the "four leading men of the Grants" cautiously had lighted a year earlier.

None lay so deeply in the shadow of invasion as the Grants people. This was a time when politic men should be thinking most earnestly of their personal safety and how to achieve it; this was a crisis in which the timid would cling to the more powerful state of New York that still claimed the Grants territory.

On January 15, 1777, delegates met in convention at the village of Westminster and chose this moment of extreme peril to divorce their land from New York and to proclaim that:

"The New Hampshire Grants of right ought to be and hereby is declared forever and hereafter to be considered a separate, free and independent jurisdiction or state: by the name and to be forever hereafter called and known and distinguished by the name of New Connecticut."[2]

Later, the new state was rechristened "Vermont," a name having no grammatical justification in any language.

There could not have been a time apparently less opportune for this independent gesture. Vermont's early leaders were sublimely audacious, dismayingly canny or incredibly lucky—perhaps all three. For the moment, scant notice was taken of their declaration. New York was too occupied with the approaching invasion to pay the insurgents adequate heed.

At Ticonderoga, the task of holding together the bodies and souls of his command, as well as the travail of maintaining discipline among troops who were never too wretched to start intercolonial rows, was wearing down Wayne mentally and physically.

He might have worried less if he had known that Carleton's army had gone into winter quarters and that the governor-general himself had been retired from the field. On August 22 orders were sent by the king through the Colonial Secretary, Lord George Germain—a scaly person who after being thrown out of the army for cowardice had prospered as a bureaucrat—bidding Carleton return to Quebec as soon as he had driven the invaders from Canadian soil.

The governor general was further instructed to exercise his considerable talents for appeasement upon the habitants, whose esteem for British rule was only a little higher than the Americans'. He also was directed to detach "Lieutenant General Burgoyne or such other officer as you shall think most proper with that part of your forces which can be spared from the immediate defense of your province to carry on such operations as shall be most conductive to the success of the army acting on the side of New York."[3]

Carleton thus was removed from command of the still projected invasion, though he had the privilege of choosing his successor. Lieutenant General Burgoyne, to make certain that he himself got the post, journeyed that winter back to London and there "humbly laid myself at His Majesty's feet for such active employment as he might think me worthy of."[4] He was appointed.

Gentleman Johnny Burgoyne was a many-faceted, gaudy personage—soldier, poet, playwright and member of Parliament; and never quite first-rate in any of the roles. A better man might have been chosen to play his part in the impending campaign that was designed to split the young nation in twain—and probably would have failed as completely.

The planners of the 1777 offensive were influenced more by British reverence for precedent than common sense. The French armies had always advanced up Champlain and so would the present holders of Canada. Vaudreuil in 1758 had designed a diversionary thrust via Oswego and the Mohawk Valley. Now, Colonel Barry St. Leger, with 1,700 regulars, Tories and Indians, was ordered to make an exactly similar attack.

The campaign's one original concept was the expectation that General William Howe would move up the Hudson from New York and, meeting Burgoyne and St. Leger marching downstream, break the rebellion's back. It was a complex plan and it offered the alert and resolute defenders prime opportunity for smashing it in detail.

Spring brought the complacent Burgoyne back to Canada. There, with Carleton's magnanimous co-operation, he prepared for a campaign in which, following his initial victory, he did everything the wrong way. Meanwhile, internal strife was weakening the lakes' defenses.

Gates had resumed his post at Ticonderoga. The general wore a smugly confident air while he waited for his winter's labors to bear fruit. When Congress, by a one-vote margin, reconfirmed Schuyler as commander of the Northern Department, Gates lost his temper, resigned and scuttled back to Philadelphia to resume his lobbying. Brigadier General Arthur St. Clair, an experienced soldier against whom the Fates bore a chronic grudge, succeeded him.

St. Clair inherited works which Gates had spread so far on either shore of the lake that at least 10,000 men were required to defend them. Ticonderoga had an indifferent garrison of 2,800, and at Champlain's lower end, Burgoyne was marshaling 7,200 crack troops.

There were 250 Canadians and Tories in Gentleman Johnny's army and some 400 Indians. The rest were acclimated, professional soldiers with an immense train and more than the normal complement of cannon. Carleton had turned over to Burgoyne almost all the German mercenaries and seven of the ten British regiments in the province. Each of the three the governor-general maintained to keep order in Canada had been divested of its grenadier company and its light infantry company. These were composed of the strongest, most active men and were assigned to the expedition.

It was a polished and powerful machine that began to move southward in early June and the men who guided it were accomplished veterans. Even the junior officers were of more than ordinary ability. Thirty-five of them were to become British generals. The spent and prostrate New York frontier had little with which to oppose invasion save Fort Ticonderoga and its undersize garrison. St. Clair dared not summon the militia until the actual attack was ready to break upon him. He had not enough provisions to feed them.

Ticonderoga's commander would not have long to wait. None of Carleton's deliberation of the previous year marred Burgoyne's preparations. Bands brayed and men cheered at St. Johns in early June as, brigade by brigade, the troops embarked.

Organization had been thorough. Brigadier General Simon Fraser commanded the British Advanced Corps comprising the 24th Foot and the grenadier and light infantry companies of the ten redcoat regiments in Canada. Brigadier General Henry Watson Powell, commanding the First Brigade, had under him the 9th, 47th and 53rd Foot. Brigadier General James Hamilton's Second Brigade included the 20th, 21st and 62nd Foot.

Fat General Friedrich Adolph Baron Riedesel commanded the mercenary troops. Colonel Heinrich Breymann led the German Advanced Corps of grenadiers, light infantry and a company of jägers with their short, heavy rifles. Colonel Johann Friedrich Specht commanded the Riedesel, Specht and Rhetz Regiments of the First Brigade; Colonel W. R. von Gall, the Prinz Friedrich and Hesse-Hanau Regiments of the Second. A dismounted squadron of the Riedesel Dragoons served as headquarters guard.

A Royal Artillery battalion and a company of Hesse-Hanau Artillery sweated the 142 cannon of the expedition aboard the barges. With the new, ship-rigged *Royal George,* 26 guns, and the veteran *Inflexible* in the lead, the army moved up the Richelieu toward Champlain, which glittered in the inconstant sunlight of this storm-troubled June.

Other craft that had swept the lake in 1776—*Maria, Carleton, Thunderer*—and the captured vessels of Arnold's fleet—*Washington, Lee, New Jersey*—wallowed along in the armada. Their guns had been removed that they might be more deeply laden with material. No ships had been built by the Americans to replace their smashed navy. There would have been no crews to man them, if they had been constructed. Commodore Lutwidge, on *Royal George,* commanded the flotilla.

By June 21, the expedition had paused at the mouth of the Boquet River and here Burgoyne addressed his Indian allies. Despite their debatable worth to earlier armies, he had enlisted them and already was beginning to regret it.

"I heard Gen'l Burgoyne declare," Lieutenant Hadden entered

in his diary, "that a Thousand Savages brought into the Field cost more than 20,000 men."[5]

Qualms, which he might have done well to heed more thoroughly, apparently were beginning to afflict Gentleman Johnny. He sought to wean his red allies away from their unhampered system of warfare by an oration in which he conceded that the Indians might continue to take the scalps of the dead but warned that "on no account or pretense or subtlety or prevarication are they to be taken from the wounded or even dying and still less pardonable if possible will it be held to kill men in that condition."[6]

The Indians promised with solemnity that all these strictures would be observed. On June 27, when he occupied Crown Point, Burgoyne composed a proclamation to the residents of the territory he was about to invade. It was couched in his best style, which was very bad indeed, and promised welcome to Tories, protection to neutrals and hard cash for provisions. He then warned:

"I have but to give stretch to the Indian forces under my direction and they amount to Thousands"—a monumental exaggeration—"to overtake the hardened Enemies of Great Britain and America (I consider them the same) wherever they may lurk. If notwithstanding these endeavors and sincere inclinations to effect them, the phrenzy of hostility should remain, I trust I shall stand acquitted in the Eyes of God & Men in denouncing and executing the vengeance of the state against the wilful outcasts."[7]

The general, having ordered this threat to be broadcast, gathered up his army, his mistress and his traveling wine cellar and got on with the war.

St. Clair, perforce belatedly, was calling for the militia, though on what he intended to feed them during a possible long siege remains obscure. Nine hundred men reached him, but their worth as reinforcements was offset by the fact that two Massachusetts regiments of the garrison, whose time of service expired in a few days, had announced their determination to go home. Burgoyne arrived in time to keep them at their posts.

He came up against the fort by land and water, with the British Advanced Corps marching along Champlain's west shore and the German along the east. As he closed in on July 2, the guns of Mount Independence, where Roche de Fermoy, a French soldier of fortune commanded, halted the German advance and kept clear the road that ran eastward from the hill's base to Hubbardton and Castleton in "New Connecticut." The British on the west shore pressed ahead and toward evening elements led by the artillerist, General Phillips, got up Mount Hope which overlooked the Lake George outlet and held it, despite bombardment by St. Clair.

Phillips, conceivably, was not disturbed by the cannon fire, or distracted by the blaze in the valley where St. Clair's troops were burning the outlet blockhouses before quitting a now untenable position. Quite possibly he was staring at the bulk of Sugar Loaf Mountain, tall and black against the pale evening sky, while he considered problems in ballistics.

St. Clair's guns continued to rage on the morrow, harmlessly throwing shot at the east shore German camp and upon Mount Hope. From this height as a center, British and German troops spread left and right to cut off Ticonderoga's peninsula from the mainland. Burgoyne still dwelt on *Royal George,* which lay with *Inflexible* just beyond the fort's range, and this day Phillips was rowed out to the flagship for a conference with his commander, in which Sugar Loaf Mountain frequently was mentioned.

Next morning, July 4, *Thunderer,* the floating battery, was warped up from Crown Point and artillery was trundled ashore. The following day, the British with no more vital expenditure than sweat took the key to Ticonderoga. They occupied the commanding height to which Gates, and Schuyler as well, had remained obstinately blind.

Lieutenant Twiss, chief of Burgoyne's engineers, clambered to the peak of the rugged hill, which the British renamed Mount Defiance, and found there would be no great difficulty in hauling guns thither. Phillips at once began to clear the summit for a battery of medium 12-pounders, light 24's and 8-inch howitzers.

Artillerymen started to manhandle guns up the slope and by afternoon two 12's were in position.

St. Clair, observing their brazen shine through a field glass, knew that Fort Ticonderoga was doomed. He must move swiftly or the bulk of the Northern Army would be lost. The council of war that he called decided to abandon the stronghold that night, while the guns on Mount Independence still kept open the long thin arm of upper Champlain and the road that ran east toward Castleton.

St. Clair resolved to lead the major part of his garrison overland to Schuyler. Noncombatants, women and the ailing, with 500 escorting troops under Colonel Long of New Hampshire, were loaded aboard bateaux in the darkness and rowed up narrow Champlain. Five galleys, all that remained of the American fleet, convoyed them. St. Clair sank the surviving schooner, *Royal Savage,* off Ticonderoga.

Only an able general could have extricated his otherwise doomed command so swiftly and deftly. A less resolute leader than St. Clair must have collapsed under the disobedience, blunders and downright idiocies that swarmed down to afflict his retreat.

The British slept soundly. The garrison of Fort Ticonderoga was across the bridge and on the Castleton road, with the troops that had held Mount Independence treading on their heels, before the alarm was raised and then it was supplied by one of their own people.

Roche de Fermoy, commanding at Mount Independence, conceived it a part of stealth to set fire to his quarters when he left. The flames revealed the retreating column to the British. By the time they had died down, Fraser with 750 grenadiers and light infantry from the west shore, Riedesel and 1,100 Germans from the east, had taken up the pursuit.

Misfortune dogged St. Clair. He had opened powder kegs and laid a train to blow up the main fort but whomever he had entrusted with the match failed him. He had placed cannon at the east end of the bridge to fire into the British advance. Four men whom he had detailed to the forlorn hope enlivened their vigil by emptying a keg of Madeira and were found by Fraser's men, drunk beside the loaded guns.

Nevertheless, St. Clair pushed his retreat so vigorously that he outmarched the British Army's best troops throughout the sultry day and brought the major part of his force into Castleton that night. His success was offset by the fate of the flotilla he had dispatched up the lake.

The log and chain boom, which Gates had believed would hold back British craft indefinitely, was cut by Burgoyne's sappers in half an hour. *Royal George,* with the general aboard and *Inflexible* following, passed through the opening and pursued the American craft, full sail. Gunboats carrying the 9th, 20th and 21st Foot trailed behind them.

The retreating flotilla, joyous in its deliverance, reached Skenesborough at 3:00 P.M. At 5:00 *Royal George* and *Inflexible* were upon them. The gunboats closed with the galleys, capturing two and driving three ashore, and then landed their troops. Colonel Long and his men fired the town and the stockade that overlooked it from the hill before they fell back to Fort Ann. Burgoyne left the 62nd Foot and the Prinz Friedrich Regiment under Brigadier General Powell to garrison Ticonderoga and brought the rest of his available force up to Skenesborough.

On the morrow, the invaders won another minor victory. St. Clair's main body had bivouacked at Castleton but his rear guard, composed of Warner's Vermont Regiment, the 11th Massachusetts Line under Colonel Francis and the 2nd New Hampshire Line under Colonel Hale, had chosen to disobey their general's express orders. They lagged and camped in what is now the town of Hubbardton. There, at daybreak of July 7, Fraser surprised them.

Hale and the New Hampshire men ran at the first volley but Warner's and Francis' commands resisted stubbornly until Riedesel joined the fight. Some of the Americans, including Warner, escaped. Francis was among the killed. Many were taken prisoner, but the British and Germans abandoned their pursuit of St. Clair who joined Schuyler near Fort Edward on July 12.

One by one the defenses of the frontier were being broken in. On July 8, the British Colonel Hill who with only 120 men had been ordered by Burgoyne to follow Long's retreat from Skenesborough caught up with the fugitives at Fort Ann. Long had been reinforced by militia under General Henry Van Rennselaer, but when, after some skirmishing, the British raised the Indian war whoop, the Americans retreated to the fort and, after setting it ablaze, ran still farther.

On July 16, General Phillips, who had been detailed to bear the army's heavy equipment up Lake George, approached the lake-head blockhouse by water. The small garrison hurried away after burning or sinking what it could not transport. Tidings of this withdrawal inspired Major Yates, commanding at Fort Edward, to set his post afire and retreat with 700 men.

The apparent collapse of American resistance woke panicky howlings throughout the colonies, particularly in New England where Schuyler, the aristocrat, never had been popular. Congress, too, grew hysterical and Gates doubled his industrious boring from within. Schuyler, a patient man who was doing his admirable best, was stung by waxing, undeserved criticism and wrote to Washington, July 26:

"I find by letters from below that an Idea prevails that Fort Edward is also a strong and regular Fortification. It was once a regular Fortification but there is Nothing but the ruins of it left and they are so totally defenseless that I have frequently galloped my Horse in on one side and out of the other."[8]

Still the denunciatory clamor mounted and Gates intrigued more fervently and, mile by mile, with immense effort, Burgoyne advanced his army. He had elected to move toward the Hudson from Skenesborough via Wood Creek, though Lake George obviously was the easier way.

Legend says that the British general was persuaded to take the Wood Creek route by Philip Skene who felt that the value of his property would be enhanced if the army were to build a military road across it to Fort Edward. Burgoyne defended his selection by alleging that the morale of his troops would have been harmed if they had retired from Skenesborough to Ticonderoga to begin another advance by way of George.

American hopes were at their lowest now but Burgoyne had committed the first of a series of mistakes that would destroy him. Wood Creek normally was a muddy stream, twisting through swamps. In the rainy summer of 1777, these marshes had widened and deepened, making progress additionally difficult. Schuyler's axmen slowed the British advance still further by felling trees into an egregious tangle.

It took the invasion more than three weeks to crawl through this semiliquid region to solid ground beyond. Forty bridges, one a mile long, were built over the winding creek and its attendant sloughs. Skene's property would have been improved indeed had he been able to hold it.

Schuyler's "retreating, raged, lousey, thievish, pockey army"[9] retired only a little more rapidly than the floundering British advanced. Their commander was fighting for time. General Benjamin Lincoln, who was popular in New England, had been sent into New Connecticut to organize there an attack upon Burgoyne's overextended supply line.

When the British reached Fort Edward, July 30, Schuyler, who continued to be hampered by the slowness with which the militia were rallying, fell back to Stillwater. This sound strategy increased the outcry against him. On August 19, Gates appeared in Albany with his long-wheedled authority from Congress to take command of the Northern Army.

Burgoyne's troops, now standing at the Hudson, had accomplished more than any invasion that had preceded or was to follow theirs. They had won both lakes and had reached the direct water route to Albany and Troy. They had performed most of the task assigned them in a campaign which, still imperceptibly, was beginning to collapse.

St. Leger's invasion via the Mohawk Valley had bogged down before Fort Stanwix. Howe's co-operative thrust up the Hudson never was undertaken at all. The featherbrained general was familiar with the plan of campaign and the part he was expected to play therein, but he seems, after Ticonderoga's swift fall, to have believed that Burgoyne could take care of himself. Orders definitely commanding Howe to advance to his associate's relief were mislaid in Germain's office and never sent.

When, on August 3, a spy brought Burgoyne a letter in which Howe lightheartedly wished him luck and announced that he was moving against Philadelphia, the army at Fort Edward was placed in great, if not immediately apparent, peril. Whether Burgoyne saw the danger or not, his orders were positive and bade him advance.

He obeyed them with more devotion than intelligence. The disasters that had begun to smite him should have warned a more stupid commander. On August 17 barely 400 returned of the 1,400 raiders he had sent against the American supply depot at Bennington. On August 22 St. Leger abandoned the siege of Stanwix and retreated. Burgoyne's Indians, sensitive to impending disaster, began to desert wholesale. The rest of the doomed army, which now numbered little more than 4,000 men, gathered itself and pressed forward.

On September 13 it crossed to the west bank of the Hudson. On that same day a movement was begun against Burgoyne's supply line which, if it had been more heavily mounted and more energetically led, might have destroyed him and his command at once.

At Pawlet in the Grants, Lincoln had collected 2,500 local and Massachusetts militia. Now he ordered 1,500 of these toward Lake Champlain to break British communications by seizing Skenesborough and Ticonderoga. Colonel John Brown, who had proposed early in 1775 that Ethan Allen's men be sent against the fort, was ordered to attack it now with his 500. Colonel Johnson of Massachusetts with another 500 was to assail Mount Independence while the remaining men under Colonel Woodbridge, also of Massachusetts, were to capture Skenesborough.

The triple expedition set out on the thirteenth. Johnson backtracked over the Castleton-Hubbardton route of St. Clair's retreat while Brown marched his force across country to the Narrows of the riverlike upper lake. He crossed there and advanced along a rough trail on the west shore toward Mount Defiance. His troops were eager. Their colonel had promised them, if they took Ticonderoga, unlimited looting.

On September 17, the day Brown's men reached the vicinity of the fort, Woodbridge's command took Skenesborough without a fight, and Lincoln moved with his remaining 1,000 men from Pawlet to reinforce him, lest Burgoyne strike back. By now, however, the British had abandoned the toilsomely cleared Wood Creek route in favor of the more direct way up Lake George, and Lincoln, after finding there would be no reaction, led his men, not toward Ticonderoga, but back to Pawlet.

At the fort, General Powell, the garrison's commander, was so intent on getting supplies for Burgoyne across the portage and so scornful of American arms, that he had spent no time on even the most elementary precautions. Brown's 500 lay for most of the seventeenth within eye and earshot of Ticonderoga but the British remained unaware of their presence until, before daybreak of the eighteenth, they struck.

Ebenezer Allen, a captain in the Grants rangers and Ethan's salty cousin, led sixty men up Mount Defiance to seize the blockhouse on its crest where Lieutenant Lord of the 53rd Foot and a handful of men were quartered. A single brass 6-pounder on the height had been used as a sunrise and sunset gun. It went off betimes that morning as Allen's men rushed the blockhouses and captured its little garrison.

Before the untimely explosion notified Powell that something was wrong, Brown had led the rest of his followers against the Lake George landing. Here lay fifty bateaux, seventeen gunboats and a sloop armed with three 6-pounders. All these were taken, as well as the protecting blockhouses where Captain Davis of the 53rd, a lieutenant and twelve soldiers were captured after a five-minute fight in which both officers were wounded.

The east was paling as Brown's command, eager for more negotiable plunder, hurried down the outlet. At the sawmill, a larger British force was gathered in. They awoke to find themselves prisoners. The roar of the falls had obscured the sound of firing on the Lake George shore. A hundred and fifty more bateaux and two brass cannon were captured.

In the quickening light, the invaders hurried across the outlet bridge and moved uphill toward the old French lines. In a barn, guarded by another detail of the 53rd under Captain Baird, who was captured with all his men, 100 prisoners from the Hubbardton fight were discovered. They joined their deliverers and rushed on with them toward glory and plunder. At about this time, the signal gun on Mount Defiance boomed.

The highly affronted General Powell made no attempt to defend the French lines. He pulled his men back into the fort and expressed his indignation by firing his cannon at nothing in particular. Mount Independence, which was held by the Prinz Friedrich Regiment, caught the contagion and wrapped itself in gun smoke, while the schooners *Maria* and *Carleton,* anchored offshore, discharged their batteries.

The cannonade halted Brown at the French lines and wilted out of Johnson's men, who were approaching Mount Independence by the Hubbardton road, any original intention they may have had of assaulting the works.

Ticonderoga was thoroughly alerted now and Brown and Johnson had a bear by the tail. They had neither the guns nor the recklessness needed to carry works held by men their equal in number and heavily supplied by artillery. Brown, in addition, was hampered by the 304 prisoners his men had gathered.

The colonel attempted to bluff Powell by sending him, during a lull in the salvos, a letter proclaiming that the fort was surrounded by "the Mighty Army of the Continent"[10] and demanding immediate surrender.

Powell replied in the best British tradition: "The Garrison entrusted to my charge I shall defend to the last,"[11] and went back to his shooting.

Brown had taken the key to Ticonderoga but had not the strength to turn it. Though Mount Defiance was his, he had only a few light-weight captured guns and little powder to serve them. His men, who were becoming increasingly restless in the absence of the promised loot, did drag the two cannon taken at the sawmill up to the French lines and fired them a few times at the fort, but the results were imperceptible and the spirits of the troops sank lower.

Before Mount Independence, on the lake's farther shore, Johnson had been succeeded by Brigadier General Nathaniel Warner, Lincoln's second in command, who hopefully invited the Mount Independence garrison to surrender and got no other reply than further hysterical cannon-firing.

The profligate wastage of ammunition curdled further the bilious spirit of Lieutenant John Starke, R.N., commanding *Maria*. Stark, who already had collaborated in bitter comment on Pringle's conduct during the Valcour Island battle, seems to have been galled afresh by the report Powell sent to his superiors after the Americans had withdrawn. He wrote:

"The defense of Mt. Independence is mentioned in the same letter as a gallant and spirited service. It certainly was so if men are to judge from the quantity of ammunition fired; but it is an undeniable truth that the Mount was never attacked by the Rebels, otherwise than on Paper.

"The only living creatures (except the paper messengers) who approached it after September 18th, was a poor strayed Cow that in the night of the 21st, being a thick fog, caused a general Alarm and a most thundering cannonade from all quarters of the Mount and from the vessels ensued which continued almost without intermission till day light, when the lawless plunderer who had been so daring was taken prisoner and carried into the garrison in triumph."

Starke then waxes scornful over the cannonade ordered by Powell from the batteries and the schooners, each night, "as a preventative and to scour the Woods, if the Rebels should chance to be there. . . ."

He adds in his most unpleasant vein:

"It must have been a pure and noble Flame for military glory that burned so much powder and not the effect of f——r."[12]

Before Powell ran out of ammunition, the troops of Brown and

Warner withdrew, the latter retiring by way of Hubbardton, the former sending his prisoners off under guard and embarking his men on the captured sloop and some of the gunboats.

Brown, foiled in his attempt to break Burgoyne's life line at Ticonderoga, was determined to hack at it again. A British supply dump had been built on Diamond Island in Lake George. Captain Thomas Aubrey with a battery and two companies of the 47th Foot guarded it so vigilantly that when Brown's impromptu fleet advanced upon the island September 24, he was driven off by a strong and accurate fire.

The colonel crossed to the east shore of George, beached and burned his craft and led his men back overland to Skenesborough. He had lost less than a dozen killed and wounded, had captured more than 300 prisoners, had destroyed much shipping and had induced Powell to fire away, uselessly, many tons of His Majesty's powder and ball. If the colonel had been adequately supplied with artillery and ammunition, he might have taken Ticonderoga and starved Burgoyne's army to death a month before it was beaten in the field.

The end of the campaign that was to have torn the United States in two came October 17. After a series of battles that were like the frantic lungings of a trapped animal, Burgoyne, striving belatedly to retreat, surrendered when he found that Gates by spading up entrenchments at all the fords had closed the crossings of the Hudson and held him surrounded.

Powell, when the tidings reached him, recalled the troops from Lake George, burned the works on Mount Independence, tried with indifferent success to blow up Ticonderoga and, lacking boats, marched the remnant of the lately proud army back to Canada.

Captain Ebenezer Allen and fifty rangers followed at Powell's heels and near the mouth of the Boquet River got in among his rear guard to capture horses, cattle and other booty, fifty-nine men and Dinah Mattis, a Negro slave and her child. For her, Ebenezer penned a document:

"To Whom It May Concern Know Ye Whereas Dinah Mattis, a negro woman with Nancey her Child of two months old was taken prisoner on Lake Champlain, with the British Troops some-where near Col. Gilliner's Patten the Twelfth day of Instant November by a scout under my Command, and according to a Re-solve Past by the Honourable Continental Congress that all Prisses belong to the Captivators thereof—therefore She and her Child become the just Property of the Captivators thereof—I being Con-scihentious that it is not Right in the Sight of god to keep Slaves— I therefore obtaining leave of the Detachment under my Com-mand to give her and her Child their freedom I do therefore give the said Dinah mattis and Nancy her child their freedom to pass and Repass any where through the United States of America with her Behaving as becometh and to Trade and Traffick for her Self and Child as tho She was Born free without being Millested by any Person or Persons.

"In witness whereunto I have set my hand or subscribed by name.

"Ebenezer Allen, Capt."[13]

The Grants people's peculiar love of freedom was to bring about phenomena less orthodox than Captain Ebenezer's emancipation proclamation in the years immediately ahead.

---

1 *Fort Ticonderoga Museum Bulletin*, V, 37.
2 *Records of Governor and Council* (Montpelier, 1878), I, 41.
3 Lieutenant General John Burgoyne, *A State of the Expedition from Canada, as Laid before the House of Commons* (London, 1780), Appendix II.
4 *Ibid.*, Appendix I.
5 Lieutenant James M. Hadden, *A Journal Kept in Canada and Upon Burgoyne's Campaign* (Albany, 1887), p. 61.
6 Lieutenant General John Burgoyne, *State of the Expedition*, Appendix III.
7 *Ibid.*
8 Major General Philip Schuyler, Orderly Book, in New York Public Library.
9 *Revolutionary Journal of Colonel Jeduthen Baldwin 1775-1778* (Bangor, 1906), p. 80.
10 *Fort Ticonderoga Museum Bulletin*, II, 36.
11 *Ibid.*, 37.
12 Starke Manuscript, in Fort Ticonderoga Museum Library.
13 *Records of Governor and Council* (Montpelier, 1878), I, 93.

Chapter 17

Words Defend the Frontier

THE storm gathered slowly but the first small gusts revealed its course. In September 1777, before Burgoyne's host had surrendered at Saratoga, Indians out of Canada raided into Vermont. They came up Champlain by canoe and, landing, struck at the infant village of Pittsford, plundering and burning.

The wife of Felix Powell was alone in her cabin when whooping and a towering smoke warned her. She caught up her fourteen-months-old child and crept away into the brush. All night she lay there, hushing her offspring while the raiders caroused within earshot. When they had departed and neighbors on the morrow found her, the wife of Felix Powell was clasping her elder child and her newborn baby.

The attack upon Pittsford may have compelled Moses Pierson to withdraw with his family from Clarendon that fall. He harvested his wheat before he retreated, being a thrifty man, and in January 1778 returned with his wife and an escort of Vermont militia to thresh it. The winter-locked frontier seemed so peaceful that they tarried, possibly infatuated by the excellence of the beer Mrs. Pierson had brewed. Fifty British-led Indians attacked on March 12. Two wheat buyers, Josiah Woodward and one Daniels, were killed at the first fire.

Twice, before the garrison drove off the raiders, the house was set ablaze. When all the water had been spent, Mrs. Pierson's beer was used to extinguished the flames.

These minor forays presaged heavier blows. Most of them obviously would be directed against the rashly established and increasingly lonely little republic of Vermont. The leaders who had snatched her from the grasp of New York were too astute not to see the danger clearly.

Though Burgoyne's invasion had failed, the British fleet still controlled Champlain. The center of war was moving toward Georgia and the Carolinas, stripping the American north frontier of men. Vermont's own regiment of the Continental Line, which the now ailing Seth Warner had commanded, marched away in April 1779 to Albany.

If men saw in this departure the vindictive hand of New York, a subsequent order from Washington himself filled Vermont with the desolate belief that he, too, sided with her enemies. In 1780, the commissary in charge of the supplies stored at Bennington was instructed to issue no more to Green Mountain militiamen. Governor Chittenden of Vermont, however alarmed he might have been, was not awed. He immediately slapped an embargo upon the exportation from Vermont of any foodstuffs whatever.

George Clinton, a stubborn and jealous man, now was governor of New York. It must have comforted him to see Vermont left unprotected in the mounting wind of retribution. Already, the small republic had appealed for inclusion and protection to the federated Thirteen. New York, abetted by New Hampshire and Massachusetts which still hoped to share in the partition of Vermont, had blocked action by Congress and had left the petitioner outside in a storm whose blasts waxed in violence.

British craft came up the lake in November 1779 and discharged troops and Indians who raided shore settlements as far south as Orwell. Brandon was burned. Middlebury, when the foray was spent, lay in ashes save for one barn that was built of timber too green to set afire.

Indians attacked Skenesborough in March 1780, destroying what few buildings still were whole and using their prisoners as pack animals to bear their booty northward. A larger force, convoyed by warships, came up the lake in May. Sir John Johnson, son of William, landed 600 troops and Indians at Crown Point which he used as a base for his attack upon the settlements about Johnstown, New York.

In October, Major Christopher Carleton struck a still heavier blow against the buckling frontier. Eight ships and 26 boats bore

Derick Photo, Department of Conservation and Development

LAKE CHAMPLAIN FROM MOUNT PHILO, VERMONT

Derick Photo, Department of Conservation and Development

LAKE CHAMPLAIN FROM GRAND ISLE, VERMONT

BENNETT YOUNG
1864
Leader of the Raid

FIRST LIEUTENANT BENNET H. YOUNG, C.S.A.
Leader of St. Albans Raiders.

his force of 800 British regulars, some field artillery, a company of German jägers and 375 Tories and Indians up Champlain. Carleton landed 400 men in Bulwagga Bay, south of the present Port Henry, to co-operate with Johnson in his raid on Schoharie and Stone Arabia, New York, and went on up the Lake to Skenesborough.

American defenses were now so weak that the invasion, with less than one-fifth Burgoyne's force, advanced almost as far as he in a tenth the time. Fort Ann, garrisoned by seventy-five militia under Captain Adiel Sherwood, surrendered October 10. Carleton sent forward his Tories and Indians, who raided south to Saratoga with only the lightest opposition, and marched his regulars across to the Fort George-Fort Edward Road.

Captain John Chipman held Fort George with sixty men of the Vermont line. A messenger reported to him on the morning of October 11 that he had been fired on by Indians near Bloody Pond. Captain Thomas Sill and forty-eight men, ordered out by Chipman, ran full tilt into Carleton's force. Only thirteen escaped. Chipman surrendered Fort George and its wooden interior was burned.

Carleton recalled his raiders and deliberately retired down Lake George with smoke from the burning Hudson Valley settlements soiling the sky behind him. There were barely enough boats for his troops and their soldier prisoners. The Indians followed the rough trail on the lake's west shore, driving their laden captives before them. One of these unfortunates was Bill Harris, whose clan was among the first permanent settlers of Lake George.

The legends that adorn Bill's memory indicate that he was a very tough man. He and a dozen of his fellows were put aboard boats at Bulwagga Bay and taken into Canada where they were prisoned on an island in the St. Lawrence. They escaped but were pursued by Tories and Indians and were attacked while they slept about a campfire. Bill grappled with an Indian and threw him into the embers but was struck across the head and laid senseless by Cyrenus Parks, a Tory and erstwhile neighbor.

Harris was stripped of hat, coat and shoes and left for dead.

When he revived, he found that his right arm had been broken, his head had been laid open once by the blow that had stunned him and again by a war ax and he had received, in addition, a bayonet thrust in the chest. Despite these handicaps, he started for home once more, fell in with two fellow captives and after great hardships in the wilderness reached the Connecticut in southern Vermont.

Bill, from then on, cherished a prejudice against Indians and there are lurid tales of the number he slew. He also had acquired a permanent distaste for Cyrenus Parks who spent the rest of his days in Canada since, as far as he and Harris were concerned, the war never ended.

Carleton, withdrawing, did not continue down Champlain. His ships and his troops halted at Crown Point, menacing Vermont. Militia under the hurriedly commissioned Brigadier General Ethan Allen, who had returned from British captivity a year before, occupied Castleton and near-by villages and prepared for the worst.

The state's inability to defend its widely scattered settlers had been demonstrated again, only a week or so earlier.

Lieutenant Houghton, landing at the mouth of the Winooski River, went up the valley and over the hills with 300 Indians and Tories. Buildings were burned in Tunbridge and Randolph. In Royalton, 21 houses and 16 barns were destroyed, 150 cattle and many hogs and sheep were butchered, and the raiders carried with them into Canada 26 persons and 30 horses.

A month before Royalton, Ira Allen and Stephen Rowe Bradley had appeared in Congress to plead Vermont's cause once more and had met another rebuff. They had, however, presented to the honorable body a singular and disturbing letter from Governor Chittenden in which "One-eyed Tom" had pointed out that if his state continued to be barred from the Union "she has not the most distant motive to continue hostilities with Great Britain, and maintain an important frontier for the benefit of the United States, and for no other reward than the ungrateful one of being inslaved by them."[1]

There had been unpleasant rumors floating about the country

that made this half threat of Chittenden's sound downright sinister, though Vermont's plentiful enemies considered it an outrageous bluff.

More observant eyes than Congressmen's had been watching the orphan state's increasing torment. Sir Henry Clinton, commander in chief of British forces in America with headquarters in New York, General Frederick Haldimand, new governor-general of Canada, and Lord George Germain, secretary of state for the colonies, knew the strategic importance of Vermont, and sought profit from its present plight.

If the flouted and already repeatedly seared and wounded state could be captured, or cajoled into surrender, the New York frontier would be outflanked and a passage would be opened to interior New England.

One British army had swept the lakes clear but had gone on to disaster. Before another heavy invasion was launched, it might be well to try subversion. Germain ordered Clinton and Haldimand to make the attempt.

One-half the story of what ensued is plainly to be read in surviving British dispatches. One-half, to this day, is dim and largely illegible, open to surmise and a variety of interpretations. The British statesmen kept scrupulous records. The Vermont leaders, for reasons of which the safety of their own necks was chief, committed little to writing. None of them was trained to the pen. Still less was any man among them schooled by education or experience in the devious and delicate ways of diplomacy. Chittenden was a raw if shrewd farmer; Ira Allen, a backwoods surveyor; Ethan, a blustering eccentric; Joseph and Jonas Fay, other actors in the plot, were sons of a frontier tavern keeper.

The hope that Yankee yokels could outwit polished men of the world was rather less than the chance that Vermont militia could defeat the British army in open battle. Clinton was a grandson of the Earl of Lincoln and a former officer in the Guards. He was a persuasive man with an appetite for intrigue. Haldimand, by birth a Swiss, had been educated in the Prussian service and had won in the British army repute as a soldier and administrator. Behind this competent pair stood the sharp and cynical Germain. It was he who instructed Clinton and Haldimand to attempt the seduction.

Vermont's leaders not only were unsophisticated folk; they also were hampered by events. They had been pressed into a corner where there was no room to maneuver and their insistence upon independence had alienated their American neighbors. Their own people, who were freedom's devotees, were certain to disavow and perhaps hang them if they dabbled in treason.

Meanwhile, New York, New Hampshire and Massachusetts were expectantly waiting the self-made state's collapse and partition. Raids out of Canada that already had destroyed, wholly or in part, Pittsford, Clarendon, Brandon, Middlebury, Tunbridge, Randolph, Royalton and other lesser settlements, were certain to become more frequent and more punishing if Vermont carried on the war alone. Negotiation might postpone what appeared to be otherwise inevitable downfall. The little republic's leaders prepared to negotiate.

They already had been supplied with an opportunity. In July of 1780, a stranger shuffled up the street of Arlington to Ethan Allen and thrust a letter into his hand. It was from Colonel Beverly Robinson, a Virginia-born New York loyalist who already was being of some minor aid to Benedict Arnold in that general's self-corruption.

Robinson, in his letter, offered his good offices in any attempt Allen should make toward bringing Vermont back to the British fold and promised "that you may obtain a separate government under the King."[2]

The Vermont conspirators, none of whom probably told all they knew, agree that Allen immediately showed the letter to his brother Ira, to Chittenden and to others who counseled him not to answer it.

Haldimand, who commanded at the source of Vermont's greatest danger and therefore was closer to hand than Clinton, was the person with whom the homespun diplomats preferred to deal. There is no surviving trace of how communication first was opened with Canada but on September 27, after Vermont's latest rebuff by Congress, Chittenden wrote Haldimand, proposing a cartel for exchange of prisoners, and sent it with a flag of truce to a British warship lying in Champlain. When, in October, Major Carleton swept up the lake and other raiders from Canada burned Royalton, the governor undoubtedly wished he had written earlier.

Yet his proposal got prompt result. While Carleton lingered balefully at Crown Point and Vermont's militia under Brigadier General Ethan Allen watched him from Champlain's east shore, Haldimand's agent, Justus Sherwood, arrived at Castleton, October 29, accompanied by a fifer, drummer and two privates, to confer with the general, ostensibly on an exchange of prisoners.

Sherwood was a captain in Peters Corps of loyalists and one-time resident of New Haven in the Grants. He had ridden at least once with the Green Mountain Boys, was an old friend of the Allens and a monumentally patient man.

"I authorize you," the governor had written, "to give these people the most positive assurance that their country will be erected into a separate province, independent and unconnected with every government in America."[3]

At Castelton where Patriot Allen had assembled his Green Mountain Boys for the assault upon Ticonderoga, Conspirator Allen, surrounded by ten field officers of Vermont's army, heard Sherwood's proposals for a prisoner exchange. Before the agent made these, and again on the following day, the two old friends talked privately together.

If Sherwood expected hearty collaboration he was disappointed. Haldimand's agent informed the governor-general that Allen announced that, if he were to declare for Britain now, "his own people would cut off his head." However, if her many American enemies tried to force the young republic, Vermont "rather than be ruined by Congress will ask help of Canada."[4]

Further conferences on the exchange of prisoners and other matters must wait, Allen said, upon the will of the governor of Vermont. Meanwhile, a truce must be established to cover not only the new state's territory but also the entire shores of Lakes Champlain and George. Sherwood agreed. Carleton embarked his troops and went home. General Allen, after disbanding his own army which still had a deal of the fall farm work to finish, hurried to Bennington to report publicly to the legislature assembled there and privately to his fellow conspirators.

The lawmakers listened with relief to Allen's edited but triumphant account of the truce he had wrung from the British, yet patriotic noses detected a sour smell. Had it been only the general's engaging personality that had persuaded Carleton's threatening host to go meekly back down the lake?

A disagreeable legislator named Hutchins demanded further information and another, Simeon Hathaway, proposed impeachment of Allen. The general, in a thundering rage, resigned his military commission and stormed out of the building and also out of leadership in the plot, thereby ensuring its smoother procedure henceforth. Chittenden, after abating Hathaway's and Hutchins' suspicions, appointed Ira Allen and Joseph Fay to arrange with British authorities for the exchange of prisoners.

Lake Champlain which has witnessed unnumbered improbabilities in its violent lifetime was to see none so unlikely as the taut, quiet drama about to be played by desperate men of a little and friendless nation against the power and the statecraft of Great Britain. The waters of the lake, its shores and a wooded island beyond its outlet were to furnish the background for the more important scenes.

In the hushed, impending struggle, Britain would try to win back an erring province. The imperiled Vermont commissioners would strive for nothing more specific than time—time, however brief, in which their people would be safe, the new republic would endure and invasion would not advance along the lakes' valley; time in which Congress, roused to what was happening, might admit the petitioning state into the Union; failing this, time prolonged by every possible subterfuge to the ultimate hour in the hope that luck, till now Vermont's most reliable ally, might by some unimagined stroke rescue the hard-pressed little country.

Sherwood was visited by Ira Allen and Joseph Fay, November 11. The Vermonters were cordial and agreed to complete the negotiations during the winter at St. Johns. Meanwhile, it was stipulated that the lately established truce would continue.

Sherwood left for Canada. Already the ice of a precocious winter was forming and he had a straitened and ghastly time reaching Quebec, where he arrived November 30. A month later, Colonel Barry St. Leger, commanding at St. Johns, began at Haldimand's bidding to prepare a house on Isle aux Noix where Sherwood was to receive the commissioners.

Already, by pseudo treason, the plotters had gained for their nation a six-weeks' respite. Whatever satisfaction they may have felt was curdled by the predicament of Ethan Allen.

Vermont's most celebrated citizen appears to have followed his natural bent and have talked too much, for it became general knowledge that he had been invited by Clinton to become a second Benedict Arnold. In February 1781 another spy brought him a second letter from the persistent Robinson. Allen also received an unwelcome visit from the invalid Seth Warner who asked uncomfortable questions, delivered solemn warning and profoundly disturbed his cousin.

Allen, with or without the counsel of the plotters, hastened to cleanse himself by sending both Robinson letters to Samuel Huntington, President of Congress, with a covering disclaimer in which the unhappy man insisted that the twin missives represented his only contact with the enemy and that neither of them had been answered.

This revelation shocked Clinton and sharpened the already pointed suspicions of Haldimand. The house prepared at Isle aux Noix still was empty. The Vermont commissioners did not appear.

The hard winter of 1780-1781 supplied Chittenden with a semiplausible excuse. He blamed the delay on the weather. When spring arrived, he assured Haldimand, negotiations certainly would begin.

It was early May before Ira Allen, escorted as became an ambas-

sador extraordinary by a militia lieutenant and sixteen rank and
file, embarked for Isle aux Noix. The plotters by then had won
six months' time.

Unwittingly they had accomplished more. Vermont's hesitation
and evasion seem to have heated British minds. Clinton, finding
her hard to get, became more ardent in pursuit and bent his
strategy accordingly. The truce still covered Champlain and
George. Now, the affair exerted further influence on the main
course of the conflict.

Clinton, urged by Cornwallis to come to the war's new center
in the South, listed on May 2 for Germain's perusal his reasons
for remaining in New York: "Among which its proximity to the
undecided district of Vermont is not the least in weight."[5]

Haldimand's suspicions must have ebbed and the long-enduring Sherwood must have felt a quickly unjustified satisfaction
when, on May 7, Commissioner Ira Allen and his escort arrived.

This shabby and half-comic martial pomp must be the outward
and visible sign of Vermont's impending return to grace. Sherwood was stunned to find, after greetings had been exchanged
and negotiations began on Isle aux Noix, that it was no such
thing. Progress was additionally hampered by the presence of a
Major Dundas who had been sent to expedite the prisoners' exchange and was not privy to the plot.

Commissioner Allen, Sherwood learned, had journeyed north
only to explain that nothing could be done to advance the conspiracy until after the meeting of Vermont's legislature in June.
Commissioner Allen also demanded that the impromptu, still
maintained truce be solidified into a formal armistice. It probably
was some minutes before Sherwood recovered breath, picked up
his dashed hopes and proceeded to argue.

The waters of the Richelieu ran brightly past Isle aux Noix, the
maples were unfolding small green banners to spring, but the
British agent found no room in his overcrammed spirit for vernal
or other elation. He complained to Haldimand of "Colonel Allen's
dark and intricate manner of proceeding in a negotiation."[6]

The solid little Vermont emissary with his large, poetic eyes and small slot of a mouth was as hard to land and as difficult to hold as an eel. During the eighteen days of argument, cajolery and threat, he quibbled, dodged and displayed obstinacy up to the breaking point of his adversary's temper. Meanwhile in Vermont, farmers, freed from invasion's dread, sowed their brown fields, thanks to the dexterity and balance of Ira Allen who danced on a tight wire at intense risk to his own neck and the continued existence of his state. Early and late, he still persisted in his opening statement: Nothing could be done to advance the plot until after the legislature had met.

Midway in the long-drawn-out conference, the baffled Sherwood, realizing that he was getting nowhere, appealed for aid. Haldimand sent his adjutant general, Major Lernoult, to add weight to the British argument but Allen, though outnumbered, was no more compliant.

"In short," Sherwood wrote to his chief, "Allen says many plausible things, but none to the point."[7]

By evasion, by perseverance in repeating his contention, Vermont's ambassador, inch by inch, prevailed. When his weary opponents bade him farewell, May 25, he had wrung from them an agreement to extend the truce until the legislature had dissolved and in some still less comprehensible fashion had convinced Lernoult and Sherwood of his honesty.

"I believe," the latter wrote to Haldimand, "Allen has gone with a firm determination to do his utmost for a reunion and I believe he will be seconded by Gov. Chittenden, his brother E. Allen and a few others, all acting from interest, without any principles of loyalty."[8]

As he was rowed away from the Isle aux Noix, Ira Allen may have allowed himself a moment of satisfaction. He had won for his nation another month or so of that precious commodity, time.

Yet his neck must have felt ominously stiff and the risk he had run must have disturbed him, for after reporting his success to the governor and council, he won from that body an unusual absolution signed by them all. Perhaps he intended to use it in a not improbable time of personal danger. It read:

"Whereas Colonel Ira Allen has been with a flag to Quebec for the purpose of settling a cartel for the exchange of prisoners, and has used his best policy by feigning or endeavoring to make them believe that the State of Vermont had a desire to negotiate a treaty of peace with Great Britain—thereby to prevent the immediate invasion or incursion upon the frontiers of this state, as appears by the letter he sent General Haldimand dated May 8th, 1781, enclosing a copy of Colonel Beverley Robinson's letters to General Ethan Allen and General Allen's letter to Congress, and the resolutions of the assembly of Vermont approbating the same, as also the circular letter to the several states, according to his verbal report made to us this day:—We are of the opinion that the critical circumstance this state is in, being out of the union with the United States and thereby being unable to make that vigorous defense we could wish for—think it to be a necessary political manoeuver to save the frontiers of this state."[9]

Fortified by this somewhat chaotic absolution, Vermont's commissioner reported to the legislature in Bennington. He was aware that Canadian spies sat in the gallery and that the lawmakers themselves were suspicious, but he spoke deftly. His statement and the carefully selected documents with which he embellished it were reassuring to all present.

"Is it not curious," he wrote with smugness long afterward, "to see opposite parties perfectly satisfied with one statement and each believing what they wished to believe and thereby deceiving themselves?"[10]

He had little opportunity for moralizing that summer. His correspondence with Haldimand was lively and, on the governor's side, increasingly brusque. The legislature had adjourned. Where, Haldimand kept demanding, was Vermont's promised submission to the King?

When Haldimand's patience seemed about to snap, Joseph Fay went north to win, if possible, still more time. What originally had been intended as a brief truce already had continued for nine months.

Allen himself and Jonas Fay repaired to Philadelphia. Once

more they asked Congress for inclusion in the Union and once more their petition was rejected. Joseph Fay met the Canadian commissioners Sherwood and Dr. George Smyth, an Albany loyalist, aboard the man-of-war *Royal George* on August 7.

"I wish," Fay wrote to Haldimand, August 9, "it was in my power to remove every suspicion you may have against the good intentions of the people of Vermont,"[11] which, considering the rapidly approaching crisis, undoubtedly was verity.

Royal George lay off a small fort lately built on Dutchman's Point, now Blockhouse Point, on North Hero Island. The ostensible business of the conference—the exchange of prisoners—was swiftly arranged; the real subject of the negotiation was approached with more difficulty. Fay must have had a miserable sojourn. The British commissioners were insistent. Haldimand's patience was wearing perilously thin. When Fay tried to evade any commitment, the governor general delivered an ultimatum.

"I shall not expect," he wrote, "a flag of truce from Vermont upon any other business than to signify her acceptance of my offers."[12]

This firmness did not quite awe the commissioner who managed to wring from the exasperated Haldimand a still further extension of time. Vermont, it was agreed at last, would return a final answer to the British agents on or before September 5.

Fay went home with no warmer comfort for his fellow plotters, leaving Sherwood and Smyth in an uncertain mental state. They reported to Haldimand concerning Vermont's most recent commissioner:

"He professes so much honesty, accompanied by so many gestures of sincerity that he seems to overact his part. He certainly is perfectly honest or a perfect Jesuit."[13]

Though Haldimand had set September 5 as the ultimate deadline, it was not until the seventeenth that Ira Allen and Joseph Fay met Sherwood and Smyth at Skenesborough. By then, the truce had endured for more than ten months.

The time was past for feinting, ducking and agile footwork. Haldimand belatedly suspected that he had been duped. Invasion from Canada had been stayed by the interminable dickering of Yankee hobbledehoys while American troops that might have been held in the lake region had marched with Washington to Yorktown, where guns were beginning to speak over raw breastworks.

The legions of devious words that had kept the frontier at peace for five-sixths of a year could protect it no longer. Sherwood and Smyth grimly proclaimed Haldimand's decision. The governorgeneral was ending the truce. His fleet and his army were about to come up the lake. St. Leger, commanding, had his orders. Vermont immediately would declare for the King or suffer destructive invasion.

Allen and Fay proposed delay until after the October meeting of the legislature when it was almost certain—

No. The British commissioners had heard all that before. Vermont must choose between reunion and war. At once.

Allen's face was calm, his voice admirably dry. He agreed. He had only one minor suggestion. Would it not be better, purely of course as a matter of strategy, if Haldimand himself proclaimed the royal willingness to receive the wandering sheep? Would it not be more persuasive if the offer came from the governor-general? And, not to be persistent, would not the best time for the proclamation be while the legislature was in session and could immediately reply? Allen would engage to notify Colonel St. Leger when the precisely proper moment arrived.

Haldimand granted inwardly desperate men this final brief stay. Canada's governor would prepare the proclamation. St. Leger would bring it up Champlain. Vermont's commissioners, departing on September 20, left behind them an edifying atmosphere of candor and probity in which Sherwood, who was no fool, wrote to Haldimand:

"I am fully of the opinion that Messrs. Chittenden, Allen and Fay with a number of the leading men of Vermont are making every effort in their power to endeavor to bring about a reunion with government."[14]

The legislature met October 11 at Charlestown, New Hampshire, which with other towns east of the Connecticut had entered into a brief union with Vermont. Allen and Fay, riding thither, met militia companies tramping through the brilliant fall weather toward Champlain where Brigadier General Roger Enos was assembling his command. St. Leger with his ships and his troops and the still unuttered proclamation had come up to Ticonderoga.

The Vermont conspirators received their agents' report. They had no fresh, procrastinating expedient to offer. Time had been stretched to its uttermost. Resourceful and unscrupulous minds that had immobilized Haldimand for eleven months and had kept the lakes' area at peace could present now no further subterfuge. The stroke of fortune for which the plotters had hoped still withheld itself and against their shoulder blades the plotters could feel the grim pressure of the wall at the blind alley's end.

In Charlestown, the legislature had fed on rumor and had gathered, apparently from the air, a suspicion that treachery was afoot. It was angry and ready to rage at the first opportunity, which St. Leger direly supplied.

The British commander grew worried when no word came, bidding him release the proclamation. He became nervous in the silence and, October 22, sent out an officer and twelve men to catch a live Vermonter from Enos' force who would carry a message to Chittenden. The British patrol found not one but a patrol of six and in the scuffle killed its commander Sergeant Archelaus Tupper, before the rest surrendered.

Dead men have a fell gift for upsetting diplomacy and St. Leger was aghast. He deemed that an open letter of apology to Chittenden might atone for the accident and forwarded by his recent prisoners a verbal mortuary wreath:

"Not meaning hostilities against Vermont while they chose to continue inimically disposed to the King's troops as well as to evince the friendly inclinations of His Excellency, General Haldimand towards them in the strongest manner, I have the honour to send back a scout of yours, surprised by one of mine. . . . I most sincerely lament that the necessity of service made shedding of blood unavoidable. . . . While I sympathize with the friends of the deceas'd I have directed the last decencies to be paid to his corps. A flag attends your people to pass them through all advanced Posts etc. and see the interment made and return."[15]

As though this remarkable production were not caiamitous enough, the man chosen to bear it to Charlestown was Simeon Hathaway who, in 1780, had voiced as a legislator the demand for Ethan Allen's impeachment which had helped drive him into retirement. Fortified now, he clamored his distrust in Charlestown and the already wary and irritable legislature hummed like a roused hive.

Ira Allen's deft address and Chittenden's bland assurance pacified the indignant, but the effort must scarcely have seemed worth while. Time had run out; their enemies had closed in upon the plotters and intransigent Vermont would be torn apart by renewed slaughters and burnings when it had rejected Haldimand's impending proclamation.

That proclamation never was issued. The first rumors which spread through the land were beyond belief. Then gunfire, not of war but of rejoicing, swept across Vermont and there was iublilant clamor in Charlestown.

Yorktown had fallen, the tidings ran; Cornwallis and his army were prisoners. On November 6, St. Leger's expedition returned to Canada. It was the last British force to come up Champlain in strength for thirty years.

"Thus," Ira Allen wrote, "ended the campaign of 1781 with the incidental loss of only one man on the extensive frontiers of Vermont exposed to an army of 10,000 men; yet she did not incur any considerable debt. Such were the happy effects of these negotiations."[16]

---

1 *Records of the Governor and Council* (Montpelier, 1873), II, 254.
2 Ira Allen, *History of Vermont* (London, 1798), p. 160.
3 *Vermont Historical Society Collections*, vol. II, 87.
4 Canadian Archives B-176, pp. 14-26.
5 Sparks Manuscripts, in Harvard University Library, 45, 57.
6 Canadian Archives B-176, p. 80.
7 *Ibid.*, p. 106.
8 *Ibid.*, p. 120.
9 *Records of the Governor and Council*, II, 172.
10 Ira Allen, *History of Vermont*, p. 172.
11 *Ibid.*, p. 172.
12 Vermont Historical Society Collections, II, 161,
13 *Ibid.*, p. 149.
14 Canadian Archives B-175, p. 141.
15 *Ibid.*, B-134, p. 141.
16 Ira Allen, *History of Vermont*, p. 195.

Chapter 18

Interlude

A NOTHER war had ended and the tide of settlement, recently damned by conflict, was moving north again through the Champlain-George Valley. By land and by water, obstinate, aspiring men were returning to abandoned dwellings or were finding, where raiders had passed, fireweed shining above the rain-leached ashes that had been cabins.

Two new republics controlled the valley now, though the stubborn British still maintained garrisons near Champlain's outlet on Point au Fer and on Blockhouse Point, North Hero Island. Lake George and the west shore of Lake Champlain were property of the State of New York in the lately established United States of America. The east side of the larger lake was territory of the self-created, independent nation of Vermont.

The erstwhile New Hampshire Grants, by diplomacy when this would serve and by downright audacity when temporizing failed, had withstood the efforts of New York, New Hampshire and Massachusetts to subject the district to a Polish partition. These three states, hungry for territorial gain, had blocked Vermont's attempts to enter the Union. After Massachusetts and New Hampshire had withdrawn their opposition, New York still remained vindictively hostile. While the deadlock endured, Vermont flourished as a separate republic, with its own constitution, duly elected officials, army, coinage and post-office service.

The thirteen original states were staggering under the massive burden of a war debt to which independent Vermont, that had conducted its share of the conflict on a strictly cash basis, was immune. Unoccupied land was still plentiful in the little nation; taxes were infinitesimal, settlers were pouring in. Vermont could afford to wait in waxing prosperity, for an invitation to join the Union. It did not become the fourteenth state until 1791.

During the Revolution, no single settlement on the immediate shores of Lake George or Lake Champlain had retained its inhabitants. War had ousted them all. Now, they were returning, reinforced, to revive old communities and create new. In the decade following the war, the last of the towns that now occupy Champlain's east shore had been established and organized; streams had been harnessed to saw and gristmills and the original log cabins were being replaced by the small, seemly, clapboarded farmhouses that still are typical of Vermont.

The people who in ten years' time had settled and organized all Champlain's east shore were of the same stripe as the earlier Grants pioneers. There was a sprinkling of Scots among them but otherwise the new immigrants were of English descent. Other racial ingredients were slight and accidental. Highgate, for instance, a town on the Canadian frontier, was settled by discharged German mercenaries in the belief that they were building their cabins on British soil. When the boundary line was resurveyed and the settlers learned they actually were occupying American territory, they deftly changed allegiance and kept their farms.

Impatience with the solidified standards of longer established states, and the desire to find for themselves a region where a man might own, unhampered, his property and himself, brought most of the later pioneers by boat or long land marches to Champlain's shore. Here they repeated the incredible travail of clearing and building that earlier settlers of the New Hampshire Grants had performed. These new folk, like their forerunners, were men and women of great physical strength. Weaklings were abolished quickly by the rigors of frontier existence. Old graveyards of the region still attest the brutal efficacy of the natural selection life in the wilderness imposed. Ancient headstones reveal the appalling number of children who died in infancy and also the many persons who, surviving the ordeal of childhood, lived on thereafter into their 80's and 90's.

The strong bodies of Champlain settlers housed rough and icono-

clastic mental vigor. Most of the newcomers had made the toilsome journey thither to get away from ecclesiastical, social and even
more fundamental strictures on human conduct. Like all pioneer
groups, this population was composed largely of insurgents, bold
egoists who would not fit their energies and their disbeliefs into
the rigidities of longer settled communities. Then and thereafter,
arbitrary authority, whatever its source, seldom failed to rouse the
never dormant truculence of the new towns.

John Clark, a lonely moralist of Clarendon, entered in his account book and diary in 1785 the following estimate of his fellow
townspeople:

"Some good Christians like here and there a berry on the upper-
most bows but looking round must conclude vice predominant
and irreligion almost epidemical Sabbath disregarded profanity de-
bauchery drunkenness quareling by words and blows and parting
with broken heads and bloody noses."[1]

There was a rough spaciousness about the new villages that
older Vermont towns were losing. Not a few residents in the
senior settlements moved up into the lakeside wilderness. Among
these were men of the Allen clan, though love for the invigoration
of frontier life may not have been the prime reason Ethan Allen
established himself on the Onion—now the Winooski—River in
the infant hamlet of Burlington.

The aging warrior and his kin still were neck-deep in land spec-
ulation. They owned vast tracts in the north country, and off the
mainland in mid-Champlain lay twin islands that represented
not only a real-estate venture but a variety of monument to Ethan
Allen. They had been granted to him, Samuel Herrick and their
associates in 1779 and had been named by Ethan, with his usual
becoming lack of modesty, Two Heroes, for himself and Sam.

Cousin Ebenezer Allen now owned a farm and tavern in South
Hero and thither on February 12, 1789, Ethan Allen repaired,
accomplishing, while his Negro farmhand guided the ox-drawn
sled over the ice, the first stage of a longer, unpremeditated journey.

Allen's ostensible purpose was to bring home a load of hay from
Ebenezer's but he lingered so long with cronies in his cousin's

taproom that it was toward midnight when he started home.

It was a lifeless body that reached the mainland. Somewhere on the passage of Lake Champlain that had supplied Ethan Allen with his chief fame, the strange, strong spirit had gone free.

The creation of the shore towns followed in general the pattern established by the older Grants communities with one fundamental and stimulating difference: At the doorstep of these new villages lay navigable water, no longer presenting the threat of lake-borne raiding parties and invasions but now an easy highway to White-hall or St. Johns and a trade route of shining promise. In the 1790's, a growing fleet of sloops and schooners opened a commerce with Canada or plied between Champlain's west and east shores.

Geography decreed the slower development of Champlain's New York side. In Vermont, a long breadth of plain lay between water and the aloof ramparts of the Green Mountains, and here when the clearings had been made, was astoundingly fertile soil. For most of the west shore's length, the Adirondacks pressed close to the water line and granted among their crowded masses scant profitable foothold for farming folk.

In 1822, the New York legislature, observing with concern the thin population of Essex County, offered 200 acres of land to anyone who would build a house and clear and fence 15 acres in 5 years. Few responded to this inducement. The area's most note-worthy product at this time was scenery, which had small nour-ishment value in an era of infrequent roads and no summer vacationists.

The same causes retarded any important settlement along Lake George. Until trees came to be regarded as something more than obstacles that must be cleared away, the population of the moun-tain area remained small.

It was to the more fertile, flat lower Champlain country with its strong little rivers, between Port Kent on the south and Rouses Point—where Jacques Rouse, an Americanized Nova Scotian settled probably in 1793 and sired, it is said, twenty-six children—that New York pioneers first turned.

Others, before permanent settlement began, had been aware of this district's implicit worth. William Gilliland had begun his short-lived towns here, and in 1766 a peculiar and indefinite person known as Count or Captain Charles de Fredenburg, or Vredenburg, received from the British government a warrant for 30,000 acres extending inland from the mouth of the Saranac River.

The Captain-Count built a house where Plattsburg now stands and a sawmill at Fredenburg Falls, three miles upstream. When the Revolutionary War began, he took his family to Canada and, returning to his property, vanished never to reappear. His house and his mill were burned.

The post-Revolutionary patent obtained by Zephaniah Platt, delegate from Dutchess County to New York's first provincial Congress, by Melancton Smith, also a Dutchess County patriot, and others, covered the identical territory Fredenburg had possessed. It was a far larger tract than present-day Plattsburg.

New York's practice was to establish townships of vast extent and then, as population increased, to break them up into smaller. Land included in the Crown Point patent was taken away later to form the additional townships of Ticonderoga, Moriah, Westport, Elizabethtown, Schroon, Minerva, Newcomb, North Hudson, and part of Keene as well. Portions of Plattsburg's original territory now are occupied by Black Brook, Ausable, Beekmantown, Dannemora, Saranac and Schuyler Falls.

Political organization, which was comparatively simple to establish in the small, compact Vermont towns, was more difficult on the New York shore where the early townships had a scant population scattered over a prodigious range of territory. Until this was split up into smaller communities, the problem was met according to the New England tradition.

Most of the settlers were Yankees and a majority of them came from Vermont which supplied the New York shore with more early population than the parent state provided. The "New York fever" of the later 1700's and early 1800's was a milder version of the "Western fever" seizure that inspired the land-hungry later to move out to the Ohio Country.

Settlers on Champlain's west shore brought the town-meeting

idea across the water with them but modified it to meet conditions not encountered in New England. In the extensive New York townships, not one but a number of preliminary town meetings were held at convenient places. Legislation proposed and persons nominated for office then were considered at a later, central gathering. When ballots had been prepared, duly appointed, peripatetic election officials went through the wilderness from cabin to cabin, affording all the qualified opportunity to vote.

Plattsburg which was to become the second city of Lake Champlain had a no more impressive infancy than a dozen other similar villages. The prime requisites for a successful settlement—a sawmill and a gristmill—were in operation as early as 1785 on the Saranac River, whose power was the first factor in Plattsburg's growth.

By 1811 the town had only seventy-eight dwellings though the building for the Plattsburg Academy, completed in this year, was said to be the largest structure in northern New York. Education among all the Yankee pioneers was considered secondary only to self-preservation.

It was not until the 1820's that lake craft deemed Plattsburg of sufficient importance to enter its harbor. Earlier boats had stopped at Cumberland Head where storehouses stood and from which a stage line ran to the town. The settlement of the back country, the development of roads and a waxing trade with Canada combined to make Plattsburg the metropolis of the New York lake shore.

Burlington, the principal city of the Champlain area, had a similar undistinguished beginning. It was a frontier hamlet with a population of 330 in 1791 when the University of Vermont was established there in a single brick building through the efforts of Ira Allen. It was only a moderate-sized village during the War of 1812 and the water of its bay was so shallow that cargo had to be lightered or floated to and from its trading craft.

These vessels and the lake that bore them granted the infant water-front towns an immediate stimulation that inland settlements lacked. When the first grim stage of pioneering had ended,

when the family and stock and shelter and the farm was beginning to yield more than its owners consumed, there were available
markets for surpluses and water at hand to carry them.

Trade, in the post-Revolutionary time, was hampered by the
extreme scarcity of money and was limited further by the fact
that lumber, which later was to become a commodity of constantly
increasing value, was then so plentiful as to be of dubious worth to
the Champlain people.

Forests must be removed before the settlers could get at the soil
and thus on all the new farms the tall, primeval trees went down
and the timber for which the pioneers had no immediate use was
burned. Not only was this the easiest way of getting rid of obstacles, but it was also the preliminary step in a profitable industry—the manufacture of potash, the frontier's first and, for a time,
its most important enterprise.

The production process was simple. Wood ashes were collected—no farm of that era was without its stone or brick "ash
house"—and when a sufficient supply had been assembled, they
were leached and the resulting liquid was evaporated by boiling in
iron pots. The potash, thus created, had a ready sale in Canada
and became, until a sufficient number of farms got into agricultural
production, the principal wilderness export, the foundation of
frontier economy.

Wood ashes themselves were considered legal tender. Men
bought goods with them and received them willingly from debtors.
"Home ashes" were the more highly regarded and were worth 12
cents a bushel. "Field ashes" because of the inevitable amount of
dirt and litter they contained were quoted at from 5 to 8 cents a
bushel.

Early in the time of settlement, firms were established that bought
from the pioneers the raw material and performed the process of
manufacture, often carrying it another forward step and purifying
the potash by baking so that it became a more valuable product,
known to the trade as "pearl ash." Other concerns entered the
field on a co-operative basis, renting to farmers the large iron pots
in which the leachings of the wood ashes were boiled and purchas-

ing the resultant potash at from $70 to $80 a ton. Loans were made against a prospective yield of ashes. Promissory notes often were drawn to fall due at the time of "June salts," when the product of the winter's felling and burning was leached, then boiled.

Potash was, and is, used in chemical combinations as a wide variety of medicines and in the manufacture of glass. It most frequently returned to the pioneer family as saleratus, baking soda.

As time went on and the clearings about the cabins grew, wheat came to rival potash as a medium of exchange. The forest soil, once trees had been felled and stumps cleared away, yielded abundant harvests—twenty-five bushels an acre normally and frequently as much as forty. The valley, as years went by, grew green in spring and golden in fall with wheat. Corn, which had preceded wheat as the principal crop, yielded seventy bushels to the acre. Rye and buckwheat also were sown.

Horse breeding had been an occupation of colonial Vermonters. It was carried on now in the Champlain Valley, largely for export. Ox teams were to remain the principal farm motive power for generations. A good yoke usually cost about $50. Cows were raised more for beef than for milk production in what is now one of the most important dairy regions in the East.

It was a hopeful and increasingly prosperous time and the people who at last had unlocked the valley's long-withheld resources enjoyed themselves with less than the traditional New England reticence. They were independent, vigorous and astonishingly self-sufficient. Democracy was neither a slogan nor a politician's catchword; it was inherent.

Households drew no distinction between blood kin and the hired help who were treated as members of the family. Farm hands received not more than $5 a month, but they were expected to work for this wage along with their employers, from dawn till dusk.

Pioneer farming was strenuous and, by modern standards, ruinously shortsighted. While the original rich forest loam was depleted by successive crops, only advanced thinkers replenished the land with ashes and even these applied no further fertilizer.

Manure was shoveled from the barn to lie in accumulating heaps until these became too plentiful. The farmer then moved, not the reeking hillocks but the barn, tearing it down and rebuilding it elsewhere.

The settlers' self-sufficiency was nearly absolute. It was a time of almost universal manual skill. Imports from Canada or the interior United States were largely luxuries. An ingenious people made their own necessities. Many farmers fashioned the family boots and worked bar iron into the horseshoes and implements they required. Women had time and energy to accomplish all housekeeping tasks and to spin and weave as well. A girl at marriage was expected to have not only a "hope chest" filled with garments and fabrics she had made but to be clothed from the skin out with raiment of her own manufacture.

Fruit trees were planted early, from seed. Their produce and grain were substances from which were distilled a daunting assortment of alcoholic beverages. Women brewed beer as regularly as they baked bread. There were more distilleries than gristmills in the Valley.

A pioneer standard that still endures as "neighborliness" decreed that major jobs of buildings should be general efforts to which the community gave willingly of its strength and skill and the beneficiary offered no other compensation than an abundance of drink. The host at a barn-raising, threshing or husking bee whose liquor gave out before the job was completed felt that his face had been blackened.

It was inevitable that so bold a people should increasingly resent as the years went by the continued presence of British army posts on American soil. In the early 1790's, the late enemy still maintained a garrison at Point au Fer, and at Blockhouse Point, while H.M.S. *Maria* kept station in the channel between Point au Fer and Alburg to inspect all boats going north. Her captain, John Steel, did little to endear himself to Americans by compelling passing craft to salute the British ensign and firing upon them if they refused.

There was trouble in 1792 when Deputy Sheriff Enos Wood of Chittenden County attached cattle in Alburg for a debt. When he attempted to drive them off he was pursued by Captain Dechambault, commanding at Point au Fer, and a file of soldiers. Wood and his two assistants were jailed at St. Johns. Shortly thereafter, Benjamin Marvin, Vermont magistrate at Alburg, and Samuel Mott, constable, were arrested for exercising their offices in the British-held territory and were warned to leave the area within two months.

The Valley's indignation spread throughout Vermont, and Governor Chittenden, forgetting in his wrath that his state lately had become a member of the Union, sent furious objections to Canada, direct, and was chided by Jefferson, then Secretary of State, for not having forwarded them through national channels.

In 1796 under the terms of the Jay Treaty, the small British force withdrew from the lake, thereby removing a chronic irritation. Difficulty arose again in 1799 when John Allen, a deputy sheriff of Franklin County, Vermont, seeking to arrest one John Gregg, chased him across the Canadian line before he caught him.

Gregg was bound to a sled and Allen started southward with his captive over ice which broke beneath them. Gregg was drowned. Canadian authorities forthwith indicted Allen for murder and demanded his surrender by Governor Isaac Tichenor of Vermont. Tichenor was more of a diplomat than One-eyed Tom Chittenden, and after much negotiation and a good deal of martial snorting by the Champlain people, the affair blew over.

The settlers on either shore of the lake were not an innately tolerant folk and the attitude of many toward the minions of the British king was something less than cordial. The spacious existence the valley people led was intensifying their original impatience with arbitrary authority and their passion for that impractical variety of individual liberty which permits each person to do as he pleases, in defiance of any governmental strictures.

That passion, in a little while, was to lead Champlain people into certain activities that it was difficult to distinguish from outright treason.

---

[1] David M. Ludlum, *Social Ferment in Vermont 1791-1850* (New York, 1939), p. 20.

Chapter 19

"The Almighty Has Been Pleased . . ."

THE wind that yesterday had rocked the gunboats and spoiled their aim had died during the night and smoke from the burned warehouses on the Saranac's left bank now rose steeply against the morning sky. On the ridged point between the river and the lake, Brigadier General Alexander Macomb's outnumbered force labored amid the raw earth and the unplaced timbers of the still incomplete works. Some 2,000 American regulars, plus 3,000 unreliable militia and volunteers, were preparing to stand off 14,000 of the best troops in the British army.

In the bay that was an uneven quadrangle of water, if an imaginary line from the tip of Cumberland Head to the Saranac River's mouth were used for its south side, there was activity in the fleet, too. Master Commandant Thomas Macdonough's four ships, with ten gunboats scuttling about them, were taking position in a line two miles from the Plattsburg shore and parallel to Cumberland Head, which formed the bay's east side. Small boats from the flagship *Saratoga* were carrying out kedge anchors to either side of her bows.

Disciplined tumult smothered the few brief streets of Plattsburg from which most of its normal inhabitants had fled. The fugitives had been replaced by massed strangers in red-coated uniforms and bucket-shaped leather shakos. Ten thousand already were there, and the roads smoked as more batteries and the ponderous supply train rolled in.

Light dragoons from Sir George Prevost's headquarters at Thomas Allen's farm clattered past trudging infantry. Engineer details with picks and shovels marched toward recently selected gun emplacements. Down by the river, muskets spoke singly or in brief multiple explosions.

247

It was the morning of September 7, 1814, and the catastrophe that the Champlain Valley people had dreaded increasingly since the new war's beginning now actually was falling upon them. Delay, incompetence and a farcical mismanagement had ordained this hour.

For two years, a series of animated museum pieces, unwarrantably styled United States Army generals, had conducted campaigns along the border that were chiefly notable for posturing and bluster. At last, the obvious had happened. An army was on the move via the time-hallowed invasion road—the most powerful host the valley ever had seen. On September 6, it had occupied Plattsburg. Now it waited the coming of the British fleet before storming the works beyond the village and moving irresistibly onward.

While the muskets of sniping pickets continue to bang on the Saranac's shores, it might be well to survey briefly the cumulating errors and insanities whereby the present calamity had been wrought; to go back two years and review the Champlain Valley's undistinguished part in a regionally unpopular conflict.

By 1812, when war was declared, the Northeast's martial fervor was at its lowest. Britain had become more willing to negotiate and the star of Napoleon, who it had been expected would be America's at least unofficial ally, was declining. That star set in April 1814, releasing British troops for service against the United States. Veteran regiments poured into Canada. Presently, an army of 14,000 men had gathered north of the border.

This critical hour was the consequence of the war's protracted mismanagement by American politicians who deemed themselves military geniuses and by American generals more skilled in politics than battle. All the inappropriate, stumbling gentlemen ignored the prompting of the Champlain-George Valley that led toward the vitals of Canada. No competent attempt was made to follow the ancient road of invasion. The conflict, till September 1814, had been centered in the Great Lakes with something less than a triumphant result. American ships and regiments had been dedicated to hacking at the enemy's fingers and toes instead of driving down Champlain at his heart.

The blindness of the United States' grand strategy, plus the unanimity with which generals commanding in the subordinate Champlain area fell over their own feet, had lowered still farther an originally dubious enthusiasm for the war among the immediate region's people in particular and the whole population of New England in general. Hostility toward the struggle was divided and then subdivided.

"Nearly one half of the five New England states supported the war, but were paralyzed by the other half which opposed it. Of the peace party, one half wished to stop the war, but was paralyzed by the other half, which threatened to desert their leaders at the first overt act of treason."[1]

There were shining patriots along the lake shore. There also were a number of New Yorkers and Vermonters, including a governor of the latter state, who dabbled more or less deeply in treason. No deed of the American armed forces in the Valley, ashore or afloat, had been sufficiently valorous to encourage an additional vast number of uncertain spirits. The army's accomplishments were more shabbily comic than the navy's. Each successive general surpassed his forerunner in achieving farce.

Major General Joseph Bloomfield was the first of an undistinguished series and the only one to make no glaring mistakes, which he accomplished by doing nothing at all. He fell ill in November 1812 at Plattsburg and was replaced by Major General Henry Dearborn who in mid-month marched 2,000 regulars of the garrison and 3,000 militia north to the boundary below Lacolle, Quebec. Part of Dearborn's host got lost; one detachment by mistake fired into another, and the befuddled army was repelled by Colonel Charles de Salaberry of the Canadian *Voltigeurs.* Dearborn led his army back to Plattsburg, November 23.

Major General Wade Hampton, grandsire of the Confederate leader of the same name, arrived at Burlington, July 30, 1813, to assume command of the army. He strove to revive its flagging morale by shooting major delinquents and publicly spanking minor.

One sinner was sentenced, crescendo, "to receive twenty-five

Cobbs on his bare posteriors on the parade in front of his Regiment, be put to hard labor with the ball & chain, for the remainder of the period for which he enlisted, and to have his liquor rations stopped for the same period."[2]

The general limited his other activities that summer to quarreling with his military district's commander, the malodorous James Wilkinson, who, at Sackets Harbor on Lake Ontario, was planning a modified version of Amherst's descent on Montreal.

Hampton, compelled to co-operate, crossed the lake, marched September 19 with 4,000 men from Cumberland Head to Chazy and Champlain and thence to the border from which he retreated on the plea that the summer's drought had left no water for his army to drink. When he advanced again, via the Chateaugay River, the busy Colonel de Salaberry blocked his way, and Hampton, after suffering 50 casualties, fell back to Plattsburg.

Wilkinson's imitation of Amherst had failed to carry him more than a hundred miles down the St. Lawrence. He led the bulk of his army to Plattsburg in early February 1814, and March 30, on the eve of a court of inquiry into his conduct, advanced through heavy snow to Lacolle where a small force under the British Major Hancock held fast to a stone mill, shot down a number of the invaders and drove Wilkinson back across the border.

In the spring of 1814 George Izard, a competent soldier who had been newly promoted major general, assumed command of the lakes army. A rubicund young brigadier, Alexander Macomb, was among his subordinates. The Valley troops at last had able leadership. The United States warships on Champlain had been similarly blessed for a year and a half.

In September 1812, when Lieutenant Thomas Macdonough superseded Lieutenant Sidney Smith in command, the American fleet had consisted of two gunboats built in 1809 to check smuggling, and one of them was beached at Basin Harbor and full of water. These were all the twenty-nine-year-old newcomer, with his tousled light hair and long Caledonian face, had with which to obey the order to keep Champlain clear of British ships.

Macdonough's best fortune was that, at the moment, the British possessed little more. The lieutenant was energetic and farsighted. He could look forward to a naval battle that might be fought for possession of the fair lake and the young towns on its shores. That was a future problem. Immediately he must race the British in creating a fleet by reconstructing and arming lake craft at once and by building better warships from the keel up if time served.

Macdonough visited Dearborn at Plattsburg and pried some army transports from him. He bought a lake sloop and sailed his makeshift fleet up to the shipyard at Whitehall. When spring came, he had an armed squadron—and a new wife, Lucy Shaler Macdonough, whom he had rushed away to Middletown, Connecticut, to marry—and he led his vessels proudly down the lake. His flag flew from the sloop *President,* twelve guns. The sloops *Growler* and *Eagle,* each of eleven guns, and the two revived gunboats followed. The nine-gun sloop *Montgomery* was not yet in commission but Macdonough had won the first lap of the race. The British had nothing under sail to rival him.

Success may have made the new commander reckless. The blow now dealt him might have broken a lesser man. *President* ran aground and hurt herself. Complaints came from down-lake that British craft were aprowl there, and Macdonough, mindful of his orders, sent *Growler* and *Eagle* under command of Lieutenant Smith on June 3 to rout them. Smith chased two gunboats into the Richelieu with a strong south breeze behind him and discovered when he came within range of the British batteries on Isle aux Noix that he was trapped. *Growler* and *Eagle* could make no headway back upstream with wind and current against them.

Gunboats and batteries opened. A shot tore away *Eagle's* bow below the water line; another dismasted *Growler*. Smith surrendered and half of Macdonough's effective fleet was in enemy hands. What he said about Smith has not come down to us.

Ironically it was after this disaster, on July 24, that Macdonough was promoted to master commandant.

He could find no shipwrights, and seamen were scarce. The best he could do at once was to seize some scows and hurriedly mount cannon on them. He had need for haste. Commander Daniel

Pring of the Royal Navy, whose fleet Smith immeasurably had strengthened, was a driver himself.

Pring repaired *Growler* and *Eagle,* renamed them *Shannon* and *Broke,* and, July 31, 1813, used them as the principal elements in the force that convoyed Lieutenant Colonel James Murray and 1,400 troops in 47 bateaux to Plattsburg. The American army under Hampton was concentrated at Burlington, and its general made no attempt to reinforce the endangered town. Chief defense of Plattsburg was Captain Sherry's company of New York militia which prepared to meet the enemy with the moderate ardor roused by their commander's instructions.

"Fight or run," Sherry is said to have cried, "as the occasion may require!"[3] and his warriors forthwith ran all the way to the Salmon River while Murray burned blockhouses, arsenal, armory as well as stores and warehouses, federal and private. Loss to the government was $25,000; to citizens of Plattsburg, $208,000.

Broke, Shannon and a gunboat appeared off Plattsburg, August 2, and opened a long-range bombardment of the earthworks that had been raised in what is now Battery Park. The American land guns and the cannon of Macdonough's *President,* his two gunboats and the armed scows replied. Gravest damage wrought was to the feelings of the master commandant who was forced to keep the remnant of his fleet out of harm's way while the British ranged the lake, destroying four vessels, capturing a flour-laden sloop and several other craft and marching inland to burn empty barracks and other government buildings at Swanton.

It was not until September 2 that Macdonough had an unsatisfactory revenge. He had managed by then to assemble a scratch squadron—*President,* the sloops *Preble* and *Montgomery,* each with nine guns; *Frances,* five, and *Wasp,* three. The last two were rented craft that sailed abominably but the fleet made a brave showing, and Pring, on their approach, retired into the Richelieu where Macdonough, remembering Smith's fate, refused to follow.

Pring with six gunboats ventured out of the river on December 4, burned an empty storehouse on Cumberland Head but popped back into his refuge at Macdonough's approach, and the master commandant led his fleet into winter quarters below the Otter Creek falls at Vergennes on December 21 with control of the lake firmly in his hands again.

Supremacy brought no ease. Pring was still in the race, and a sixteen-gun brig was building at Isle aux Noix. Macdonough had chosen Vergennes as the best site for the work ahead. Here, powered by the falls and fed from the bog iron beds at Monkton, Vermont, were furnaces, forges, a rolling mill and a wire factory. A road led to Boston whence shipwrights must come and another to Troy. Over this eighty teams drew naval stores all winter.

A cloud by day that was fiery by night hung above the Vergennes mills and the clamor of machinery and tools endured. On the ways stood the skeleton of an early steamboat. Macdonough appropriated it and turned it, as his answer to Pring's brig, into the sixteen-gun schooner *Ticonderoga.* Momentarily, he was ahead, but in February tidings came from the north that the British were planning a veritable frigate of 1,200 tons and carrying 30 guns. Such a giant was beyond the means at the master commandant's hand. His best answer could be only a 726-ton, twenty-six-gun ship.

He proceeded forthwith to build her. Trees for her timbers were felled March 2; her keel was laid March 7. On April 11, more than four months before her British rival took water, *Saratoga* was launched.

Fort Cassin, the battery the master commandant had established at the mouth of Otter Creek to protect his shipbuilding, proved its worth that spring. Ice left Champlain early, and on May 9 Pring with his new brig *Linnet* leading an armada of five sloops and thirteen gunboats, entered the lake and bore up its length with the intention of destroying the American fleet or blocking it in harbor. Izard at Plattsburg warned Macomb, commanding at Burlington. Captain Thornton and fifty artillerymen were trundled by wagon to Vergennes and Pring's contemplated attack evaporated, May 14, into a long range, almost harmless duel much enjoyed by the spectators.

Gunboats detached from the British fleet attempted to capture stores at Willsborough Falls in the Boquet River, but the supplies had been removed before the British appeared and one gunboat was hurt by fire from militia under Lieutenant Colonel Ransom Noble. Pring thereupon went down the lake again to remain holed-up in the Richelieu, for on May 26 Macdonough stood out past Fort Cassin with the new *Saratoga* and *Ticonderoga,* the sloop *Preble* and six gunboats. Later *President* and *Montgomery* joined him with five more gunboats.

The master commandant controlled Champlain but he was not entirely happy. From smugglers, spies and other persons of dubious loyalty he had learned that the British had not abandoned their intention of building their frigate. *Confiance* was to be her name, and in June Macdonough heard that her keel had been laid at Isle aux Noix. Forthwith he decreed still another American vessel.

The twenty-gun brig *Eagle* was launched at Vergennes August 11 and joined the fleet that was patrolling the lower reaches of the lake on August 27, two days after *Confiance* had gone down the ways.

The building contest was over. Izard and Macdonough were aware that the British were on the verge of moving up Champlain. This thrust would not be limited to raids and skirmishes. It would be the heaviest invasion the Valley ever had seen.

Since Napoleon's downfall, troops had been pouring into Canada, many of them tough, veteran regiments that had beaten the French marshals in Spain. Warwise generals—de Rottenburg, Power, Brisbane, Robinson—had arrived to supplement the less than redundant military talents of the commander in chief, Sir George Prevost. When *Confiance*—most powerful craft the lake ever had floated—was ready, the attack would be launched by army and fleet.

The Champlain area waited invasion with feelings that ranged from panic through indifference to satisfaction. It was not the most loyal area in the hard-pressed United States, nor is the record of the region at that time the most creditable in American history. Opposition of many to the war, profits wrung by more than a few from

Derick Photo, Vermont Development Commission

HARBOR ON LAKE CHAMPLAIN, VERMONT

Photo from Division of State Publicity, New York State Department of Commerce

SPEEDBOAT ON LAKE GEORGE AT HULETT'S LANDING

Adirondack Guide Photo

S.S. *Mohican* ON LAKE GEORGE

trading with the enemy made a darkness in the Valley against which the valor of patriots shone the more brightly. Obstruction of the war effort was not limited to undistinguished folk. Martin Chittenden, son of Thomas and Federalist governor of Vermont, already had attempted to hamstring the American army.

In the fall of 1813, when the garrison at Plattsburg had been depleted by Hampton's stumbling march to the north, the Third Brigade of Vermont militia under Colonel Luther Dixon had moved across the lake as reinforcement. On November 13 Martin Chittenden, styling himself in his summons "Governor, Captain General and Commander in Chief in and over the State of Vermont," recalled the state troops. He justified his peculiar command by propounding "that in his opinion, the Military strength and resources of this State must be reserved for its own defense and protection, *exclusively*—excepting in cases provided for, by the Constitution of the U. States; and then, under orders derived *only* from the Commander in Chief."[4]

Chittenden's order received, not obedience, but a prompt and blistering reply, signed first by Dixon and then by most of the brigade officers, acknowledging receipt of "a most novel and extraordinary Proclamation" and refusing, with a storm of invective that must have made Chittenden catch at his breath and hold fast to his hat, to comply.

"We consider your proclamation," the epistolary mutiny announced, "as a gross insult to the officers and soldiers in service, inasmuch as it implies that they are so *ignorant* of their rights as to believe that you have authority to command them in their present situation or so *abandoned* as to follow your insidious advice. We cannot regard your proclamation in any other light than as an unwarrantable stretch of executive authority, issued from the worst motives, to effect the basest purposes. It is, in our opinion, a renewed instance of that spirit of disorganization and anarchy which is carried on by a faction to overwhelm our country with ruin and disgrace . . . and although it may appear incredible to your Excellency, *even soldiers* have discernment sufficient to perceive that the proclamation of a governor when offered out of the line of his duty, is a harmless, inoffensive and nugatory document. They regard it with mingled emotions of pity and contempt for its author and as a striking monument of his folly."[5]

The rank and file of the Third Brigade, which comprised the entire militia force of Franklin County, Vermont, was less intransigent. Its removal to New York had left forty miles of border without defense. Furthermore, it was harvesttime and the little frontier farms needed their men. Many of the militia turned their backs on the duty their officers so glowingly had extolled and went home. One of the deserters, Silas Gates of St. Albans, was shot and killed by Alva Sabin of Georgia, Vermont, who was one of a detail sent out under Sergeant Henry Gibbs to round up the runaways. Sabin was tried for murder but got off when the jury disagreed.

There were less equivocal obstructionists than Chittenden on either lake shore. Prevost wrote to Lord Bathurst, secretary for war and the colonies, August 27, 1814:

"Two-thirds of the army are supplied with beef by American contractors, principally of Vermont and New York,"[6] and Izard at about this time complained to the War Department:

"On the east side of Lake Champlain the highroads are insufficient for the cattle pouring into Canada."[7]

Men were willing not only to feed but also to arm their country's foes. Macdonough on June 29 seized near the border two spars he believed were intended for *Confiance's* fore and mizzenmasts, and, July 7, four more that were apparently designed for her main and three topmasts.

The sorest blow to American defenses was dealt, not by British adherents in the Valley, but by that self-elected military genius, John Armstrong, Madison's secretary of war.

An army, some 14,000 strong, was marshaled just over the border. The British fleet, now commanded by Captain George Downie, waited for the mighty *Confiance* to be armed and rigged before entering the lake. While the landslide hung and Izard with 6,000 indifferent troops at Chazy and Champlain waited for it to plunge, Armstrong lightheartedly ordered him to march at once to Sacket's Harbor on Lake Ontario with 4,000 of his command.

Izard received the dispatch in mid-August and obeyed under protest on the twenty-ninth. The better part of the American army sailed down Champlain. By September 1, Prevost was across the border; was at Champlain on September 3 and Chazy September 4. Macomb, now commanding some 1,500 competents and no more than that number of invalids, replacements and casuals, had fallen back to Plattsburg.

The chubby general might have retreated still farther with small discredit. Fourteen thousand of Britain's best troops were marching toward him and to face them at the moment he had less than 2,200 able men—Captain Sproul's detachment of the 13th Infantry, 200; Captain M'Glassin's company of the 15th, 50 strong; fragments of the 6th, 29th, 31st, 32nd and 34th Infantry Regiments, totaling 1,771; 77 casuals and 802 invalids. The odds against Macomb were almost seven to one, yet, if he were to stand, there was no better place to meet invasion than the already fortified ridge between the Saranac's mouth and the lake.

Here trenches had been dug, cannon mounted and there was a large redoubt, Fort Moreau, which Macomb now flanked by two smaller—Fort Brown, close to the river, and Fort Scott, on the lake shore. Where the ridge projected, thumblike, into the lake, two blockhouses stood with a third, uncompleted, near by.

Macomb moved his invalids to Crab Island, south of the mouth of Plattsburg Bay, and gave them a fieldpiece for their protection. He worked furiously to improve his position, all the while begging with equal frenzy for militia reinforcements. Before the British came, 700 New York troops, including Captain Gilead Sperry's dragoons in inappropriate red jackets, had assembled. General Benjamin Mooers commanded them.

All available craft were ferrying Vermonters across the lake. Chittenden, clinging obstinately to his original peculiar contention, had refused to order the militia from the state but had consented to call for volunteers. Macomb had asked Vermont for 2,000 men. He got 2,500, under General Samuel Strong.

Macdonough's fleet that had been watching the narrow channel through the islands bore full sail up lake and into Cumberland

Bay, with an ingenious battle plan already forming in its commander's long head. He had lost the ill-starred *President* through storm damage and had released *Montgomery* as a transport. This was his available force:

Saratoga, ship: Master Commandant Thomas Macdonough, 732 tons, eight long 24's, six 42-pound and twelve 32-pound carronades.

Eagle, brig: Lieutenant Robert Henley, 480 tons, six long 18's, twelve 32-pound carronades.

Ticonderoga, schooner: Lieutenant Stephen Cassin, 350 tons, eight long 12's, four long 18's, five 32-pound carronades.

Preble, sloop: Lieutenant Charles Budd, 80 tons, seven long 9's.

Six 70-ton gunboats, each armed with one long 24 and an 18-pound columbiad, and four forty-tonners, each carrying a long 12.

The young master commandant considered the force Downie would bring against him:

Confiance, ship: Captain George Downie, 1,200 tons, twenty-seven long 24's, four 32 and six 24-pound carronades.

Linnet, brig: Captain Daniel Pring, 350 tons, sixteen long 12's.

Chub, sloop: (ex-*Shannon,* ex-*Growler*), Lieutenant James McGhie, 112 tons, one long 6, ten 18-pound carronades.

Finch, sloop: (ex-*Broke,* ex-*Eagle*), Lieutenant William Hicks, 110 tons, six 18-pound carronades, one 18-pound columbiad.

Five 70-ton gunboats with a total armament of three long 24's, two long 18's, five 32-pound carronades; four 40-tonners carrying a total of four 32-pound carronades and three of 30 tons, each armed with a long 18.

To the landsman, the fleets might seem evenly matched with the odds slightly favoring the British. They had the larger complement—917 trained man-of-war's men against Macdonough's scratch force of 820—and more guns—92 to the American 86. To a canny seaman like the master commandant, it wasn't so simple as that.

Downie had a great preponderance of big, far-reaching cannon—thirty long 24's to the American fourteen. In a fight of his own choosing, the British commander might lie beyond range of most of the American armament and break Macdonough's ships apart. Hadn't Downie boasted that he could defeat the enemy with *Confiance* alone? The big craft with her twenty-seven 24's probably could do precisely that with adequate sea room and wind.

Macdonough would have to get his ships in close and stay there. He must pin the British down where the blows of his heavy, short-ranged carronades would hurt. This was the master commandant's problem as his squadron moved into the bay off Plattsburg, past the downward reaching arm of Cumberland Head.

Macomb and Macdonough in the brief remaining pause before the tempest could only make ready the materials then in hand. No further reinforcement possibly could join them before the invasion rolled in by land and water.

Prevost was advancing with the deliberation of the consciously omnipotent, protecting his supply line, more as a military formality than with any thought of need, by leaving the 88th Foot at Champlain and the 39th at Chazy. Two regiments were hardly missed in the host that pressed forward in the greatest and the last invasion of the Valley and reached Sampson's, south of Chazy on September 5.

The infantry marched in four brigades. Major General Manley Power led the 3rd, 5th, 58th foot and a battalion of the 27th; Major General Thomas Macdougal Brisbane, the 6th, 18th, 49th and one battalion of the 8th. The regiments guarding the supply line had been taken from Major General Frederick Robinson's command, leaving him only another battalion of the 27th and one from the 76th. Canadian *voltigeurs,* chasseurs and light infantry were included in a Light Brigade with, like an echo from the earlier war, an organization of mercenaries, the Regiment de Meuron, Swiss professionals that the British first had hired in 1796.

Four troops of the 19th Light Dragoons, a company of engineers, a rocket battery with its terrifying weapons advanced with the infantry and in the dust of their passage clanked the artillery—four 24-pounders, two 12's, one 8-inch howitzer and three battalions of light 6's.

Lieutenant General Francis Baron de Rottenburg was in immediate direction of the army, and Prevost, as commander of all

British forces in North America, exercised supreme authority over both troops and fleet and already was writing peevish dispatches to Downie, urging haste.

On the bright, windy morning of the sixth, the slow, red river flowed out from Sampson's and split. One stream, composed of Power's and Robinson's men, slanted to the right on the Beekmantown road that led into Plattsburg and to the upper bridge across the Saranac. The rest of the army followed another track that crossed Dead Creek near its mouth and reached the lake shore some three miles north of the village.

Troops sent out by Macomb to dispute the advance scarcely delayed the plodding veterans. What opposition they offered never checked the strong streams of scarlet coats and bobbing leather shakos. Not once did either British column deploy, but pressed stubbornly onward toward the resistance and brushed it aside. The baleful approach of Power and Robinson frightened the militia that waited under Mooers by the stone church at Beekmantown. Their retreat became a stampede when they mistook their own red-coated dragoons, ranging the hills in the rear, for British cavalry.

Major John E. Wool and 200 regulars, who had been ordered forward to stiffen the militia, gave way more stubbornly but were pressed back, and the 2 field guns under Captain Leonard that tardily reinforced them at Halsey's Corners had barely time to fire before they were forced to limber up and whirl away to avoid capture.

The New York dragoons and 110 riflemen, scouting under Lieutenant Colonel Appling far out on the Dead Creek Road, soon were pushed in upon Captain Sproul who with 200 men and 2 cannon guarded the bridge across the sluggish stream. The Americans were barely able to destroy the structure before the British reached it.

Appling and Sproul, falling back still farther, made contact with Wool and retreated with him through Plattsburg village and across the lower of the Saranac's two bridges, tearing it up and thereafter using its planks in a breastwork to protect the crossing.

Mooer's fugitive militia had retired across the upper bridge and had served it likewise.

Power's and Robinson's troops were entering Plattsburg now. Brisbane's, having repaired the Dead Creek bridge, were advancing by the curved road that skirted the bay. Gunboats sent in by Macdonough opened on the column but the wind was driving white-maned waves across the water and the craft plunged and rolled so wildly that their aim was uncertain. They withdrew when British batteries began to reply from the shore.

Prevost occupied Plattsburg but did not try to force the Saranac, contenting himself with posting sharpshooters in the warehouses at the riverside. Macomb abolished this annoyance by setting fire to the buildings with hot shot.

On the morning of the seventh, Prevost began to build earthworks and place his batteries. During four successive days, he made no attempt upon the American fortifications but lethargically waited for Downie's tardy squadron. Had the British commander in chief taken the enemy's works, as it seems probable he could have done by an all-out assault, cannon on the height must have driven Macdonough from the bay and thwarted the victory for which the master commandant was preparing with every stratagem an admirably farsighted mind could devise.

By September 7, Macdonough was ready for battle. He had employed local geography to handicap Downie to the utmost. He had stationed his four principal craft one hundred yards apart in a line parallel to the downward-reaching Cumberland Head and closer to it than to the Plattsburg shore. The British, to get at the American fleet, must enter the bay where normally winds were light and unreliable.

Downie, in all probability, would come up the lake with a north breeze behind him and, rounding Cumberland Head, then would be forced to beat upwind to reach his enemies. All Champlain war vessels, British and American, were light of draft and too flat-bottomed to handle well close-hauled.

The British captain would have trouble in coming to grips with the American ships as Macdonough had placed them. Furthermore unless Prevost roused from his torpor and won his land battle before the fleet appeared, Downie would not dare attack along the wider stretch of water between Macdonough's line and the Plattsburg shore, since that would subject his ships to fire from the fortified ridge. He must, the master commandant was sure, choose the narrower breadth between the American craft and Cumberland Head. This would impose a close-range fight in which Macdonough's every gun could reach the enemy, who would have sacrificed the long-range superiority granted by his thirty 24-pounders.

There was one more advantage that might be gained by anchored craft that waited an enemy attack. Macdonough employed it. He planted a kedge anchor off each of *Saratoga's* bows, to starboard and port of the big bower anchor that held her, with a line leading from each of the kedges to the ship's corresponding quarter—her sternward side. A stream anchor, midway between kedge and bower in size, was hung from Saratoga's stern ready to let fall.

The ship now could be warped—turned end for end—thus bringing her unengaged broadside battery to bear if the other were silenced. It is probable that *Eagle, Ticonderoga* and *Preble* were similarly prepared, though *Saratoga* was the only craft to employ the device.

At some time during this waiting period, Sailing Master Daniel Stellwagon wrote out Macdonough's battle orders. The document recently was found by Captain H. A. Baldridge, U.S.N. (retired), Curator of the United States Naval Academy Museum, among a mass of papers sent to the Academy in 1888 from Brooklyn Navy Yard. It reads:

"Order of Battle

"The Saratoga will lead, the Schr will follow close after then the Brig, then the Preble. The Gallies (gunboats) will keep our large Vessels between them & the Enemy and will fire at Intervals or when they can bring their Guns to bear between the Saratoga, Schooner, Brig & Preble, or a little ahead of the Saratoga or astern of the Preble.

"The black dots denotes the Enemy the round marks our vessels, straight lines our Galleys, the 3rd division ahead, then the 2nd Division then the 1st Division."

Here follows Stellwagon's diagram and the order concludes: "The Galleys will remember to Keep our large vessels between them & the Enemy, and fire when they can get a chance."[8]

At some time after this undated order was written, the line of battle it prescribes was altered. *Eagle* headed it, followed by *Saratoga, Ticonderoga* and *Preble.*

Macdonough now had done all possible to make ready for the engagement. He waited. So, with less warrant, did Prevost who was resolved to delay his assault until Downie's squadron should appear.

The British captain was having a disheveled and unhappy time. He was continually prodded by dispatches from Prevost, urging haste, but he could not move without *Confiance,* and the frigate was not ready. Drafts of men from the warships in the St. Lawrence were coming in slowly. The last of them arrived September 6. *Confiance* hauled from the Isle aux Noix wharf on the seventh. Vessel and men were to have no opportunity for a shake-down cruise. The frigate actually sailed before she was completed and the last gangs of riggers and outfitters left her on September 11 only two hours before she came under fire.

Adverse winds, blowing strongly from the south, also delayed Downie's fleet. It was a little before 7:00 on the morning of the eleventh that watchers on the fortified ridge saw British topsails moving beyond Cumberland Head in a light north breeze and the men of the American fleet heard offshore cannonading as *Confiance* "scaled" her hitherto untried guns—cleared their bores by firing light powder charges.

Macomb's men had small subsequent opportunity to watch the approach of the enemy fleet, for Prevost's bugles were calling in Plattsburg, his long silent batteries were opening, and beyond the village heavy red assault columns formed.

This was the moment for which the torpid Prevost had insisted upon delaying the attack that he might advantageously have launched at any time within the last four days. His inertia had strengthened Macomb's command by militia reinforcements and had lifted its morale to the point where it was beginning to hit back. On the stormy night of September 9, Captain M'Glassin and fifty United States regulars had forded the Saranac, had fallen upon a British rocket position, had destroyed it and put its detail to flight.

The British fleet hove to east of Cumberland Head and, while the gunboats caught up, Downie was rowed forward to inspect the American position. He determined to turn the head of Macdonough's line. While the sloop *Chub* and the brig *Linnet* assailed *Eagle,* Downie purposed to lay *Confiance* across *Saratoga's* bows and rake her. Meanwhile, the sloop *Finch* and the gunboats were to assail first *Preble* and then *Ticonderoga.*

At 7:40 the British made sail and, on rounding Cumberland Head, found it impossible to execute their commander's plan entire. The wind that had blown satisfactorily out on the lake came to the bay only in light, baffling gusts. At the head of the line, *Chub* and *Linnet* were having difficulty in taking position, and *Confiance* was moving up slowly.

She came on, white ensign rippling and all canvas drawing, a towering craft and contemptuously silent though along the American line guns were flashing and booming. *Linnet,* while passing *Saratoga,* had thrown a broadside at her which had accomplished little beyond smashing a crate in which a gamecock was penned. The bird flew to the rails, flapped his wings and crowed, while *Saratoga's* gunners cheered the omen.

Shot from *Eagle* and the American flagship were falling closely short about *Confiance,* but the tall frigate moved on beyond the leaping spray without reply. At last, Macdonough's guns began to reach her. A ball from a long 24, aimed by the master commandant himself, ranged across *Confiance's* deck. Others carried away her two port bow anchors. Downie now abandoned his original purpose. His ship, still silent, anchored with deliberate precision 300 yards off *Saratoga's* beam.

Not until all had been secured did *Confiance* let go her broadside. The shock of the double-shotted 24's, fired at close range, was like a collision. *Saratoga* heeled so violently that half her men were cast asprawl upon her deck. Many were killed, among them Peter Gamble, Macdonough's first lieutenant. More were wounded. While splinters still were falling, the survivors scrambled up and rushed back to their guns. In one of their responding broadsides Captain Downie died.

A 24-pound shot struck the muzzle of a gun behind which the British leader was standing, driving it backward from its carriage against his midriff, smashing his watch, killing him almost instantly but, beyond a bruise, leaving no mark of injury upon his body.

Noise like the uneven rolling of a colossal drum now ran along the embattled vessels and a deepening smoke with a flickering in its heart spread above them. Out of the cloud drifted what remained of the British *Chub*.

Eagle's broadside had caught the sloop full force. Smashed and helpless, she struck her flag and was taken by Midshipman Platt and a boat crew from *Saratoga*.

While *Linnet* and *Confiance* slugged it out with the American flagship, the sloop *Finch* and the British gunboats were active at the south end of the line. *Ticonderoga's* fire at last disabled the enemy sloop and the fitful wind drove her toward Crab Island where invalids, healed by excitement, opened on her with the fieldpiece Macomb had placed there and forced *Finch* to surrender.

Two British ships were out of the battle but Macdonough had lost *Preble*. Furiously attacked by the British gunboats, she at last could take no more but cut her cable and withdrew, leaving *Ticonderoga* to bear the full brunt of the assault.

A fury of cannonading and yelling raged about the schooner. Foam boiled around the threshing sweeps as the British tried to board, but *Ticonderoga's* guns blasted them with grapeshot and sacks of musket bullets and at last drove them off. The gunboats withdrew. Meantime, at the head of the line, the dogged pounding of ship by ship went on. In the heavy battle smoke, *Confiance* was firing high, bringing down *Saratoga's* spars, one of which in falling stunned Macdonough for an instant, but dealt less damage to the ship herself. After the action, it was found that *Saratoga* had been hulled 55 times and *Confiance,* 105.

Yet fire from the American flagship was slackening. One by one, her guns were being silenced. Twice she had been set afire by red-hot shot from the furnace *Confiance* carried, and still heavier punishment was in store for her.

Eagle, severely mauled by *Linnet* with some aid from *Confiance,* had one of her cables shot away and swung so that her guns no longer could bear. Lieutenant Henley accordingly cut her other cable, ran the brig down under topsails to a new position between *Saratoga* and *Ticonderoga* and resumed action, but her withdrawal left the flagship exposed to the combined fire of *Confiance* and *Linnet.*

As *Saratoga's* few remaining guns were hushed, Macdonough began to work the device he had prepared, days before, for such an emergency. To continue the battle he must warp his ship and bring her port battery to bear. Boatswains' whistles shrilled above the crashing British guns. There was a splash as the stream anchor, hanging at *Saratoga's* stern, was let go (Fig. 1). Seamen stumbled over the littered deck, bearing the stream-anchor line forward to the port bow while others cut the cable of the bower anchor.

Men heaved on the line running to the starboard kedge and brought the ship's quarter up to that anchor while the line to the port kedge was passed beneath *Saratoga.* The vessel now hung at right angles to her former position with her stern to *Confiance* (Fig. 2) but already men in her port bow had begun to heave strongly on her stream-anchor line. *Saratoga's* prow came around, swung farther still to the south (Fig. 3) and at last, when the ship had been turned completely end for end, her port battery came to bear.

The sorely wounded *Confiance* shook at the blow from hitherto unused guns. At 10:30 the British flagship had had enough. She struck her flag, and at 10:45 *Linnet* could endure no further battering and also surrendered.

The last cannon had spoken from the broken, leaking ships. American gunboats that had started in pursuit of the fleeing British

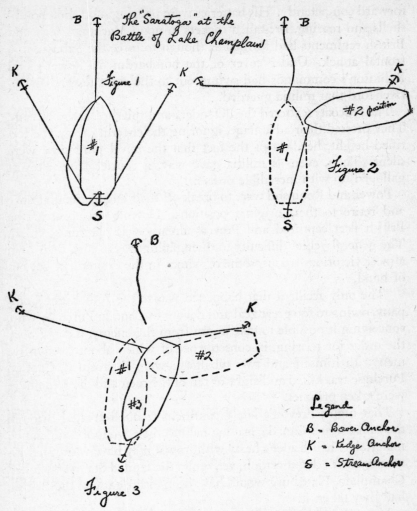

The "Saratoga" at the Battle of Lake Champlain

Figure 1

Figure 2

#2 position

Figure 3

Legend
B = Bower Anchor
K = Kedge Anchor
S = Stream Anchor

How Macdonough reversed the *Saratoga* in Plattsburg battle.

small craft were recalled to help save the larger vessels from sinking. In the sudden quiet, men could hear, like enduring echoes of their own battle, the roar of guns on the Plattsburg shore.

Prevost's assault, however belatedly decreed, had been moving forward competently. His batteries were pouring solid shot, bombshells and roaring, fire-tailed rockets in upon Macomb's fort, and British regiments had formed as though to force the Saranac in a frontal attack. Under cover of the bombardment, Power's and Robinson's commands had swung out to the right toward an upriver ford that militia guarded.

The redcoats scattered the defenders and splashed across stream. They pressed their advantage, ignoring the cheering from the fortified height, heedless of the fact that the naval guns now were silent. Then, even as militia gave way, a courier from Prevost galloped up with incredible orders.

Power and Robinson were to break off their engagement at once and retire to their original positions. Downie was beaten, the British fleet captured and Prevost already was planning retreat. The generals' chief difficulty in disengaging was to curb their own almost victorious troops, some of whom in the excitement got out of hand.

"The only accident that happened was to the 76th Light Company, owing to too great zeal and daring in Captain Purchase who, conceiving it possible to take a gun from the enemy, did not obey the order for retiring, in consequence of which about twenty-five men with himself and two subalterns were intercepted, Captain Purchase was killed and eight or ten of the men and the remainder were taken prisoner."[9]

That night, Prevost's lately confident troops retreated through the rain toward Canada, leaving behind their wounded and much material. Their leader's hasty withdrawal may have warranted his countrymen's denunciation, yet, while the United States controlled Champlain, Plattsburg would have been of little use to the British, had they taken it.

Macomb let the enemy plod away through the storm with only minor attempts at pursuit. He probably was profoundly relieved to see them go. His claim that the British army lost 2,500 in killed and wounded is a fantastic overestimate. 600 would be a more plausible guess. American army dead, injured and missing were about 150.

In the lake battle, the British had lost 300 wounded and killed: the Americans, 200. Macdonough had not spent his men's lives vainly. He had broken up the gravest danger that ever threatened the Champlain Valley and indirectly had helped end the war. Already his messenger was on the way to the secretary of the navy with the following letter:

"U.S.S. Saratoga
"off Plattsburgh, September 11th, 1814
"Sir:
The Almighty has been pleased to Grant us a signal victory on Lake Champlain in the capture of one Frigate, one Brig and two sloops of war of the enemy—I have the honor to be
"Very respectfully,
"Sir, your ob't Serv't
"T. Macdonough, Com."[10]

He dismissed his achievement too briefly. Its consequences were emphatic and far-reaching. British negotiators who were imposing upon American emissaries punitive peace terms had an immediate change of heart when news of Macdonough's victory reached them and hurriedly revised their hitherto excruciating demands.

"The battle of Lake Champlain," Admiral Mahan has written, "more nearly than any other incident of the War of 1812 merits the epithet 'decisive.' "[11]

---

[1] Henry Adams, *History of the Administration of James Madison* (New York, 1930), Book VIII, p. 1.

[2] "Garrison Orders of the 11th and 12th Infantry," printed in *The Moorsfield Antiquarian*, I, No. 2, 85, Aug. 1922.

[3] Duane Hamilton Hurd, *History of Clinton and Franklin Counties* (Philadelphia 1880), p. 156.

[4] Abby Maria Hemenway, *The Vermont Historical Gazetteer* (Burlington, 1686), I, 671.

[5] *Ibid.*, p. 672.

[6] *Report on Canadian Archives* (Ottawa, 1896), Lower Canada, p. 35.

[7] *Official Correspondence of General Izard with the War Department* (Philadelphia, 1816), pp. 56-57.

[8] Manuscript in U. S. Naval Academy Museum.

[9] Major General Frederick Robinson, Diary in *Royal United Services Institution Journal*, Aug. 1916, p. 512.

[10] Manuscript in U. S. Naval Academy Museum.

[11] A. T. Mahan, *Sea Power in its Relation to the War of 1812* (Boston, 1905), II, 381.

Chapter 20

Transition

THE guns once more were silent but the people of the Champlain-George Valley regarded peace with suspicion, though it brought to an area long retarded by strife a bright promise of prosperity. Men, returning to their farms, their mills, their young commercial enterprises, still looked apprehensively northward.

Six times war had rolled thence through the valley. There was no warrant that it would not gather again below the lake and sweep over it once more. Thrice within the memories of the no more than middle-aged, British fleets had invaded Champlain. The American government was moving now to block a possible fourth attack.

Island Point juts out from the New York shore, north of the village of Rouses Point and just south of the Canadian line. The army purposed to raise a fort on this site, a powerful stronghold whose guns, commanding Champlain's outlet, would bar the lake to hostile craft. Engineers under Colonel Joseph Totten began to build in the summer of 1816.

The construction, though ambitious, did little to advance Totten's repute as an engineer. The walls were of stone and brick but the footing beneath them was ill-established and the structure almost at once began to crack and crumble. The stronghold was not begun at a propitious time for either federal or private enterprise in the northern Champlain region. That twelvemonth is still remembered as "Eighteen Hundred and Froze to Death."

Spring had come early with plentiful warm rain that roused hope of bumper crops but the weather grew so cold that apple trees did not blossom until June and snow fell on the sixth, seventh

270

and eighth of that month. The storm was followed by a hard freeze in which many lately shorn sheep perished, though their owners tried to save the quaking flocks by lashing their late fleeces back about bared bodies. There were snow flurries in July and August but no rain fell and in the parched forests fires kindled and raged. A heavy frost, September 10, ruined what hardy vegetation still endured. Six inches of snow came on October 18.

Fish from the streams and the lake were the principal human diet during the following winter. There was almost no fodder for sheep or cattle and they perished wholesale. Imported rye sold for $3 a bushel and corn for $2.50. Flour was from $15 to $17 a barrel.

Uncommonly fine growing seasons followed that year of dearth, but recent privation and the dread of more launched the first of the mass migrations from the Champlain region. Men who had dwelt too briefly beside the lake to know that the rigors of 1816 had been unique abandoned their farms and moved out to the alluring Ohio Country, leaving behind them depleted communities. All the residents of Worcester, Vermont, departed save one stouthearted family.

Nerves had been so rasped by the late war and the more immediate year of cold that the authorities attempted to conceal from the remaining residents the tale of still another, newly discovered calamity.

British commissioners to the peace conference at Ghent in 1814 had insisted that the new treaty provide for a resurvey of the United States-Canada boundary. This was begun by representatives of the lately warring nations two years later. In 1818, surveyors who were tracing the 45th parallel westward from New Hampshire found to their consternation that in the Champlain area the hitherto accepted line lay about three-fourths of a mile north of the true latitude.

The survey that Governor Henry Moore of New York had supervised in company with William Gilliland during 1766 had been lamentably inaccurate, and territory that heretofore had been considered the property of New York and Vermont, as well as the new Federal reservation with a half-built fort, plainly belonged to Britain.

Though the commissioners tried to keep their discovery from the ears of an already exasperated people, their attempt fared no better than most secrets several persons share. Canadians gloated and Americans uttered defiance. The army at once stopped work on the stronghold, which thenceforth was known derisively as "Fort Blunder," and the stone, brick and metal were carried away piecemeal by dwellers in the region. No final decision was reached in the dispute until 1842 when, by a provision of the Webster-Ashburton Treaty, the line as misestablished by Moore's surveyors was confirmed.

In 1844, American engineers tried again, beginning a new stronghold on Island Point, a little to the west of the original. It was to be a powerful structure, stone-walled and mounting, when complete, ninety cannon. Work was pursued sporadically for twenty-six years. Little was undertaken while peace seemed secure. Tension, whenever it arose between the United States and Britain, immediately resulted in further building.

William A. Wheeler, later President Hayes's vice-president and in 1862 a New York representative in Congress, wrote on January 17 of that year, when the nation was teetering on the verge of war with Britain over the Mason and Slidell crisis:

"I have prevailed upon the Comm. of Ways & Means to insert in the Fortification Bill, for Fort Montgomery $50,000 for the bal. of the fiscal year (ending June 1st next) and $100,000 for the next fiscal year. . . . We may thank the Trent affair for these liberal amounts.

"If thieves," Wheeler pursues mordantly, "are needed to prey upon these expenditures, we can forward them from here to order."[1]

During the Civil War, the still unfinished Fort Montgomery most nearly fulfilled its purpose. Artisans working there were formed into a military company and, when friction between the United States and Canada was most acute, manned the stronghold's uncompleted batteries.

From 1870, when work on the fort permanently was suspended, until 1908 when the post was abandoned, Montgomery, which covered three acres, was garrisoned by an ordnance sergeant and a watchman. Stone from the north wall was removed in 1908 to serve as fill for the Rouses Point-Alburg bridge. Its remaining ruins are a finis mark, a colophon in decaying masonry, to an era of antagonism and violence.

In the early decades of the nineteenth century there were abundant distractions at hand to keep the Valley dwellers from brooding too rancorously on the Fort Blunder fiasco. Many of these were galling counterirritants. One, at least, was a diversion. The scandal of the Mooers, New York, wolf ring in 1821 filled the district with the unscrupulous glee that effervesces in American frontier communities whenever constituted authority is outsmarted.

Details of the operation of the ring, which may have centered in Mooers but certainly spread throughout Clinton and into Franklin County, are still reasonably clear. The identity of members of the conspiracy is dim, since most of the documents dealing with the combine long ago mysteriously vanished from official files.

Wolves, which in the earlier days had been a plague to settlers, largely had vanished from Clinton and Franklin Counties by 1820, but towns, counties and state still offered bounties, totaling $40 per wolf, for the creatures' slaughter. This was a large price to pay for any animal, feral or domestic, in times of financial stringency and a number of ingenious persons who seem to have been bound together by a common aversion for hard work at small wages considered the matter and then took action.

In 1821 it appeared that a horde of wolves suddenly had invaded Mooers and surrounding territory. It was true that sheep continued to graze unharmed and no person encountered the intruders alive, yet hunters began to appear before justices of the peace with two, three or even a half-dozen wolf heads and demand bounty certificates. For years such bounties in either county never had exceeded $1000 annually. During this one twelvemonth in Franklin County alone $10,600 was paid out for slaughtered wolves.

There were cries of fraud from citizens outside the ring, but in 1822 still larger bounty payments were made. It was charged that justices of the peace were in the conspiracy and that identical wolf heads were presented over and over and each time were accorded certificates. Tumult and the harvest of trophies waxed together. If the hunters continued to demand reward for their wolf heads, it would be only a matter of brief time before the involved counties went bankrupt.

The mysterious plethora of wolves in the two counties came at last to the attention of the state legislature. Investigation is said to have established that the prospering hunters were not ridding their neighborhoods of marauders but actually were importing them.

The ring, it was charged, was buying wolf heads by the gross from Canada. They cost little there and were worth $40 apiece in New York. When wolf heads were not available, the ring members were willing to accept husky dogs' heads in their place.

Incomplete records show that before the legislature cut the bounty to $10 per wolf and forbade any county to pay out more than $1000 for heads in any one year, 500 of the predators had allegedly been slain in Franklin County and 275 in Clinton. When the bounty was reduced, wolves immediately ceased to ravage the region. Many otherwise respectable citizens were said to have been involved in the conspiracy but their names and the documents that cited them have vanished.

The Mooers wolf ring contributed a lively episode to the Valley's domestic annals which otherwise dealt largely with brief prosperities, disappointments, thwartings and the serial defeat of a region limited in its resources by newer, richer areas.

Only people as obstinate, ingenious and resourceful as the lakes' folk could have maintained a flourishing economy in the face of afflictions supplied by disaster, by mounting competition from the West and by their own profligate use of what appeared to be the Valley's illimitable natural wealth.

Wheat, by 1820, had become the prime crop of the lately cleared fields on Champlain's either shore. No other equal area in the young nation grew the grain so plentifully. A bushel of wheat had supplanted a bushel of ashes as a currency unit in a time still stigmatized by a shortage of actual cash. At the height of the wheat growers' prosperity, weevils invaded the Valley, ruining crop after crop and driving farmers out of large-scale agriculture into animal husbandry.

Sheep to a major and cattle to a minor extent became the region's chief enterprises. The tariff on wool and the introduction of Merinos covered the erstwhile wheatfields with flocks that made Vermont for a decade one of the country's foremost sheep-raising states. The peak of production was attained in the early 1840's. A slow decline set in thereafter and became more rapid when the Civil War ended and Western competition grew still more redoubtable. As the profits from sheep raising diminished, Valley farmers turned increasingly for support to cattle.

Cows and oxen had entered the region with the pioneers but generations passed before the animals were raised commercially for milk production. Originally they were of no particular breed, though Devons and Shorthorns appeared early, but the lush Valley grazing gave them a stature and substance that spread the fame of "lake cattle."

Ayrshires, imported by Scots, were the first of the specialized dairy varieties to be introduced. Guernseys appeared in the 1840's and Jerseys in the 1850's when the sheep market was declining. These breeds, with Holsteins which arrived in large numbers during the 1870's, still form the backbone of Champlain farm economy though in this industry, too, the rivalry of the West has imposed changes.

Cheese and butter originally were the area's principal dairy products. Vermont, for a space, led in their manufacture but was driven from pre-eminence and forced to turn in the early 1900's to milk raising by the competition of the Midwest. The pattern imposed on industry had been inevitable in a region whose scenic loveliness has been its one inexhaustible asset. A swift rise into prosperity, a more abrupt decline, has been the story, in graph, of many Valley enterprises.

Lumber and iron both conformed to that production curve. In either industry, fine but limited resources were run by ambition and energy into quick depletion, so that only vestiges of once great enterprises remain.

The day when the log rafts' brown herds moved over Lakes George and Champlain ended long ago. The time when the smoke of forges dimmed the west shore of the greater lake and the thump of trip hammers went far across the water has almost as wholly gone by, but the enterprises in their heyday made Champlain a great highway of commerce.

The forests with which originally the twin lakes were framed were to the early settlers successively obstacles, raw material for potash and, finally, as mills and men increased, an apparently unlimited source of wealth. They were so vast, lumbermen proclaimed, that they would last for centuries—and forthwith proceeded to destroy them in a single human life span. It required little more than sixty years, once the industry achieved large-scale production, to slaughter the great, primeval woodland of the Champlain watershed.

The towering white pines, many of them more than 200 feet high and unafflicted by their present multitude of diseases, fell first, and white oak and spruce marched close behind them toward practical extinction. Subsequently, the demand for tanbark doomed the hemlocks, the later rise of the pulp industry swept away poplar, basswood and birch of whatever size, and the charcoal-burning for iron forges completed the destruction.

The massacre proceeded more rapidly on the east shore where population was greater. Stephen Mallet, whose name still adheres to Mallet's Bay, north of Burlington, sent the first raft of Vermont oak timber to Canada in 1794. The traffic increased, though it was not devoid of danger. Rafts were torn apart by sudden Champlain storms and not a few of them were smashed and members of their crews drowned in the rapids of the Richelieu.

Thus, the enterprising Clinton County lumber firm of Keggs, Stafford & Hoyle forwarded the first raft of New York timber north toward Canada in 1812. A tempest broke it up off Valcour

Island and beached most of the logs at Shelburne, Vermont. The raft was toilsomely reassembled and continued its voyage. It reached Canada just after war had been declared and forthwith was confiscated.

The occasional rigors of the northward voyage were mild, compared to the difficulty of getting logs from Whitehall over execrable roads to the Hudson, and the tide of trade ran into Canada with increasing strength until 1823, when the Champlain-Hudson Canal was opened. Thereafter the trend reversed itself and flowed up-lake instead of down. Barges and sailing craft in increasing numbers carried lumber southward, but by then the best of the timber on the Vermont shore was gone. Axes and saws had slain almost all the white pine. By 1835, the east slope of the Champlain Valley had been practically cleared of its magnificent primeval stand.

The despoiling of the basin's western rim began later but was conducted no less ruthlessly. In their arrogant belief that the forests of the Adirondacks were inexhaustible, lumbermen were criminally wasteful. Hillsides were shorn clean, but only the best timber was utilized. Felled hemlocks were stripped of their bark for tanneries, and the logs then were left to rot. No reforestation was undertaken in the cleared areas.

On the steep slopes that frame Lake George, hosts of ancient trees were taken and in their places lay the slash left by lumber crews. The logs, once launched, moved up or down the lake— southward to Caldwell whence they were trucked to Glens Falls; northward through the outlet and, from Ticonderoga, up or down Champlain.

From the mouths of all the streams stout enough to float log drives and turn sawmills, schooners, sloops and barges, deep laden with squared timbers, planks and boards plied the lake while crews of from 15 to 20 men toiled at the sweeps of lumber rafts whose standard length was 160 feet, width 140 and depth from 25 to 30 tiers of logs. Meanwhile, the forest dwindled and the blight of cutover land spread across the hills.

It was on this brief, rich commerce that the erstwhile village of

Burlington, Vermont, fed and grew. As the demand for lumber mounted and the Valley's supply diminished, imports from Canada became continually heavier. A law closing the Champlain-Hudson Canal to foreign craft made Burlington a transshipment center. The influx of Canadian timber was quickened by the opening in 1845 of a canal about the Richelieu's difficult rapids. When the railway reached Burlington in 1849, the town was well on its way toward becoming the lakes' great lumber center, whence wood, finished and unfinished, was borne to Boston for distribution throughout New England and carriage overseas.

The peak of Valley timber production was passed by the mid-century. On the Vermont shore, the disappearance of the forest was not calamitous, since its abolition bared more fertile land for farming. In the Adirondacks, the situation was tragic. Those rugged slopes were too steep, their soil was too thin for profitable agriculture, and erosion followed in the wake of the logging crews. Champlain's west shore had been thoroughly deforested before New York State belatedly considered locking the stable door.

Horatio Seymour was appointed in 1872 chairman of a commission to study the condition of the state's natural resources— forests, water power and wild life. Despite the aggrieved howls of the lumber interests, New York passed a law in 1883 prohibiting further sale of state lands and in 1885 established the first conservation commission. Ten years later, this became the body that today scientifically controls all state forests to insure their perpetuation.

The Champlain Valley's importance as a highway for lumber traffic ceased abruptly in 1897, when a duty of $2 a thousand feet was imposed on Canadian wood products. What earlier had been the principal sustenance for Burlington's growth now was cut off, but the vigor that the commerce in timber had granted to the city enabled it to survive the shock and diversified manufactures—wood products, textiles and the processing of maple syrup—in which Burlington already had concerned itself, insured its continuing prosperity.

On the rest of Champlain's Vermont shore, lumbering had ended, save for small cutting of new trees, and the region was passing through the second stage of its development, with the third and present already in view. Cultivation of the cleared and fertile land waxed as the forests diminished, but mass production by the great Western farms increasingly pinched Valley agriculture. Though the dairy industry flourished and apple orchards became plentiful, the region was transforming itself as roads and transportation improved, more and more into a resort country where hotels, boardinghouses and lakeside camps multiplied and a growing number of city dwellers bought property for summer and, not infrequently, permanent homes.

The development of the Valley's west slope from wilderness to its present situation did not follow precisely the course of the east. On Lake George and in some Champlain areas, the trees, once felled, bared only unprofitable hillsides. Many vigorous communities relapsed into an apathy, from which the influx of vacationists is only now reviving them.

Certain lake towns, particularly in Essex County and to a lesser degree in Clinton, enjoyed during and immediately after the lumber boom additional prosperity through the development of the iron deposits within their limits. In this the Vermont shore towns had only a slight and early share.

"Bog Iron," a red hematite deposit that through the decay of the marshy soil about it has practically mined itself, was produced profitably in Monkton, Addison County, in the post-Revolutionary era and was used in outfitting Macdonough's fleet. Other slim resources were worked briefly at Brandon and elsewhere, but there were no iron beds in Vermont comparable to those on the New York shore.

The Adirondack slope of the Champlain Valley contains deposits great and small of magnetic iron (Fe_3O_4)—a black variety of the mineral which, when mined and crushed, can be separated from its surrounding rock dust by magnets.

Philip Skene's forge at Skenesborough may have been fed by ore from this region, since he held a grant of land in what is now the Port Henry area. Otherwise, Adirondack iron production developed tardily and reached its peak in 1880 when New York produced 23 percent of the metal mined in the United States, chiefly from Essex and Clinton Counties.

Slow settlement of Champlain's west shore, preoccupation with the lumber industry and a lack of the capital requisite for mine development, all were factors in delaying production. As the forests dwindled and wealth consequently increased, men became aware of fortunes that lay beneath their feet.

There had been many indications that iron was abundant in the area. Surveyors' compasses had been unsettled by the metal's attraction; there were outcroppings in pastures and, in one instance, ore had been bared by an uprooted tree. Work in a small way had been carried on in the Cheever Mine, in the present Mineville district, back of Port Henry, and on Arnold Hill, in Peru township, during the early 1800's, but it was not until the late 1840's that production gained momentum. In 1841 the Champlain-Hudson Canal carried only 132 tons of ore southward; in 1864 it bore 103,000 tons.

A dozen towns in Essex and at least half that number in Clinton County were engaged at one time or another in iron mining. Blast furnaces were raised at Ticonderoga, Crown Point, Port Henry, Ausable Forks and elsewhere beside the lake. Many of the enterprises, handicapped by scant deposits and scanter capital, perished swiftly. Among the longer-lived were the Arnold and Palmer Hills mines in Peru, the Hammondville beds west of Crown Point which produced the armor for the Civil War ironclad *Monitor,* the Lyon Mountain deposits, far inland from Champlain at Dannemora but linked by rail with Plattsburg, and—one of the largest magnetic iron deposits in the world and the only Champlain mines to be worked continuously since their beginnings—the Mineville bed in the bleak upland above Port Henry.

The opening of the Mesabi Range in the Lake Superior region during the 1890's brought into the market low-cost iron with which most of Champlain's mines could not compete. One by one they expired and only rubble-filled holes and gaunt decaying buildings are their memorials. Even the Dannemora workings suspended operations for a space, though later they were purchased and revived by Republic Steel. Only the Mineville property continued production.

This field, from its beginning, has been blessed with a bed of high-grade iron whose limits still have not been wholly determined, plus a continually able management. In 1862 Witherbee, Sherman & Co. completed the purchase of all the profitably productive properties in the area. Until 1938 when the company's holdings were released to Republic Steel for a forty-year term, the Witherbee, Sherman concern, though handicapped by its distance from fuel and market, survived Western competition that had ended many similar Adirondack enterprises.

The tilted skips still are bringing iron to the surface in Mineville. Fifty million tons of ore already have been taken from a bed that still appears inexhaustible. Witherbee, Sherman's blast furnaces were shut down when Republic Steel leased the property. This concern, during its tenancy, has produced some 8,000,000 tons of ore from the three mines now operating—the Old Bed, the Harmony and Fishers Hill. Another 1,500,000 tons probably will be shipped in 1946.

Assembly-line production prevails in Mineville. The ore moves mechanically up from the depths and thence to successive great buildings where an institutional cleanliness and an appalling noise incongruously dwell together and complex engines with a minimum of human supervision grind, concentrate, sinter and at last dump the glowing, clinkerlike end product into cars that bear it to company blast furnaces elsewhere.

Mineville's export is a small survival of the more prosperous day when fleets of barges, deep laden with iron, moved out from now sleepy lakeside villages and crept up Champlain to cram the canal with their number. Ore moves now by rail, not water. The time when the lake was a crowded commercial highway and the prowess of its steamers excited the whole region ended years ago. Steam traffic followed the pattern of many Valley industries from a heyday into abrupt decline.

------

[1] Letter in the collection of Hugh McLellan, Champlain, N. Y.

Chapter 21

Steamboats of the Lakes

JOHN and James Winans, brothers and forward-looking men, built the steamship *Vermont* at Burlington, close to where the offices of the Champlain Transportation Company now stand, and launched her in the spring of 1808. This was less than a year after Fulton's *Clermont* had puffed and splashed her way from New York to Albany in thirty-two hours.

Vermont was slid widewise into the water and stuck on the ways. The superstitious, with more accuracy than usual, saw an augury of future disasters in the mishap. The craft had a brief, misfortune-hounded existence but she was nevertheless the first steamer to ply commercially on an American lake, as well as the ancestor of a succession of increasingly splendid vessels that were to traverse Champlain and George for more than a hundred years.

Commerce came belatedly to the twin lakes that for the first two centuries of their existence in history were dedicated almost exclusively to war. Philip Skene launched a sloop for trade with Canada in 1771, and his new schooner *Liberty* became a prize for Ethan Allen's men in 1775. Samuel Deall, a New Yorker with an interest in Ticonderoga real estate, in 1768 launched on Lake George a "petti-auga." This odd word, of no discernible ancestry, was applied to an equally unusual craft—a flat-bottomed contraption with leeboards in lieu of a keel, two masts and two sails, "all managed by one man who was also helmsman and very frequently drunk."[1]

Early attempts at commercial navigation died after the Vermonters captured Ticonderoga. Traffic was resumed slowly at the war's end but gathered momentum as settlers came into the region and identified the broad highway of the lakes as the smoothest road to fortune.

282

An ingenious people contrived a variety of craft with which to open trade with Canada. Zephaniah Platt, at Plattsburg, was commodore of a large fleet of bateaux by 1785. At Burlington, Essex, Whitehall and elsewhere, men turned to building lake vessels. Some were constructed according to residents' own landlubberly ideas; some were produced by imported shipwrights.

Between 1790 and 1815 more than thirty sailing craft were launched upon Champlain. Most of these came eventually into the hands of Gideon King, leading citizen of the growing village of Burlington. He entered the lake trade with two self-built cutters and by his driving tactics acquired a practical monopoly of the carrier trade and the half-derisive, half-envious title of "Admiral of the Lake."

King's sloops and schooners bore into Canada from Vermont horses, beef, pork, lumber, potash and pearlash, maple sugar and flax; ashes, peltry and iron from New York. Canada, in return, exported such products from overseas as rum, gin, wines, tea, coffee, chocolate, linens and woolens.

None laughed more loudly than "the Admiral" and his crews when, June 1808, *Vermont* waddled out into the lake on her maiden voyage and the swifter sailing craft ran circles around her. The steamer was to be a source of malicious merriment during all her harried existence.

No picture of her survives but she probably was built on the general lines of *Clermont*—a flush-decked, bargelike affair with tall stack and unhoused paddles. She had no pilot house and was steered by a tiller in the stern. In calm, when her engines ran smoothly, which was seldom, she could scuttle along at six miles an hour. She made amends for this perilous speed by frequent break downs.

Vermont's schedule called for one round trip a week between Whitehall and St. Johns. This often took ten days and sometimes a fortnight. Possibly her misfortunes and the mounting exasperation of her captain, John Winans, drove the steamer to suicide. On October 15, 1815, while proceeding up the Richelieu River, *Vermont* shook loose her connecting rod, stabbed it through her side and sank, mourned by none, above Ash Island. More from thrift than fondness, the Winanses salvaged her engines.

Vermont's ignominious life and death seem to have disgusted James Winans but did not dismay John or daunt a number of associates who had got themselves incorporated as "The Lake Champlain Steamboat Company" in 1813. The concern began a new steamer at Vergennes, eight miles up Otter Creek. Her frame had not been completed when Macdonough snatched her away, and, having no faith in steam, built her into the schooner-rigged *U.S.S. Ticonderoga*. When the War of 1812 ended, the company tried again.

Phoenix, a larger boat than *Vermont,* was laid down at Vergennes, equipped with secondhand engines from a Hudson River craft and put into service in 1815. In the following year, *Champlain,* built by John Winans and with *Vermont's* salvaged engines installed, joined her. After a few months' invalidism, new machinery was placed in *Champlain* and Winans had his engines on his hands again.

Each Wednesday and Saturday *Phoenix* and *Champlain* left from opposite ends of the Whitehall-St. Johns run. Fare for the entire distance was $9, "with board and lodging." Compared to *Vermont's* unreliabilities, the new steamers were models of punctuality though not wholly prompt in the modern sense, as this footnote to their schedule attests:

"As the time at which the boat may arrive at the different places above-mentioned may vary a few hours, according to the advantage or disadvantage of the wind, those wishing to come on board will see the necessity of being on the spot two hours before the time."[2]

Folk of that leisurely age who were inured to the whimsicalities of sailing craft probably did not deem this an unreasonable request.

John Winans and his durable marine engines were initiating steam traffic on other, hitherto virgin water. In 1817 the man built a vessel at the head of Lake George and installed his unique machinery. Few details and no picture of the craft have come down to us, which is regrettable, since *James Caldwell,* in lieu of an orthodox stack, boasted a brick chimney.

The boat, soon after the beginning of her career, was struck by lightning, yet this indication of divine displeasure did not daunt Winans who was her captain as well as designer and builder. *James Caldwell,* when her engines were not breaking down, wheezed herself the entire length of Lake George in a single day, progressing about as rapidly as a stout oarsman could row. As a spectacle, she must have been successful; as a commercial enterprise, she was something less.

Champlain steamers from the beginning enjoyed a hearty revenue from freight which, when the Chambly and Champlain-Hudson canals were opened, increased enormously in bulk and value. Lake George craft were almost wholly dependent upon passenger traffic. No more than 7 percent of their income ever was derived from other sources.

In the time of *James Caldwell* passengers were few. The boat burned by her dock at the lakehead in 1821. The cynical said she took fire "from overinsurance."[3] This time, Winans did not salvage the engines.

Two years elapsed before *Caldwell's* successor was built. Meanwhile, the Lake Champlain Steamboat Company was incurring almost enough misfortune to gratify the ill wishes of Gideon King and other adherents to sail. *Champlain* burned at Whitehall in September, 1817. The company replaced her the following year with *Congress,* a craft almost double her forerunner's size.

On September 5, 1819 *Phoenix* stood out from Burlington for St. Johns. It was a calm, moonlit night when passengers, in accordance with company rules, turned in at 10:00. Within two hours a northwest storm smote the steamboat, and at its height she caught fire.

Captain Jehaziel Sherman, skipper of *Phoenix,* was ill ashore and his twenty-two-year-old son, Richard W., was in temporary command. He met the crisis with precocious fortitude, quelling panic, regulating, pistol in hand, the rush for the boats and remaining aboard when the last of them pushed off. By the light of the wind-blown flames, the boats reached Providence Island, set the rescued ashore and rowed back to the blazing vessel. Of the ten persons who had been left aboard her in the confusion, young Sherman and four others were hauled alive from the water. The others, including the stewardess, a Mrs. Wilson, were drowned.

The company began at once a steamer of 343-tons displacement, a third larger than *Congress*. She was christened *Phoenix II* and made her first voyage in 1820.

The alacrity with which boats that had perished were replaced by larger, handsomer craft was due not only to the courage of their owners but also to something equally basic in the Yankee character. Despite reiterated misfortune, despite the continued scoffing of sail men, steamers had become something more than a novel experiment. For all their defects and disasters, they actually were making money for their owners.

Residents of the Valley were growing steamboat-minded. Merchants were consigning more and more freight; an increasing number of passengers were risking themselves on the tall-stacked, spark-snorting, high-sterned vessels that rushed up and down Champlain at the unheard-of speed of eight miles per hour.

Steamers were becoming something more important than ingenious contraptions to the lake people. The popular instinct for animism was turning them into creatures native to the Valley, as indeed they were since they were built at the shore line of regional materials and had been formed to deal with the peculiar local conditions of wind and water.

Lake steamboats acquired, as all such craft will, personalities of their own so emphatic that they quickened human affection and comically violent loyalties. Men grew familiar with them all, recognizing each from afar, identifying them in the blackest night by whistle blast or bell stroke, acquiring favorites among the increasing fleet and growing ever more willing to bet on their prowess, or, in time of crisis, to punch the nose of a beloved's traducer.

On Lake George, despite *James Caldwell's* lamentable record, a new steamer was building. *Mountaineer* was completed in 1824.

HORSE RACING ON THE ICE AT LAKE GEORGE

CROWN POINT BRIDGE

Ruins of Fort St. Frédéric in foreground.

ROAD APPROACHING PORT KENT ON LAKE CHAMPLAIN

She was small by Champlain standards of the time—only of 125-tons displacement—but the larger lake never produced creations as unusual as the craft and her captain.

Mountaineer was 100 feet long and 16 wide. Her hull was sketchily framed but this deficiency was remedied by a layer of boards running lengthwise, a second layer, running from keel to gunwale, then a sheathing of tar paper and finally another horizontal layer of boards. All this basketry was held together with wooden pins. Legend recites that, in rough weather, *Mountaineer* proceeded with alarming and Oriental writhings.

The boat was scheduled to make the run between Caldwell, now Lake George Village, and the lake's north end in something less than seven hours, but her arbitrary yet chivalrous skipper, L. C. Larabee, made faster trips by not making stipulated stops and letting would-be male passengers chase him instead. If a woman, particularly a pretty one, wished to be taken aboard, Larabee would pause and even escort her overside. If a man wanted passage, he had to work to get it.

Such an aspirant was obliged to hire a rowboat and an oarsman who, when the steamer approached, rowed furiously in pursuit of a yawl towed by *Mountaineer*. If this were overtaken, the prospective passenger tumbled in and was hauled aboard over the steamboat's stern. Otherwise, he failed to obtain passage. Due possibly to her singular skipper, *Mountaineer* was not a profitable enterprise.

On Champlain, the supply of steamboats was beginning to outstrip the demand. Seven craft were plying the lake under varied ownership and, among so many, profits were diminishing. In 1826 a new concern, the Champlain Transportation Company, was incorporated. By grace of its surviving vestige it claims to be the oldest commercial steamboat company in the world.

Luther Loomis of Burlington was the new concern's first president and its officers and directors were lake men. During its long lifetime, the company has been the possession of various corporations and persons. The buccaneering Daniel Drew controlled it from 1849 to 1858, then sold it to a syndicate headed by Legrand

B. Cannon of Burlington. Thereafter, the corporation was owned by the Rennselaer & Saratoga Railroad and when the Delaware & Hudson leased that line became the latter concern's possession.

The Champlain Transportation Company was generally fortunate in its management and particularly so in the quality and loyalty of its servants. James Roosevelt, president from 1895 to 1900, was father to Franklin D. Roosevelt. Captain Henry T. Mayo, in company service for fifty years, sired Admiral Henry T. Mayo, U.S.N. Richard W. Sherman, the lake's most celebrated captain, was grandfather of James S. Sherman, Vice-President of the United States during the Taft administration. Captain Andrew I. Goodhue's daughter was Grace Goodhue Coolidge. Captain Ell B. Rockwell had been forty-eight years with the company when he died, still in service, in 1928 at the age of ninety-eight.

The company had from its birth a prime and simple intention: To acquire and keep a monopoly of the steam carrier trade on Lake Champlain. By 1835 it had accomplished its purpose and henceforth defended its self-bestowed domain with nineteenth century vigor, starving out the stubborn by cutting rates or, when rivals appeared too redoubtable, including them on its board of directors and absorbing their property.

The first steamboat the company launched was the largest, finest and fastest the lake had borne. *Franklin* was built at St. Albans and completed in 1827. Her displacement was 350 tons, compared to *Champlain II's* 343, and her speed was 10 miles an hour against her rival's 8. *Vermont,* third of that name and built in 1903 as the last major creation of the Champlain Transportation Company, displaced 1195 tons and steamed at 23 miles an hour.

The concern when it had erased its last competitor owned seven lake steamboats, some of which it immediately scrapped. To celebrate its victory it raised passenger and freight rates that had been dragged ruinously low during the struggle for supremacy and decreed a new steamer to be called *Burlington.* She was built at Shelburne Harbor, Vermont, in 1837 under the critical eye of her captain-to-be, Richard W. Sherman, at the then unprecedented cost of $75,000.

Burlington was larger and faster than any earlier lake steamer. Her engines drove her 405-tons' displacement at 15 miles an hour and she also represented what 1837 and Captain Sherman deemed the peak of elegance and luxury. Passengers accustomed to the utilitarian interiors of other lake steamboats gasped when they boarded *Burlington* and frequently proceeded to set down on paper the raptures inspired by her magnificence. None praised these more highly than that not too catholic admirer of America, Charles Dickens, who celebrated Captain Sherman's prowess as an interior decorator thus in *American Notes:*

"The steamboat which is called the *Burlington* is a perfectly exquisite achievement of neatness, elegance and order. The decks are drawing rooms, the chairs are boudoirs, choicely furnished and adorned with prints, pictures and musical instruments; every nook and corner of the vessel is a perfect curiosity of graceful comfort and beautiful contrivance. Captain Sherman, her commander, to whose ingenuity and excellent taste these results are solely attributable, has bravely and worthily distinguished himself on more than one trying occasion. . . ."

Such praise was likely to inflate the ego of a man less proud of himself than Captain Sherman. He found the material elegance he had created was not enough and proceeded to polish his crew as well, drilling them continually in their duties and deportment.

Burlington's man-of-war precision, her baroque interior that dazzled foreigners, did not equally please homespun natives of the Valley. The tariff of $5 for cabin passage from Whitehall to St. Johns hurt them intensely in a less aesthetic region. Lake people began to sneer at Captain Sherman who, from his burnished and highly decorated boat, sneered right back at them. He was a chin-whiskered autocrat whose face, as displayed in a contemporary woodcut, wore a bilious look which was probably the engraver's attempt to depict haughtiness. His martinet airs rasped other than local nerves.

President Van Buren, in 1840, took passage through the lake on *Burlington* and, when asked if he did not wish to meet her skipper, said dryly:

"I know him. He thinks the world is a steamboat and he the captain."

"Dandy Dick" Sherman was making himself unpopular with his neighbors at a time when his employers were in need of native support.

One of the steamboat lines the Champlain Transportation Company had abolished was the Champlain Ferry Company and among the expired concern's directors had been Peter Comstock of Whitehall, one-time operator of packet canal boats and an energetic and uncomfortably persistent person.

While *Burlington* still was on the ways, Comstock began at Whitehall a rival craft which, he loudly promised, would surpass the Champlain Transportation Company's boat in size, speed and elegance. The probability of another fight and lesser dividends alarmed *Burlington's* proprietors who, after much gagging and groaning over the price Comstock demanded for his unfinished craft, purchased it for $20,000 and did their legal best to tie its builder's hands.

On September 13, 1836, Comstock accepted the post of company agent at Whitehall. For a salary of $1000 yearly he bound himself for six years from the previous April 1 not to "build, construct or run or aid and assist and abet in the running, building or constructing of any steamboat or steamboats on Lake Champlain other than those in which the said Champlain Transportation Company may have an interest."[4]

Comstock's erstwhile steamer *Whitehall* was completed less elaborately than *Burlington* and became her sister ship on the day run through the lake. Harmony seemed to have been ensured, but it continued only for the duration of Comstock's bondage. When six years had elapsed, he promptly began another steamer. The Champlain Transportation Company's directors, faced by the prospect of a rate war or else another purchase of Mr. Comstock and his new boat, chose, this time, to fight.

Accordingly they waited until *Francis Saltus,* named for a New York capitalist who was president of the Peru Iron Company, was commissioned in the spring of 1845, and then put *Burlington* on the same schedule after cutting the fare to $3. *Saltus* was a fine, fast craft but she was smaller and less ornate than her rival. The directors of the Champlain Transportation Company were bewildered to find how large a proportion of the lake folk preferred the Comstock craft. Dandy Dick's scorn of yokels was coming home to roost.

This was not a quiet financial struggle like that which had won supremacy for *Burlington's* owners. This was a country-wide brawl in which everyone took sides, even to the extreme of balladry:

> Dick Sherman is so very slick
> The fops all flock around him thick
> As humbugs round a pot of honey.
> So Dick's cologne brings him the money.
> > Ha, ha, ha! That's the fun
> > For Dandy Dick and the *Burlington*.

> Oh, Dicky is a gallant lad!
> He makes the ladies very glad.
> He smiles and smirks with great parade
> And then makes love to the cabin maid.
> > Ha, ha, ha! That's the fun
> > For Dandy Dick and the *Burlington*.

> His decks are scrubbed with so great care
> That cowhide boots can't come in there.
> If you can't make your money rattle,
> You must go forward with the cattle.
> > Ha, ha, ha! That's the fun
> > For Dandy Dick and the *Burlington*.[5]

Dandy Dick and his *Burlington* were suffering the usual fate of those who aspire to aristocracy in a violently democratic region. His employers hastily withdrew their prize boat from competition, put her with *Whitehall* on the night run and substituted the humbler *Saranac* as competitor to *Saltus*. *Saranac* was the smaller and somewhat slower craft but her fare for deck passage the length of the lake had been reduced to 50 cents. Comstock was obliged to meet this ruinous rate.

Mississippi steamboating at its most untrammeled hardly surpassed the uproar of that violent summer. The whole lake region took sides in the contest and backed its favorite with cash and not infrequently with fists.

Saltus and *Saranac* steamed at the same moment from either side of the Whitehall pier, often leaving a fight in progress behind them, and raced the length of Champlain and down the Richelieu to St. Johns. Hoots, insults and occasionally more substantial missiles were exchanged by passengers on the striving craft and assaults enlivened each landing.

Though *Saltus* was somewhat faster, *Saranac's* stokers at need added pitch pine and barrels of tar to her fires. If *Saltus* employed the same fuel and forged ahead again, Saranac would skip a stop, heedless of the distress of passengers who wished to get off, and thus recover the lead.

The aquatic brawl progressed down-lake and returned next day from St. Johns. Disturbances at the landings became so vigorous that, to abate them, company directors ordered bar service on *Saranac* suspended but hastily reversed themselves and directed that it be resumed when it was found that passengers, undistracted by drink, simply spent more time in fighting.

The Champlain Transportation Company swung another haymaker at Comstock by reducing deck passage on *Saranac* to 25 cents. Both boats were losing an alarming amount of money, but the company was the better supplied. In the fall Comstock quit the contest, but he did not surrender to his adversary. The Troy firm of Grant, Coffin & Church took over and carried on the war during the 1846 season, but the end drew near.

The Champlain Transportation Company was building a new steamer that would finish the fight. In the spring of 1847 Captain W. W. Anderson of the concern's 648-ton, 19-mile-an-hour *United States* held his boat at the Burlington pier until *Saltus* had cast off and was well down the lake. *United States* then stood out, overhauled *Saltus* and with derisive tooting stormed past. That fall Grant, Coffin & Church sold out to their rival and the monopoly was re-established.

The immediately following years saw the peak of lake traffic. Two company liners made the day run between Whitehall and St. Johns; two more steamed the same course at night. Smaller boats plied as ferries across the lake's breadth. Though steam carriers increased, sailboats still were plentiful.

After the opening of the Chambly canal about the Richelieu's rapids in 1841, the ingenious firm of Follet & Bradley in Burlington incorporated as "The Merchants Line," equipped its herd of canal barges with sloop rigs and sent them up and down the lake by wind power, thus saving time and tonnage expense. Independent sloops and schooners were alert for cargoes and the lake was alive with sails through which the tall white steamers moved. The golden age for lake commerce ended when the railways came.

In 1851 the Rutland Railroad reached Burlington and the St. Lawrence Railway, a future segment of the Delaware & Hudson, arrived at Rouses Point. Their competition was not more than the Champlain Transportation Company immediately could bear but much of what heretofore had been water-borne freight began to move overland. Follet & Bradley failed in 1854, and two years earlier the steamboat company had reduced its own domain by fixing its northern terminus at Rouses Point.

An empire was failing but as it approached its fall, the Champlain Transportation Company reached out for new dominion. In 1868 it bought control of the Lake George Steamboat Company. It was not, from its immediate aspect, a provident investment.

Since 1838 when that peculiar craft *Mountaineer* had been replaced by a larger steamer, *William Caldwell,* Lake George craft, when they had run at all, had been operated to comply with the schedules of Lake Champlain steamboats. Travelers down the lesser lake were landed at Baldwin, near George's outlet, and were taken by stage to Montcalm Landing where a Champlain Transportation Company liner waited for them.

The Lake George service was unreliable and misfortune followed the boats. *William Caldwell* which had made little money was condemned in 1848, and it was not till 1850 that *John Jay* took her place. On July 29, 1856, she burned off Island Harbor. The Glens Falls *Republican* for August 5 reported:

"The boat was driven on the rocks and almost careened over. The tiller ropes were burned off and she was left to the mercy of the waves. After striking the rocks, she shot out into the lake some thirty or forty rods. At this point, the passengers became alarmed."

Five women and a man were drowned. The hard-pressed company managed to resume service by placing *John Jay's* engines and boilers in the new *Minne-ha-ha* which was completed in 1857 under a weight of mortgage heavier than her cargoes. The concern limped along through the lean years of the Civil War and must have sold out to the Champlain Company with great relief. No one imagined that, in the years ahead, the Lake George concern would become the more profitable.

The Champlain Transportation Company's independence ended in 1870, when the Rennselaer & Saratoga Railroad acquired a majority interest. It leased its line and all its holdings to the Delaware & Hudson and the steamboat company became a subsidiary of its latest, greatest rival.

There was no immediate diminution in the Champlain concern's activity. It brought out in 1871 *Vermont,* second of the name and, as was usual with the firm's new vessels, the largest, finest craft the lake had seen. Two years later, it purchased the car ferry, *Oakes Ames,* from the Delaware & Hudson and, since her name smelled of financial corruption, rechristened her *Champlain.*

Champlain's career was brief. Her pilot on the night of July 16, 1875, rammed her, full tilt, into Split Rock Mountain below Westport and broke her back. No one was injured and the passengers walked ashore on an improvised gangplank, save one who later was found sleeping tranquilly in his half-submerged cabin. He proved to be a law student who had been overcelebrating his passing of his bar examination.

The completion of the railroad from Whitehall to Ticonderoga in 1874 threatened still another province of the Champlain Transportation Company's domain. The concern in 1879 again reduced service, quitting the lower as well as the upper reaches of the lake and reducing its once proud fleet to *Vermont,* which plied between Plattsburg and Ticonderoga, and a ferry steamer that plodded a quadrilateral course from Burlington to Port Kent, Plattsburg and St. Albans. This craft was replaced in 1888 by *Chateaugay,* which later was remodeled into an automobile carrier.

Dusk was falling on Champlain's steam traffic, but the hitherto valetudinarian Lake George branch of the company suddenly was growing hale. In 1882 the Delaware & Hudson sent a line north from Glens Falls to the lakehead and, with the railway, came a host of tourists, most of whom soon or late booked passage for a trip through the lake. The Lake George line, always chiefly dependent upon passengers, until now had had unsatisfactorily few, but the railroad brought them in abundance.

Four more large steamers were launched on Lake George— *Mohican,* 1894; *Sagamore,* 1902; *Mohican II,* 1908; and *Horicon,* 1911. The Champlain Company with a final gesture brought out the third *Vermont,* largest of its line, in 1903 and, diminuendo, the excursion steamer *Ticonderoga* in 1906. The end was approaching. The automobile was hastening the fate the railways already had foreshadowed. When a paved motor highway was completed along Lake George's west shore the days of her steamship line also were numbered.

Captain George Stafford, native of Plattsburg and skipper of *Mohican* during the last years of the Lake George Steamboat Company, bought the vessel in 1938 when the concern was dissolved. *Horicon,* the other surviving craft, was broken up.

Mohican still makes a round trip through the lake each day of the vacation season. When Walter P. Harris, her pilot, first took a steamboat up George and back in 1895, he made thirty-two landings. *Mohican,* today, makes four.

In 1937 Horace W. Corbin of Grand Isle bought the Champlain Transportation Company and since then has been divesting himself of the line's remaining craft. The ferry *Chateaugay* was sold to a Lake Winnepesaukee, New Hampshire, firm, sliced into segments and trucked across the mountains to her new home. *Vermont,* cut down and equipped with Diesels, has been transformed into a freighter which her new owners will operate between the lake and New York, via the Champlain-Hudson Canal. Negotiations are under way, as this is written, for sale of *Ticonderoga,* last of the fleet.

The Champlain Transportation Company's shipyards were leased during World War II by a construction firm which, for the first time since Macdonough's day, launched naval craft on Champlain—patrol boats, lighters and tugs. Corbin recently sold the yards.

The company which, first to last, operated a score of steamers on Champlain limits itself now to running Diesel-driven ferries between Burlington and Port Kent, Charlotte and Essex and from Grand Isle to Cumberland Head. Corbin plans to build more modern craft of airplane carrier design—each 150 feet long with space on their "flight decks" for 50 cars.

If *Ticonderoga* is sold, her new owners intend to retain her on the lake as an excursion craft. When "Old Ti's" whistle has spoken for the last time, a romantic era will have ended. Something beautiful and heart-stirring will have departed from Champlain, leaving an emptiness behind it.

---

[1] B. F. De Costa: *Lake George, Its Scenes and Characteristics* (New York, 1868), p. 118.

[2] Champlain Transportation Company, *The Steamboats of Lake Champlain* (Albany, 1930), p. 30.

[3] *Ibid.,* p. 37.

[4] D. A. Loomis Papers, in Wilbur Library, University of Vermont.

[5] Champlain Transportation Company, *The Steamboats of Lake Champlain,* p. 66.

Chapter 22

The Smoldering Border

P EACE, for sixty years after the end of the War of 1812, maintained an uncertain and often precarious sway in the north Champlain area. There remained no wide stretches of wilderness to keep two nationalities safely apart. Settlements in New York and Vermont stood face to face with Canadian villages and the dwellers in the communities on either side of the line had a long heritage of enmity.

Friction was inevitable and practically continual. Again and again its engendered heat set the frontier to smoldering. It was the reluctance of British and American statesmen to dare a third war and not the pacifism of the border folk that, on frequent occasions, prevented open conflict.

The Webster-Ashburton Treaty fixed the United States and Canadian boundary in the Champlain area, but no mortal mind or expedient could bring into order or completely classify the jumbled sympathies and antipathies that perpetually stewed in this region.

Canadians and Americans, in general, heartily disliked and thoroughly suspected each other, but the situation could not be dismissed so simply. Erstwhile citizens of the United States who had cherished loyalty to Britain now dwelt north of the border. Canadians with American sympathies had moved south of the line. Many of them had settled immediately after the Revolution at Point au Roche in Beekmantown on Champlain's west shore, and others elsewhere in the valley.

There were further complexities. Many Canadian dissenters, some of whom were to become open rebels, depended on their southern neighbors for support and sympathy in their hatred of His Majesty's government and this abundantly was available. Numerous secret societies—"Hunters' Lodges," "Sons of Liberty" and the

297

like—that purposed to emancipate Canada flourished on both sides of the line. The situation was scrambled further by the fact that the Champlain Valley contained pro-British residents, as the treasonable commerce of the late war had emphasized.

While the resentment of Canadians to arbitrary British rules increased, minor friction was chronic all along the border. American miscreants continually were dodging arrest by skipping across the line. Frequently in their flight they bumped into offenders against Canadian law, running earnestly in the other direction. International amity was not improved by the fact that overzealous officers of both nationalities often invaded foreign soil, kidnaped the erring refugees and haled them back to justice.

In November 1837 Canadian dissatisfaction boiled over into open rebellion. Louis Joseph Papineau, a legislator whose oratory surpassed his fortitude, inspired the revolt and soon after the guns began to go off sought refuge in Vermont. Martial law was declared in Canada, and on December 6 a column of "liberators" largely equipped by Vermont adherents marched north from Swanton Falls to attack loyalists at the head of Missisquoi Bay and were put to flight after two had been killed and two wounded.

The defeat did not diminish the Champlain Valley's enthusiasm for the rebels, and the region broke out in a rash of mass meetings. Volunteer companies were raised, ostensibly to protect the border, and the situation became so tense that Generals Winfield Scott and James E. Wool were ordered to the frontier to prevent further overt acts.

The revolt continued into the following fall. Twice, expeditions formed on American soil and advanced toward Canada, only to fall into the hands of United States authorities. The firmness of Scott and Wool and the refusal of Governor Silas H. Jenison of Vermont to be stampeded by a bellicose electorate prevented graver violations of neutrality, but American popular adherence to the insurgents' cause affronted Canadian officialdom, and memory of it undoubtedly influenced the Dominion's conduct when the United States had to deal with its own rebellion.

During the American Civil War, Canada displayed and intensified the general British sympathy for the South, welcomed the commissioners of the South, restored escaped prisoners via the West Indies and, despite official Union protests, harbored a group of Confederate soldiers and officers who actually, in 1864, invaded the United States from the north.

It was three o'clock on the cloudy afternoon of October 18 when the raiders attacked St. Albans. There were only twenty-two of them, yet this handful for the better part of an hour paralyzed a town of some 4,000 inhabitants. The invaders chose their time well and struck on a particularly relaxed instant of an uncommonly dull day.

Tuesday had been market day and on the following afternoon Main Street was steeped in the apathy that always followed the weekly inpouring of farmers. Some leading St. Albans citizens were absent, since the legislature was sitting in Montpelier and the Supreme Court was in session at Burlington, yet the raiders were fantastically outnumbered. There were hundreds of men at work in the railroad shops alone. Nevertheless, there was a minimum of resistance and none of it was organized. The raid was so swift and smooth and savage that it stunned.

It was launched when the town clock struck thrice. A thick-lipped, surly, shock-headed youth, lounging beside the Green, near where St. Albans' three banks stood close together on Main Street, gave a signal to other loitering strangers. Each of them was distinguished by the leather satchel he wore slung across his shoulder.

The foray had been brought to the verge of precipitation by careful planning of sundry agents. James A. Seddon, confederate secretary of war, had been an instigator. Clement Claiborne Clay, Jr., Jacob Thompson and George W. Saunders, southern commissioners in Canada, had expedited and implemented the scheme, and Bennet H. Young, first lieutenant, C.S.A., had been chief instrument in the plot.

Young, a Kentuckian, had escaped to Canada from the Union prison camp at Camp Douglas, near Chicago. He had recommended himself to the commissioners who had sent him by sea to

Richmond, where, July 16, 1864, he had received his commission from Secretary Seddon. The twenty-year-old boy reappeared in Canada, chose his force from the large number of Confederates available and made one or more visits to St. Albans before October 10, when he and two subordinates registered at the Tremont House. Two others put up at the American House.

Six more raiders arrived at the Tremont House on October 16, and six additional reached the St. Albans House and five the American House October 19 in time for dinner. This influx of strangers apparently roused no suspicion, though the earlier delegations were incautiously inquisitive. They peered into banks, stores and livery stables, tried to borrow guns for a "hunting expedition," and Young himself obtained permission to inspect the estate of Governor J. Gregory Smith. Whatever plans for a kidnaping the raiders may have cherished were thwarted by the Governor's absence in Montpelier.

St. Albans' vigilance may have been lulled by the fact that Young and his comrades then present decorously attended church on Sunday, October 16. Furthermore, one of the young men staying at the Tremont House was addicted to reading his Bible aloud, and the impression got around that he and his associates were theological students on a holiday. Enlightenment was abrupt and stupefying.

The last stroke of the town clock still hung in the air when men ran up the steps of the three banks and entered, revolver in hand, while others, similarly armed, began to herd citizens across Main Street toward the Green that faced the thoroughfare. Others plundered Fuller's and Field's livery stables of their horses and ransacked Bedard's harness store for saddles and bridles. There was astonishment, fear, but no immediate resistance outside the banks or within.

Albert Sowles, cashier, was the only official in the First National Bank when the strangers entered, though in a corner General John Nason, almost ninety, deaf and vague of mind, sat and read a newspaper. Sowles stared into the muzzles of three revolvers while the raiders warned that the cashier was a prisoner of the Confederate Army and would be shot if he resisted.

"This," one raider cried, "is in retaliation for the acts of General Sherman against our own people."[1]

Sowles stood helpless while the intruders stuffed their satchels with currency from drawers and safe. Old General Nason, peering over his paper, piped:

"What gentlemen are these? It seems to me they are rather rude in their manners."[2]

At this moment, William H. Blaisdell, a truculent man, climbed the steps of the bank, which occupied a gabled building at what is now the foot of Fairfield Street, and pushed open the door. At once he was seized by the raiders who had been stowing $58,000 in currency into their satchels, and he and Sowles were ordered to march across muddy Main Street to the dazed and growing group of captives in the Green.

On the bank's threshold, Blaisdell suddenly grappled with his escort. The two men reeled and, still locked, fell and rolled down the steps together. Another raider pressed the muzzle of a cocked revolver against Blaisdell's ear and he submitted. From his chair in the bank, the ancient general objected:

"Two against one is not fair play."[3]

Men, later identified as Marcus Spurr and Thomas Bronsdon Collins, were the first to enter the fenced precinct of the St. Albans Bank, which occupied the first floor of a dwelling that stood where Kingman Street now joins Main. The subsequent disheveled proceedings impelled the two intruders to yell for reinforcements, and three others joined them.

For a space they all had their hands full. Martin A. Seymour, clerk, was docile under the threat of the leveled pistols, but Cyrus N. Bishop, assistant cashier, leaped into the directors' room and tried to hold the door shut. It was burst in so violently that he was bumped severely on the forehead. Scarcely had Bishop been overcome when Samuel Breck entered the bank to pay off a note for $400 due that day. He promptly was relieved of his money, though he protested with anguish that this was not the bank's but his own personal cash.

The three captives were placed under guard in the directors' room, where Bishop had wished to stay anyway, and presently were joined by another unfortunate, Morris Roach, who had come in to deposit $210 for his employer, Joseph Weeks, merchant. This sum was added to the loot the raiders were stuffing into their satchels. They took $73,522 but overlooked in the press of dealing with visitors $50,000 more in sheets of banknotes, signed but not yet cut.

Before the plunderers departed, some humorist among them insisted that the captives swear allegiance to the Confederate States of America. When the oath had been taken by Bishop, Seymour, Breck and Roach, the newly obligated rebels were locked in the directors' room.

In the Franklin County Bank, a flat-roofed, two-story structure occupying the institution's present site, Marcus W. Beardsley was talking to Jackson Clark, sawyer, when the raiders rushed in, promising at the pistol's point to burn the whole town if either captive resisted. Clark immediately was pushed into the bank's open vault where Beardsley, after surrendering the concern's cash, joined him. The door was closed upon them with the cheering promise that the bank immediately would be set afire, and they spent a hideous half hour, expecting to be baked alive, before they were released. Seventy thousand dollars were taken from the Franklin County Bank.

Outside on Main Street, which was ankle-deep in mire from the autumn rains, rose the clump and slither of horses' hoofs and men shouted. A shot sounded and then another. St. Albans was rousing from its temporary paralysis. The bank looters ran to join their comrades.

Some of these already were mounted and galloping up and down the thoroughfare, revolvers in hand. Others were continuing to take prisoners to the Green and still more were holding up wagons and freeing horses from harness. Captain George P. Conger, a discharged veteran of the 1st Vermont Cavalry, was driving into St.

Albans when a terrified fugitive met him with tidings of the raid. The captain left his wagon and, advancing on foot, was captured and added to the prisoners on the Green. He waited his chance and, slipping away, ran through the American House and out the back door. At about this time, the first shot was fired.

Collins H. Huntington of St. Albans was walking along Main Street toward the school from which he intended to bring his children home when a stranger ordered him over to the Green. Huntington, believing he was dealing with a drunk, walked on.

"If you don't go over, I'll shoot you," the man warned.

"Oh, no," Huntington said lightly, "I guess you won't shoot me," and forthwith was shot. The ball, deflected by a rib, caused only a flesh wound.[4]

Guns were going off elsewhere now and St. Albanians not already captured were scuttling for cover. On Main Street the horses the raiders were assembling snorted and plunged. E. D. Fuller, whose livery stable had been swept bare, had lost his temper and found an unreliable revolver. Thrice, from behind a tree, he aimed at the confusion before him and pulled the trigger, but the weapon refused to fire.

On the porch of the American House from which he was shouting orders to his men, Young shot at Fuller. He missed the livery stable owner, but E. J. Morrison of Manchester, New Hampshire, a contractor who had been at work on the new Welden House and was running for shelter in Miss Beattie's millinery store, lurched and fell over. The bullet had passed through his right hand and into his abdomen. Morrison, who died two days later, was the raid's sole fatality. Ironically, he had been a violent sympathizer with the South.

The raiders were mounting. A few horses had been saddled, the rest were bareback. Young, while his men assembled, galloped up and down Main Street. Leonard Cross came to the door of his photography salon and called to ask the cause of the celebration.

"I'll let you know," Young shouted, shot at him and missed.[5]

Leonard Bingham fired at a raider and was grazed by the bullet sent in return. Elsewhere on Main Street Henry Watson wrapped his arms about his abdomen and cried that he had been mortally wounded. Investigation revealed a spent bullet that had cut through his breeches' waistband but had only bruised the skin beneath.

The raiders rode off, yelling through the storm of mud thrown up by their horses and, in token of farewell, hurling incendiary bombs against Main Street buildings. The only structure set afire was the American House privy.

Captain Conger, who finally had succeeded in borrowing a gun, aimed at the retreating horsemen but the weapon missed fire. He and F. Stuart Stranahan, a lieutenant on Custer's staff then home on leave and a future lieutenant governor of Vermont, began to organize pursuit. Stranahan found a horse and galloped to the governor's house to get arms. Mrs. Smith, his sister-in-law, met him at the door, pistol in hand. She had learned of the raid and, recalling that Union troops had burned the homes of the Governor of Virginia and the Governor of Georgia, had expected that her husband's dwelling would be set afire. She thrust her weapon at Stranahan.

"Here, take this pistol," she cried. "It is all I have yet found and, Stuart, if you come upon them, kill them, kill them, kill them."

"I never," Mrs. Smith relates, "felt so murderous. The frenzy of battle was upon me. The blood of the old Norse kings stirred in my veins."[6]

Her sanguinary yearnings undoubtedly were shared by an unfortunate farmer of Sheldon who, jogging along the road on his horse, was overtaken by the fleeing raiders, threatened, robbed of his steed and left with a spent animal as the flight rushed on. While he still was swearing over this outrage, Conger's and Stranahan's posse stormed into view.

Here, the wretched man presumed, came more trouble and he strove to avoid it. He fled cross-lots with bullets whistling about him, since the pursuers took him for one of Young's men, and found refuge at last in the heart of a swamp. This and other delays, for the raiders tried, but not always with success, to burn the bridges they crossed, enabled the fugitives to beat the posse across the frontier.

It is doubtful whether twenty-two men ever created greater or wider-spread alarm. For a space, panic that magnified the raid into the first step of a full-scale Confederate invasion via Canada shook the Champlain Valley. Temporarily, all northbound rail traffic was halted. Steamers berthed near the border were moved out into the lake. Their crews were armed and each craft henceforth was supplied with a guard of a noncom and seven soldiers.

Troops were rushed to the frontier towns. Muskets were issued to citizens from the arsenal at Vergennes. The St. Albans and First National Banks offered $10,000 reward for the return of their stolen U. S. Treasury notes. The endemic suspicion of British motives was not allayed by the assurances of Viscount Monck, Canada's governor general, that the raiders would be brought to justice, and the subsequent legal proceedings increased regional Anglophobia.

Canadian authorities at last succeeded in arresting fourteen of the twenty-two raiders. All of them when captured were dripping with American cash, and $86,000 of the stolen $201,522 was taken from them and sequestered. Beside Young, Spurr and Collins, those made prisoner were Samuel Eugene Lackey, Alamanda Pope Bruce, Charles Moore Swager, Caleb McDonnell Wallace, Joseph McGrorty, John Scott, William H. Hutchinson, Dudley Moore, James Alexander Doty, Samuel Simpson Gregg and Squire Turner Teavis.

All save McGrorty, who was thirty-eight, were youngsters in their late teens or early twenties and each of the fourteen claimed he was a duly enlisted soldier in the Confederate Army. In response to Secretary of State Seward's demand that they be extradited forthwith, Canadian law started to move ponderously.

The prisoners were lodged in the Montreal jail, and a city magistrate, Charles J. Coursol, began taking evidence on November 7. He threw out the case December 13, on the pretext that the warrants under which the defendants were held were defective. Young and his associates were freed, rearrested and arraigned again before Judge James Smith of the Canadian Superior Court.

The case dragged on until March 29, 1865, when the prisoners again were released. Judge Smith ruled that they all were members of the Confederate Army and under orders. He held that since Britain recognized the Confederacy as a belligerent power, the raiders were not criminally responsible and therefore could not be extradited. Canada's return to the St. Albans banks of $80,000 of their looted funds did not wholly soothe the American sense of grievance.

The St. Albans affair and its aftermath intensified border animosity and inspired on both sides of the line much loose talk and vague threats of invasion and counterinvasion. Americans and Canadians alike seemed willing to take matters into their own hands and at least one British officer seriously contemplated storming and capturing Fort Montgomery with his command, though his martial intention eventually was immersed in alcohol and transformed into amity.[7]

Captain Gustave A. Drolet was quartered in April 1865 with his 10th Company of the 3rd Battalion, 65th Canadian Volunteers, at Lacolle, Quebec, a few miles across the border from Rouses Point. He seems to have been subject to dreams of glory which boredom intensified and, after consultation with his lieutenants who heartily endorsed the project, determined to capture the still unfinished American stronghold. This would probably bring on a war, he reflected, but it would at least banish his ennui.

Captain Drolet accordingly borrowed a buggy and, with his orderly, drove south to reconnoiter. Cannon that began to boom at the fort made him wonder whether his hostile purpose had been discovered, but it was not until he reached the village of Champlain and found his buggy, his orderly and himself unwillingly incorporated in a parade that he learned the cause of the gunfire. This was the day of Abraham Lincoln's burial and most of the region's population had assembled in Champlain for memorial exercises.

The would-be captor of Fort Montgomery found that the parade was halting and breaking up before a church. He entered with the mourners. The presiding minister, during the obsequies, spoke approvingly of the presence of a representative of Her British Majesty in the congregation. When the service was ended, American officers, deeply affected by this gesture of international amity, insisted that Captain Drolet accompany them back to the fort for dinner.

The meal seems to have been chiefly memorable to the guest of honor for the quantity of bourbon he and his fellow diners consumed. He recalls that many toasts were drunk, including one to the British Army and another to Queen Victoria—one of the officers referred to her as "Old Vic"—and Captain Drolet immediately challenged him to mortal combat which was averted by more bourbon. He also remembers that he did not get back to Lacolle until twenty-four hours later and forthwith canceled his hostile intentions against Fort Montgomery.

Most persons of the border region cherished their grudges more vindictively. The enduring anger of St. Albans' people expedited a vicarious reprisal against Britain. In 1866 and again in 1870, bands of Irish zealots, the Fenian Brotherhood, with their grotesque scheme for freeing Ireland by invading Canada with a handful of men, were welcomed, less for their *opera-bouffe* cause than for the opportunity their intention offered the lately plundered town to pay off an overdue grudge.

The Fenians, a St. Albanian has written, "were induced to come here because they were confident we would mete out the same kind of neutrality that Canada had taught and practiced at the time of the St. Albans raid."[8]

The soldiers of the Brotherhood who gradually assembled in St. Albans during the early days of June 1866 were in civilian clothes and unarmed. On June 5, some 700 of them slopped northward through the rain to invade Canada. They bore slight resemblance to a conquering host, but the good wishes of the citizenry accompanied them.

The sodden men who plodded through the mud to Franklin constituted the right wing of the Fenian army that its commander,

Thomas W. Sweeney, formerly colonel of the 16th Infantry, U.S.A., optimistically planned to hurl into Canada from sundry points on the frontier.

This was the first brief flowering of the Fenian Movement in America. The organization was the more public offshoot of a subversive secret society established in Ireland. The movement had come into the open in America, had held national conventions and had adopted for about-to-be-freed Ireland a constitution modeled on the United States's. The Fenians were proficient in issuing proclamations and passing resolutions, but all their adventures in the field accomplished only anticlimax. The body overestimated prodigiously the number of fighting men it could muster and held, furthermore, the mistaken conviction that Canadians by the thousand would welcome invasion.

Sweeney's right wing camped wherever in Franklin it could find shelter from the rain of the night of the fifth, while its commander bivouacked in the drier precincts afforded by the Tremont House in St. Albans. The soaked 700 had received some arms and equipment which had been deposited earlier with sympathizers along the line of march, and on the morrow moved across the border.

Captain W. Carter, commanding three companies of Canadian militia, had been awed by rumors which magnified the size of the invasion and fell back hastily from the frontier, leaving it defenseless. The Fenians crossed the line, June 6, but on that day lost their commander.

The United States was enforcing a more vigorous variety of neutrality than St. Albans had displayed. General Sweeney was arrested in his hotel room; Hugh Henry, United States Marshal, and D. C. Denison, state's attorney, confiscated arms and supplies that were to be forwarded to the advancing host, and President Johnson sent General George Gordon Meade hurrying north to check the invasion.

The general, when he arrived in St. Albans, met the Fenian army retiring from the front. It had advanced only as far into Canada as St. Armand and Frelighsburg, a few miles over the border. There, lack of the confiscated arms and food halted the forward movement, and the arrival of Canadian troops put the host to flight with the loss of a few killed and wounded and fifteen captured.

Meade received the disgusted warriors' paroles, arranged with the railway for transportation to their homes, attended a ball in his honor at St. Albans and then moved on to quash other tentative invasions at Malone, Watertown and Ogdensburg, New York, by garnisheeing their arms and ammunition.

Four years later, the Fenians tried again. This time they were led by John O'Neill, president of the Fenian Society and former captain of Union cavalry, who professed his belief in "steel as a cure for Irish grievances."[9] The new invasion was planned on a narrower front, with the left wing advancing from Malone, New York, and the right, under O'Neill's personal command, moving down the Champlain Valley from St. Albans.

Once again, the leader was fantastically misinformed concerning the number of men who were ready to follow him. O'Neill in his "Official Report" charges that J. J. Donnelly of Massachusetts promised "he would have ten or twelve hundred men at or near St. Albans on the morning of Tuesday, May 24th,"[10] and that E. L. Lewis pledged 600 more from Vermont and New York. The Fenian leader met his subordinates at the stipulated place and time, but Lewis brought only about 150 men and Donnelly, 30.

Despite inclemencies of fortune and the weather—it was raining again—the handful took the road the previous army had followed to Franklin and once more, en route, were issued arms, ammunition and, in some cases, green-faced blue uniforms. Late arrivals had swelled the strength of the host to 240 men before, on May 25, it moved out of Franklin for the border, followed, since the weather had cleared, by a train of spectators and pestered by George P. Foster, United States marshal, who overtook the advance with a hard-driven team and warned the army to cease and desist.

Foster, unable to check the invasion with words, drove ahead. He crossed a brook-traversed valley through which the boundary line ran, just north of Alvah Richards' farm, and sought out the Canadian militia on wooded Eccles Hill beyond, to tell them, probably unnecessarily, what was about to happen.

O'Neill, when he reached the southern rim of the valley, deployed part of his command along the ridge and ordered thirty-five skirmishers, profusely officered by Colonel John H. Brown and Captains Cronin and Murphy, to advance across the bridge that spanned the brook and feel out the enemy.

Thirty-five armed farmers who occupied Eccles Hill had been reinforced by a company of the 60th Battalion of Canadian militia, under Colonel Brown Chamberlin, just before the advance began. These men opened fire as O'Neill's skirmishers crossed the border and John Rowe of Burlington went down into the road, shot through the heart.

Rowe's comrades discharged their guns and broke for shelter, some of them finding it beneath the bridge, others scurrying into a near-by tannery or the Richards' farmhouse, where O'Neill had taken station and from which he now retired to bring up the remainder of his force.

Part of this, the distracted general found, had joined in the stampede spectators had started when firing began. The rest, with Rowe's dead body asprawl in the road below them, refused to advance. O'Neill, searching in the rear for further reinforcements, was scooped up by Marshal Foster, whirled away to St. Albans and jailed there. That night, the remnant of the Fenian army abandoned its second Canadian invasion and trailed back to St. Albans. Again they were disarmed and sent home.

Once more General Meade, this time accompanied by General Irvin McDowell, found the invasion he had been ordered to halt had vanished before his arrival. He reached St. Albans May 28 and hurried on to Malone, where the advance of the Fenian left wing had come to an equally ignominious conclusion.

Two hundred years of border battle and bitterness ended in the year 1870. Coincidentally, work ceased on the protective Fort Montgomery in that same twelvemonth. The deserted stronghold's broken walls attest a mutual confidence and friendship along the boundary that, seventy-six years ago, still was unknown. No further strife, other than the struggle against recurrent epidemics of smuggling, has marred that serenity, and in this unhallowed enterprise neither nation has been blameless.

[1] Edward A. Sowles, "History of the St. Albans Raid," *Proceedings of the Vermont Historical Society* (St. Albans, 1876), p. 11.

[2] *Ibid.*, p. 12.

[3] Abby Maria Hemenway (ed.) *Vermont Historical Gazatteer,* II, 306.

[4] *Ibid.*, p. 307.

[5] L. N. Benjamin (compiler), *The St. Albans Raid* (Montreal, 1865), p. 73.

[6] Mrs. J. Gregory Smith, "An Incident of the Civil War," *The Vermonter,* (St. Albans, Jan. 1899), p. 103.

[7] Gustave A. Drolet, *Zouaviana* (Montreal, 1893), Chap. I.

[8] Edward A. Sowles, "History of Fenianism and Fenian Raids in Vermont," *Proceedings of the Vermont Historical Society* (Rutland, 1880), pp. 1-43.

[9] John O'Neill, "Official Report," (Foster, New York, 1870), p. 3.

[10] *Ibid.*, p. 15.

Chapter 23

Sorrel Barber and Silver Gray

ROAD that joins two nations is certain to bear legitimate commerce in time of peace and armaments in war. A third, less celebrated variety of traffic may move furtively along the linking highway.

If neighboring peoples are restricted by tariff or embargo from trade with each other; if one nation has produce that the other nation wants, goods continue to move, despite the law and enforcement officers. In the early nineteenth century, the Champlain Valley became a smugglers' route. It has never completely abandoned this role, since then.

A disreputable enterprise on which the region periodically has waxed fat was inaugurated by no less a person than a President of the United States. Among the accomplishments of Thomas Jefferson, the establishment of the Champlain smuggling racket is not generally listed, yet he was its involuntary but actual founder and his ingenuous scheme for punishing Britain by stifling American foreign trade brought the nefarious industry into being.

Jefferson proclaimed his embargo, December 22, 1807, with little consideration for what the Champlain Valley residents deemed the rights of freemen, less for frontier economy, and no apparent regard whatever for the nullifying influence geography would exert on his measure. The President's ingenuous scheme for punishing Britain by strangling American trade was immediately unpopular in the north country, where the sole practical avenue of commerce ran down-lake and, via the outlet or Missisquoi Bay, into Canada.

When, on March 12, 1808, the embargo was intensified by a supplementary law, forbidding intercourse with Britain or its pos-

312

sessions by land as well as by sea, the Valley people felt that the president was vindictively plotting their ruin. Even Jefferson adherents lost their tempers and shouted their protests in the mass meetings that were held on either lakeside, while many persons discarded moral strictures and embarked defiantly on a lawbreaking that frequently was hard to distinguish from insurrection and finally led some men into barefaced treason. Champlain folk never have taken kindly to having their tails twisted, even by an august hand.

Settlers, who lately had suffered great hardship in pursuit of a more spacious freedom than interior America granted, were vociferously unwilling to let Mr. Jefferson run their lives and ruin their livelihoods. The measure that purposed to block the Valley's only available trade route would, if obeyed, set the area's economy back again into its grim, primitive stage.

Unless Mr. Jefferson could convert a whole stiff-necked people to his peculiar expedient, the embargo was destined to fail. The course immediately taken by the more recklessly indignant was prompted by the situation of Champlain itself.

On either lake shore lay wilderness with suggestive valleys, passes and trails across the border, a sieve through which the prohibited trade with Canada easily might flow, and Champlain's lower end with its devious channels twisting among the northern islands was a Creator-ordained smugglers' highroad.

If the Valley people could not sell their beef, pork and potash to Canada, why then, the overheated protestants declared, their produce had been made worthless by a stroke of the Jeffersonian pen. The President had announced, in effect, that it was against the law for the north country to prosper. Very well; a large and angry portion of the electorate would prosper illegally.

Here was the lake and yonder was the market with only a scattering of increasingly apprehensive customs officers to keep goods from moving either way across the border—raw materials into Canada; finished products which the frontier craved into New York and Vermont. Someone of Enosburg in the latter state fathered a ditty that soon most of the Valley was singing:

There was old Sorrel Barber
And also Silver Gray
Who swore they'd go a-smuggling
Until the Judgment Day.

Barber and Gray almost at once had a swarm of energetic emulators, recruited alike from among the adventurous and the commercially-minded. While Champlain ice endured, sledloads of potash were teamed from St. Albans and the islands to British territory on upper Missisquoi Bay. When the snow had departed, residents of Enosburg, Franklin, Georgia and other border towns often were roused from sleep by hushed voices and the sound of a myriad hoofs moving through the darkness as droves of cattle passed, guarded and hurried along toward Canada by one man to each half-dozen beasts.

These drovers' journeys were not always peaceful since law officers, aided by Jefferson Republicans, tried with diminishing success to sustain the embargo. So many brawls arose in Georgia, so many heads were cracked during frequent clashes between smugglers and the law-abiding, that it unofficially was rechristened "Hellgate."

When not engaged in their nefarious and increasingly profitable commerce, the miscreants enlivened their leisure by bedeviling the unhappy customs officers. These received innumerable letters relating in horrid detail what was about to happen to them. Several of the more energetic found significantly empty coffins on their doorsteps. Jabez Penniman of Colchester, Vermont, collector of customs for the area, confessed to Albert Gallatin, Secretary of the Treasury, April 1, 1808, that it was impossible to enforce the embargo without the aid of troops. His troubles were just beginning.

When ice left Champlain that spring smuggling redoubled. Rafts laden with produce waited for a dark night when the wind blew from the south and then slipped past the customs house on Windmill Point and down the Richelieu. Other craft joined in the profitable trade. Many of them were light, sweep-driven boats that nested in the intricacy of straits and bays among the islands of the lower lake.

Gallatin instructed Penniman to buy and arm revenue craft of his own and to enlist crews. The 1st Regiment of Franklin County Militia was called out by Vermont to aid the customs collector. The Valley's misbehavior shocked Jefferson who, in a proclamation published in the May 9 issue of *The Vermont Journal,* charged the smugglers with "forming insurrections against the authority of the laws of the United States." He also warned "such insurgents and all concerned in such combinations instantly and without delay to disperse themselves and retire peaceably to their abodes."

Undispersed smugglers on June 25 stole the revenue cutter Penniman had purchased, armed and sent to Windmill Point.

The illicit trade with Canada proceeded briskly on land and water. Men from the north packed goods in through woods to secret places of deposit. They made social calls on friends south of the line and, when they departed, took all the cattle that had been assembled there north across the border with them. Sheds were built on hillsides that ran down to the line and filled with hogsheads packed with contraband. At the proper time, the down-hill side of the shed which was hung on hinges was raised, the hogsheads rolled out and gravity bore the goods over the border. Herds of northward-moving cattle still filled the roads at night.

The Franklin County militia regiment failed so completely to diminish the traffic that official suspicion of its integrity grew continually stronger. At last it was dismissed, and troops from Rutland County, who had fewer relatives and friends in the smuggling area, took their place. The Franklin men were indignant and adopted resolutions protesting against the insult to their honor.

On Champlain, smugglers' craft were playing a deft game of hide and seek with revenue men among the crooked waterways about the Hero Islands, Alburg peninsula and Isle La Motte. Major Charles K. Williams, later to be governor of Vermont, was stationed with a militia command at Windmill Point and Penniman had outfitted a new twelve-oar cutter, *The Fly.*

The revenue craft chased many boats but caught few, for it was heavily built and it was a favorite trick of smugglers when they were pursued too closely to run for the thin strip of dry land connecting the two halves of North Hero Island. Here the light, fugitive craft were hauled across and relaunched beyond a barrier that *The Fly,* ponderous as it was, found insurmountable.

Most notorious of the smuggling fleet was *Black Snake,* a tardaubed, converted ferryboat, propelled by fourteen sweeps and captained by the rascally William Mudgett whose daring and success became a lake byword and an increasing pain to both Penniman and Major Williams. When they learned, August 2, 1808, that *Black Snake* had slipped by night into the Winooski River and was tied at Joy's Landing, three miles downstream from Burlington, the major detailed Lieutenant David Farrington of Brandon, Vermont, Sergeant David B. Johnson and twelve privates to take *The Fly* up-river and capture the smuggler.

The expedition, all participants were aware, was unlikely to be a picnic, for *Black Snake* mounted a swivel and her crew were tough men and were armed. Ten of them were on the bank above their moored boat when *The Fly* came round a bend of the serpentine stream. As she drew nearer, Mudgett shouted to Farrington:

"Don't lay hands on that boat. I swear by God I'll blow the first man's brains out who lays hands on her."[1]

He leveled his musket, but Farrington nevertheless came alongside *Black Snake* and sent Sergeant Johnson and six militiamen aboard her. While the smugglers brandished their guns and howled, the sergeant cast off and followed *The Fly* toward the river's far shore, although Samuel Mott, with the dismounted swivel trained on them through a tree crotch, threatened to fire.

A musket went off. Its ball struck up spray between the retreating craft. A ragged volley from the bank followed and, on *The Fly,* Private Ellis Drake dropped, shot twice through the head. The pacifistic Farrington continued his retirement to the scorn of Captain Jonathan Ormsby of Burlington who appeared on the far shore and demanded that the lieutenant turn about and make the smugglers prisoners.

At this instant the swivel let go. Five of its slugs struck and killed Ormsby; three more slew Private Asa Marsh. Farrington fell with wounds in his left arm, right shoulder and forehead. Sergeant Johnson, a less temperate man than his superior, ordered both boats back across the river. The troops swarmed up the bank and captured all the smugglers but two.

One of *Black Snake's* crew, Cyrus Dean, was hanged, November 11, for murder. Captain Mudgett's trial ended in a jury disagreement. David Sheffield, Samuel Mott and Francis Ledgard were found guilty of manslaughter and each was sentenced to ten years' imprisonment. All were pardoned before their terms expired.

There was compensating comedy later that year when smugglers fell upon the customs house at Windmill Point while only a lone sentry was stationed there and appropriated sixty barrels of potash that recently had been confiscated. Laughter rose more loudly over the subsequent predicament of Samuel Buell, collector of the port at Burlington, though he did not share in the mirth.

Buell captained a cutter that put off from Windmill Point to overhaul a suspicious craft and was the first to board her. He also was the last, for the cutter's crew shied away from the muzzles of smugglers' muskets and left their leader a prisoner.

The collector, his captors resolved, was too hot-blooded for his own good and something remedial should be undertaken. Accordingly, after careful sounding, they lowered him up to his chin in the cold water of the Richelieu, and left him there. The embittered Buell, when he had got to shore and had returned to Windmill Point, told his fainthearted crew:

"I wouldn't give a damn for as many such men as you as could stand between here and Hell."[2]

In 1809 the United States Navy was summoned to aid in enforcing the embargo. Two gunboats, destined five years later to be the beginning of Macdonough's fleet, were built on Champlain, yet smuggling went profitably on, by land, by water and, in winter, by ice. The smugglers were durable men.

Duncan Macgregor of Alburgh, an eminent miscreant, was returning from Canada with a sledload of contraband rum and cutlery when the ice of Windmill Bay gave way beneath him. Macgregor managed to cut his sled loose before it dragged his horses under and, soaked to the skin, succeeded in hauling one animal out upon firmer ice. Together, they rescued the other horse.

Macgregor then found with dismay that the zero cold was freezing his wet clothing so hard and stiff that he could neither walk nor, in his increasingly rigid state, mount a horse. Ingenuity did not desert him. The smuggler rehitched his team, lay down, gripped the whiffletree, shouted "Giddap!" and, sliding along on his ice-shod anterior, was drawn to shore and thence to Joseph Mott's farm. There he was thawed out and went back to dredge up his sled and its load.

The embargo was causing deprivation in New York City and was filling owners of depleted stores with an intense craving for goods. It also was damming up a great supply of merchandise in Canada. Big business now entered the smuggling trade which heretofore had been a matter of small, individual enterprises.

Cornelius Peter Van Ness, a future governor of Vermont, succeeded the lately jettisoned Samuel Buell as Burlington's collector of the port. He and other citizens—Gideon King, "Admiral of the Lake," among them—became partners with New York merchants in an ingenious scheme to break the embargo while leaving it apparently intact.

Van Ness granted that he would be obliged to arrest Americans who brought goods in from Canada, but he and his associates convinced themselves that the measure applied only to their own countrymen. Obviously, they told one another, the law was not intended to regulate the trading of, say, a Spaniard. By odd coincidence there was then in Burlington a Spanish subject, one Manzuco, and he, with the blessing of Van Ness & Co., became titular owner of the sloop *Saucy Fox*.

LAKE GEORGE FROM ABOVE LAKE GEORGE VILLAGE

NORTH BEACH, BURLINGTON, ON LAKE CHAMPLAIN

MODERN CHAMPLAIN DIESEL FERRY

The craft plied between Burlington and St. Johns, carrying potash and other produce to Canada and bringing back goods that were forwarded most profitably to merchants in New York. The collector of the port and his subordinates never interfered with these voyages. They piously contended that they had no authority to hamper Spanish trade.

Manzuco's activity was ended by the outbreak of the War of 1812, but a more frolicsome representative of the New York merchants, John Banker, Jr., succeeded him. Banker had obtained from the New York collector of the port a commission empowering him to fit out a privateer on Lake Champlain for the destruction of British trade. He bought a small sailboat, appropriately christened it *The Lark* and began to cruise in search of enemy craft.

The Banker privateer was of less than a ton's burthen and her battery consisted of two muskets. Once, in a moment of unscrupulous elation, her captain discharged his broadside into an Essex-Charlotte ferryboat. *The Lark* captured an astonishing number of prizes.

Banker would run his boat down to Rouses Point, anchor near the line and wait. Barges, deep laden with goods, would come out of Canada and submit meekly to capture. The privateer would convoy the "enemy craft" to Burlington and appoint a prize master. He would forward the cargoes to Banker's principals in New York who had paid Canadian shippers in advance for the barges and their contents. The enterprise eventually was halted by the federal government which confiscated *The Lark*.

From 1812 to 1814 smuggling discreditably reached apogee, to the aid and comfort of the enemy and the mounting indignation of commanders in the Champlain region who time and again detailed troops to smash the treasonable trade, and never succeeded. With the conflict's end, illicit commerce diminished. Its chief importance in the ensuing years was a secret traffic, not in goods but in human beings.

Most of the runaway slaves who had reached New York passed through the Champlain Valley on the final stage of their journey to Canada and freedom. While the lake was open, local anti-slavery societies relayed many fugitives from Troy or Albany to Whitehall, frequently by canalboat. They were concealed on steamers or sailboats and borne down Champlain to British territory. In winter, when ice had closed this route, Negroes traveled north on Vermont's underground railway.

Brethren of Ebenezer Allen, who in 1777 had issued his personal emancipation proclamation for the slave Dinah Mattis and her child, were not likely to be laggard in aiding other such seekers for freedom. The underground railway along Champlain's east shore was established early. It followed the general course of the present highway that runs the length of the state at the foot of the Green Mountains' westward slope. Antislavery societies flourished in most of the towns along its course and a succession of agents smuggled the runaways to Canada via Bennington, Manchester, Wallingford, Rutland, Middlebury, Vergennes, Burlington, St. Albans and Swanton.

The underground railway handled an increasingly heavy traffic during the 1840's and 1850's with a minimum of publicity. Hatred of slavery and sympathy for its victims were too nearly universal in Vermont for partisan clashes to arise. The secrecy of the commerce makes close estimate of its beneficiaries impossible, but it is certain that hundreds of men and women were borne north through the lake or its shore to freedom.

Smuggling of all varieties dwindled during the latter half of the nineteenth century yet never wholly perished. When there was profit to be made by evading the customs laws, the spiritual descendants of Sorrel Barber and Silver Gray remained faithful to their heritage.

The smuggling of Chinese into the United States reached epidemic proportions in the 1880's, particularly on Champlain's west shore where the railway from Canada was afflicted by a horde of yellow stowaways. Those who were discovered filled the jails of the region and in several towns, Port Henry among them, additional prisons had to be built to house the overflow.

This variety of smuggling had only a brief flowering but when prohibition parched America while liquor remained plentiful in Canada, the ancient trade burst into a long, resplendent blooming. The attempt to abolish it was no more successful than had been the effort, a century earlier, to enforce Jefferson's embargo.

Silver Gray's and Sorrel Barber's twentieth-century avatars saw at once the profits that would reward energetic lawbreakers and went gleefully to work. By swift powerboats that dashed past Rouses Point at night or snaked their way through the labyrinthine waters below the mouth of Missisquoi Bay, by automobiles and by trains, by wagons that lumbered over back roads with ostensible loads of hay or cordwood, even by packhorses that followed dim forest trails, the new contraband came south across the border.

As usual, repressive forces were fantastically outnumbered. Company B of the United States Customs Patrol whose beat extends from Champlain's west shore to Coos County, New Hampshire, was increased from thirty-five to sixty-five men for the emergency's duration. This meant that, if the whole force watched the border twenty-four hours a day, the patrolmen would be posted about two miles apart.

The customs navy on Lake Champlain which had consisted of two launches was reinforced by an additional four and a forty-foot cabin cruiser that served as mother ship. These augmentations were not enough to strangle water-borne smuggling. The tide of contraband continued to rise.

Rumrunning, in its early Champlain stage, was an enterprise, operated by individuals, but the American talent for organization soon transformed the trade. Leaders rose among this new generation of smugglers, and within a brief time most of the Canadian liquor and beer was borne into the United States by either the Parker or the Conway gang. These groups waged with customs officials an immensely profitable, resourceful and generally bloodless warfare.

Little of the viciousness that stained urban liquor traffic got into the Champlain branch of the industry. The customs men and rumrunners in general were striving against neighbors whom they knew and, often, liked. Only one deliberate killing was recorded in the entire campaign.

Murray M. Tucker, now captain of Company B, and his patrol mate, E. B. Webb, tried to halt a liquor truck north of St. Albans. The driver mortally wounded Webb and shot Tucker through the right hand. The killer was captured and imprisoned for life.

Two more customs men lost their lives by accident during the prohibition era. One died when the car in which he was chasing a smuggler skidded and overturned. The other fell overboard while boarding a rum-running craft at night. His body never was found.

At least one smuggler perished. John Conway, founder and leader of the Conway gang, set out from Burlington by launch with several associates for Grand Isle. His companions on arrival there reported that their chief had fallen overboard. No trace of him ever was discovered.

In general, the strife was viewed by participants as a violent game for high stakes. Wits rather than weapons were the deciding factor in most clashes. Each side employed spies, informers and much canny subterfuge. If the Parker gang could convince the customs patrol that liquor was to be shipped south through Highgate, enough agents might be massed there to give the rum caravan clear passage by way of Sheldon. If the customs men could make Conway's followers believe the Rouses Point channel was heavily guarded, they might be able to trap a smuggling craft sneaking out of Missisquoi Bay.

By land, the gangs moved their liquor in fleets of laden passenger automobiles with a pilot car in front and another at the rear of the procession. The leading car scouted before the advance, uttering warning horn blasts if it detected a trap. The following machine guarded against pursuit.

If the road in front were blocked or the caravan were about to be overhauled from behind, the gang deserted cars and cargoes and fled. A successful later trip would compensate for the present loss.

Company B during prohibition captured more than 300 cars.

Since, by law, these were offered for sale at their appraised value, many immediately were repurchased by their former operators and, often, were taken again by the federal agents. It was a vigorous but not a vindictive strife.

On the lake, the contest most nearly resembled aquatic, nocturnal tag. In a straightaway race, the power-packed craft of the smugglers could outdistance, even when laden, the patrol boats. It was customs strategy to lay ambushes and close in upon the runners before they could abandon stealth for speed.

Even if a boat were boarded, agents needed to be swift in overcoming its crew. Otherwise, the liquor might be cast overside before it could be seized. One ingenious beer smuggler carried his cargo dangling in sacks from the boatrail and abolished evidence, when necessary, by slashing the tethering cords.

Tidings came to the customs that a big, fast boat lay, filled with liquor, in the Richelieu River close to the boundary line waiting for darkness before running the blockade. A patrol craft was posted on either side the channel at Rouses Point and a stout rope was stretched between them on the surface. It was hoped this obstacle would foul the rumrunner's propeller or at least check her until agents could board.

Toward midnight, the smuggler drove across the line with the roar of wide-open engines. Searchlights of the lurking craft fell upon her as she came abeam and surged into the rope. It delayed her momentarily and in that space a customs boat bore down on her.

Opposing gunwales ground for an instant. An agent got aboard the rumrunner before she got free of the obstruction and shot off into the gloom. The vainly pursuing customs men saw something fall from the fugitive and, sweeping black water with their searchlights, discovered and retrieved the erstwhile boarder who was bobbing about in his life jacket, unconscious, and with a lump on his head.

The agent as he stumbled aft on the craft had encountered a member of her crew who had wasted no time in argument but had smitten the invader with a baseball bat and had knocked him overside. The empty boat was found next day, hidden in brush at the mouth of Otter Creek. Her ownership never was determined but she was identified by a piece of her metal work that had broken off and had remained embedded in the customs craft's gunwale.

Repeal once again has reduced smuggling activity in the Valley, but contraband of various importance still moves furtively across the border. Southward are borne gold stolen from Canadian mines and such unglamorous items as Swiss watch movements, cattle feed and butter. Northward, a reversal of the late tide, go liquor in small amounts and larger secret shipments of cigarettes.

Once more the boom time has passed, yet inheritors of the Silver Gray-Sorrel Barber tradition are ingenious enough to keep B Company of the Customs Patrol, now reduced to its normal complement of one captain, one lieutenant, three sergeants and thirty men, continually alert. The game of wits goes on.

Captain Tucker's men, after long and involved intelligence work, halted a car near St. Albans and triumphantly confiscated its load. They had believed that opium was to be smuggled into Vermont and here were hundreds of small dark blocks wrapped in red paper and Oriental in aspect and odor. Car, shipment and strangely unprotestant driver were detained while analysis was made of samples of the cargo. When the report came, the agents' faces grew redder than the red "opium" wrappers. They enclosed nothing more narcotic than blocks of ground figs.

The customs men have no way of knowing whether, while this decoy engaged their attention, the actual shipment of opium came through successfully elsewhere, but they have the rueful feeling that probably it did. The north country still has its normal number of Sorrell Barbers and Silver Grays and the valley that reaches into Canada remains ideal terrain for their enterprises.

---

[1] Abby Maria Hemenway (ed.) *Vermont Historical Gazetteer,* II, 345.
[2] *Ibid.,* p. 495.

Chapter 24

Fish and Strangers

Some early, unidentified and obviously morose visitor to Lake George delivered himself of an aphorism that tourists and vacationists still quote. "The natives of this region," he proclaimed, "live upon fish and strangers."

When the first cabins got a precarious foothold on the lake's steep shores, this peculiar diet was not immediately adopted. There were forests, at the outset, for the settlers profitably to destroy. The area prospered from export of logs and tanbark, potash and pulp, while the tall firs and hardwoods endured.

The monumental pines that had suffused the Great Carrying Place with an appropriately foreboding gloom went first. Thereafter, the hills were stripped of all negotiable timber. When the boom time ended, when the assets had been spent, there remained little for Lake Georgians to feed upon but scenery, which was highly unnourishing, fish—and strangers.

The last have been the area's most plentiful and palatable stimulus. They have adorned the lake with summer hotels, some elaborate and luxurious and some not. They have strung its fair shores with mansions, both seemly and otherwise, with cottages, cabins and camps. Summer colonists and holiday makers, who together outnumber the seven thousand-odd natives more than twenty to one, supply these permanent residents with more than sufficient nutriment to keep them from feeding necessarily on fish.

The transition of Lake George from a lumbering to a vacation area was painless and gradual. While the log rafts still were floating to the sawmills at Ticonderoga in larger herds yearly, the first temeritous summer people arrived. They were of a tougher, more adventurous breed than their descendants, for the region still was frontier and was accessible only by the Old Military Road which

325

was then in a state to try the fiber of the stoutest traveler. The dusty, bruised and thoroughly shaken up pioneer visitors, on arrival at the lake, found their chief comfort in scenery, for there were at the beginning of the nineteenth century only two rudimentary hotels.

James Caldwell, the imperious original proprietor of most of the land in the township that now bears his name, built the Lake House where Lake George village's Shephard Memorial Park now runs down greenly to the water. In Bolton, then entering its heyday as a lumber town, the Mohican House was constructed.

Neither hostelry, originally, was designed for the vacation trade. Each was established to care for the uncritical wants of woodsmen and timber buyers but the first small trickle of summer people swelled quickly into a profitable stream and other hotels and boardinghouses followed in the pathway the Lake and the Mohican House had blazed. Both these were enlarged and remodeled many times in their long existences. The Mohican, an ungainly, verandahed two-and-a-half-story structure, with a painted wooden warrior glowering out over the lake from the top of its flagpole, had almost rounded out a century when it was torn down in 1898.

While the massacre of negotiable timber proceeded, vacationists were only a contributory source of Lake Georgian incomes, yet each year they became a more profitable one and each year the region did more to attract them. Tea Island in Bolton now is destitute of tea, but it was so named for the teahouse that was established there in 1828. Other equally mild amusements were provided for summer visitors. The natives were becoming increasingly aware that, when the timber was gone, they would be obliged to subsist on fish—and strangers.

The prime attractions which, a hundred and forty years ago, brought the first few vacationists to a region that now yearly receives its tens of thousands, have been preserved or restored. Foresight, which is not typically American and is quite as commercial as esthetic, has kept Lake George much as it was when its discoverer first saw it.

The narrow, island-adorned water encourages intimacy and unity. The hills that stand knee-deep in the lake have left no space for the growth of large towns, if indeed these ever could have been established on a waterway that led from one unimportance to another. The rocky, unproductive land surrounding Lake George and the rapids at its outlet prohibited the settlement, the growth, the trade and the traffic that its larger sister has known.

Champlain, with canals at its north and south ends, supplied a direct and level route from interior New York to Canada. Champlain's valley with its ore and timber, its plentiful water power and stretches of rich agricultural land bred wealth and energy denied the Lake George area. Resorts became a major consideration on the greater lake comparatively late in its career.

When the armies no longer came down from the north, when the massacre of the forests had ended, resort life became George's single, redeeming importance. Originally it had been a surpassingly lovely lake. It might have sunk into a desolate region of denuded hills and polluted water. The people of New York recognized its beauty and set about maintaining it.

Lake George is still a cool, bright place that presents new loveliness with each alteration of light and shade. Boathouses and the gables of buildings jut through its lakeside foliage, and on the infrequent level spaces, green lawns run back to hotels and summer dwellings. Otherwise, the region retains its pristine fairness. The once ravaged hills that soar and swoop against the sky have been reclothed in carefully administered forests, state and privately owned. The lucid water itself is kept untainted. No filth, no refuse sullies it. Even the single steamer that now plies Lake George has self-contained septic tanks.

Intrinsically the blue green depths, the heart-stirring heights, the fir-plumed islands are as they were at the beginning. The lake's destiny was plain even then. After a century and a half of violently dramatic history, before the last British war on this continent had ended, Lake George had begun to achieve the inevitable. Events, some purposeful, some inadvertent, moved it ever more swiftly on its way.

Steam traffic came to the lake in 1817 and immediately hitherto remote stretches of the shore line became accessible to vacationists. Where the wheezing *James Caldwell* touched, new hotels were established and summer colonies were born. The steamboat accidentally brought to the area it served a still more glamorous luster. A stout choleric gentleman who watched the loveliness of Lake George unfold from *James Caldwell's* deck was challenged by a friend to write a novel against this background. Thus it came about that James Fenimore Cooper published *The Last of the Mohicans* and stamped the region with a new, romantic impress.

Cooper also tried vigorously to bestow a new name upon the lake. With others, he had girded against the meaningless and guttural appellation that had been inflicted on the water and proposed as a substitute, not St. Isaac Jogues' own title, but "Horicon," insisting, with no warrant, that this had been the lake's original name. Cooper's campaign failed but the township that was carved out of Hague and Bolton in 1838 called itself "Horicon" and lake steamers have borne the same name.

The tide was coming in. The little village of Caldwell, which later was to be incorporated as Lake George, found that the profits it made from summer visitors exceeded what the winter's lumbering produced. In 1848 a plank highway was laid from Glens Falls to the Lake. In the following year, the railway reached Glens Falls.

Passengers who heretofore had arrived at Lake George in a thoroughly disheveled, if not dislocated, condition, now traveled the ten miles from the railhead in glittering red coaches, drawn by six horses. From the ruins of the stockade at Half Way Brook, arose a tavern which offered as refreshments to the travelers punch for the gentlemen and lemonade for the ladies, as well as ice water free to all—and seldom available.

Each year, more of the affluent made the pilgrimage to the lake. Each year new hotels and boardinghouses opened their doors. In 1858, a hostelry which, like many of its predecessors, and successors, was designed to be the abiding final word in luxurious entertainment of the stranger raised its gigantic and surprising bulk on a pine-shaded knoll above the mounded earth that marks the grave of the fort Montcalm captured and destroyed.

Lake Georgians of that era looked upon the Fort William Henry Hotel with justified awe and considered it the ultimate in summer hostelries. Compared to its predecessors, it was immense and, matched against anything extant today, bewilderingly ornate. All the orders of architecture, including some additional that the builder had thought up himself, were represented in its mass. Grecian pillars, thirty feet high, supported a mansard roof that was crowned by a proud dome. It had further distinctions.

"The house," a contemporary reporter explains, "is elegantly furnished throughout and supplied with all the modern improvements, including gas, which is manufactured at the works erected on the grounds, especially for that purpose."[1]

The original Fort William Henry burned in 1909 and has been replaced by a second hotel of the same name, a more restrained structure of stucco and red tile.

Lake George now was launched on what plainly was to be its predestined career, yet the wilderness retreated unwillingly. Roads were few and were either blanketed with dust or deeply mired. Traffic between the lake-shore villages and hotels was almost entirely water-borne.

Indians from Canada still were included among the summer visitors. Yearly until the 1870's, canoe flotillas followed the immemorial waterway to the head of George where their crews raised themselves a temporary village. Thereafter they whiled away the warm months with the traditional Indian pastimes of hunting, fishing and despoiling the paleface, no longer by tomahawk but by selling him a variety of useless articles of alleged Indian manufacture.

They and the rest of the company that came to the lake each summer were a floating population that was bound to the region by no material ties. It was not until the 1860's that the first summer resident established here a home of his own.

This pioneer was Rufus Wattles of New York, a gay bachelor, who purchased in Bolton township Recluse Island and built himself a cottage there. Legend holds that Recluse Island was once the temporary abiding place of a Jesuit, Father Bernard, after a flight from the Iroquois. Legend also maintains that there was little of the monastic in Householder Wattles' Lake George career. He is said to have been equally interested in sailing and young ladies, but so deft at either sport that no reef or designing mama ever stranded him.

The mid-Victorian enthusiasm for communion with nature inspired others to follow the Wattles' example. More houses were raised on the lake shore and the islands. None of these enterprising builders sought solitude quite so enthusiastically as the artist, J. Henry Hill, who lived alone on Phantom Island in Bolton township from 1870 to 1876, won for himself the title of "The Hermit of Lake George" and eventually was removed from his hermitage to an insane asylum.

Meanwhile, still another author was reburnishing the history of the region and stressing its romantic beauty. In 1865 Francis Parkman published the first volume of his monumental narrative. The minds of readers turned from the squalor of a more recent war to dwell upon the distance-enchanted events of ancient conflict.

Champlain and George were growing increasingly accessible; comfortable steamboats were available to carry the tourist the length of a valley where one might feast one's eyes on scenic splendor, moon over the ruins of Fort George, Crown Point and Ticonderoga and pleasantly combine culture and enjoyment. "The Northern Tour," inspired by Parkman, became a fashionable enterprise and thereby Lake George's stature as a summer resort was increased, but it was not until 1882, when the Delaware and Hudson Railroad built a spur line north to Caldwell, that the social life of the region burst into flower.

Freight cars brought new luxuries to the area and passenger coaches bore the luxury-loving. The elect who had disdained the comparative simplicity Lake George heretofore had offered the visitor found it pleasant now, after the sinful delights of Saratoga, to journey still further north and rest for a space in a cool tranquillity where boating and croquet were the most demanding enterprises. Society sanctified the region with its approval and a whole new generation of hotels sprang up to care for Society's needs, while the more ancient were thoroughly refurbished.

Whiskered gentlemen and their bustled womenkind took their ease at a wide variety of hostelries. At the head of the lake stood the Fort William Henry, the Lake House, the Fort George, the Crosby-side, while at Bolton the ancient Mohican House was rivaled by the Wells House, the Bolton House, the Locust Grove House, the Lake View House and others. In 1882 the original Sagamore Hotel was built on Green Island.

There were still other hotels on either lake shore, but Society's exclusives were unwilling to be anything except august and aloof in the region they had blessed and proceeded to build dwellings of their own. They were not the simple cottages of an earlier time. Society decreed mansions, some of them downright dreadful, most of them English, French or even Swiss in architecture, but all of them spectacular.

In Caldwell and Bolton the mountains stand back a little way from the water and on the shore made available by this recession the elect contrived their estates. That area was christened spontaneously "Millionaires' Row." The east side of the lake, with its more forbidding shores, maintained and still cherishes a simpler way of life, with modest cottages and camps, but the west side, in this boom time, became a fresh-water version of Newport, with formal gardens, fountains, imported servants, steam yachts and, later, naphtha launches on the lake and ornate revelry conducted in accordance with social protocol. It was a bright little, tight little world from which hotel patrons and natives were excluded. The natives did not object. They were living affluently on strangers.

Society in the heyday of the Lake George sojourn may have been stuffy and smug but it still had its insurgents and prank players. The Lake George Sea Serpent was contrived by one of these. Harry H. Watrous, president of the National Academy of Design, had a villa on the lake and among his near neighbors was the socially elect, if slightly malodorous, Colonel William Mann of *Town Topics* notoriety. Possibly as revenge for the number of occasions when Mann frightened society by threat of scandalous exposure, Watrous spent long weeks in the summer of 1904 building, painting and horrendously decorating a submersible monster to scare the colonel.

With the help of an engineer, the artist contrived an apparatus that would raise and lower the effigy, sank it in the lake and waited in hiding ashore until Mann and a party of guests came rowing by. Watrous then pulled the appropriate wire and a hideous, dripping creature emerged alongside Mann's boat, stared hungrily into the bewhiskered face of the colonel and sank from sight as Watrous pulled another wire.

The hoax was not exposed until after the colonel had telegraphed to a number of learned societies accounts of his thrilling experience.

The natives still are living well, though the baroque splendors of an earlier day have faded. There was no spectacular collapse of the social dynasty, only a gradual transmutation due to many influences. Society, whimsically, came to consider other regions more fashionable. Pyramiding taxes made the maintenance of the Millionaires' Row palaces an ever stiffer ordeal. Finally, the advent of the automobile and the powerboat turned all Lake George's most secluded precincts into places easily reached by the unanointed. A few descendants of the mansion builders still occupy their ancestral residences each summer. Elsewhere, caretakers keep the courts where Society gloried.

The change has been the antithesis of decay. When the first rash adventurer in linen duster and goggles guided his one-cylinder job into the village of Lake George, a new and more vital era began. Motorized millions have followed him. Old roads have been improved and new have been cut through erstwhile wilderness. Where the yachts of the wealthy once glided, swarms of speedboats and outboards range the lake to its farthest haven. The gas engine has changed Lake George from a remote, aristocratic summer colony into a vigorous, still expanding resort for the world and his wife.

Some pulpwood still is cut yearly from the carefully maintained forests that have reclothed the despoiled mountains. A few lean farms still exist. Otherwise, the area, from the wide-winged Sagamore Hotel, shining white and stately above its lighthouse-guarded pier on Green Island, to the smallest cottage with its hopeful "Tourists Accommodated" sign has a single, enveloping purpose.

The concrete highway that caracoles over the west shore hills on its way from Champlain and Canada links isolated lakeside communities, hotels and boardinghouses. It skirts Millionaires' Row and the wide variety of elaborate fences—picket fences, board fences, concrete fences, cobblestone fences, wrought-iron fences, even chain fences—with which the elect keep themselves and their premises unspotted from the world, and runs southerly downhill into what was once the little lumbering village of Caldwell and now is the county seat, Lake George.

The community is a hotel and shopping center with lately acquired overtones of Coney Island. Here are neon lights and bingo games, saloons, slot machines to infinite variety and a miniature golf course. Offshore, in the summer, yachting regattas are held, and in the winter, harness horses race over a course laid out on the ice.

The time when Lake George, village and region, relapsed on Labor Day into eight months' hibernation has passed with the social exclusiveness of Millionaires' Row. Excellent ski slopes now bring an increasing number of visitors during the once apathetic months of winter.

The area is in the process of turning itself from a strictly summer into an all-year-round resort, with foliage-viewing and hunting in the fall, winter sports thereafter and in the spring lake and stream fishing.

The transformation more than satisfies the natives. While they have the strangers, the strangers are welcome to the fish.

The fishing, to be sure, isn't so good as it used to be—it never has been, anywhere—but Champlain and George still offer a creditable supply. The lesser lake is stocked regularly with landlocked salmon, brook and lake trout and smallmouthed bass; the larger has a reasonable abundance of northern and walleyed pike, pickerel, bass, landlocked salmon and less gamy species. The Atlantic salmon that once spawned in the rivers emptying into lower Champlain make the inland voyage no longer, though in early days they thronged so thickly in the streams that men on nervous horses hesitated to ford. Sturgeon, once plentiful in Champlain, grow continually scarcer.

The fish population of either lake never was great enough to make large-scale commercial capture profitable and has been left in general to sportsmen, though the wartime food shortage impelled New York to authorize the netting of non-game varieties from her share of the waters. This enterprise has yielded more than 100,000 fish yearly, chiefly perch, bullheads and sunfish.

Fishing, in Champlain particularly, furnishes year-round sport for the fanatics who esteem any variety of angling above sedentary comfort. The most violent of these, when winter prohibits further casting or trolling, risk personal breakage and exposure to frostbite and chilblain by rushing furiously from one agitated tipup to another in the frigid sport of ice fishing. When February sends across the lake blasts so keen that they would daunt an Eskimo, the most incurable addicts resort to smelt fishing.

Cabins on runners that have been beached for nearly a year are drawn out upon Champlain, and the ice is chopped away below holes in their floors. Within these edifices, the infatuated sit on narrow plank benches for a prodigious number of hours, each man twitching the jigstick from which depends a long line, bright sinker and baited hook. Occasionally he hauls up, hand over hand from the jade depths, a small silvery fish. Continually he listens to the barefaced lying of his fellow residents and breathes malodorous fumes from the kerosene stove. Stupefaction from such noxious vapors can best be averted by repeated dosages of *spiritus frumenti*. Even this is not a completely reliable antidote, since men who have resorted to it too trustfully have had trouble in getting back to shore and have been known to fall, on landing, into deep swoons.

Champlain's transformation into a resort area has been more deliberate and is less complete than George's. Mills and factories still are more important to Winooski, Plattsburg, Burlington, St. Albans, Port Henry, Ticonderoga Village and Whitehall than the tourist trade, yet the catering to the wants and whims of vacationists has become an increasingly important industry, and hostelries ranging in splendor from the vast bulk of the Hotel Champlain at Bluff Point on the west shore to modest "tourist homes" welcome holiday makers from May to November.

Clubs with central buildings and attendant broods of cottages stand on the lake shores. Summer camps for boys and girls increase yearly beside Champlain. Motorboats of countless variety, sailboats, skiffs and canoes move over water that, in earlier years, bore only armed flotillas. Champlain and George, twin ancient warpaths, have been transformed in the fourth century of their recorded history into playgrounds.

---

[1] S. R. Stoddard, *Lake George* (Glens Falls, 1873), p. 33.

Chapter 25

Family Fort

ICHEL CHARTIER DE LOTBINIÈRE, raised from his grave and set down upon the rugged point he knew so well almost two centuries ago, could be pardoned for not immediately identifying his situation. It is doubtful whether he would recognize the lake before him, so changed has its setting become. Where there was forest, now there are disciplined farms: where unbroken wilderness lay, houses today stand singly and clustered in communities and, north of the point, the stainless sky Lotbinière knew is smudged by the smoke of mills.

Governor General de Vaudreuil's engineer would feel lost in this altered land until he looked up to the ridge that is the peninsula's spine. There, like a kindred miracle to his resurrection, still crowning the height as he had ordained it, he would see his own proud work, the stronghold he had named "Fort de Vaudreuil," and the army of Montcalm had called "Carillon," and the conquering British, "Ticonderoga."

Gray, solid and unchanged, it looks out over the narrow water. Apparently it is the very fort, exact in detail, that Lotbinière built. Actually it is a necromancy, a reincarnation contrived by a family that for generations has loved Ticonderoga, and it has been principally accomplished by one member of the clan, Stephen H. P. Pell—"Pell of Ticonderoga"—who inherited a ruin and from it has recreated the ruin's original form and substance.

Among the million property owners of America with the wide variety of their holdings, Pell of Ticonderoga is the one private citizen who is proprietor of a full-statured, heavily armed fort. Though the post is strong and continually made stronger, though yearly more iron and bronze cannon thrust their black or green

336

muzzles from the walls, the Republic has not attempted to interfere. Instead, the federal government has encouraged the stronghold's growth by the gift of additional guns. It scarcely could do less when a passion for historical accuracy and the contagious enthusiasm of one man have lifted out of decay and brilliantly restored what is in essence a national monument.

Fort Ticonderoga is again the stronghold Lotbinière first built, yet, despite the thousands of the curious and the reverent who yearly pass through its reconstructed gateway, the garrison is entirely spectral and numbers among its ghostly company not only the unnamed thousands, red and white, who fought on the blood-steeped peninsula but also many who in their time were among the great of the earth and, tarrying at Ticonderoga, left vestiges of their personalities here.

Champlain fought the first skirmish of a 150-year war near where the fort later was to rise. Montcalm defended the post. Abercromby failed and Howe died before it. The destinies of Amherst, of Putnam, Stark, Schuyler, Ethan Allen, Benedict Arnold, Anthony Wayne, Arthur St. Clair, Burgoyne, Sullivan, Koscuisko, Knox, André and Rogers of the Rangers all were influenced to greater or less degree by their sojourns at Ticonderoga. Benjamin Franklin paused at the post in the Republic's first year. George Washington visited it at the war's end.

The fort today, despite its batteries of ancient guns, despite the long and violent saga in which it played a vital part, no longer is a bulwark of empire but a museum and a library of continually greater importance. It has been raised from its tomb in the last quarter-century but the association of Ticonderoga and the Pell family runs back a hundred and sixty-nine years. The Pells and the fort first met in 1777.

Captain Joshua Pell, in that year, tarried for a space at Ticonderoga. Captain Joshua did not come to the stronghold directly from the ancestral manor of Pelham in the late province and now state of New York. He approached it more circuitously.

In 1775 the Pell family like many others was split by the outbreak of the Revolution. Joshua remained loyal to his king, jour-

neyed to London and thence to Quebec and came up Champlain
with Burgoyne's army.

There is no record in Captain Pell's diary, now in the possession
of his collateral descendant, Pell of Ticonderoga, of its author's
emotions on viewing for the first time the place that was to become so intimately associated with later generations of his kin.
Probably, in retrospect, Captain Joshua cherished a cool attitude
toward the stronghold since it had proved to be only a way station
on the road to disaster. Joshua Pell had accompanied the doomed
regiments of Burgoyne from Ticonderoga to Saratoga and surrender.

The captain's loyalty was rewarded at the conflict's end by a
land grant in Canada. Thither he and his loyal brothers repaired
and thence, twice yearly, Joshua's nieces and nephews traveled the
length of Champlain, to and from the ancestral Pelham Manor
where they were educated. It was a nephew, William Ferris Pell,
who was great-grandfather to Pell of Ticonderoga, that first felt
the fascination of the place to which none of his descendants has
been immune.

"My ancestor," Stephen Pell relates, "fell in love with Ticonderoga. He visited the fort's ruins on every opportunity. Years
later, he told his daughter-in-law, who was my grandmother, that
even as a little boy he promised himself that he would own it some
day."

William Ferris Pell had become a prosperous importer when
circumstances brought the place within his reach. Crown lands, at
the Revolution's end, became the property of the states in which
they were situated. New York devoted hers to education and bestowed the 3,000-acre Ticonderoga domain on Columbia and
Union Colleges, neither of which had any immediate use for a
crumbling fort.

The first Ticonderoga Pell leased the tract soon after the War
of 1812 and became its actual owner in 1820, barely in time to keep
the fort from disappearing piecemeal. By then thrifty and lar-
cenous pioneers from either side of Champlain, filled with the
rugged frontier spirit of self-help and help-yourself, were doing

their creditable best to abolish the erstwhile proud possession of a French and of a British king.

Window frames which obviously had been doing no one any good on a completely empty building had been pried out and re-installed in settlers' dwellings. Barracks floors had been stolen and relaid in homes and stables. It would have been waste effort, the plunderers agreed, to spend time quarrying material for a residence or barn when here, for the taking, were great bastions of finished stone. One enterprising vandal, before Pell intervened, had revived the old French kiln and was burning to lime what portions of the fort his associates had not managed to cart away.

There was indignation when the property's new owner prohibited further distribution of Fort Ticonderoga throughout the countryside. The protests of some of the vandals who for years had lived beside and off the stronghold became so vehement that Pell actually had to pay them to move away.

The new proprietor made no attempt to revive the fort. He limited himself to protecting what portion of the ruin remained by building a fence about it. They proved a deterrent but not a preventive to further depredation. James Kent Pell, son of William Ferris, returned to the property one spring, years later, to discover that a new steamboat pier had been built on the lake shore during his absence and that the stone of which it was composed had been pried from two redoubts and the walls of the "covered way" whereby Ethan Allen and his men had advanced on Ticonderoga.

In time, persistence, occasional pugnacity and the fact that little remained above ground worth taking weaned the Pells' neighbors from their nefarious ways, and rain and frost were left to pursue their more deliberate demolition.

William Ferris Pell built a summer home, "Beaumont," below the ridge on which the fort stands. The place burned in 1826 and in the following year another, larger dwelling was raised. Its center unit with its Greek revival façade is linked with two smaller by glassed-in corridors. Behind the new house, which was called "The Pavilion," lay vestiges of "Le Jardin du Roi." The first Ticonderoga Pell revived the garden, and subsequent generations have maintained it.

Pontleroy, Montcalm's engineer, laid out the plot a hundred and ninety years ago. Great trees were felled to make way for this wilderness echo of France. The garden endures much as it originally was designed. It is an oblong, formal precinct whose flowers must have comforted a garrison homesick for the more splendid exactitudes of Versailles. The British who continued to cultivate it called it "The King's Garden." An air of grave antiquity broods over it. Even the buttressed brick walls, with which its present owner has enclosed it, wear the look of age.

One more disaster visited the site of uncounted ancient tragedies during the new owner's lifetime. In 1838 William Ferris Pell's eldest son, Archibald, who most nearly shared his father's love for Ticonderoga, determined to celebrate his parent's return to the property by firing one of the few cannon left in the ruin. The piece burst and killed him.

William Ferris Pell died, leaving ten children. No will of his was ever found and his descendants still cherish the conviction that one scapegrace son, finding the document and learning of his small inheritance under its provisions, destroyed it. With ten equal claimants to the patrimony, the chance was small that the Ticonderoga property would remain intact, yet it did. Though none of the younger Pells was able to maintain it, the family with its odd affinity for the fort set its face against division. Profitable offers repeatedly were made for portions of the tract. They all were refused.

Tenant farmers occupied the land and the Pavilion for a time was used as a summer hotel. Years went by; the grass crept higher about the remains of the old stronghold, and William Ferris Pell's children were succeeded by his grandchildren and great-grandchildren. Ticonderoga still was held as a unit, a general family possession, though the shares of some of the later proprietors had shrunk to as little as one-sixtieth of the whole.

Stephen Pell, in whom his great-grandsire's affinity for the place burned high, bought out the other owners in 1909. Many of these, when they learned of his then modest plans for restoration, gave him their shares outright. Pell of Ticonderoga, his wife Sarah and her father, Colonel Robert M. Thompson, began their enterprise. It proceeded slowly. The fort did not leap into being but came back stone by stone.

"I told Mr. Rockefeller recently," said Stephen Pell, "that he could wave a golden wand and recreate Old Williamsburg but that we, after each forward step, had to wait for more funds before we dared take another."

There were other reasons beside financial for the early deliberate progress. The outline of the stronghold still was discernible in the mounded rubble and crumbling walls but research was needed before the reconstruction could be accomplished accurately, and Pell of Ticonderoga has a religious respect for historical verity.

Investigation revealed that all French forts of the mid-eighteenth century were as nearly identical as their sites would permit. They might vary in size and in armament but each was built in the star-shaped form prescribed by the greatest military engineer of his time, Marshal Sébastien de Vauban. Lotbinière had no need to design his fortification. He simply adapted the Vauban plans to this hilltop site.

The terrain forbade a completely symmetrical construction. Ticonderoga was built as what the French term a *"fortification irregulier."* It was a gigantic, unbalanced asterisk of masonry centering on an oblong *"place d'armes"* or parade ground. This was surrounded by barracks that, in the fort's reincarnation, have become the museum and library. On the west bastion, Lotbinière raised a square watchtower which afforded a wide view over Champlain and the Lake George outlet.

Now, after thirty-six years of work with intervening pauses until more funds accrued, Fort Ticonderoga is five-sixths restored. The rebuilding of the tower is the only major project still uncompleted.

"And we've been ready for several years to finish that," said Stephen Pell, looking wistfully at the unfinished pile. "The money is in the bank. We're waiting now only for workmen."

He stood, a stalwart elder, on the counterscarp and surveyed his accomplishment. The banner that whipped in the lake wind above the red-roofed, dormer-windowed barracks was a replica of the standard first raised here by patriot troops—the "Cambridge Flag," thirteen red and white stripes with the Union Jack in the upper left canton. This was the emblem Arnold's fleet flew in the Valcour Island fight.

Bastions and demilunes bristled with cannon, and beyond the outer works to north, south and east, the land went steeply down to the shining narrow water where George and Champlain unite. Few men have been more gratifyingly surrounded by the realization of a dream. Pell of Ticonderoga blinked approvingly at the line of visitors streaming in from the office.

"When we started our work, it was a private, intimate enterprise. We had no idea then how far it would lead."

His and his wife's and his father-in-law's purpose was, at the beginning, merely to put together a broken fort, but at once matters more important than displaced stonework were unearthed by the diggers. The soil about Ticonderoga teems with relics of American, British, French occupations. It also yields an abundance of earlier Indian artifacts. These troves were housed in a rudimentary museum.

Stephen Pell chuckled as the sightseers plodded past.

"It was Mrs. Pell who first saw what we had here. She turned it from a family enterprise into a public institution. While I was overseas during the First World War, the work went on. So many people came to see it that my wife thriftily decided to charge admission. We have done so ever since."

Ticonderoga was well established as a museum when its owner came back from Europe where he had served first in the French and then in the American Army. He also brought back with him a wound, the Legion of Honor and Milo S. King, lately a major in the A.E.F., a small, quiet man with an appalling knowledge of ancient ordnance and an enthusiasm that has been whetted by the years he has served as General Manager.

The zest that all members of the Pell staff share for the reconstruction is contagious and has been a prime factor in its accomplishment. The financial aid and the more personal assistance volunteered by a variety of persons have made the fort and the museum it houses so complete a summation of Champlain Valley history.

"I try not to think," Pell of Ticonderoga says when asked what the enterprise has cost him personally. He is less reticent in acknowledging the help he has received from friends and even strangers who have fallen under the spell of the place.

Because of this zeal, the fort is now armed with the largest collection of eighteenth-century cannon in the world. The British and United States governments have contributed guns. H. Jermain Slocum, a family friend, was so filled with fervor for the enterprise that he traveled at his own expense through Central America and the West Indies, preaching the gospel of Ticonderoga and soliciting from Latin dictators freewill offerings of ancient artillery. His crusade resulted in gifts from the Haitian, Dominican, Panamanian and Nicarauguan governments, as well as the Dutch.

Only two of the guns now mounted on Ticonderoga's walls actually saw service in the old fort. One, an 8-foot, iron 18-pounder was dug out of the rubble where it had lain since the last British garrison, retreating into Canada in 1777, had attempted to blow up the stronghold. The other has a more involved history.

General Knox, while hauling guns from the Ticonderoga batteries to the Continental Army about Boston in the winter of 1775-1776, lost one in crossing the frozen Hudson. A sled fell through the ice, carrying its burden with it. Years later, it was retrieved and, until the outbreak of the latest World War, stood on the common of a river town whose residents were so blind to its value that they contributed it to a scrap drive.

News of this atrocity roused Milo King to indignant haste. He raced cross-country to the junk dealer who had bought the cannon, only to find that it already had been broken into three pieces. Nevertheless, King purchased it, had it trucked to Ticonderoga and succeeded in having it welded.

"It looks as sound as any of the others," he grins, "and it cost us only ten dollars. We'd gladly have paid two hundred to get it."

Though excavation has not been prolific in its yield of cannon, fragments of small arms in all stages of decay have been recovered by the thousand as well as relics more intimately linked with the stronghold's past. Only lately, the great iron hinges and studs of the gate through which Ethan Allen and his men stormed were recovered. They have been fitted into new timber and now are back in place.

Much of the eloquent material in the fort's museum has been purchased; more has come, as loans or outright gifts, from persons who have been inspired, as Americans with veneration for their country's history must be, by the scope and excellence of its contents. Here are Indian relics, as well as items that exemplify completely the military lives of three nations from the French wars to the 1812 conflict—uniforms, weapons, equipment, portraits, maps. Here, too, is a mass of implements and furnishings that illustrate civilian existence of colonial and postcolonial times.

No trace of dust or rust, none of the aroma of mice and must that provides so dubious an atmosphere for most exhibitions of antiques, gets into the shining chambers of the Fort Ticonderoga Museum. Each article is cleaned and repaired before it is put on display. The collection of small arms, which is no less noteworthy than the heavier ordnance, is polished, oiled and obviously in working order. No matter how incomplete an old weapon may be when received, Milo King is almost certain to find, among the remnants of arms that have been dug up on the premises, the spare parts with which to mend it.

The collection grows like a rolling snowball. The more distinguished the museum's material becomes, the more willing persons grow to make it still more significant. Heirlooms that families have cherished, jealously and emptily, for generations are beginning to come, unsolicited, to Fort Ticonderoga. Many of them are correctly deemed beyond price.

Citing at random, it would be difficult to set a cash value on George Washington's spurs, Philip Schuyler's military stirrups, epaulettes and fowling piece, Ethan Allen's powder horn or the blunderbuss that he, in a rare moment of amity, presented to Benedict Arnold.

Here also, are Champlain's astrolabe; Israel Putnam's, Arthur St. Clair's and Alexander Hamilton's swords; Sir William Johnson's punch bowl; a Stars and Stripes made by Betsy Ross which is probably the oldest American flag in existence, and the silver bullet that bore Sir Henry Clinton's blighting last message to the desperate Burgoyne.

Clinton, in the hope of reducing the pressure on "Gentleman Johnny," raided up the Hudson from New York in October 1777. He captured Fort Montgomery in the Highlands but his force was too small to warrant farther advance. On October 8, he wrote in a fine hand on thin paper the following dispatch to Burgoyne:

"Nous y voici and nothing between us and Gates. I sincerely hope this little success of ours may facilitate your operations. In answer to your letter of the 28th by C.C., I shall only say I cannot pretend to order or even advise for obvious reasons. I heartily wish you success."

The paper was enclosed in threaded hemispheres of silver that, when screwed together, formed a ball about the size of a musket bullet, and was entrusted to a spy who tried unsuccessfully to work his way through Gates' lines. The unfortunate man, upon capture, swallowed the silver ball. It required two heroic doses of tartar emetic before it came into patriot possession for, after the first upheaval, the spy swallowed it again.

"The silver bullet" fell into the hands of General James Talmadge and eventually became the property of Henry O. Talmadge, his contemporary descendant, who after much diplomatic persuasion deposited it in the Museum.

"For a time," Pell of Ticonderoga related, "we almost despaired of getting it. Then Talmadge told me one day: 'You know, my wife has gone over to your side.' I knew then that the silver bullet was ours."

The fort library contains not only practically all published material on Lakes Champlain and George but also an invaluable manuscript collection. Among its treasures are Ethan Allen's letter announcing Ticonderoga's capture, a love letter from Robert Rogers to his long-suffering wife, British officers' denunciatory round robin after the Valcour Island battle, the papers of Philip Skene. More important still is the continually growing mass of humbler Colonial and Revolutionary writings—letters, diaries and orderly books of uncelebrated men. What they set down with no thought of posterity not infrequently mars theories that repetition has established as a fact.

Fort Ticonderoga, like a giant magnet, is drawing into herself a conglomerate mass of data bearing upon the history and the humble daily life of the early Champlain-George Valley. The absorption will continue. He who revived the stronghold is seventy-one but his work will long outlive him.

The enterprise now is administered by a corporation, the Pell Family Association, of which Robert and John, sons of Stephen, are assistant director and secretary-treasurer. The purpose that William Ferris Pell saw dimly and the fourth and fifth generations of his line now execute has become too vitally important for the death of any one man to blight. The fort and its new purpose wisely remain exclusively a family enterprise.

The French built an earlier, almost equally important stronghold sixteen miles down the lake. Today, dark stones protruding through the unkempt grass of a bleak little park are all that remains of Fort St. Frédéric. No attempt at excavation, no restoration is visible in the dreary precinct. In imagination, enterprise, accomplishment, the Pells of Ticonderoga have little in common with the proprietor of Crown Point, which is the sovereign state of New York.

Chapter 26

Flotsam

WITHOUT a perspective, the pattern becomes blurred. At the distance of centuries, the influence of the twin lakes upon peoples and their histories can be seen. More immediate matters remain of doubtful consequence until time has sifted them.

The clouded water, moving northward from Champlain's South Bay; the clear overflow of Lake George, joining and going onward to the distant Richelieu, are the only future certainties. No one can predict how much of what now seem importances the Valley will retain in its eventual design. It may link and preserve the apparently unrelated. It may let much that men believe enduring pass out of human recollection and slip away like flotsam on the lakes' slow, northward flow.

Time alone will tell what will be kept and what erased. Time is deliberate and careful of speech.

Champlain's one venture in communism is flotsam impossible to salvage entire. Philip Skene's settlement, at a distance of almost two centuries, is more sharply discernible than the details of the Dawn Valcour colony after the lapse of seventy years. Only fragmentary accounts of the experiment still survive and there are gaps in the narrative that surmise alone can bridge.

There could have been more salubrious sites for an exemplification of free love and the rest of the half-baked gospel according to François Fourier than Valcour Island, south of Cumberland Head, on the lake's west shore. The community founded there endured little more than a year. It seems to have been the joint creation of Orren Shipman of Colchester, Vermont, and John Wilcox, a Midwesterner. Shipman supplied the property, heavily mortgaged; Wilcox furnished the doctrine and a nucleus of settlers.

Valcour Island's proprietor, a peculiar person who voyaged about Champlain with his wife and another woman straining at the oars and who for some obscure reason was styled "Professor," read in a Chicago magazine articles by Wilcox extolling the advantages of communal living and straightway caught fire. He wrote the author, offering the island as a site for such a colony but omitting any mention of how onerously the place was entailed. When Wilcox and his handful of pilgrims came east, Shipman joined the community himself. It was incorporated in October, 1874, as "The Dawn Valcour Agricultural and Horticultural Association" and its membership, possibly because of the most spectacular of its dogmas, was disproportionately male.

By the time the experiment's first winter was over, the comrades were entangled in a communal brawl. Love, it appeared, though free, had become increasingly scarce among them. On March 13, 1875, Orren Shipman's suit against John Wilcox was dismissed in the Winooski, Vermont, court. In April, Shipman's wife published a circular charging that the colony's members were intent on running her husband into bankruptcy.

Some of the original settlers now deserted and there were dismayingly few converts to take their places. Wilcox prevailed upon the holders of the Valcour Island mortgages to foreclose on Shipman and turn the property over to the colony. During July, the Plattsburgh *Republican* published a series of articles by the Minerva of the movement, a Mrs. H. Augusta White. She expounded the principles of the association but though she proclaimed "Social Freedom in its broadest sense means simply the right of each to regulate his own sexual relations as they please,"[1] few recruits responded.

The approach of another Champlain winter chilled further the failing ardor of the faithful and, in November, the mortgage holders foreclosed again and the Dawn Valcour Agricultural and Horticultural Association's frostbitten members abandoned their enterprise and departed. Local families, capitalistic and continent by conviction, farmed Valcour Island extremely profitably thereafter.

The United States, after the War of 1812, did not wholly relinquish the site it had fortified at Plattsburg, but in 1815 established a small infantry post there that in 1890 was enlarged to a regimental. Three years later, Fort Ethan Allen, onetime largest cavalry post in the country, was founded in the east shore town of Colchester.

The Vermont fort led a colorless existence, but reminiscence of ancient strife, now half-forgotten, still clings to the Plattsburg reservation. It was here that Theodore Roosevelt began his once-memorable feud against Woodrow Wilson which expedited American preparedness for World War I yet barred the erstwhile Rough Rider and his friend, Major General Leonard Wood, from active service therein.

Wood, who already had made himself painful to the administration by his insistence that the United States should arm, announced in May 1915, after the sinking of the Cunarder *Lusitania,* that an officers' training school would be held at Plattsburg if 100 civilians would volunteer. This was not to be a government enterprise but was to be financed by Bernard Baruch and others.

Not 100 but 1,200 candidates offered themselves. While they were training, Theodore Roosevelt spoke at the camp with such impolitic vehemence that Wood was reprimanded by Lindley Garrison, Secretary of War, for permitting the address. The general kept still, but Roosevelt leaped to his defense, fists flying, and began his long and vituperative assault upon the administration.

That winter, graduates of the first Plattsburg camp were instrumental in establishing the Military Training Camps Association. The system it sponsored for turning civilians into reserve officers was continued until World War II.

The Plattsburg post, as this is written, is an army convalescent hospital. Fort Ethan Allen, no longer active, is occupied in part by GI students at the University of Vermont and their wives.

The Plattsburg camps were responsible, indirectly, for Lake Champlain's most dramatic resurrection. L. F. Haggelund, a salvage engineer from New York, received his officer's training there during the First World War and years thereafter returned to realize an ambition. In the summer of 1932, he sought and eventually found the hulk of the schooner *Royal Savage* that had been beached and burned during the Valcour Island naval battle.

Champlain already had yielded the drowned body of one member of Arnold's fleet. The schooner *Revenge,* survivor of the engagement, had been scuttled off Fort Ticonderoga when St. Clair had evacuated the post. She had been located by Stephen H. P. Pell and in the winter of 1909 had been raised and drawn ashore.

Haggelund, in a diver's suit, got cables under *Royal Savage's* remains and raised them. He found little of historic interest in the charred and sodden wreck, for it had been thoroughly plundered years earlier. He then considered a more difficult enterprise.

Somewhere between Valcour Island and the lake's west shore, the galley *Philadelphia,* sunk by the British on the day of battle, must repose. It was not until the summer of 1935 that Haggelund assembled an expedition to try for her.

J. Ruppert Schalk of New York was partner in the adventure. The yacht *Linwood* served as base of operations and a professional diver, William Lilja, was included in her crew. In late July the company began a systematic dragging of the area. The hooks caught and held at twilight on August 1. Next morning, Lilja went down and found they actually were fast in the galley. He brought up three cannon balls as proof thereof.

A derrick from Burlington, under direction of the diver, salvaged *Philadelphia's* 3 cannon and on August 9 raised the galley herself from her 159-year submersion. Her hull, still approximately intact, was 59 feet long, with a 15-foot beam, and was planked both inside and outside her ribs. Three British cannon balls had pierced her side and a fourth was lodged between her inner and outer skin. Teeth and bones of the men who had died aboard *Philadelphia,* pewter buttons, corroded iron and fragments of glass were found.

The galley, lashed to a lighter, was towed to the Champlain Transportation Company's shipyard. There she was housed on a barge and taken on a tour of the lake towns. *Philadelphia* now lies, still on her barge, at Fort Ticonderoga where *Revenge* also reposes.

Change came so gradually to the Valley that its people scarcely were aware of its approach until it manifested itself in the mid-1920's. The lake that for centuries had been the main thoroughfare through a difficult region was becoming an obstruction to travel.

Railways had foreshadowed the transformation. Paved roads now stressed it. Champlain with its once proud fleets of sail and steam and its monopoly of regional traffic had sunk below the importance of a secondary highway. The water that had been the principal stimulus to the area's growth had turned into an obstacle to tourists. Men moved to by-pass it.

The first and greatest of the lake bridges, 2,900 feet long and 90 feet above water at the center of its span's flat arc, linked Vermont and New York across the Crown Point narrows. When it was opened, August 26, 1929, it gave motor traffic unimpeded passage, east and west.

Two more bridges at Champlain's north end were completed in 1937, granting land passage through the islands and again joining New York to Vermont. The long causeway and small drawbridge between Swanton and Alburg extends 4,290 feet. The approaches to the Rouses Point-Alburg draw, fashioned largely of stone from Fort Montgomery's east wall, are more than a mile in length.

New York State resolved in 1946 to raise the bridges that cross the Champlain-Hudson Canal from their present eleven-foot height to twenty feet. This may have been only the slumberous stirring of a moribund enterprise. It just possibly may have been the first small forward step in a tremendous project that might alter the life and aspect of the Valley, restoring a museum-piece lake, whose present chief virtue is its beauty, to more than its ancient rank as a trade thoroughfare.

The Champlain-Hudson Canal, which in 1829 joined Whitehall to Troy and thereby turned the commerce of the lakes' area away from Canada and toward interior America, may again implement a new prosperity.

The man-made waterway that clambers over the low divide at Fort Ann enjoyed so healthy a youth that it has been a long time dying. Barges and packets crammed its locks during its early years and filled its reaches with lusty, brawling traffic. Tolls in 1824 were only $46,000 but in 1828 they had climbed to $107,000 and in 1850, despite growing competition from railways, had reached $133,000.

The impetus of this early prosperity carried the canal a long way. Despite aggrieved howls from railroads, tolls were abolished in 1882. Improvements have been frequent. The latest, undertaken in 1917, were marred, canal enthusiasts contend, by railway influence. The twelve-foot-deep channel, the generous locks were ample for the traffic the waterway then was expected to bear, but the bridges that carried roads across the canal were a mere eleven feet above its surfaces.

Only craft of special design could pass beneath these semi-obstacles and few boats save low, self-propelled barges have since then traveled the canal. Traffic is dwindling. In 1935, 351,000 tons of freight were carried; in 1945, 326,000. Northbound cargoes, principally petroleum products, weighed 194,000 tons; southbound, almost entirely pulp and paper, 132,000 tons. In 1864, 103,000 tons of Adirondack iron, alone, passed south through the locks.

The greater clearance twenty-foot bridges ensure will permit pleasure craft to use the canal. It will bring to Champlain by inland passage, lakeside optimists believe, a free-spending fleet of yachts and power craft barred by their dimensions from passing beneath eleven-foot bridges. Vacationists hereafter will be able to approach the Valley by water as well as by land.

This is the immediate encouraging prospect. Long-range and still entirely theoretical proposals which include radical alteration of the Champlain-Hudson Canal look forward to an equally complete revolution in Valley existence.

The Champlain-Hudson Cutoff thus far exists only in pamphlets, engineers' preliminary drawings and the records of hearings, but imaginative dwellers in the region speak as though the great project already had been undertaken. It must remain imprisoned on paper until the time—if that time ever arrives—when the St. Lawrence Seaway actually is undertaken by the United States and Canada. The Champlain-Hudson Cutoff is dependent upon this still more immense accomplishment.

The St. Lawrence Seaway, by a system of dams and locks at the river's rapids, would open the Great Lakes to direct ocean commerce so that cargoes might move from any lakeside city, without transshipment, to any port in the world. When, or if, this spacious dream becomes a reality, the Champlain-Hudson Cutoff will be a logical consequence.

The plan provides for enlargement of the Champlain-Hudson canal to handle ocean-going craft, the deepening of Champlain's own channel and the creation of a new ship canal from the upper Richelieu cross-country to the dilation of the St. Lawrence, upstream from Montreal, that is called Lake St. Francis.

Primarily, the establishment of such a waterway would open a short cut for Great Lakes craft to any point on the United States Atlantic Coast and in South America. The proposed route from Lake St. Francis to New York harbor would be about 500 miles. The present course that ships from Montreal must steam—down the length of the St. Lawrence and looping around Nova Scotia—to reach Manhattan is some 1,500 miles. More than three days would be saved by the cutoff which also would reduce transportation expenses about $2,000 per average cargo ship.

Secondarily—and this is the point at which cutoff enthusiasts begin to shout and wave their arms—the lake would be transformed by the scheme into a navigable estuary of the Atlantic and each of its shore towns into an incipient seaport. Industries would flourish; resources that have been left undeveloped because of excessive freight costs could then be profitably exploited; agriculture, in which the Valley once led the nation, would renew its youth. Wealth would follow in the wakes of the cargo ships of the Seven Seas.

It still is only a glowing dream, far from fulfillment, but it is more practical than most such visions. In time, it may bring Champlain a commerce and a prosperity such as its people in the heyday of the lake's earlier trade never imagined, or it may prove to be only flotsam that a shift in the future's tide has borne away.

There are reactionaries who have no enthusiasm for the proposed violation of the Valley's peace and the spoilation of its waters by the world's grime-strewing, oil-spewing merchant fleets. These unaspiring folk prefer Champlain as it is today—calm, comely, and, like its lesser sister, reposing at ease after dark centuries of strife.

Few lakes have witnessed more transforming violence in their brief recorded lifetimes than Champlain and George.

The red, vanished nations; the wars of French upon English and British upon Americans; the armed hosts that filled the Valley; the forts that rose, endured and fell away; the cannon thunder over Valcour Island and Cumberland Head; the drab, mute settlers who came and cleared and at great cost possessed the land; the travail and the torment and the unnumbered dead—all these send faint echoes of themselves across the shining waters when the sun goes west beyond Burlington Bay and its long light leaves George to climb the eastern hills.

The lakes wait, mountain-enfolded, serene and fair for what the future still hides, twin lovely ladies whose presents reveal no trace of their lurid and violent pasts.

---

[1] Plattsburgh *Republican*, July 14, 1875.

ACKNOWLEDGMENTS AND
BIBLIOGRAPHICAL NOTE

ACKNOWLEDGMENTS

THE roster of persons who freely have offered the sum of their own long studies to improve a stranger's book is too lengthy, and the author's debt to each of them too large for more than the citation of some of their names here.

Among those who not merely permitted their mental storerooms to be ransacked but turned them inside out in this book's behalf are:

Captain H. A. Baldbridge, U.S.N. (retired), Curator of the U. S. Naval Academy Museum, Annapolis, Maryland; Dr. Albert B. Corey, New York State Historian, Albany, New York; Mr. George W. Davis, Vermont Fish and Game Director, Montpelier, Vermont; Professor Leon W. Dean, University of Vermont, Burlington.

Lt. Commander F. W. Filbury, U.S.N., Annapolis, Maryland; Vice Admiral Aubrey T. Fitch, Superintendent of the U. S. Naval Academy, Annapolis, Maryland; Mr. Lewis B. Francis, Brooklyn, New York; Mr. Stewart Holbrook, Portland, Oregon; Professor Elbridge C. Jacobs, Vermont State Geologist, Burlington, Vermont.

Mr. Milo S. King, Fort Ticonderoga, New York; Dr. Gustave Lanctot, Dominion Archivist and Deputy Minister, Ottawa, Canada; Mr. Joseph R. Linney, Plattsburg, New York; Mr. R. L. Linney, Mineville, New York; Mr. Hugh McLellan, Champlain, New York; Mr. Francis Myers, Mineville, New York; Mr. Earle Williams Newton, Director, Vermont Historical Society, Montpelier, Vermont.

Mr. Stephen H. P. Pell, Fort Ticonderoga, New York; Mr. L. F. Perry, Ticonderoga, New York; Mrs. Marjorie L. Porter, Plattsburg, New York; Mr. Frederick D. Richards, Treasurer of the New York Historical Society, Glens Falls, New York; Captain F. L. Riddle, Head of the Department of Seamanship and Navigation, U. S. Naval Academy, Annapolis, Maryland.

Captain Murray M. Tucker, U. S. Customs Patrol, St. Albans, Vermont; Mr. Sterling Van de Water, Pompton Lakes, New Jersey; Mr. Alvin G. Whitney, Assistant Director, New York Geological Survey, Albany, New York; Mr. Joseph Winterbotham, Burlington, Vermont.

An author who for many months has been the major affliction of sundry libraries and librarians also makes special and grateful acknowledgment to the generosity and patience of Mr. Sylvester L. Vigilante, Head of the American History Collection, New York Public Library; Mrs. Doris J. Harvey, Wilbur Library, University of Vermont, Burlington; Miss Fannie Rothman, Fletcher Free Library, Burlington; Mr. J. Thacher Sears, Crandall Library, Glens Falls, New York; Miss Eleanor Murray, Fort Ticonderoga Museum Library, Fort Ticonderoga, New York; Miss Helen Hale, Plattsburg Library, Plattsburg, New York.

BIBLIOGRAPHICAL NOTE

PRIMARY material embodied in this book has been drawn not only from the *Proceedings* of the New York and the Vermont Historical Societies, from the manuscript collections of the New York Public Library, the Canadian Archives at Ottawa, the Wilbur Library of the University of Vermont and from the invaluable material embodied in the Fort Ticonderoga Museum Library and its published "Bulletins" but also has been taken from the generously offered collections of Valley historians—chief among them Mr. Frederick B. Richards of Glens Falls, New York, Judge Berne A. Pyrke of Albany and that prodigious collector of North Country lore, Mr. Hugh McLellan of Champlain, New York.

The geological history of the Champlain-George Valley may be found more fully in Charles Schuchert *Outlines of Historical Geology* (New York, 1931); D. H. Newland and Henry Vaughan, *Guide to the Geology of the Lake George Region* (Albany, 1942); William J. Miller, *The Geological History of New York State* (Albany, 1924) and Elbridge C. Jacobs, *Report of the State Geologist* (Burlington, Vermont 1935-1936 and 1941-1942).

Chapters on the discovery of Lakes Champlain and George are based on Samuel de Champlain's own *Voyages,* edited by W. L. Grant (New York, 1907) and *The Jesuit Relations and Allied Documents,* edited by Reuben Gold Thwaites (Cleveland 1896-1901).

The Valley's part in the French Wars is set forth most vividly in Francis Parkman's great historical studies. Of these, *Pioneers of France in the New World, The Jesuits in North America, Frontenac and New France, The Old Regime in Canada, A Half Century of Conflict* and *Montcalm and Wolfe* are most helpful. Contributory primary material can be found in *Documents Relating to the Colonial History of New York State* (Albany, 1855) and *The Documentary History of the State of New York* (Albany, 1851) both edited by E. B. O'Callaghan. B. F. De Costa, *Notes on the History of Lake George* (New York, 1871) deals thoroughly with the lesser lake's share in the conflict while the region's most important affray is drawn full length in Morris P. Ferris, *The Battle of Lake George* (New York, 1903). A single phase of the strife is completely covered by Frederick B. Richards, *The Black Watch at Ticonderoga* (Fort Ticonderoga Museum, n.d.).

In examining the French Wars, as well as later epochs, Writers Project, *Warren County, New York* (Glens Falls, N. Y., 1942), *New York* (Albany, 1940) and *Vermont* (Cambridge, Mass., 1940) are geographically helpful.

Early settlement of the lakes region is illuminated by Peter S. Palmer, *History of Lake Champlain* (Albany, 1866), Winslow S. Watson, *Pioneer History of the Champlain Valley* (Albany, 1863), which embodies the bulk of the William Gilliland diaries. This phase also is covered in W. E. Lamb, *The Lake Champlain and Lake George Valleys* (New York, 1940) and A. de Lery MacDonald, *The Seigneurie of Alainville on Lake Champlain* (Baltimore, 1929).

Basic material on Vermont's first struggles for freedom is to be found in Ira Allen, *History of Vermont* (London, 1789), *The Records of Governor and Council* (Montpelier, 1873) and *The Documentary History of the State of New York*. Charles M. Thompson, *Independent Vermont* (Boston, 1942), Walter Hill Crockett, *A History of Lake Champlain* (Burlington, Vermont, 1909) and *Vermont, The Green Mountain State* afford continuous narratives of the early and later strife on Champlain's east shore.

The capture of the lakes' strongholds by Allen and his men is discussed most thoroughly in Allen French, *The Taking of Ticonderoga* (Cambridge, Mass., 1928), and B. F. De Costa, *Notes on the History of Lake George*. Both volumes are carefully documented and definitive. Ethan Allen, *Narrative* (Fort Ticonderoga, 1930) is his own characteristic and prejudiced story of what happened. John Pell, *Ethan Allen* (Boston, 1929) supplies a vivid, modern version.

The Revolutionary struggle for the lakes is almost hidden beneath the frequently conflicting volumes that deal with it. Basic is John Fiske, *The American Revolution* (Boston, 1891). *Correspondence of the American Revolution,* edited by Jared Sparks (Boston, 1863), supplies much primary material and sound general narratives are Justin H. Smith, *Our Struggle for the Fourteenth Colony* (New York, 1907) and

Henry Belcher's *The First American Civil War* (London, 1911). Hoffman Nickerson, *The Turning Point of the American Revolution* (Cambridge, 1928), is a thorough study of the events leading up to Saratoga. These are discussed from a partisan viewpoint in General John Burgoyne, *A State of the Expedition from Canada* (London, 1780) while the lesser man's opinion of that campaign is set forth in *The Journal of Captain Pausch,* edited by W. L. Stone (Albany, 1886) and Lieutenant James Hadden, *A Journal Kept in Canada and Upon Burgoyne's Campaign* (Albany, 1887). Howard Swiggett, *War out of Niagara,* describes events that dovetail with raids launched up Champlain.

Much of the extant material concerning Vermont's perilous flirtation with Canada has been published in James Benjamin Wilbur, *Ira Allen, Founder of Vermont* (Boston, 1928) while some additional primary sources have been uncovered by Clarence White Rife in his *Vermont and Great Britain* (New Haven, 1922). *The Records of Governor and Council* (Montpelier, 1873) again are useful here.

Best source material for the era of settlement that succeeded the Revolution is to be found in the county histories, notably Franklin B. Hough, *History of St. Lawrence and Franklin Counties* (Albany, 1853); Duane H. Hurd, *History of Clinton and Franklin Counties* (Philadelphia, 1880), Frederick J. Seaver, *Historical Sketches of Franklin County* (Albany, 1918); *History of Essex County,* edited by H. P. Smith (Syracuse, 1885); W. L. Stone, *Washington County, N. Y.* (New York, 1901); Writers Project, *Warren County* (Glens Falls, 1942) and Winslow C. Watson, *Military and Civil History of the County of Essex* (Albany, 1854).

Development of Vermont's lakeside is most thoroughly covered by Abby Maria Hemenway who compiled and edited the gigantic *Vermont Historical Gazetteer* (Burlington, 1868-1891). This prodigious symposium of reminiscences from hundreds of sources is invaluable for its colorful if disjoined narrative of all important and a myriad unimportant yet revealing events in early Vermont.

For the War of 1812, Henry Adams, *History of the Administration of James Madison* (New York, 1930) gives a long-range view of the conflict as it affected the Valley. Benson J. Lossing, *Field Book of the War of 1812* (New York, 1869) and James Hannay, *History of the War of 1812* (St. Johns, N. B., 1901) shorten the perspective. Much source material is to be found in University of the State of New York, *The Centenary of the Battle of Plattsburgh* (Albany, 1914) *The Lake Cham-*

plain Tercentenary, edited by Henry W. Hill (Albany, 1911) New York State Committee, State Centennial, *The Battle of Plattsburgh* (Albany, 1914), Henry Harmon Noble, *Battle of the Boquet River* (Albany, 1913); Plattsburg Centenary Commission, *Dedication of the Thomas Macdonough Memorial* (Plattsburg, 1924).

Theodore Roosevelt's *The Naval War of 1812* (New York, 1882) gives a rousing account of the lake campaign. Admiral A. T. Mahan's *Sea Power in Its Relation to the War of 1812* (Boston, 1905), is a longer, more scrupulous narrative. Fletcher Pratt, *The Navy* (New York, 1941) is also of value.

County histories and *The Vermont Historical Gazetteer* again are the main dependence for the post-1814 development of either lakeshore, while the character and prejudices of Green Mountaineers-is analyzed carefully and candidly by David L. Ludlum, *Social Ferment in Vermont* (New York, 1939).

Light is thrown on the St. Albans Raid by Edward A. Sowles, *History of the St. Albans Raid* (St. Albans, 1876). Hemenway furnishes additional details. So does James T. Walsh, *Story of the St. Albans Raid* (St. Albans, 1939) and Mrs. J. Gregory Smith, "An Incident of the Civil War," *The Vermonter,* Vol. IV, No. 6 (St. Albans, Jan., 1899). Bennet H. Young gives his version of the foray in "Secret History of the St. Albans Raid," *The Vermonter,* Vol. VII, No. 6 (St. Albans, Jan., 1902). The Canadian view of the attack is expressed in *The St. Albans Raid,* compiled by L. N. Benjamin (Montreal, 1868), and J. Douglas Barthwick's *History of the Montreal Prison* (Montreal, 1866).

Edward A. Sowles, "History of Fenianism and Fenian Raids in Vermont," *Proceedings of the Vermont Historical Society* (October 19, 1880) and John O'Neill, "Official Report" (New York, 1870) are the most nearly authoritative after-views of the fiasco.

Steam commerce on the lakes is dealt with thoroughly in The Lake George Steamboat Company, *Steamboats of Lake George* (1930) and The Champlain Transportation Company, *Steamboats of Lake Champlain* (1930) while a mass of associated material can be found in the D. A. Loomis papers in the University of Vermont's Wilbur Library.

The industrial development of the area is set forth insofar as timber is concerned by James Elliot Defebaugh, *History of the Lumber Industry in America* (Chicago 1907) and by Stewart Holbrook, *Holy Old Mackinaw* (New York, 1938) while the rise and fall of iron mining is described by Dr. George F. Bixby, *History of the Iron Industry on*

Lake Champlain (Proceedings, N. Y. Historical Society, Vol. X), Frank S. Witherbee, *The Iron Ores of the Adirondack Region* (St. Louis, 1916) and *A History of the Iron Industry in Essex County* (n.p., 1906).

The story of Vermont's underground railway is told with carefully documented thoroughness in Wilbur H. Siebert, Vermont's Anti-Slavery and Underground Railroad Record (Columbus, O., 1937).

Volumes dealing with the transformation of the area into vacation country include S. H. Stoddard, *Lake George* (Albany, 1873); J. Bonsal, *The Northern Tour* (Philadelphia, 1879); Warwick S. Carpenter, *The Summer Paradise in History* (Albany, 1914), W. Max Reed, "Lake George and Lake Champlain" (New York, 1910).

INDEX

INDEX